GERMAN SENTENCE PROCESSING

STUDIES IN THEORETICAL PSYCHOLINGUISTICS

VOLUME 24

The titles published in this series are listed at the end of this volume.

GERMAN SENTENCE PROCESSING

edited by

BARBARA HEMFORTH

Freiburg University,
Freiburg, Germany

and

LARS KONIECZNY

Saarland University,
Saarbrücken, Germany

KLUWER ACADEMIC PUBLISHERS
DORDRECHT / BOSTON / LONDON

A C.I.P. Catalogue record for this book is available from the Library of Congress.

ISBN 0-7923-6104-0

Published by Kluwer Academic Publishers,
P.O. Box 17, 3300 AA Dordrecht, The Netherlands.

Sold and distributed in North, Central and South America
by Kluwer Academic Publishers,
101 Philip Drive, Norwell, MA 02061, U.S.A.

In all other countries, sold and distributed
by Kluwer Academic Publishers,
P.O. Box 322, 3300 AH Dordrecht, The Netherlands.

Printed on acid-free paper

Printed in the Netherlands.

CONTENTS

PREFACE

The present volume contributes to the growing body of work on sentence processing. The goal of work in this area is to construct a theory of human sentence processing in general, i.e., given a grammar of some particular language and a general characterization of the human sentence processing mechanisms, the particular processing system for that language should follows automatically. At least that's the goal. What is needed in order to pursue this goal is systematic in-depth analysis of the sentence routines of individual languages. With respect to German, that is precisely what the present volume delivers.

In sharp contrast to a decade ago, the study of German sentence processing is flourishing today. Four lively and active centers have emerged. The University of Freiburg is one prominent center, represented in the present volume by the editors Barbara Hemforth and Lars Konieczny (who was at Freiburg for many years) as well as by Christoph Scheepers (who is now in Glasgow) and Christoph Hölscher. The University of Potsdam has recently begun an interdisciplinary collaboration on sentence processing involving Matthias Schlesewsky, Gisbert Fanselow, Reinhold Kliegl and Josef Krems. The University of Jena has several investigators trained in linguistics and interested in language processing. That group is represented here by Markus Bader and also includes his colleagues Michael Meng and Josef Bayer. Finally the relatively young Max Planck Institute of Cognitive Neuroscience at Leipzig has a lively group of people working with Angela Friederici on various aspects of sentence processing. The group is represented here by Paul Gorrell.

The chapters of this book provide a snapshot of the findings emerging from these research centers. What is so encouraging to my mind is the combination of novel questions being asked, on the one hand, and the systematic way in which they are being pursued, on the other. Thanks to the contributors in this volume, we may already know nearly as much about processing German sentences as we know about processing English sentences, despite the fact that processing studies of (British and American) English began in earnest much much earlier. In any case, with this volume on processing German, psycholinguistics has taken a substantial step forward.

Lyn Frazier
Amherst, Massachusetts
April 3, 1998

ACKNOWLEDGEMENTS

During the time we were preparing this volume, we were generously supported by a grant from the German Research Foundation (DFG, He 2310/ 2-1). We would like to thank Gerhard Strube, the head of the Cognitive Science Center in Freiburg, for his ongoing support, Lyn Frazier for urging us to edit this volume, Harald Seelig, Nick Ketley, and Michael Walter for helping us preparing the manuscript, and Lisa for her patience.

COGNITIVE PARSING IN GERMAN:
AN INTRODUCTION

Barbara Hemforth[*] and Lars Konieczny[+]
*University of Freiburg
+Saarland University

Research in human sentence processing is a genuinely cross-linguistic project. Since most theories of human parsing make predictions based on the architecture and the mechanisms of the human sentence processor in general, these predictions are assumed to hold for all human comprehenders irrespective of their mother tongue. Ideally, the only difference between processing phenomena in different languages should be due to different grammatical features of the respective languages. In this view, it should be possible to plug the grammar of a particular language into the sentence processor and have all sorts of syntactic complexity phenomena or preferences in ambiguity resolution fall out (Frazier, 1987). This enterprise can obviously only be pursued if theories of human language processing are applied to and tested in as many languages as possible. Nevertheless, by far the majority of research in human sentence processing has been carried out in English. This picture is now changing, however. More and more cross-linguistic studies on human language processing are being published on a wide variety of languages.

This volume aims at participating in the project of broadening the theoretical and empirical basis of human sentence processing research. All authors of this volume share the basic idea of a principle-based sentence processor although they differ with respect to their assumptions on what the general principles governing this processor are. Exploiting the peculiarities of German syntax, they develop research questions which are relevant for psycholinguistics in general, but which cannot be as easily tackled in other languages.

The general picture that emerges from the papers in this volume strongly supports the relevance of purely structural or syntactic preferences in parsing. It is shown that word ordering preferences as well as attachment preferences in various constructions cannot easily be attributed to frequency, semantics, or thematic roles.

1

B. Hemforth and L. Konieczny (eds.), German Sentence Processing, 1-23.
© 2000 *Kluwer Academic Publishers. Printed in the Netherlands.*

In this introduction, we will briefly sketch out the background of sentence processing research in Germany. We will then discuss some of the major syntactic features of German which make it particularly interesting for psycholinguistic research. An overview of the chapters will be given in the final section.

THE PSYCHOLINGUISTICS OF SENTENCE PROCESSING IN GERMAN

For a rather long time, psycholinguistics of sentence processing was virtually nonexistent in German, at least as an interdisciplinary enterprise in psychology and linguistics. Turning away from a competence based theory of sentence processing in the late sixties/early seventies, German psychology of language did not find an easy way back to cooperative work with syntacticians.[1] Hörmann (1976) claimed somewhat sarcastically that the emphasis on "syntax as the rich sister of poor semantics" had always been misguided, since the human language processor had not developed to judge grammatical well-formedness of sentences but to convey meaning. According to this view, psychological research should concentrate on the content of utterances, on the messages to be exchanged between discourse partners.

Accordingly, models of human language processing were developed, concentrating on higher order processes. Syntactic information was only considered to be relevant for cases where general world knowledge and the current discourse situation did not render a fully consistent interpretation (e.g., Herrmann, 1985), an approach we have termed the "syntax-as-last-resort"-approach (cf., Hemforth, 1993). This perspective was not only taken in the early seventies where it was presumably prevalent nearly everywhere, but is still the point of view of many German psychologists of language. Herrmann and Grabowski (1996) for example, follow a psychological tradition of language oriented research that they see as considerably distinct from the "anglo-saxon mainstream" (Herrmann & Grabowski, 1996, p. 133): they claim that language (spoken language in particular) deviates strongly from what we learn in grammar lessons.[2] To what extent these deviations are in any way linguistically systematic should be of only marginal interest to psychologists. Herrman and Grabowski claim that there is no such thing as a grammar (in the sense of a Universal Grammar, for example) but only a variety of alternative theoretical reconstructions of human language behavior. Any kind of grammatical realism is therefore supposed to be misleading.

Without doubt, this is a possible perspective. Unfortunately though, there was virtually no alternative to this research tradition in Germany for quite a while. Whereas the "anglo-saxon mainstream" became more and more differentiated, allowing for different schools and traditions, linguistically informed syntax-oriented research on human sentence processing was rather sparse in Germany until the late eighties / early nineties. This situation is now changing considerably. Several research groups in psychology as well as in linguistics have taken up the effort to thoroughly investigate the interplay of the peculiarities of German syntax and general parsing strategies. This volume gives a non-exhaustive overview of this line of research with contributions from Markus Bader from the University of Jena, Matthias Schlesewsky, Gisbert Fanselow, Reinhold Kliegl, and Josef Krems from the University of Potsdam, Paul Gorrell from the Max-Planck Institute of Neuropsychological Research in Leipzig, Lars Konieczny from the University of Saarbrücken, and Christoph Scheepers, Christoph Hölscher, and Barbara Hemforth from the University of Freiburg. The idea for this volume originated in the psycholinguistic research group in Freiburg in 1995 (at that time including Barbara Hemforth, Lars Konieczny, Christoph Scheepers, and Gerhard Strube) and was inspired by Lyn Frazier who we would like to thank for her invaluable support.

SOME FEATURES OF GERMAN SYNTAX

The major features of German which have been exploited for psycholinguistic experimentation are: its relatively free word order, its rather rich morphology, and the variable positioning of the main verb. We will present these features in a little more detail in order to form a linguistic background for the chapters in this volume which rely heavily on these peculiarities in German syntax. We will first present some of the relevant phenomena, before we discuss standard syntactic representations assumed for these constructions in the framework of government and binding theory (e.g., Stechow & Sternefeld, 1988).[3]

Ordering of verbal arguments

English is a language with a relatively fixed ordering of verbal arguments with a general subject-verb-object ordering. Even in cases where the object may precede the subject such as in wh-questions (1b) or relative clauses (2b), the functional role of each constituent can be read from the surface ordering, since the subject generally directly precedes the finite verb.

(1) a. I wonder which doctor visited the patient.

b. I wonder which patient the doctor visited.

(2)   a.   The doctor who visited the patient ...

         b.   The doctor who the patient visited ...

In contrast to this direct correspondence of surface ordering and functional role, constituent ordering in German is rather flexible, although a general subject-before-object preference is well established (e.g., Gorrell, this volume; Hemforth, 1993; Hemforth, Konieczny, & Strube, 1993; Konieczny, 1996, Konieczny et al., this volume; Mecklinger et al., 1995; Scheepers, 1996; Scheepers et al., this volume; Schlesewsky et al., this volume). Only the case marking on the which-phrase in (3a,b) or the relative pronoun in (4a,b) tells us whether this constituent is the nominative marked subject (3a, 4a) or the accusative marked direct object (3b, 4b) of the sentence.

(3)   a.   Ich frage mich, welcher Arzt den Patienten besuchte.

                  I wonder [which doctor]$_{nom}$ [the patient]$_{acc}$ visited.
                  "I wonder which doctor visited the patient."

         b.   Ich frage mich, welchen Patienten der Arzt besuchte.

                  I wonder [which patient]$_{acc}$ [the doctor]$_{nom}$ visited.

(4)   a.   Der Arzt, der den Patienten besuchte, ...
                  The doctor, who$_{nom}$ [the patient]$_{acc}$ visited ...
                  "The doctor who visited the patient"

         b.   Der Arzt, den der Patient besuchte, ...
                  The doctor who$_{acc}$ [the patient]$_{nom}$ visited ...

In verb second sentences like (5a-e), virtually any constituent may appear before the finite verb, in a position which is often called the Vorfeld-position. The examples in (5a-d) show sentences with approximately the same meaning but different constituents in the Vorfeld: a nominative marked subject in (5a), a dative marked object in (5b), and an adverb in (5c). (5d) shows that even the VP may be fronted.

(5)   a.   Der Student begegnet dem Professor nur selten in der Cafeteria.
                  [The student]$_{nom}$ meets [the professor]$_{dat}$ only rarely in the cafeteria.

b. Dem Professor begegnen der Student nur selten in der Cafeteria.

[The professor]$_{dat}$ meets [the student]$_{nom}$ only rarely in the cafeteria.

c. Nur selten begegnet der Student dem Professor in der Cafeteria.

Only rarely meets [the student]$_{nom}$ [the professor]$_{dat}$ in the cafeteria.

d. Dem Professor in der Cafeteria begegnen möchte der Student nicht.

[The professor]$_{dat}$ in the cafeteria meet would like the student$_{nom}$ not.

roughly: The student would not like to meet the professor in the cafeteria.

Not only can virtually any constituent be moved to the Vorfeld-position, the ordering of arguments following the verb is also fairly unrestricted. The examples in six show some of the possible variations of (5c) with an NP[dat] < NP[nom] < PP ordering in (6a), a PP < NP[nom] < NP[dat] ordering in (6b) and a NP[dat] < PP < NP[nom] ordering in (6c).

(6) a. Nur selten begegnet dem Professor der Student in der Cafeteria.

Only rarely meets [the professor]$_{dat}$ [the student]$_{nom}$ in the cafeteria.

b. Nur selten begegnet in der Cafeteria der Student dem Professor.

Only rarely meets in the cafeteria [the student]$_{nom}$ [the professor]$_{dat}$.

c. Nur selten begegnet dem Professor in der Cafeteria der Student.

Only rarely meets [the professor]$_{dat}$ in the cafeteria [the student]$_{nom}$.

The flexibility in the ordering of verbal arguments gives us the opportunity to disentangle surface position and syntactic or thematic function. Ordering preferences may therefore be investigated in much more detail than in relatively fixed order languages as is evident in the papers by Bader, Scheepers et al., Schlesewsky et al., and Konieczny et al., in this volume.

Positioning of the main verb

In most languages discussed in the psycholinguistic literature, the position of the finite verb is rather consistent. In English (7), it generally follows the subject and precedes all other arguments, whereas it follows all arguments in Japanese (8).

(7) a. The doctor visited the patient.

    b. Yesterday the doctor visited the patient.

(8) Roozin ga kodomo o yonda,
    Old man$_{nom}$ child$_{acc}$ called.
    The old man called the child.

In German, different positions of the finite verb are possible depending on the syntactic context: (A) the finite verb precedes all of its arguments, (B) it follows them, or (C) it follows one argument and precedes all others. The examples in (5) show that in German main clauses the finite verb appears in the second position with exactly one constituent preceding it. If the first constituent is a verbal argument(5a,b), condition (C) holds. If the Vorfeld-position is filled with an adverb (5c), all verbal arguments follow the finite verb (A).

In German subclauses like (9), the verb generally follows all of its arguments (B).

(9) a. Daß der Arzt den Patienten besuchte, ...
    That [the doctor]$_{[nom, masc]}$ [the patient]$_{[acc, masc]}$ visited, ...

    b. Daß den Arzt der Patient besuchte, ...
    That [the doctor]$_{[acc, masc]}$ [the patient]$_{[nom, masc]}$ visited, ...

What makes this variability in verb positioning so interesting? The role of verb information in sentence processing is one of the central topics in psycholinguistic research (e.g., Adams, Mitchell, & Clifton, 1994; Clifton, Frazier, & Connine, 1984; Clifton, Speer, & Abney, 1991; Ferreira & Henderson, 1990; Ford, Bresnan, & Kaplan, 1982; Mitchell, 1987; Konieczny, Hemforth, Scheepers, & Strube, 1997). The argument structure of verbs has been shown to influence attachment preferences in various kinds of constructions, often at a very early point in the analysis (e.g., Britt, 1994; MacDonald, Pearlmutter, & Seidenberg, 1994; Tanenhaus, Carlson, & Trueswell, 1989).

(10) a.   The woman positioned the dress on the rack,

     b.   The woman wanted the dress on the rack.

(11) a.   The thesis enjoyed by the professor ...

     b.   The thesis examined by the professor ...

A language with a fixed verb position allows us to vary the kind of preference induced by a verb as well as the strength of this preference. However, it is not possible to vary the availability of this information. The relevant information is either available before the arguments are processed as in English or not available until the end of the clause, as in Japanese. Unfortunately, though, English and Japanese not only differ in the positioning of lexical heads but in many other respects. A direct comparison of the influence of verb positioning is therefore not possible by simply comparing these languages. Languages with variable verb positioning give us the opportunity to answer questions on the influence of the availability of verbal information within one language. For example, we can investigate which attachment preferences hold in the absence of verbal information in clause-final constructions (12), and we can find out in how far these preferences can be influenced if verbal arguments are read in the context of the relevant verbal information (13) (Konieczny et al., 1997; Konieczny, Hemforth, & Völker, this volume).

(12)   Ich sah, daß die Frau den Mann mit dem Fernglas ... bemerkte / beobachtete.

     I saw that the woman the man with the binoculars ... noticed / watched.

(13)   Die Frau bemerkte / beobachtete den Mann mit dem Fernglas.

     The woman noticed / watched the man with the binoculars.

Verbs not only carry information about the number of arguments they subcatergorize for but also information about their thematic structure and the ordering of arguments with respect to their thematic prominence. Scheepers et al. (this volume) exploit the possibility of variable verb positioning to investigate the influence of verb specific thematic prominence on ordering preferences. The verb-final property of German subclauses is used to investigate "default" attachment or ordering preferences in many of the experiments presented in this volume (e.g., Bader; Schlesewsky et al.; Gorrell).

Case marking, gender marking, and number marking

Noun phrases in German are mostly overtly marked for case as was evident in many of the examples presented so far (comparable, for example, to Finnish, Hyönä et al., in press). The case marking system is however far from perfect in that there is a considerable amount of ambiguity, in particular with respect to the nominative and accusative cases. Only masculine singular noun phrases with determiners are unambiguously case marked. All feminine and neuter NPs and plural masculine noun phrases show no overt difference between nominative and accusative case marking (see Bader, this volume for a more detailed discussion of case syncretism). Therefore, sentences like (14a) are globally ambiguous between a subject-first reading and an object-first reading. Sentences like (14b) and (14c) are only disambiguated by the unambiguous case-marking on the second NP, forcing an object-first reading in (14b) and a subject-first reading in (14c). (14d) is disambiguated by the number-marking on the clause-final verb.

> (14) a.   Die Ärztin besuchte die Patientin.
>   The doctor$_{[nom\ or\ acc,\ fem]}$ visited the patient$_{[nom\ or\ acc,\ fem]}$
>   The doctor visited the patient. or The patient visited the doctor.
>
>   b.   Die Ärztin besuchte der Patient.
>   [The doctor]$_{[nom\ or\ acc,\ fem]}$ visited [the patient]$_{[nom,\ masc]}$.
>   The patient visited the doctor.
>
>   c.   Die Ärztin besuchte den Patienten.
>   [The doctor]$_{[nom\ or\ acc,\ fem]}$ visited [the patient]$_{acc}$.
>
>   d.   Daß die Ärztin die Patientinnen besuchen, …
>   That [the doctor]$_{[nom\ or\ acc,\ sing]}$ [the patients]$_{[nom\ or\ acc,\ plur]}$
>   visit$_{plur}$ …

An ambiguity between dative and genitive case can only be found for feminine singular NPs (see Bader, 1990; Konieczny et al., 1997). The NP "der Schülerin" (the pupil) in (15) is locally ambiguous between a genitive modifier of the preceding NP "der Lehrer" (the teacher; 15a) and a dative object of the verb "schickte" (sent; 15b). (15c) and (15d) show the corresponding sentences with an unambiguously genitive (15c) or dative (15d) marked masculin NP.

(15) a.   Daß der Lehrer der Schülerin gestern einen Brief erhielt, ...

That the teacher [the pupil]$_{[dat\ or\ gen,\ fem]}$ yesterday a letter received, ...

That the teacher of the pupil received a letter yesterday, ...

b.   Daß der Lehrer der Schülerin gestern einen Brief schickte, ...

That the teacher [the pupil]$_{[dat\ or\ gen,\ fem]}$ yesterday a letter sent, ...

That the teacher sent a letter to the pupil yesterday, ...

c.   Daß der Lehrer des Schülers gestern einen Brief erhielt, ...

That the teacher [the pupil]$_{[gen,\ masc]}$ yesterday a letter received, ...

That the teacher of the pupil received a letter yesterday, ...

d.   Daß der Lehrer dem Schüler gestern einen Brief schickte, ...

That the teacher [the pupil]$_{[dat,\ masc]}$ yesterday a letter sent, ...

That the teacher sent a letter to the pupil yesterday, ...

Finally, indefinite plurals as well as proper nouns are ambiguous between nominative, accusative, and dative case marking as exemplified in (16). The main verb "unterstützen" (support) in (16a,b) requires a nominative subject and an accusative object. The case marking on the second NP forces the initial proper noun to be the nominative-marked subject NP in (16a) and the accusative-marked object in (16b). Since "helfen" (to help) requires a dative-marked object and a nominative-marked subject, the proper noun has to be a dative object in (16d) where the second NP is the unambiguously nominative-marked subject.

(16) a.   Pastor Steffen unterstütze den Mann mit vielen Spenden.

[Pastor Steffen]$_{[nom,\ acc,\ or\ dat]}$ supported [the man]$_{acc}$ with many donations.

b.   Pastor Steffen unterstütze der Mann mit vielen Spenden.

[Pastor Steffen]$_{[nom,\ acc,\ or\ dat]}$ supported [the man]$_{nom}$ with many donations.

c.   Pastor Steffen half dem Mann mit vielen Spenden.

[Pastor Steffen]$_{[nom,\ acc,\ or\ dat]}$ helped [the man]$_{dat}$ with many donations.

d.   Pastor Steffen half der Mann mit vielen Spenden.
          [Pastor Steffen]$_{[nom, acc, or dat]}$ helped [the man]$_{nom}$ with many
          donations.

Ambiguities in the case-marking system give us the opportunity to vary the point of disambiguation in attachment and ordering ambiguities as well as the kind of information used for disambiguation. The case-marking on the first NP may tell us whether we are reading a subject-first or an object-first sentence if the NP is masculine singular (5a,b, 9a,b). However, the disambiguating information may also appear at a much later point, for example the case marking of a NP further downstream, or the number marking on the clause final verb (14d). There may even be no disambiguating information within the clause (14a). Although garden-path effects in non-preferred object-before-subject sentences tend to be stronger after an ambiguous first NP and even more so with a disambiguating clause-final verb, a penalty for the non-preferred reading can already be established if the first NP is unambiguously not nominative-marked (Hemforth, 1993; Konieczny, 1996; Schlesewsky et al., this volume). Since determiners, adjectives, and nouns are all case-marked, even finer-grained analyses are possible. The determiner of the first NP in (17a) is ambiguous between an accusative singular and a dative plural reading. Being incompatible with nominative in any case, the very first word in the sentence tells us that we are reading a non-preferred object-before-subject sentence. Konieczny (1996) presents evidence from an eyetracking experiment showing that processing load is increased for unambiguous object-first sentences on the adjective of the first NP, i.e. even before the head noun of the first noun phrase was read (see Hyönä & Hujanen, in press, for comparable results in Finnish). This cannot be due to reading times for accusative NPs being longer in general because an accusative marked NP following the verb, as in (17b), is read faster than the corresponding nominative marked NP in (17a). This very early preference shows that functional roles are assigned highly incrementally and certainly before the main verb is processed as the head of the sentence. Gorrell (this volume) presents a detailed account for this kind of evidence (see also Schlesewsky et al., this volume).

(17)   a.   Den alten Mann besuchte der kleine Junge.
                  The$_{[(acc, sing) or (dat, plur)]}$ old $_{[(acc, sing) or (dat, plur)]}$ man$_{[sing; nom, dat, or acc]}$ visited the little boy$_{nom}$.

       b.   Der alte Mann besuchte den kleinen Jungen.
                  The old man$_{nom}$ visited the little boy$_{acc}$.

The kinds of constructions presented so far enable a fairly detailed investigation of the role of morphological information in sentence processing. In general, a very differentiated picture arises: morphological features differ with respect to their validity as a cue for an initial misanalysis and as a guide for reanalysis. Bader (this volume), for example, shows that the strength of the garden-path due to initial mis-assignment of case varies depending on the particular case-marking involved. Moreover, number marking on the finite verb seems to be a better cue for an initial misanalysis than case-marking (see also Meng, 1997; Kaan, 1997). Morphological features are not always processed correctly: the perception of number marking on a finite verb seems to be influenced by the local environment, i.e. in particular by the number marking of preceding NPs (Hölscher & Hemforth, this volume).

Parallel constructions

The constructions so far are rather complicated because they rely heavily on the peculiarities of German. We have argued that these peculiarities give us the opportunity to look at old research questions from a new perspective and to bring up new topics which have been neglected in psycholinguistic research to date. A more straightforward way to contribute to the crosslinguistic enterprise, however, is to find constructions in different languages which are as similar as possible and compare them. Then we can test whether predictions developed for one language can be applied to another one.

PP-attachment preferences in German main clauses like (18) are an example for a construction that is at least superficially highly comparable to its extensively studied English counterpart (e.g., Frazier, 1979; Ford, Bresnan, & Kaplan, 1982; Rayner, Garrod, & Perfetti, 1992; Spivey-Knowlton & Sedivy, 1995). Konieczny et al. (1997) present results from an eyetracking experiment which pattern very well with many experiments on English PP-attachment in that the actual preferences seem to depend on the expectation of thematic roles triggered by the main verb (e.g., McClelland, St. John, & Taraban, 1989; Tanenhaus, Carlson, & Trueswell, 1989).

(18)   Susan verzierte den Kuchen mit dem Obst.
              Susan decorated the cake with the fruit.

The construction investigated most often in crosslinguistic experiments is the relative clause attachment ambiguity exemplified in (19) and (20) where a relative clause may be attached to one of two (19) or even three (20) nouns (see Brysbaert & Mitchell, 1996; Cuetos & Mitchell, 1988; Frazier & Clifton, 1996; Gibson et al., 1996; Gilboy et al., 1995; Hemforth et al., 1994, in press;

Kamide & Mitchell, 1997; De Vincenzi & Job, 1995). This kind of attachment ambiguity is particularly interesting because it occurs in many languages of the world (e.g., Dutch, English, French, Italian, Japanese, Spanish, among many others). Most interestingly, the preference pattern for two-site attachments (19) differs between languages. Whereas most languages like Dutch, French, German, Italian, Japanese, and Spanish show a clear preference to attach the relative clause to the first NP ("der Sohn", the son), either no preference or a preference for attachment to the second NP was established in English. A much more consistent picture seems to arise with respect to three-site attachment ambiguities like (20). In all languages investigated so far, e.g., English, Spanish (Gibson et al., 1996) and German (Hemforth et al., this volume), attachment to the third NP is the preferred reading followed by attachment to NP1 and NP2. Consequences for a general theory of the human sentence processor derived from the crosslinguistic data are discussed in more detail in Hemforth et al. (this volume).

(19)   der Sohn des Schauspielers, der in Paris arbeitete
             the son of the actor who worked in Paris

(20)   der Lehrer des Sohns des Schauspielers, der in Paris
             arbeitete
             the teacher of the son of the actor who worked in Paris

Some attachment ambiguities cannot easily be transferred to German because of the German punctuation system. In general, non-elliptical sentence coordinations have to be separated by a comma in German. Therefore, the NP/S-conjunction ambiguity in (21) which has been investigated in English and Dutch (Frazier, 1987b) can only be studied in German reading experiments if the obligatory comma is omitted. A preference for NP-conjunction (consistent with the English and Dutch data) which was found for German (Hemforth, 1993) can thus easily be interpreted as an artifact resulting from the incorrect punctuation.

(21)   Tom kissed Marcie and her sister laughed.
             Tom küßte Maria(,) und ihre Schwester lachte.

This problem can be solved by choosing a different kind of conjunction ambiguity. Since only the conjunction of full sentences requires a comma, we used NP/VP-conjunction ambiguities in several experiments (Hemforth, 1993, Konieczny, Hemforth, & Scheepers, this volume). Sentences like (22) are locally ambiguous between an NP-conjunction (a book and a teddy bear) and an elliptic VP-conjunction (gave the daughter a book and [gave] a teddy bear to his son).

(22)   Tom schenkte der Tochter ein Buch und einen Teddy dem Sohn.
              Tom gave the daughter a book and a teddy (to) the son.

Parsing phenomena in German: A brief summary

Taking sentence processing research in English as a starting point, looking at German is fruitful for psycholinguistics in several ways. There are structures which are at least superficially highly similar so that parsing principles derived from experiments on English can be tested for their applicability to a new language, i.e. for universality. Additionally, the range of phenomena can be extended, in particular because of the flexibility in the ordering of constituents and the fairly rich morphological system.

GERMAN SENTENCE STRUCTURE

In this section, we will briefly present a standard account on German sentence structure (e.g., Stechow & Sternefeld, 1988). Of course, this standard account is not undebated. Paul Gorrell and Markus Bader in particular discuss deviations from the representational assumptions presented in this section which are central to their line of argumentation. We will not enter the linguistic discussion of the standard sentence structure in this section but refer to the respective chapters for more details.

Figure 1 shows the standard sentence schema for German in the framework of Government and Binding Theory. This general schema includes the complementizer phrase (CP, formerly S'), the inflectional phrase (IP, formerly S), and the verbal phrase (VP) with their respective head positions (C^0, I^0, V^0), specifier positions and complementizer positions. ISpec is supposed to host the subject which is assigned nominative case in this position. C^0 can be filled by a complementizer (e.g., "daß", that), I^0 carries finiteness features such as tense, number, person etc. and may be lexicalized as an auxiliary (e.g., "hat", has, or "wurde", was), the verb heads the verb phrase. Although the finite verb may occur as the second constituent of the sentence as well as in clause final position, it is widely assumed that it is base-generated in the final position. Verb-second sentences are considered to be a derived structure where the finite verb is moved to C^0, normally the position for the lexicalized head of the complementizer phrase (CP). If the head of CP is filled as in (23), the finite verb has to remain in its clause-final position.

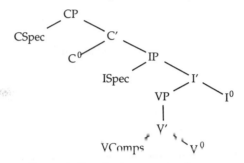

Figure 1: Standard sentence schema

(23) $[_{CP}[_{C'} [_{C0}$Daß]
                   $[_{IP} [_{ISpec}$[der Arzt]]
                        $[_{I'} [_{VP}[[_{V'} $[den Patienten] $[_{V0}$besucht]]]
                        $[_{I0}$hat]]]]
              That the doctor the patient visited has, …

In verb-second sentences, virtually any constituent may be moved to CSpec, resulting in a variety of possible orderings as exemplified in (5) above. Figure 2 shows a SVO-ordering with coindexed traces (t_n) in the base positions of moved constituents.

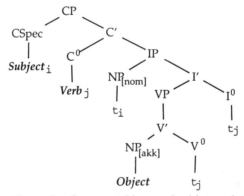

Figure 2: : German subject-verb-object ordering

Gorrell (this volume) argues that only non-subject first ordering results from movement to CSpec. Following Travis (1991), he claims that no CP but only an IP is built for SVO-ordering. In this case, the subject remains in ISpec.

The CSpec-position (or Vorfeld or topic-position) is also the position where wh-phrases move in sentences like (23).

(24) $[_{CP}[_{CSpec}$ [Welcher Arzt]$_i$
            $[_{C'}$ $[_{C0}$ hat$_j]$
            $[_{IP}$ $[_{ISpec}$ $t_i]$
            $[_{I'}$ $[_{VP}$ $[[_{V'}$ [den Patienten] $[_{V0}$ besucht]]]
            $[_{I0}$ $t_j]]]]$
            [Which doctor]$_{nom}$ has [the patient]$_{acc}$ visited?
            Which doctor has visited the patient?

The flexible ordering of constituents in subclauses where no constituent may cross the filled C^0-position in standard German[6] is assumed to be realized by an operation called *scrambling*. For these cases, an additional position has to be created for the moved constituent. It may be assumed that for object-before-subject subclauses a position is created by adjunction to IP (see Figure 4 compared to the subject-before-object ordering in Figure 3), so that the object can end up before the subject position. The additional structure building involved in object-before-subject subclauses plays an important role in Gorrell's approach (this volume).

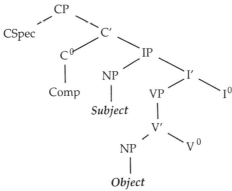

Figure 3: Subject-before-object ordering in subclauses

We will not go into more detail with respect to German sentence structures here. More details are provided in the different chapters in this volume. In the remainder of this introduction, we will give a brief overview of the chapters.

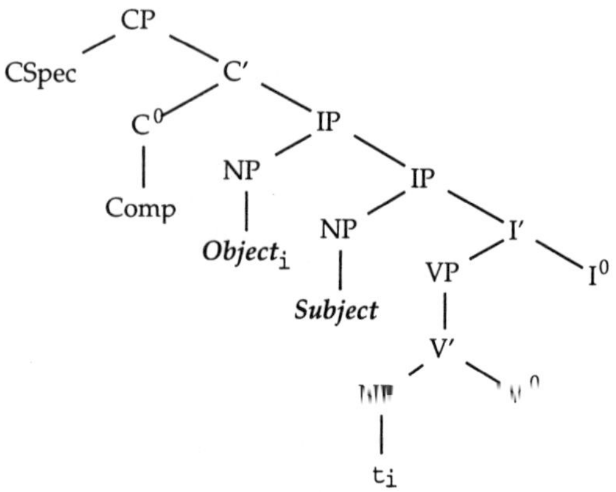

Figure 4: Object-before-subject ordering in subclauses

OVERVIEW

The chapters in this volume are roughly organized into three groups. The first three chapters tackle the question of constituent ordering preferences (Gorrell, Schlesewsky et al., Scheepers et al.). The next two chapters are concerned with attachment ambiguities (Konieczny et al., Hemforth et al.). Finally, the chapters by Bader, Konieczny et al., and Hölscher and Hemforth, discuss what happens if comprehension goes wrong in one or the other way.

Ordering preferences

Paul Gorrell offers a transparent account of syntax and parsing for German subject-before-object (SBO) preferences in verb-final and verb-second clauses for both declaratives and wh-clauses. The underlying principle *Simplicity*, derived from Chomsky's Principle of *Full Interpretation* (PFI), prevents the postulation of vacuous structure and unjustified movement of constituents at every point during incremental sentence processing. Given that subject-NPs are base generated in the Spec-IP position and object-NPs in Comp-VP, object-NPs must be moved into a position above IP, namely into the Spec-CP position. Hence, while object-before-subject (OBS) orderings require the postulation of a CP, SBO sentences without complementizers generally remain IPs. This difference in complexity is roughly the reason why SBO is generally preferred in German, since the parser will adhere to the base-generated (and simplest) structure unless there is item specific information (like case) forcing movement and therefore the postulation of further nodes. Gorrell manages to demonstrate the power of his analysis on a variety of constructions.

Matthias Schlesewsky, Gisbert Fanselow, Reinhold Kliegl, and Josef Krems present a series of experiments in order to establish the syntactic nature of the SBO preference in German. They attribute the SBO preference partly to differences in memory load during the incremental processing of SBO and OBS structures. Here, the basic assumption is that a phrase can only be attached to the current structure if its mother node has already been identified. The identification of a phrase, then, depends on whether or not its specifier (or the head) has already been encountered. Since subjects are base-generated in the IP-Spec position, whereas objects are (only) V-comps, the IP can immediately be attached to the CP only if a (potential) subject-NP is identified in the clause initial position, which is not so for an object-NP. Here, the IP and the VP have to be stored and maintained in working memory until attachment is justified, hence inducing measurable processing cost.

Christoph Scheepers, Barbara Hemforth, and Lars Konieczny investigate lexical effects on subject-object ordering preferences. They address the question of whether the SBO preference found in many experiments can be reduced to a preference to order constituents according to the thematic hierarchy (Agent > Experiencer > Theme ...). In a series of experiments, Schceepers et al. varied the linking of functional roles (Subject, Object) and thematic roles (Experiencer, Theme), exploiting an alternation of certain psych-verbs: for p-statives like "fürchten" (to fear), the Experiencer role is linked to the subject and the Theme role to the object. On the other hand, for p-causatives like "ängstigen" (frighten), the Theme is linked to the subject and the Experiencer to the object. Scheepers et al. report an early functional ordering preference which is only modified by thematic ordering preferences late in the sentence.

Attachment ambiguities

A strongly crosslinguistic perspective is taken by Barbara Hemforth, Lars Konieczny, and Christoph Scheepers in their investigation of modifier attachment. They review several sentence processing theories in the light of empirical evidence on relative clause attachment and prepositional phrase attachment in two-site ambiguities (the daughter of the teacher who ...), as well as relative clause attachment and conjoined NP-attachment in three-site ambiguities (the doctor of the daughter of the teacher who ...). The phenomena to be accounted for by a theory of sentence processing include language specific attachment preferences, modifier specific attachment preferences, and a consistent influence of thematic prepositions. Three-site relative clause attachment ambiguities are shown to depend on the position of the modifier: adjacent relative clauses show a N3 > N1 > N2 preference whereas for extraposed relative clauses, a N1 >= N3 > N2 preference was established. Hemforth, Konieczny, and Scheepers argue for a modular model of sentence processing where different subprocessors work fairly independently according to their own set of principles. The particular preference patterns found for relative clauses (and conjoined NPs) are assumed to be due to a combination of discourse-based anaphoric processes (relative pronoun resolution) and syntactic attachment processes.

Generally, the phenomenon of garden-pathing demonstrates only prefer ences in resolving local ambiguities towards one of several possible readings. A recent proposal for initial parsing preferences is the Parametrized Head Attachment principle (PHA, Konieczny et al., 1997). PHA emphasizes the role of certain properties of lexical heads and their linear order in the input string. Lars Konieczny, Barbara Hemforth and Nicole Völker (this volume) investigated whether PHA preferences can be neutralized by referentially biasing contexts. The results indicate that a referential bias cannot override PHA.

Reanalysis and misinterpretation

The ease or difficulty of recovery from a garden path has been demonstrated to not only depend upon characteristics of the error signal and the kind of revision to be accomplished, but also on certain properties of the ambiguous region itself. Lars Konieczny, Barbara Hemforth and Christoph Scheepers provide evidence on the role of the head position, i.e. the distance of the semantic head of the ambiguous phrase to the disambiguating region, in German NP/VP coordination ambiguities. They conducted an eye-tracking study to investigate the details of the on-going process of reanalysis. Their results are two-fold: For one, the head-position effect was clearly established despite the lack of a lexical frame ambiguity (Ferreira and Henderson, 1990). Second, the garden-path effect was delayed if a relative clause boundary had to be passed before disambiguation, and regressive eye-movements were strongly decreased in these cases, indicating that clause boundaries play a crucial role in reanalysis.

Markus Bader directs attention to factors of reanalysis difficulty apart from syntactic restructuring and provides striking evidence for the role of prosodic and lexical-morphological information. In his examples demonstrating prosodic effects, reanalysis turned out to be difficult only if prosodic revision was involved. This effect could be experimentally established by introducing focus particles like "only" and "even" before locally ambiguous dative or possessive pronouns. Without the focus particles, neither of the two readings seemed to cause a particular penalty on the disambiguating region. With focus particles, however, disambiguating towards the dative interpretation elicited a strong garden-path effect. Bader argues that readers assign a neutral intonation pattern during reading as long as they are not forced to do otherwise. Without focus particles, the neutral intonation is consistent with both the dative and possessive interpretation. The introduction of a focus particle, however, requires revision towards a non-neutral intonation pattern for the dative inter-pretation only, thus eliciting the garden-path effect.

Turning to syntactic function ambiguities, Bader proposes a model based on inherent case assignment preferences. If morphologically permitted, ambiguous NPs receive structural case (nom, acc), before lexical case (gen, dat), and within structural case, nominative is preferred over accusative. If reanalysis requires reassignment from structural to lexical case, the lexicon has to be reaccessed eliciting a measurable penalty. The strength of the garden path effect, then, is shown to depend upon the salience of the lexical features involved in disambiguation. More salient features (like number) elicit stronger garden-path effects than less salient features (like case) and also drive the subjects more often to (erroneously) judge a sentence as ungrammatical before attempting reanalysis.

The number feature also plays an interesting role in a research tradition on agreement errors recently established by Bock and colleagues (Bock & Eber-hard, 1993). In studies on language production, they observed an increased number of agreement errors in only one out of four conditions of complex NP-verb agreement: if the subject-NP consisted of a singular head NP modified by a plural NP, the number feature of the verb was often falsely set to plural as well, more often than in any other combination of the number feature within the complex NP. In this volume, Christoph Hölscher and Barbara Hemforth present two experiments which investigate this agreement effect in German. In the first experiment, a completion study, results known from studies on English could in general be replicated. The second study, however, an eyetracking study looking at agreement effects in language perception, reveals an agreement-mismatch effect even before the verb. The results suggest that the number-mismatch effect reflects peculiarities of complex NP construction, and that German might differ from English with respect to number processing.

NOTES

[1] This seems to be true not only for German psychology, however. An American colleague recently told us that it is out of fashion for psychologists to work on syntax.

[2] Grammar is understood here as a prescriptive school grammar, whereas the role of modern linguistic grammar theories is not discussed.

[3] We do not make any commitments with respect to a particular grammar theoretical approach. Even within the GB-framework, there is a considerable debate on what the adequate representations of these constructions are (see e.g., Gorrell, this volume). Our own approach (Hemforth, 1993; Konieczny, 1996) works within the HPSG-framework (Pollard & Sag, 1987, 1994). We chose GB-based representations mainly because they underlay many of the theoretical assumptions in different chapters of this volume (e.g., the chapters by Bader, Gorrell, Scheepers et al., and Schlesewsky et al.), and because the GB-framework and its successors are presumably the most common ones within linguistics.

[4] This schema is rather simplified since several levels of verbal projections may be assumed for different features like a tense phrase, an agreement phrase, etc.

[5] This is again a simplification. Fanselow (1992), for example, assumes that the subject is base-generated within VP where it receives its thematic role from the verb and then moved to IP where it gets its case. Haider (1993) claims that all cases in German are lexically assigned (see also Bader, this volume) and denies the existence of an IP in German.

[6] Although this is possible in Bavarian, for example.

REFERENCES

Adams, B., Clifton, C., & Mitchell, D. (1994). *Lexical guidance in sentence processing: Further evidence for a filtering account.* Unpublished manuscript.

Bader, M. (1990). *Syntaktische Prozesse beim Sprachverstehen: Theoretische Überlegungen und experimentelle Untersuchungen.* Unpublished master's thesis, University of Freiburg, Freiburg, Germany.

Bock, K., Eberhard, K. M. (1993). Meaning, sound and syntax in English number agreement. *Language and Cognitive Processes, 8(1),* 57-99.

Britt, M. A. (1994). The interaction of referential ambiguity and argument structure in the parsing of prepositional phrases. *Journal of Memory and Language, 33,* 251-283.

Brysbaert, M., & Mitchell, D. (1996). Modifier attachment in sentence parsing: evidence from Dutch. *Quarterly Journal of Experimental Psychology, 49A,* 664-695.

Clifton, C., Frazier, L., & Connine, C. (1984). Lexical expectations in sentence comprehension. *Journal of Verbal Learning and Verbal Behavior, 23,* 696-708.

Clifton, C., Jr., Speer, S., & Abney, S. P. (1991). Parsing arguments: Phrase structure and argument structure as determinants of initial parsing decisions. *Journal of Memory and Language, 30,* 251-271.

Cuetos, F., & Mitchell, D. (1988). Cross linguistic differences in parsing: Restrictions on the issue of the late closure strategy in Spanish. *Cognition, 30,* 73-105.

De Vincenzi, M., & Job, R. (1995). An investigation of late closure: The role of syntax, thematic structure and pragmatics in initial and final interpretation. *Journal of Experimental Psychology: Learning, Memory, & Cognition, 21(5),* 1303-1321.

Fanselow, G. (1992). *The return of the base generators.* Unpublished manuscript.

Ferreira, F., & Henderson, J. M. (1990). Use of verb information in syntactic parsing. *Journal of Experimental Psychology: Learning Memory and Cognition., 16(4),* 555-568.

Ford, M., Bresnan, J., & Kaplan, R. M. (1982). A competence-based theory of syntactic closure. In J. Bresnan (Ed.), *The mental representation of grammatical relations* (pp. 727-796). Cambridge, MA: MIT Press.

Frazier, L. (1979). *On comprehending sentences: Syntactic parsing strategies.* Bloomington, IN: IULC.

Frazier, L. (1987). Sentence processing: A tutorial review. In M. Coltheart (Ed.), *The psychology of reading. Attention and Performance XII* (pp. 559-586). Hove/London/Hillsdale: Lawrence Erlbaum.

Frazier, L. (1987). Theories of sentence processing. In J. Garfield (Ed.), *Modularity in knowledge representation and natural-language understanding* (pp. 291-308). Cambridge, MA: MIT Press.

Frazier, L., & Clifton, C. (1996). *Construal.* Cambridge, MA: MIT Press.

Gibson, E., Pearlmutter, N., Canseco-Gonzalez, E., & Hickock, G. (1996). Recency preference in the human sentence processing mechanism. *Cognition, 59,* 23-59.

Gilboy, E., Sopena, J., Frazier, L., & Clifton, C. (1995). Argument structure
    and association preferences in Spanish and English complex NPs. *Cognition, 54,* 131-167.

Haider, H. (1993). *Deutsche Syntax - generativ: Vorstudien zur Theorie einer
    projektiven Grammatik.* Tübingen: Narr.

Hemforth, B. (1993). *Kognitives Parsing: Repräsentation und Verarbeitung
    sprachlichen Wissens.* Sankt Augustin: Infix.

Hemforth, B., Konieczny, L., & Scheepers, C. (1994). Probabilistic or univer-
    sal approaches to sentence processing: How universal is the human lan-
    guage processor? In H. Trost (Ed.), *KONVENS94* (pp. 161-170). Berlin:
    Springer.

Hemforth, B., Konieczny, L., & Strube, G. (1993). Incremental syntax pro-
    cessing and parsing strategies. *In Proceedings of the 15th Annual Confer-
    ence of the Cognitive Science Society, July, 1993* (pp. 539-545). Hillsdale,
    NJ: Erlbaum.

Herrmann, T. (1985). *Allgemeine Sprachpsychologie.* Grundlagen und Prob-
    leme. München, Wien, Baltimore: Urban & Schwarzenberg.

Herrmann, T., & Grabowski, J. (1996). Kurzgefaßt: "Sprechen: Psychologie
    der Sprachproduktion.". *Psychologische Rundschau, 47,* 117-136.

Hörmann, H. (1976). *Meinen und Verstehen. Grundzüge einer psychologis-
    chen Semantik.* Frankfurt am Main: Suhrkamp.

Kaan, E. (1996). *Processing subject-object ambiguities in Dutch.* Unpublished
    doctoral dissertation, Rijksuniversiteit Groningen, Groningen, Holland.

Kamide, Y., & Mitchell, D. (1997). Relative clause attachment: Nondetermin-
    ism in Japanese parsing. *Journal of Psycholinguistic Research, 26,2,* 247-
    255.

Konieczny, L. (1996). *Human sentence processing: A semantics-oriented
    parsing approach* (IIG-Bericht Nr. 3/96). Freiburg: Universität Freiburg,
    Institut für Informatik und Gesellschaft.

Konieczny, L., Hemforth, B., Scheepers, C. & Strube, G. (1997). The role of
    lexical heads in parsing: Evidence from German. *Language and Cognitive
    Processes, 12,* 307-348.

MacDonald, M., Pearlmutter, N., & Seidenberg, M. S. (1994). The lexical
    nature of syntactic ambiguity resolution. *Psychological Review, 101:4,*
    676-703.

McClelland, J. L., St. John, M., & Taraban, R. (1989). Sentence comprehen-
    sion: A parallel distributed processing approach. *Language and Cognitive
    Processes, 4,* 287-336.

Mecklinger, A., Schriefers, H., Steinhauer, K., & Friederici, A. (1995). Pro-
    cessing relative clauses varying on syntactic and semantic dimensions: an

analysis with event-related potentials. *Memory and Cognition, 23,* 477-494.

Meng, M. (1997). *Die Verarbeitung von W-Fragen im Deutschen: Präferenzen und Reanalyseeffekte.* Doctoral Dissertation, University of Jena.

Mitchell, D. C. (1987). Lexical guidance in human parsing: Locus and processing characteristics. In M. Coltheart (Ed.), *Attention and Performance XII: The psychology of reading.* London: Lawrence Erlbaum Associates Ltd.

Pollard, C. & Sag, I. A. (1987). *Information-based Syntax and Semantics.* In CSLI Lecture Notes (No. 13, Vol. 1). Stanford: Center for the Study of Language and Information.

Pollard, C., & Sag, I. A. (1994). *Head-Driven Phrase Structure Grammar.* Chicago, London: University of Chicago Press and CSLI Publications.

Rayner, K., Garrod, S., & Perfetti, C. A. (1992). Discourse influences during parsing are delayed. *Cognition, 45,* 109-139.

Scheepers, C. (1996). *Menschliche Satzverarbeitung: Syntaktische und thematische Aspekte der Wortstellung im Deutschen.* Unpublished doctoral dissertation, University of Freiburg, Germany.

Spivey-Knowlton, M. & Sedivy, J. (1995). Resolving attachment ambiguities with multiple constraints. *Cognition, 55,* 227-267.

Stechow, A. von, & Sternefeld, W. (1988). *Bausteine syntaktischen Wissens.* Opladen: Westdeutscher Verlag.

Tanenhaus, M., Carlson, G., & Trueswell, J. C. (1989). The role of thematic structures in interpretation and parsing. *Language and Cognitive Processes, 4,* 211-234.

Travis, L. (1991). Parameters of phrase structure and verb-second phenomena. In R. Freidin (Ed.), *Principles and parameters in comparative grammar* (pp. 339-364). Cambridge, MA: MIT Press.

THE SUBJECT-BEFORE-OBJECT PREFERENCE IN GERMAN CLAUSES

Paul Gorrell

Max Planck Institute of Cognitive Neuroscience, Leipzig

> *Misunderstanding, in fact,*
> *is only a particular type*
> *of understanding*
> M. Bierwisch[1]

SUMMARY

This chapter extends the parsing model outlined in Gorrell (1996). In that article the focus was on German verb-second declarative clauses. Here I will discuss the 'subject-before-object' [SBO] preference which is evident in a number of different types of structurally-ambiguous German clauses. I will argue for an approach which unifies both the processing of verb-second and verb-final clauses, and the processing of declarative and wh-clauses. I will argue that, in the processing of verb-final clauses, the parser makes crucial use of item-independent regularities concerning clause structure, argument structure, and case assignment. Further, I will argue that the subject preference observed in ambiguous wh-constructions follows from the general, grammar-based, principle of minimal structure building which is also responsible for the SBO preference in declarative clauses. The syntactic analysis which underlies this approach treats wh-subjects as occurring in the same base-generated position as non-wh-subjects.

INTRODUCTION

It is a common observation that, despite the ambiguity, there is a strong 'subject-before-object' [SBO] preference in the interpretation of German sentences such as those in (1). Recent experimental work suggests that there is a similar, if less persistent, SBO preference in ambiguous wh-structures such

25

B. Hemforth and L. Konieczny (eds.), German Sentence Processing, 25-63.
© 2000 *Kluwer Academic Publishers. Printed in the Netherlands.*

as (2), e.g. Mecklinger et al 1995; Schriefers et al 1995; Meng 1996; Schlesewsky et al (this volume).

(1) a.   Die Frau sah das Kind
              the woman saw the child

     b.   daß die Frau das Kind sah
             that the woman the child saw

(2) a.   Welche Frau sah das Kind
             which woman saw the child

     b.   Das ist die Frau, die das Kind sah
             this is the woman who the child saw

The ambiguity is due to two factors: (i) the feminine, singular, determiner *die/welche* and the neuter, singular, determiner *das* serve as both the nominative and accusative forms, and (ii) the grammar of German permits object NPs to precede subject NPs, as the unambiguous sentences in (3) illustrate. I will refer to this as object-before-subject [OBS] order.[2]

(3) a.   Den Mann sah der Chef

     b.   ... daß den Mann der Chef sah

I will argue that an analysis in which wh-subjects remain in base-generated position unifies the SBO preference in declarative and wh-clauses as a general preference for base-generated structures, i.e. for the simplest structure compatible with the grammar and the input (Frazier 1978; Gorrell 1995a)[3]. I will not attempt here to give an exhaustive treatment of the parsing of ambiguous structures in German. Nor will I attempt to explicate all the factors that influence sentence processing[4]. Rather I will focus on simple subject-object ambiguities as they relate to the contrasts between: (i) verb-second and verb-final clauses, and (ii) declarative and wh-clauses. The goal of this paper is to motivate both an approach to syntactic structure and a model of syntactic processing which interact in such a way that the SBO preference observed in the processing of different types of German clauses follows from one basic principle: the prohibition on vacuous structure. This has both a grammatical aspect (the Principle of Full Interpretation of Chomsky 1986a) and a parsing aspect (the Simplicity principle of Gorrell 1995a, 1996).

Before turning to a discussion of the proposed parsing model and its specific predictions, it is necessary to clarify the type of structural representation computed by the parser. Further, as the SBO preference will be the focus of the discussion, we will need to define the terms *subject* and *object*.

SYNTAX

I assume the syntactic component of a grammar to be the representation of structural regularities which are independent of the idiosyncratic properties of lexical items. It is useful to distinguish two levels of regularity: general and category. The *general* level refers to properties which are fully category- and item-independent. For example, a common constraint on the form of phrase-structure trees is that branches may not cross (for discussion, see Partee, ter Meulen & Wall 1993). X-bar theory, e.g. the generalization that a lexical category X project to an XP (of which it is the *head*) is a fully general property of syntactic structures[5]. Another general constraint is the Principle of Full Interpretation [PFI] of Chomsky (1991) which precludes superfluous (syntactically unjustified) elements in a structure. The PFI yields a number of more specific syntax-level constraints: e.g. comparatively-complex structures resulting from deviations of base-generated order, or intermediate nodes between a lexical category and its phrasal projection, must serve some syntactic function. A related principle is the Theta Criterion which insures a one-to-one mapping between arguments and argument-structure slots. Also, various properties of long-distance dependencies must meet general syntactic conditions (e.g. Subjacency).

A *category* property is one which holds of a particular syntactic category. For example, it is a property of verbs in German that they follow their complements, whereas German nouns precede their complements. Also, it is a category property of verbs in German that subjects receive nominative case and direct objects receive accusative case. Although exceptions to category properties exist, we do not want to miss the generalization by listing for each verb, e.g., that its direct object is assigned accusative case. Exceptions will be treated as an item-level property, listed individually for each verb. Clearly we want the grammar to capture the generalization. From the parsing perspective, as Frazier (1989) observes, we do not want the parser to have to, repeatedly, take the steps to conclude for each sentence that the nominative NP is the subject *yet again*. The approach taken here is that grammatical statements concerning category regularities (whether they are termed lexical or syntactic) serve to do much of the work often given to phrase-structure rules. This will become clear in the discussion of argument structure below.

An *item* property is one which must be listed as part of an item's lexical entry. Such a listing may specify an exception to a category-level property, e.g. verbs such as *helfen*, which assign dative case to their direct object, are exceptions to the category-level property of accusative-case assignment. Bader (1996) and Bader et al (1996) discuss an interesting array of ambiguities which arise from item-specific case-assignment properties. The distinction they draw between item-independent and item-specific case assignment is consistent with the manner in which I want to make use of category properties which pertain to verbs.

The distinction between levels of regularity relates to an issue which has important implications for theories of syntactic processing. This is the distinction between the use of syntactic and lexical information (e.g. Frazier 1989; MacDonald et al 1994). But, parsing considerations aside, how do we distinguish the two information types? For example, Chomsky (1995:235) states that, "I understand the lexicon in a rather traditional sense: as a list of 'exceptions,' whatever does not follow from general principles"[6] An apparently different view is given in Grimshaw (1991:3), where it is argued that, "The position taken in much earlier work, that the lexicon is idiosyncratic... simply cannot be maintained. It fails to explain the high degree of regularity of the lexical system..." But the difference between these views is only apparent, as it is clear from Chomsky's discussion that he is not denying the existence of lexical regularities, but rather narrowly defining the term *lexicon* to exclude regularities- which are factored out as general properties of phonology, morphology, syntax, and other components of the grammar.

Grimshaw (1991) focuses on argument-structure [a-structure] regularities and proposes a prominence theory of a-structure in which the arguments of a predicate are structured in terms of relative prominence (with prominence being sensitive to thematic and aspectual information). This structured a-structure, and the way it is linked to syntactic structure, constrains the structural relations between verbs and their arguments in a phrase-structure representation. What will be important for the parsing model to be outlined below is that a theory of argument structure presupposes the existence of item-independent regularities which the theory captures. It will not matter here whether or not the relevant generalizations are considered lexical or syntactic, and I will use the term *item-independent* to refer to both. What is important is that any theory of grammatical knowledge which seeks to avoid redundancy must state the generalizations in some fashion independent of particular lexical items. I will argue that it is these regularities which the parser makes crucial reference to in processing verb-final clauses.

The manner in which a-structure maps onto a syntactic representation is central to how we define *subject* and *object*. Consider a verb such as *kaufen* ('buy'). This verb has two nominal arguments: the *agent* of the action and the *theme* of the action.[7] What can we predict about the appearance of these arguments in a syntactic structure? As the discussion in Grimshaw (1991) makes clear, it is not an idiosyncratic property of *kaufen* that the agent role will appear in the highest, base-generated, position. Grimshaw's proposal is that a-structure has its own internal structure, which reflects properties of thematic information (the thematic hierarchy) and aspectual information. The thematic hierarchy (Jackendoff 1972) is a particular way of organizing thematic relations such as *agent, theme, experiencer,* etc. For example, in (4) the leftmost thematic role (agent) is highest on the hierarchy and the rightmost lowest.

(4)   agent, experiencer, theme

As Grimshaw (1991) states, "the hierarchy is properly understood as the organizing principle of a-structures." Thus a verb such as *kaufen* will have an argument structure such as (5).[8]

(5)   (agent (theme))

In this structure, *agent* is outside of, or more prominent than, the *theme* argument. As this is a general property of a-structures, we actually would not need to state it for specific verbs.

Argument Structure and Syntactic Representation

Next we need to see how this a-structure maps into a syntactic representation. As we do this we will fill in additional item-independent information that is represented in syntactic structures. The basic intuition is that prominence in the a-structure representation directly determines prominence in the syntax. A German clause (including the VP) is right branching (cf. the Basic Branching Conjecture of Haider 1993). Therefore the most prominent position is also the leftmost, as shown in (6).

(6)

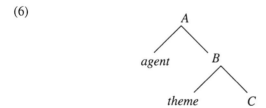

A syntactic structure contains more information than that given in (6). For example, the simple verb-final clause *(daß) der Mann das Buch kaufte* ('that the man bought the book'), contains a verb and a VP, which gives us (7).

(7)

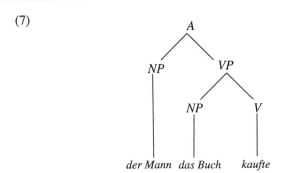

der Mann das Buch   kaufte

It can be seen here that the 'agent-before-theme' property follows from: (i) the properties of a-structure; (ii) the properties of syntactic structure; and, (iii) the condition of prominence compatibility which constrains the mapping from one to the other. But what is the node 'A' in (7)? Following Grimshaw (1993), I will assume that it is a verbal projection. By 'verbal' I mean that it is specified [+V,-N].[9] In this respect it is identical to the VP. I will assume that this higher verbal projection has its own head. For ease of exposition I will use a common label for this head and its projection (I and IP). The 'I' refers to *inflection* and it is the argument in IP, the subject, which participates in inflectional agreement with the verb. In addition to IP, a further layer of structure is needed to include the complementizer *daß* in the representation. As with IP, Grimshaw analyzes this projection as a [+V,-N] phrase. I will refer to it as CP, with a C head. This gives us the basic verb-final clause structure in (8).[10] Note that CP is head initial, with C preceding its IP complement. IP is also head initial, with I preceding its VP complement. VP is head final.

(8)

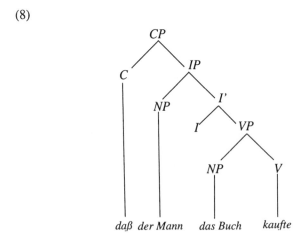

daß der Mann   das Buch   kaufte

We can now define the *subject* as the structurally most-prominent argument of a verb in a base-generated structure. An *object* is simply an argument that is not a subject.[11] Given this, the SBO order is simply the base-generated order and, as we will see below, the SBO preference reduces to a preference for the base-generated structure. I will further assume that a category property of verbs is to assign nominative case to subjects and accusative case to direct objects.[12] Therefore, only exceptions to this property need to be listed. In (9) I have informally listed the grammatical regularities that will be relevant below.

(9) a. Case-assignment defaults:
          (i) subject receives nominative case
          (ii) object receives accusative case

     b. CP and IP are head initial; VP is head final

     c. Clause structure is right-branching

Note that the case-assignment defaults are generalizations that must be captured by the grammar. Chomsky (1986a) distinguishes *inherent* and *structural* case assignment. Structural case is assigned to a syntactic position whereas inherent case is assigned as an idiosyncratic property of a verb (such as the dative case assigned to the direct object of *helfen*).[13] Given our syntactic assumptions, we can say that the most prominent argument position is assigned nominative case. The object is assigned accusative case. These are grammatical properties in the same way that verb position is a grammatical property.

Consider now a verb-second clause such as (10a) and its structure in (10b).

(10) a. Der Mann kaufte das Buch

     b.

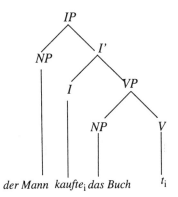

der Mann kaufte~i~ *das Buch*   *t*~i~

There are a number of important differences between the structure (10b) and (8). The first is the number of layers of verbal projection. That is, (8) contains a VP, IP and CP, whereas (10b) contains only a VP and an IP. This follows from the Principle of Full Interpretation [PFI], which requires that only the minimum structure necessary be generated (see also Travis 1991). The complementizer *daß* is a C and projects to a CP. In the absence of a complementizer or other CP constituent in (10a), (10b) is the minimum structure. One other important difference evident in (10b) is the position of the verb. It is in the head position of the IP projection [HEAD, IP] and coindexed with a phonologically-null category (a trace) in the base-generated verb position. Given PFI, this coindexed chain must be a required property.[14] Following Travis (1991), I will assume that the verb in [HEAD, IP] satisfies the requirement that the head of a projection must be "identified" in some way. Informally, we can say that, in German, a head is identified if: (i) it contains a lexical item; or, (ii) it is coindexed with a more-prominent lexical item; or, (iii) it is selected by a complementizer.

In (10b) the head of IP is identified by the presence of the verb and the head of VP is identified by being coindexed with the verb. In (8), the head of VP is identified by the presence of the verb and the head of IP is identified by being selected by the complementizer *daß*. This latter property of identification accounts, in part, for why the verb is in its base-generated position whenever a complementizer is present. The reason the verb is not permitted in [HEAD, IP] in (8) follows from the PFI, i.e. the coindexed chain is not required to meet a grammatical condition and therefore would be superfluous- and superfluous structure is what the PFI precludes. In general, deviations from base-generated positions are predicted to be either forced or ruled out (see Gorrell, in prep. for discussion).

Another deviation from base-generated position is the OBS order seen in (3) above. I will not discuss here the various discourse properties (e.g. focus properties, etc.) which may serve to justify the more-complex structure, but see Höhle (1982) and Bader (1994, 1996) for discussion. Here I only wish to illustrate the relevant properties of the representation. Similar to the verb position in (10b), the appearance of an object "to the left of" its base generated position is the result of a coindexed chain, as shown in (11), where (11a) is the structure for (3a), and (11b) the structure for (3b).[15]

(11) a.

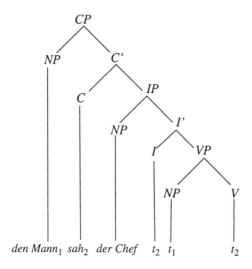

den Mann₁ sah₂ der Chef   t₂ t₁   t₂

b.

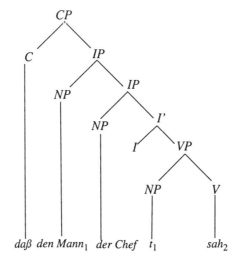

daß den Mann₁ der Chef   t₁   sah₂

In (11a), the accusative NP *den Mann* is in the specifier of CP position, i.e. specifier of the highest verbal projection. In matrix clauses, this is the position of operators with clausal scope. Below we will see that wh-operators also appear in this position. Here, we can assume that the NP has the status of a focus operator. Given that there is a CP structure, the head must be identified. This is accomplished by the presence of the verb. The heads of IP and VP are identified by being coindexed with the verb. In (11b), *den Mann* appears in a position adjoined to IP (i.e. a new IP is generated without a new head). In all other respects this structure is identical to (10b). What will be most relevant when we turn to parsing considerations is that the SBO structure is less complex than the OBS structure.

Wh-Structures

An important goal of this paper is to unify the parser's preference for SBO structures in declarative clauses with a similar preference observed in wh-clauses. Given this, the most straightforward way to achieve this result would be to show that SBO structures in wh-clauses are less complex than comparable OBS structures. The key is to analyze ss in a way that is increasingly becoming the accepted view within syntactic theory. This is the proposal that wh-objects, but not wh-subjects, are in a pre-clausal position (e.g. this has been proposed, in various forms, by Gazdar 1981; Chung & McCloskey 1983; Gazdar et al 1985; Chomsky 1986; Grimshaw 1991; and Pollard & Sag 1994). The basic point of the analysis is that wh-subjects simply occupy the same position as non-wh-subjects.[16] Thus the structure for (12a) is (12b), but the structure for (13a) is (13b).[17]

(12) a.   Welcher Mann sah den Chef
          which man-N saw the boss-A
          'which man saw the boss'

     b. $[_{IP}$ welcher Mann $[_I$ sah$_1$ $[_{VP}$ den Chef t$_1$

(13) a.   Welchen Chef sah der Mann
          which boss-A saw the man-N
          'which boss did the man see'

     b. $[_{CP}$ welchen Chef$_2$ $[_C$ sah$_1$ $[_{IP}$ der Mann $[_I$ t$_1$ $[_{VP}$ t$_2$ t$_1$

The structures in (12b) and (13b) display the same variance in clause structure that is seen in declarative main clauses, as shown in (14) and (15). That is, the wh-subject structure in (12) contains two layers of verbal projection (IP and VP), whereas the wh-object in (13) requires three layers (CP, IP and VP).

(14) a.   Der Mann sah den Chef.
'the man saw the boss'

b. $[_{IP}$ Der Mann $[_I$ sah$_1$ $[_{VP}$ den Chef t$_1$

(15) a.   Den Chef sah der Mann.
'the man saw the boss'

b. $[_{CP}$ Den Chef1 $[_C$ sah$_2$ $[_{IP}$ der Mann $[_I$ t$_2$ $[_{VP}$ t$_1$ t$_2$

For both the wh-structures in (12) - (13) and the declaratives in (14) - (15), the OBS order is more complex than the SBO order. This was true as well for the verb-final declarative clauses discussed in the last section. The structures (12b) and (13b), although differing in complexity, fulfil the requirement that the wh-phrase be in the highest specifier position of the clause, i.e. a position where they have clausal scope (Grimshaw 1993). Given this, the IP analysis of wh-subjects follows from the PFI, i.e. there is no motivation for the more-complex CP structure.

Extending this analysis to relative clauses, we have the complex-NP structures (16b) and (17b), with irrelevant details omitted.

(16) a.   Der Mann, der den Chef sah
the man$_{Nom}$who$_{Nom}$ the boss$_{Acc}$ saw
'the man who saw the boss'

b. $[_{NP}$ Der Mann $[_{IP}$ der $[_{VP}$ den Chef sah

(17) a.   Der Chef, den der Mann sah
the boss$_{Nom}$ whom$_{Acc}$ the man$_{Nom}$ saw
'the boss whom the man saw'

b. $[_{NP}$ Der Chef $[_{CP}$ den$_1$ $[_{IP}$ der Mann $[_{VP}$ t$_1$ sah

Here we see that the subject-relative clause in (16) displays the SBO order of a base-generated clause. That is, the nominative relative pronoun *der* occupies the subject position [SPEC, IP] in (16a) just as the nominative NP *Der Mann* occupies [SPEC, IP] in (14b). On the other hand, the accusative relative pronoun *den* occupies [SPEC, CP] in (17b) just as the accusative NP *den Mann* occupies [SPEC, CP] in (15b). In each case the wh-operator (i.e., the relative pronoun) is in the specifier of the clause's highest projection, where it has clausal scope.

Just as we saw that verb-second declarative clauses can vary as to the number of layers of verbal projection, wh-questions and relative clauses can vary as well. Base-generated, SBO, wh-clauses contain two layers (IP and

VP).[18] More-complex, OBS, wh-clauses require three layers (CP, IP and VP). Given the parser's sensitivity to comparative structural complexity when processing ambiguous strings, we now have the basis for unifying, not only the parsing principles required for processing verb-second and verb-final clauses, but also the processing of declarative and wh-clauses.

THE PARSER

In general I will assume the basic properties of the parsing model of Gorrell (1995a, 1996). Here, I will outline only the properties of the parser which are relevant for the processing of subject-object ambiguities in German. The focus will be on the lexical and syntactic regularities which the parser makes use of. One important property that is central to the parser's operations is the incremental application of the PFI. This principle, as noted above, precludes the appearance of superfluous elements in a syntactic representation. Gorrell (1995a) refers to this parsing principle as Simplicity, as given in (18).[19]

   (18)   Simplicity: No vacuous structure building.

Simplicity is the constraint which governs structure building. What *drives* the computation of a phrase marker is the principle of Incremental Licensing [IL], given in (19).

   (19)   Incremental Licensing: The parser attempts incrementally
                   to satisfy principles of grammar.

IL, similar to Pritchett's (1992) principle of Generalized Theta Attachment [GTA], expresses the concept that the parser's incremental structure-building operations are responsive to properties of grammar. As we have seen, grammatical properties are closely tied in many respects to lexical properties, e.g., the constrained mapping between a-structure and syntactic structure. I assume that the parser is responsive to both the idiosyncratic properties of lexical items, as well as generalizations concerning the form of a-structure and phrase markers. Although there has been considerable discussion concerning the interplay between item-specific and item-independent information in parsing (e.g. Frazier 1989; Mitchell 1989; Ferreira & Henderson 1990; Trueswell et al 1993; MacDonald et al 1994), it is clear that the pre-verbal structuring of arguments in verb-final clauses requires the use of item-independent information. This may be in the form of clause-level frequency information (e.g. SBO is the more frequent order) or it may be in the form of complexity differences (e.g. SBO is the less complex structure). Notice that the example of SBO order is not simply an 'accidental' confound. Syntactic theory construction often indirectly reflects frequency information. For example, the determination of an unmarked, or canonical, word order quite often takes into account the variety of contexts in which a given structure may be used, with the unmarked order generally the one with the widest applicability across contexts and the marked order usually requiring specific situations or presuppositions. It does not seem unreasonable to suppose that grammar construction in language acquisition is responsive to similar factors. For contrasts such as that between SBO and OBS order, we can think of the grammar as a handy way of, among other things, keeping track of certain types of frequency information.[20]

Similar remarks apply to the default case assignments. It may be that there is a lexical 'repetition threshold' that, when reached, causes the property to be factored out as a generalization (with sub-generalizations obviously possible). For present purposes, we need only assume that the parser can make use of grammatical generalizations such as those concerning nominative and accusative case assignment, and show how they interact with the preference for base-generated structures in the absence of any counterindication (i.e. with the parser's incremental application of the PFI).

Parsing Declarative Clauses

We can illustrate some of the basic properties of the parser by considering the temporary ambiguity in (20).

(20)   Die Frau kaufte ...
              the woman bought ...

The initial NP *Die Frau* is ambiguous between a nominative and an accusative reading. The parser will attach this NP as the subject of the verb, in [SPEC, IP].[21] This is the minimal structure justified by the input and it is consistent with the syntactic regularities concerning case assignment.[22] For example, Bader et al (1996) state that the parser prefers nominative case over accusative case assignment if it is grammatically permissible. Given the assumptions outlined above, the parser is making use of the default 'subject gets nominative case,' where *subject* is understood as the leftmost (most-prominent) NP in a base-generated structure. As the subject of *kaufen*, the NP *Die Frau* will receive an agent theta role. The verb is now in the head position of IP. This IP selects a VP complement and the verb is coindexed with a trace in the V position. If the post-verbal NP is consistent with an accusative reading (e.g. *das Buch*), then this NP will be attached into object position. On the other hand, if the post-verbal NP is nominative, then additional structure building is required. Specifically, an extra layer of verbal projection is computed. Informally, this 'pushes' the initial NP up into the [SPEC, CP] position.[23] This parse sequence is consistent with the observation of Hemforth (1993) that if the case marking of a post-verbal NP forces the object reading of a case-ambiguous initial NP, extra processing resources are required.

In Gorrell (1995a) I argued that, for English, clause structure was not computed until there was information in the input which justified the computation of clausal nodes (originally proposed by Pritchett 1988 and Abney 1989). For example, given the input *the man*, the parser would only compute an NP, not a full clause with this NP attached as subject (but see Frazier & Rayner 1988). But Hemforth (1993) also found a processing cost associated with string initial accusative NPs. This suggests that clausal structure is computed for string initial NPs prior to the appearance of the verb, presumably based on morphological case and item-independent information. Consider the following structures, tested in an eye-movement study by Konieczny (1996).

(21) a.   Die hungrige Füchsin bemerkte den fetten Hahn.
            the hungry fox noticed the fat rooster$_{Acc}$
            'the hungry fox noticed the fat rooster'

      b.   Der hungrige Fuchs bemerkte den fetten Hahn.
            'the hungry fox$_{Nom}$ noticed the fat rooster$_{Acc}$'

      c.   Die hungrige Füchsin bemerkte der fette Hahn.
            'the fat rooster noticed the hungry fox$_{Nom}$'

      d.   Den hungrigen Fuchs bemerkte der fette Hahn.
            'the fat rooster$_{Acc}$ noticed the hungry fox$_{Nom}$'

Konieczny (1996) reports that total reading times for the initial NP were significantly longer for the unambiguous accusative NP in (21d), as compared to the nominative and case-ambiguous NPs in (21a-c). Interestingly, *first-pass* reading times did not differ. What did differ significantly were total regression path durations [TRPD]. Koniecnzy argues that this result is incompatible with a simple difference in structure building (e.g. IP for an initial nominative NP; CP for an initial accusative NP) and suggests that the results indicate "a reanalysis process induced by the fact that the top-down prediction of a *subject-NP* could not be verified." (p. 110) Konieczny argues that, if the difference were due to structure building, then this should have been reflected in first-pass reading times. Note that first-pass reading times fail to reveal any effect of case information. There are two possibilities. The first is that first-pass reading times only reflect structure building of the NP (hence no difference given identical structures). That is, no clausal structure is not computed until the syntactic relevance of case information is available. Given this, the TRPD data reflect the additional (initial) structural building required for clause-initial accusative NPs, and not reanalysis of a computed structure. The second possibility follows from the proposal of Frazier (1989) and Friederici (1995) that item-specific information is initially unavailable to the parser, whose first-pass operations must rely on item-independent information.[24] We can incorporate Konieczny's analysis into this account if we interpret "top-down prediction of a subject-NP" as an item-independent preference for minimal structure that is disconfirmed by (subsequent) item-specific information. That is, the NP is initially processed *as if it were case ambiguous*, and the preference for the minimal analysis results in an IP structure which, when accusative case information becomes available, must be revised.

Each possibility assumes some delay in the use of case information, which is what the first-pass reading times indicate. Ruling out the first possibility would require demonstrating that regressions are specifically tied to syntactic reanalysis operations. But this would be difficult to demonstrate, given that numerous factors contribute to regressions. For example, for unambiguous word strings, Henderson & Ferreira (1995) found that, although initial reading times for a word were unaffected by manipulating the ease or difficulty of a following word, regression durations *were* significantly affected.[25] This pattern was observed despite the fact that there was no ambiguity or reanalysis involved. Thus we are left with two possible explanations for the results reported by Konieczny (1996). Neither are inconsistent with the parsing model proposed here.

To illustrate the parse sequence in verb-final declaratives, we can begin with a base-generated SBO clause containing only case-unambiguous NPs (22a).

(22) a. ...daß der Mann den Chef sah
         that the man$_{Nom}$ the boss$_{Acc}$ saw
         'that the man saw the boss'

     b. ...daß den Chef der Mann sah
         'that the man saw the boss'

The complementizer *daß* heads a CP and, as a C, subcategorizes for an IP. Next, the nominative NP *der Mann* is processed and attached as subject of the clause (in [SPEC, IP]). In contrast to (20), here there is prior evidence (C selecting an IP) for a clausal structure and the attachment as subject follows from the interaction of Simplicity and the item-independent regularity concerning nominative case assignment (i.e. it is the default subject case). Thus, this attachment can be made before the verb. It is important to stress here that the attachment into subject position is a reflection of the parser's use of a grammatical property. That is, in the absence of a lexical exception, nominative is the (item-independent) case assigned to subjects. This approach differs from the 'head-driven' model of Pritchett (1991). Pritchett proposed that neither VP nor IP nodes would be projected until their heads were processed, i.e. at the end of a clause for structures such as (22).[26] Then, the accusative NP *den Chef* is input and the parser attaches this NP into object position (making use of the default status of accusative case assignment). Next, the verb *sah* is input and its argument-structure slots accessed. Both subject and object NPs are assigned theta roles.[27]

Next consider the parse of the OBS structure in (22b). Here *den Chef*, as a clause-initial accusative NP, must be analyzed as a focused constituent and attached into a preposed position created by adjunction to IP. In contrast to the subcategorized, pre-computed, structure to which the initial nominative NP in (22a) was attached, here the adjoined structure must be computed in response to, rather than in advance of, the appearance of the accusative NP, and after its focus status is determined (this determination may be affected by discourse factors). As discussed above, this sequence is consistent with the results of experimental work which shows that clause-initial (unambiguous) accusative NPs produce increased processing difficulty (e.g. Hemforth 1993; Friederici et al, submitted; Konieczny 1996). Next the nominative NP *der Mann* is processed and attached as subject. When the verb is processed, a trace of the preposed NP is attached in direct-object position (this coindexed trace is assigned a theta role by the verb and transmitted to the NP).

The sentences in (23) show how case-ambiguous phrases are processed.

(23) a.   ...daß die Frau den Mann sah
               that the woman the man$_{Acc}$ saw
               'that the woman saw the man'

      b.   ...daß die Frau der Mann sah
               that the woman the man$_{Nom}$saw
               'that the man saw the woman'

The feminine determiner *die* is both the nominative and accusative form. As with sentence (22a), the parser will attach this first NP in (23a) into subject position (the minimal analysis), because it is a licensed position and the form of *die Frau* is compatible with a nominative reading.[28] The rest of the parse is identical to (22). The parse of (23b) differs only in that the appearance of the unambiguous nominative NP *der Mann* forces the first NP to be reanalyzed as a focused NP, as in (22a)).[29] Consider the sentences in (24), from Friederici et al (submitted).[30]

(24) a.   Er wußte, daß die Sekretärin die Direktorinnen gesucht hat
            He knew that the secretary the directors sought has
            'He knew that the secretary has sought the directors'

      b.   Er wußte, daß die Sekretärin die Direktorinnen gesucht
            haben
            He knew that the secretary the directors sought have
            'He knew that the directors have sought the secretary'

The embedded clauses in (24) are ambiguous until the final auxiliary. Disambiguation is by number specification. For example, the singular auxiliary in (24a) forces an SBO reading of the clause whereas the plural auxiliary in (24b) forces an OBS reading. For high-span readers tested in an ERP experiment, the auxiliary forcing an OBS reading produced a late-positive component when compared with the auxiliary which forced the SBO reading. This late-positive component is associated with processing difficulty and confirms the subject preference for this type of ambiguity. Friederici et al also tested sentences such as (25) in order to investigate when the preference became evident.

(25) a.   Sie wußte, daß der Sekretär die Direktorin gesucht hat
            She knew that the secretary$_{Nom}$ the director$_{Acc}$ sought has
            'She knew that the secretary has sought the director'

      b.   Sie wußte, daß den Sekretär die Direktorinnen gesucht
            haben
            She knew that the secretary$_{Acc}$ the directors$_{Nom}$ sought have
            'She knew that the directors have sought the secretary'

Here the clause-initial NPs were unambiguous (*der Sekretär* in (25a) is unambiguously nominative, forcing the SBO reading; *den Sekretär* in (25b) is unambiguously accusative, forcing the OBS reading). When comparing the clause-initial unambiguous NPs, Friederici et al (submitted) found that the accusative NPs produced a larger late positivity than the nominative NPs. Again, these data are consistent with the view that OBS clauses involve more structure building than comparable SBO clauses. As noted above, the initial NP in an SBO structure can be attached into a subcategorized phrase (the IP), but an initial NP in an OBS structure must be attached into a layer of verbal projection that is unanticipated and must be computed in response to the appearance of the NP. These data provide clear evidence for the early onset of an SBO preference in verb-final declarative clauses.

Parsing Wh-Structures[31]

In discussing the grammatical similarities between SBO declaratives and wh-clauses, and between OBS declaratives and their wh-counterparts, I pointed out that the analysis of wh-subjects as appearing in the same position as non-wh-subjects had the welcome result of unifying the complexity differences of the two clause types. SBO clauses are uniformly less complex than OBS clauses, whether or not they are declarative or wh-structures[32]. First we need to establish that simple wh-questions display the subject preference already observed with declarative main clauses.

Experimental evidence for a subject preference in ambiguous wh-structures is reported in Meng (1996). In a self-paced reading study, Meng tested sentences with initial case-ambiguous wh-phrases such as those in (26), as well as case-unambiguous structures. Disambiguation is by the number specification on the auxiliary.

(26) a.   Welche Lehrerin der Stadtschule hat die Eltern angerufen
             which teacher of the city school has the parents phoned
             'which teacher of the city school phoned the parents'

      b.   Welche Lehrerin der Stadtschule haben die Eltern angerufen
             which teacher of the city school have the parents phoned
             'which teacher of the city school did the parents phone'

Meng reports a clear garden-path effect at the auxiliary (e.g. *haben*) when the wh-object reading is forced. Interestingly, in a second self-paced reading experiment, Meng found that if the disambiguation was by the post-auxiliary NP (e.g. *Welche Bewerberin hat der Chef ...* 'Which applicant has the boss-N...'), there was no evidence of processing difficulty (as measured by reading times compared to an unambiguous structure). Meng argues that revision is more difficult when an agreement mismatch signals the error because the mismatch (assuming an initial wh-subject analysis) is a syntactic violation, i.e. a subject-verb agreement error. On the other hand, he argues that revision in the unambiguous NP condition is comparatively easy because no syntactic violation is produced, simply the need to change the computed structure[33]. No matter how this difference is interpreted, the results of Meng's experiments clearly indicate a subject preference for ambiguous wh-questions that is established when the wh-phrase is processed.

Similar results using self-paced reading are reported in Schlesewsky et al (this volume) for structures such as (26), but with a simpler wh-phrase (e.g. *Welche Frau* instead of *Welche Lehrerin der Stadtschule*). Schlesewsky et al (this volume) also tested 'long-distance' wh-structures, i.e. sentences in which the initial wh-phrase is associated with an argument position in an embedded clause, as shown in the examples in (27). Disambiguation was either by the number specification on the verb (27a) or by the case marking on the post-verbal NP (27b,c).

(27) a.   Welche Frau glaubst Du sahen die Männer am Freitag im Park
            which woman believe you saw$_{pl}$ the men on Friday in the park
            'which woman do you believe the men saw on Friday in the park'

      b.   Welche Frau glaubst Du sah der Mann am Freitag im Park
            which woman believe you saw the man$_{Nom}$ on Friday in the park
            'which woman do you believe the man saw on Friday in the park'

      c.   Welche Frau glaubst Du sah den Mann am Freitag im Park
            which woman believe you saw the man$_{Nom}$ on Friday in the park
            'which woman do you believe saw the man on Friday in the park'

The results confirm a clear subject preference for the ambiguous wh-phrase. Reading times were significantly longer when disambiguation forced the wh-object reading.[34] In order to understand the subject preference in long-distance wh-structures, we need to compare the embedded-clause structures for the subject (28a) and object (28b) readings.

(28) a.   Welche Frau$_1$ glaubst Du [$_{IP}$ t$_1$ sah$_2$ [$_{VP}$den Mann t$_2$

      b.   Welche Frau$_1$ glaubst Du [$_{CP}$ t$_1$ sah$_2$ [$_{IP}$der Mann t$_2$ [$_{VP}$ t$_1$ t$_2$

In these embedded-clause structures, in the absence of a complementizer, the verb is in the head position of the highest projection (as we saw in (10b) and (11a) above). In (28a), the highest projection is IP. In (28b) it is CP. Giving a detailed grammatical justification for the more-complex structure would take us too far afield (but see Gorrell, in prep.). Briefly, within transformational accounts, the wh-object reading requires more structure because the (structural) distance between the wh-phrase and the VP trace is too great[35]. Within phrase-structure approaches (e.g. Gazdar 1981; Pollard & Sag 1994), there is only one layer of verbal projection for long-distance wh-subjects (the VP), but there is a full clause for long-distance wh-objects. What all these approaches have in common, and what is most relevant here, is that the wh-object reading requires a more-complex structure than the wh-subject reading. Grammatical details aside, clear evidence for the more-complex CP structure in (28b) is given by the fact that the verb *sah* precedes the embedded-subject NP (*der Mann*), which is in [SPEC, IP], as was seen in (13b). Therefore the verb must be in a pre-II' position, i.e. within CP.

The parse sequence for the embedded clause with an ambiguity such as (27b,c) is as follows. When the verb *sah* is processed, the parser attaches it into the head position of a verbal projection and also attaches a trace of the wh-phrase in specifier position. If the next phrase processed is an accusative NP, as in (27c), then this is simply attached within the VP. On the other hand, if the next phrase is a nominative NP, then the parser must compute additional structure so that the preceding trace and verb remain within the highest verbal projection (now a CP) and the nominative NP is attached into [SPEC, IP]. This is formally identical to the parse sequence of any (temporarily) ambiguous OBS structure. The generalization across the different types of wh-structures considered here is that wh-subjects are less complex than wh-objects, and that the parser exhibits a consistent preference for the simpler structure.

Schlesewsky et al (1996) report the results of three experiments which suggest a subject preference for case-ambiguous wh-phrases associated with embedded *daß* clauses. They tested sentences such as those in (29), with disambiguation by the case marking of the NP following *daß*.

(29) a.   Welche Studentin glaubst Du daß der Professor beobachtet?
             which student believe you that the professor$_{Nom}$ observed
             'which student do you believe the professor observed'

      b.   Welche Studentin glaubst Du daß den Professor beobachtet?
             which student believe you that the professor$_{Acc}$ observed
             'which student do you believe observed the professor'

In one experiment using a self-paced reading task, reading times were significantly faster for the determiner *den* in (29b), which forced a subject reading of the wh-phrase, than to *der* in (29a), which forced an object reading. We can see the reason for this subject preference if we examine the parse sequence in detail. Similar to (28a) above, the parser will initially compute the structure given in (30). Note that, for all the test sentences, the case marking of the wh-phrase was incompatible with a matrix-object reading (see fn. 33).

(30)   Welche Studentin$_1$ glaubst Du [$_{IP}$ t$_1$

In contrast to (28), the next word processed is not a verb in a V2 clause, but the complementizer *daß*, which heads a CP. When *daß* is processed, a CP is projected and inserted into the structure, with an intermediate trace (t'1), as shown in (31). Given the presence of the CP, this intermediate trace is required for a wellformed link between the wh-phrase and the trace in [SPEC, IP], as discussed above with respect to (28b).

(31)   Welche Studentin$_1$ glaubst Du [$_{CP}$ t'$_1$ daß [$_{IP}$ t$_1$

Because the subject position ([SPEC, IP]) is filled by the trace t$_1$, this structure is consistent with the subsequent appearance of an accusative NP, as in (29b). The appearance of a nominative NP, as in (29a), makes reanalysis necessary, accounting for the longer reading times for the nominative determiner in Schlesewsky et al's (1996) materials[36]. Further, this parse sequence follows from the general preference for minimal structure. A CP is not postulated until there is evidence for it. Also, an intermediate trace is only posited when it is required.

Note that this analysis of the subject preference as a subcase of the preference for minimal structure differs from 'fill-the-first-gap' approaches such as the Active Filler Strategy [AFS] of Frazier & Flores d'Arcais (1989, p.332), given in (32).

(32)   Assign an identified filler as soon as possible; i.e. rank the
                 option of a gap above the option of a lexical noun phrase
                 within the domain of an identified filler.

Consider a recent study by Boland et al (1995), who tested wh-questions in which the wh-phrase was associated either with the object of a simple transitive verb, or with verbs (such as datives) which provide more than one potential gap site for the wh-filler. Boland et al (1995) found a clear plausibility effect at the verb for the simple transitive verbs (i.e. implausible fillers producing "stopped making sense" judgments at the verb), i.e. where there was a grammatical imperative to fill the direct-object gap. But such an effect was absent for the multiple-gap verbs when the first gap was implausible, but the second gap was consistent with a plausible interpretation, e.g., *Which audience did the salesman show (the movie to).* A fill-the-first-gap approach such as the AFS incorrectly predicts a consistent preference to fill the first object position in the Boland et al (1995) multiple-gap condition. This prediction was disconfirmed. But, if the putative AFS-induced subject preference is a preference for the simpler structure (and not a preference to fill the first gap), then we have a straightforward explanation for the lack of an AFS effect in the Boland et al (1995) results.

Consider also wh-structures such as (33).

(33) a.   Who did you give a book to?

     b.   Who did you give a book?

The AFS, incorrectly to my ear, predicts that (33b) should be easier than (33a). This is because, for the position immediately following the verb, an AFS-parser would "rank the option of a gap above that of a lexical NP." Clifton & Frazier (1989) note the problem but offer no solution. Again, the lack of an AFS effect is entirely predictable if there is no item-independent bias for filling the first gap position- simply a general preference for minimal structure. It may well be that, once the subject-object complexity difference is analyzed as a separate phenomenon, the processing of gaps within verb-initial VPs is best accounted for by a lexical-expectation model similar to Fodor's (1978a) original proposal[37]. Given our syntactic assumptions, the subject-object contrast always involves a complexity difference. For example, the subject preference reported by Frazier & Flores d'Arcais (1989) for ambiguous versions of Dutch wh- and non-wh-structures similar to the German examples discussed above are also predicted by the IP analysis of wh-subjects[38].

More recently, Schriefers et al (1995) tested the subject preference in German relative- clause structures using a self-paced reading task. They used feminine case-ambiguous NPs and relative pronouns, with disambiguation by a clause-final auxiliary verb whose number specification was only compatible with the clause as either a subject relative (34a) or an object relative (34b).

(34) a.   Das ist die Managerin, die die Arbeiterinnen gesehen hat
            this is the manager who the workers seen has
            'this is the manager who has seen the workers'

     b.   Das sind die Arbeiterinnen, die die Managerin gesehen hat
            these are the workers who the manager seen has
            'these are the workers who the manager has seen'

In a semantically-neutral condition (as illustrated by the examples in (34)), they found that the reading times for clause-final auxiliary verbs were faster for subject relatives than object relatives. As with the Frazier & d'Arcais (1989) study, the on-line results reported by Schriefers et al (1995) are what would be predicted by an analysis in which subject relatives are structurally less complex than object relatives, as shown in (35a,b).[39]

(35) a.   Das ist [$_{NP}$ die Managerin [$_{IP}$ die [$_{VP}$ die Arbeiterinnen gese-hen hat

      b.   Das sind [$_{NP}$ die Arbeiterinnen [$_{CP}$ die$_1$ [$_{IP}$ die Managerin [$_{VP}$ t$_1$ gesehen hat

Mecklinger et al (1995) report evidence of a similar preference in an ERP study. For fast comprehenders (as determined by question-answering RTs), the clause-final auxiliary in the object relatives was associated with a positive component significantly larger in amplitude than in the subject relatives. In a recent study, Friederici et al (submitted) found a late-positive component when the clause-initial relative pronoun was unambiguously marked for accusative case, forcing an object-relative reading. This is clear evidence of an early subject preference in these structures and appears to disconfirm one prediction of the parallel model outlined in Gibson et al (1994). This parallel parser will build structures compatible with both the subject and object relative clauses, and, as Gibson et al state, "the account proposed here predicts that the preference will not be present until the verb is processed." (p. 402)

MEMORY LOAD AND THE SBO PREFERENCE

In the previous sections I proposed that the subject preference produced by ambiguous wh-phrases is actually a subcase of the general preference for minimal structure. An alternative proposal, which has much in common with the preference for minimal structure, is that the parser prefers structures which are comparatively less costly in terms of memory load. Schlesewsky et al (this volume) put forth a specific memory load account of the subject preference.[40] The proposal is that subject phrases do not require the storage of lexical material and related structure whereas clause-initial object wh-phrases do. Therefore, unambiguous wh-subjects will involve less processing cost than unambiguous wh-objects. For ambiguous wh-phrases, the subject reading is preferred as it is argued to be processed more quickly than the object reading.[41] As the explanation for the subject preference with unambiguous phrases is somewhat different from the subject preference with ambiguous phrases, I will discuss them separately.

In contrast to the CP-IP distinction discussed above, Schlesewsky et al assume that both SBO and OBS clauses are CPs. Therefore, with respect to the grammar, there is neither a global difference in syntactic complexity, nor a local difference at the point when the wh-phrase is processed. However, there is a *parser-induced* difference as follows. Given an unambiguous nominative wh-phrase, the parser attaches this phrase into [SPEC, CP] and attaches the IP to the parse tree. For an unambiguous accusative wh-phrase, the parser will also attach this phrase into [SPEC, CP], but the IP and VP nodes cannot be attached (see below) and must be stored on a memory stack. It is this storage which produces the additional processing cost. This difference in the processing of clause-initial nominative and accusative phrases follows from the following attachment procedure:[42] The identification of α implies the postulation of all nodes grammatically required for α. Only those nodes can be built into the structure already parsed for which the specifier (or the head) has already been identified. The other nodes must be stored.

Thus if α is a nominative wh-phrase, then an IP is grammatically required because [SPEC, IP] is the base-generated subject position. This IP can be attached without delay because it is the complement of the head of CP (which has been identified through the wh-phrase). On the other hand, if α is an accusative wh-phrase, a VP is identified because this is the base-generated site for an accusative NP. But this VP cannot be attached because an IP has not been identified, and the attachment site for VP is IP. Schlesewsky et al (this volume) state that then IP and VP must be stored (p. 88). But it is not clear why IP, if postulated, must be stored and not attached to the parse tree, i.e. attached to CP. Of course if IP is attached to CP, there is no reason that VP could not be attached to the IP. It must be the case that, if IP is postulated, it is because there is item-independent information that, given a CP, there must be an IP (cf. Crocker 1994). But this still leaves unexplained why attachment of a postulated phrase into an available, grammatical, attachment site, is precluded. Of course if attachment were permitted, there would still be a complexity difference. But then memory load would have no role in the explanation.[43]

Suppose instead that IP is not postulated (as suggested by Schlesewsky et al's discussion immediately following their example (21)). Then only VP is postulated and it must be stored until IP is computed. But then the difference between the subject and object structures in terms of memory load is the status of VP. For subject phrases, the VP can be attached to the IP. For object structures, the VP must be stored on the memory stack. But note that now an additional assumption is required. For the subject phrase, more structure (CP, IP and VP) is computed than for the object structure (CP and VP).[44] Thus the cost of extra structure building for the subject phrase must be more than offset by the benefit of not needing to store the VP node. I assume that similar remarks apply to declarative structures as well. That is, either the SBO preference for declaratives requires a distinct explanation, or memory-load considerations are applicable in a way similar to wh-structures. Putting aside the less-preferred option of a distinct explanation, consider the parse of (37a,b), where the adverb *gestern (yesterday)* is in first position and the verb precedes both subject and object.

(36) a.   Gestern sah der Mann den Chef.

       b.   Gestern sah den Mann der Chef.

Given the schedule of parsing operations required by (36), a phrasal node is attached into the structure when its specifier or head is identified. In (37a,b) the verbal head sah precedes the accusative NP *den Mann*. Thus, in each case, a VP has already been identified and attached into the structure.[45] Given this, there is no difference in memory load between the SBO and OBS clauses and the prediction is that there is no processing difference between *der Mann* and *den Mann* in these structures. Of course other factors may be appealed to, but the question is whether or not, once this is done, there is any reason to retain a memory-load explanation for the processing cost of unambiguous OBS structures.

Turning to the processing of ambiguous wh-structures, Schlesewsky et al argue that for "ambiguous structures we propose a subject preference because the subject alternative can be pursued faster and will therefore block its alternatives." (p. 88). *Modulo* the appeal to (36), this is similar to the proposal of Frazier & Fodor (1978) that the principle of Minimal Attachment follows from the fact that "the structural hypothesis which the parser pursues is the first one it recognizes."[46] (p. 322) The basic intuition is that the least-complex structure is computed fastest. However, the role of memory load is not clear here. But, as noted above, it must be the case that the storage of a VP on the memory stack is more costly than the computation of additional structure. That is, the subject reading results in the computation of a locally more-complex structure. Here the cost must be temporal as it is (comparative) speed of computation which is at issue. Therefore, for ambiguous wh-phrases, the more-complex subject analysis must be computed more quickly than the object analysis. Presumably it is the use of the memory stack which slows down computation. But if this is the case, then the proposal runs into the same empirical problem as was seen with unambiguous structures. Consider (38).

(37) a.   Gestern sah die Frau der Chef.

       b.   Gestern sah die Frau den Chef.

       c.   Gestern sah die Frau die Lehrerin.

In (38a,b), the initial (post-verbal) NP is ambiguous. The prediction is that there is no memory-load induced subject preference, i.e. equal ease in processing *der* versus *den* Chef in (38a,b), as well as no SBO preference in (38c). As with (37), this is because the prior processing of an inflected verb permits the computation of both an IP and a VP, producing attachment sites for both subject and object analyses of the first NP. Comparative structural complexity may play a role, but if it does, then there is no need to invoke memory load as an explanation.

At the beginning of this section I stated that memory-load explanations are compatible with the present proposal that the SBO preference is a subcase of the preference for minimal structure. This compatibility is due to the common belief that the minimal structure will be less costly in processing terms than more-complex alternatives. But an important question is whether or not the processing system directly or indirectly seeks to reduce potentially unnecessary use of short-term memory resources. For example, one possibility is that the parser directly computes the comparative memory-load cost for alternative analyses of ambiguous input and chooses the least costly option. But this would involve a new calculation at every ambiguous point in every sentence.

It seems more plausible to assume that the parser indirectly exhibits a preference for less-complex structures. The present proposal is that the parser does this by an incremental application of the Principle of Full Interpretation (Simplicity). It was argued in Gorrell (1995a) that this is needed in any event to prevent the parser from computing superfluous structure in advance of any lexical or syntactic justification. Principles such as Schlesewsky et al's (36) do capture the spirit of this proposal by limiting the amount of structure computed (or attached) in advance of lexical justification. But it is precisely this constraint on structure building that is doing the real work. With respect to ambiguity resolution, an appeal to memory load adds nothing to the explanatory power of the proposal.

Note that this is not an argument that complex structures do not exact a cost in terms of memory resources. Rather, the claim is that the preference for minimal structure, of which the SBO preference in German clauses is a subcase, is not a direct result of the parser selecting, at each choice point, the structure least likely to burden short-term memory. I have not offered a functional explanation for the parser's use of Simplicity. It may well reflect the need to keep processing load to a minimum as the parse proceeds. It clearly has that benefit (as Frazier has often argued for Minimal Attachment). But establishing a benefit does not entail a causal relation, nor does it provide an explanation.

SUMMARY

The use of argument-structure information and category-level regularities by the parser allows us to look at the distinction between lexical and syntactic information in a new way. The distinction which is relevant for the parser is between item-specific and item-independent information. This chapter has not addressed the issue of how the parser resolves conflicts between the two information types (Frazier 1989; Mitchell 1989; Ferreira & Henderson 1990; Trueswell et al 1993; MacDonald 1994). But the incremental processing of verb-final clauses makes it clear that the parser must be able to make use of item-independent information. It may well be that the parser does not place tighter restrictions on the variation in the relative string position of phrases observed in the languages of the world, precisely because of the availability of item-independent information (whether lexical or syntactic).

One important general principle which the parser makes use of in incremental sentence processing is the PFI. From the PFI we have derived a complexity account of the SBO preference, which is to be preferred for conceptual reasons. From a grammatical perspective, the analysis of wh-subjects as IP structures is consistent with recent work in syntactic theory which posits strong economy constraints on linguistic representations. Similar constraints appear to be a factor in acquisition. Consider the English questions in (39a) and (40a), with the relevant structures given in (39b) and (40b).

(38) a.   who likes John

      b. $[_{IP}$ who $[_{VP}$ likes John

(39) a.   who does John like

      b. $[_{CP}$ who$_1$ does $[_{IP}$ John $[_{VP}$ like t$_1$

Chomsky (1986b) observes that a conclusion consistent with the well-formed (39a) and (40a) is that English has wh-movement (i.e. wh-phrases in CP) except for subjects.[47] This might follow from what has been termed the 'vacuous movement hypothesis' [VMH]. This is the hypothesis that grammars do not have deviations from base-generated structures which fail to affect the surface order of lexical items. Similarly we might suppose that the language learner would not posit such a structure for (39a), given the lack of evidence. What I have argued for here is that the parser's use of the PFI gives it a VMH property. That is, the parser will not compute a more-complex structure in the absence of relevant evidence. Within parsing theory, this was originally formulated in Fodor (1978b) and called Superstrategy. Fodor argued that, "the human parsing device processes a word sequence that is heard or read *as if it were the terminal string of a wellformed deep structure....* In particular, a constituent that appears where it could not appear in a wellformed deep structure is tagged as a filler..."(p. 249) [emphasis in original] In current terms, this is precisely the proposal that the parser assumes a base-generated order in the absence of some counterindication (such as an accusative NP which "appears where it could not appear" in a base-generated structure). In the twenty years or so since Superstrategy was first proposed, work in syntax and in parsing theory has increasingly focused on issues of economy of representation. Fodor assumed a fairly indirect relation between the grammar and the parser. In part, this indirect relation was required because, at the time, syntactic theory had not advanced to the point where it could incorporate general principles of economy (such as the PFI) that parsing considerations necessitate (cf. the Minimal Attachment Principle of Frazier & Fodor 1978, the Minimal Chain Principle of De Vincenzi 1991, and the Minimal Everything Principle of Inoue & Fodor 1995).

The parser exhibits a preference for minimal structure across a wide range of ambiguities, construction types, and languages (Frazier & Fodor 1978; Frazier 1990b; De Vincenzi 1991; Gorrell 1995a; Inoue & Fodor 1995, among others). Thus there is a conceptual advantage to analyzing the SBO preference in German declarative and wh-clauses as a preference for the minimal structure. First, we are able to explain additional phenomena without additional devices. Second, we eliminate unnecessary properties and further restrict the theory of syntactic processing. This is not possible with construction-specific strategies such as the AFS, which are only applicable to filler-gap dependencies with an identifiable filler. For the range of ambiguities considered here, the general preference for the simplest structure, which follows from the incremental application of the PFI, is all that is required.

Author's Note

I have benefited from having the opportunity to discuss a wide range of issues in German sentence processing with Markus Bader, Josef Bayer, Gisbert Fanselow, Angela Friederici, Thom Gunter, Barbara Hemforth, Reinhold Kliegl, Michael Meng, Axel Mecklinger, Matthias Schlesewsky, Ed Stabler, Peter Staudacher, Karsten Steinhauer, and Craig Thiersch. Special thanks are due to Evelyn Ferstl for numerous discussions during the preparation of this chapter. Some of the material in this chapter was presented at the University of Potsdam (April 1996) and I wish to thank the audience there for many valuable comments. I am also grateful to Lars Konieczny and Marica de Vincenzi for comments on an earlier draft of this chapter.

NOTES

[1] Bierwisch (1983, p. 117).

[2] See the papers in Corver & van Riemsdijk (1994) for various syntactic approaches to this type of word-order variation.

[3] I will use the term base-generated position to refer to the position in a syntactic structure that is directly projected from a-structure information (see Section 2 below). Simply put, a base-generated position is the position of an argument in the unmarked structure.

[4] See Bierwisch (1983) and Bayer (1995) for discussion of the role of syntax in sentence comprehension. Haegeman (1991) contains a useful introduction to many of the grammatical terms used below.

[5] MacDonald et al (1994) appear to treat X-bar structures as individual lexical properties, thereby requiring that each lexical item specifically list the general property (among others) that it projects to a phrasal category. Thus syntactic regularities are reduced to lexical coincidences. It may be that the intent is to list only unpredictable properties, but this preserves the distinction between item-specific (lexical) and item-independent (syntactic) information, even if the latter has been moved into the lexicon.

[6] As Di Sciullo & Williams (1987:3) remark, "The lexicon is like a prison- it contains only the lawless, and the only thing the inmates have in common is lawlessness."

[7] I will not distinguish between the semantic roles theme and patient.

[8] Technically, Grimshaw's a-structures do not contain theta-role labels. I use them here for convenience. Aspectual information is relevant for accounting for apparent exceptions to the relation between the thematic hierarchy and a-structure. For example, for verbs such as *frighten*, the theme argument appears to be more prominent than the experiencer argument, as in (i).
(i) Sincerity frightens John
But there is a cause aspect to the theme role (e.g. *Sincerity causes John to experience fear*) that gives it additional a-structure prominence. This cause property is missing in verbs such as *fear* and, as expected, the experiencer role is more prominent than the theme, as shown in (ii).
(ii) John fears Fred

[9] See Gorrell (1996) for discussion. The proposal is similar in many respects to that of Haider (1993).

[10] As Crocker (1994) observes, it is a property of functional categories such as C and I that their complement-taking properties are "fixed." That is, C always takes an IP complement and I always takes a VP complement. See Grimshaw (1993) for one approach to deriving this generalization. See Gorrell (1991) for an overview of the use of the complementizer phrase in generative grammar. Alternative analyses to the one assumed here are given in, for example, Schwartz & Vikner (1989) and Haider (1993). See Gorrell (in prep.) for a detailed discussion of the syntactic structures assumed in this chapter.

[11] I will not consider German double-object structures in this paper, so the subject-object distinction will be sufficient.

[12] Just as it is a category property of German nouns to assign genitive case to their complements.

[13] See Bader (1996) and Bader et al (1996) for an extensive discussion of this contrast and its relevance to German sentence processing. It should be pointed out that my treatment of case assignment begs a number of important case-theoretic questions concerning how English and German differ.

[14] A *chain* refers to a lexical phrase or word and its associated traces.

[15] The fact that deviations are 'to the left,' follows from the interaction of the right-branching property of clauses and the requirement that traces be coindexed with a more-prominent phrase or lexical item.

[16] See Gorrell (in prep.) for a syntactic analysis of this proposal

[17] I will use 'N' to designate nominative NPs an 'A' for accusative NPs

[18] Note that, although interpretations of processing studies with subject relative clauses often assume a movement analysis (e.g. Zurif et al. 1993; Swinney and Zurif 1995), the data are consistent with either analysis of wh-subject structures, as the authors cited point out.

[19] See Gorrell (1995a; in press) for a discussion of Simplicity with respect to the Minimal Attachment principle of Frazier & Fodor (1978).

[20] I am unaware of any case where a base-generated order is less frequent than a more-complex counterpart. Of course deviations from base-generated order do not necessarily reflect frequency information, as Schlesewsky et al (this volume) observe for wh-structures. Here there is simply no wellformed counterpart, at least in German and English.

[21] See below for a discussion of when the parser builds clausal structure.

[22] See Inoue (1991), Pritchett (1991), Weinberg (1993) and Gorrell (1995b) for the use of case information in Japanese sentence processing.

[23] Recall that CP, IP and VP are all specified as [+V,-N], so this 'raising' from [SPEC, IP] to [SPEC, CP] is simply additional structure building. See Gorrell (1996) for details.

[24] For more recent discussion of this proposal see Frazier & Clifton (1996) and Friederici & Mecklinger (1996).

[25] The ease or difficulty of a following word was determined by frequency. For example (i) versus (ii), where *autumn* is less frequent than *winter.*
(i) ...until autumn
(ii) ... until winter

[26] See Gorrell (1996) for discussion of case ambiguities in German with respect to the predictions of Pritchett's (1991, 1992) model. Note also that the parse sequence given here for verb-final clauses is consistent with the evidence presented in Bader & Lasser (1994) against 'pure' head-driven parsers.

[27] The present model makes no predictions concerning the temporal relation between object attachment and theta-role assignment to the subject. Further, I take it to be an open question whether or not regularities concerning theta roles (c.g. subjects tend to be agents) allow for pre-verbal theta-role assignment. See Trueswell, Tanenhaus & Kello (1993) for a discussion of ambiguities in English.

[28] Similar remarks apply to NPs (e.g. proper names) and languages (e.g. Dutch, English) where case-marking is seldom overt. What is relevant is compatibility or incompatibility with item-independent regularities.

[29] See Gorrell (1996) for a detailed discussion of this reanalysis.

[30] Friederici et al. (submitted) also investigated the processing of relative-clause structures. I discuss these in the next section.

[31] In this section I will restrict the discussion to German wh-structures. There are a number of studies in Dutch which report a preference for an object interpretation for embedded wh-structures (e.g. Jordens 1991; Frazier 1993). See Kaan (1996) for a thorough treatment of this topic, as well as discussion of main-clause preferences. Gorrell (in press) briefly discusses the Dutch data from the perspective of the model proposed here.

[32] When sentences are presented in isolation, reanalysis appears to be more efficient with wh-structures than with declaratives (Friederici et al. submitted).

This is presumably due to the fact that OBS wh-structures have a sentence-internal justification for the noncanonical order (i.e. the necessity of preposing a wh-phrase), whereas OBS declarative clauses typically require sentence-external justification.

[33] This lack of a reading time difference with the NP disambiguation may explain why Stowe (1986), who also used a self-paced reading task, failed to find evidence for a subject preference with embedded questions such as (i).
(i) My brother wanted to know who Ruth will bring us home to at Christmas.
In (i) the NP *Ruth* disambiguates, forcing an object reading of the wh-phrase.

[34] The disambiguation by the unambiguous NP was significant only in the subject analysis. Both subject and items analysis were significant for the verb-agreement condition. Note that a verb such as glauben requires a dative object (e.g. *der Frau* or *Welcher Frau*) so the form of the initial wh-phrase is incompatible with a matrix-object reading.

[35] For example, within the Barriers framework of Chomsky (1986b), the extra structure is the product of adjunction. Concerning the position of the trace, the generalization is that a link between a wh-phrase in matrix [SPEC, CP] and an embedded clause position requires a trace in the specifier position of the highest verbal projection: [SPEC, IP] in (28a); [SPEC, CP] in (28b). See Gorrell (in press) and the parse sequence in (30) and (31) below.

[36] See Gorrell (in press) for a detailed discussion of this reanalysis within the framework of Structural Determinism (Gorrell 1995a, 1996)

[37] This may offer a solution to a problem that Matt Crocker (personal communication) points out for the Structural Determinism of Gorrell (1995a). That is, if the parser first posits a gap immediately after the verb in (32a), then the correct analysis should involve the retraction of precedence relations. See Schlesewsky et al (this volume) for more discussion of wh-ambiguities with double-object constructions, and Gorrell (in press) for a discussion of the AFS effects discussed in Frazier & Clifton (1989) and De Vincenzi (1991).

[38] Following den Besten (1983), Frazier & d'Arcais (1989) assume that the pre-verbal position in Dutch verb-second clauses is always a filler position, i.e. within CP. Thiersch (1978) gives a similar analysis for German. See Gorrell (1996) and Travis (1984, 1991) for detailed motivation of the IP analysis of declarative SBO clauses.

[39] See Holmes & O'Regan (1981) for an eye-movement study showing that French subject relative clauses produce less processing difficulty than object

relatives. See also Fodor, Bever & Garrett (1974:346) for a discussion of experiments with English relative clauses showing a processing advantage for subject relatives.

[40] See also Kluender & Kutas (1993).

[41] As discussed below, this is similar to how minimal-attachment effects were derived in the Sausage Machine model of Frazier & Fodor (1978).

[42] Cf. the left-attaching parsing strategy of Stabler (1994:323).

[43] Note also that the subject-object contrast follows from the arbitrary exclusion of complements as justification for phrasal node attachment into the existing structure. That is (36) requires the identification of the specifier (or the head). Given that the syntactic framework assumed by Schlesewsky et al includes heads, specifiers and complements as core relations, why are complements excluded? Note that it is the reference to specifier in (36) that produces the immediate subject advantage (because subjects are specifiers of IP). One technical point: unless the VP-internal subject hypothesis is assumed (i.e. subject phrases bind a trace in [SPEC, VP]), (36) predicts that VPs in verb-final clauses cannot be built into the structure until the final verb (the head of VP) is processed.

[44] Presumably, the chain between the wh-phrase and its trace in [SPEC, IP] is computed as well. It is unclear if a chain is created between a wh-object and a position on a memory stack at this point in the parse. If not, then we have a subject preference, not only despite the additional number of phrasal nodes computed, but also despite the computation of a chain (which is not computed at this point in the parse for the object phrase).

[45] Assume that the parser will compute an IP, given the presence of an inflected verb.

[46] See Gorrell (1987, 1989) for a version of this within the context of a ranked-parallel parser.

[47] Another advantage of the IP analysis of wh-subjects is that it gives a straightforward account of the lack of 'do support' in structures such as (35b). That is, the CP structure in (36b) has a head that needs to be identified (see the discussion of Example (10) above) and, given that the grammar of English prevents main verbs from appearing in CP, the pro-verb do is used to identify the head. The structure in (35b), lacking a CP, has no requirement of do-support.

REFERENCES

Abney, S. (1989). A computational model of human parsing. *Journal of Psycholinguistic Research, 18*, 129-144.

Bader, M. (1996). *On reanalysis: Evidence from German.* Unpublished manuscript. Friedrich-Schiller-University, Jena.

Bader, M. (1994). *Sprachverstehen: Syntax und Prosodie beim Lesen.* Unpublished doctoral dissertation, University of Stuttgart.

Bader, M., Bayer, J., Hopf, J-M., & Meng, M. (1996). Case assignment in processing German verb-final clauses. *MIT Occasional Papers in Linguistics 9: Proceedings of the NELS 26 Sentence Processing Workshop.*

Bader, M., & Lasser, I. (1994). German verb-final clauses and sentence processing: Evidence for immediate attachment. In C. Clifton, L. Frazier & K. Rayner (Eds.), *Perspectives on sentence processing* (pp. 225-242). New York: Erlbaum.

Bayer, J. (1995). Psycholinguistics. In J. Jacobs, A. von Stechow, W. Sternefeld & T. Venneman (Eds.), *Syntax: An international handbook of contemporary research, Volume 2.* Berlin: de Gruyter.

Bierwisch, M. (1983). How on-line is language processing? In G.B. Flores d'Arcais & R.J. Jarvella (Eds.), *The process of language understanding* (pp. 113-168). New York, NY: John Wiley & Sons Ltd.

Boland, J., Tanenhaus, M., Garnsey, S., & Carlson, G. (1995). Verb argument structure in parsing and interpretation: Evidence from wh-questions. *Journal of Memory and Language 34*, 774-806.

Chomsky, N. (1995). *The Minimalist Program.* Cambridge, MA: MIT Press.

Chomsky, N. (1991). Some notes on economy of derivation and representation. In R. Freidin (Ed.), *Principles and parameters in comparative grammar* (pp. 417-454). Cambridge, MA: MIT Press.

Chomsky, N. (1986a). *Knowledge of language: Its nature, origin and use.* New York: Praeger.

Chomsky, N. (1986b). *Barriers.* Cambridge, MA: MIT Press.

Chung, S., & McCloskey, J. (1983). On the interpretation of certain island facts in GPSG. *Linguistic Inquiry 14*, 704-713.

Clifton, C., & Frazier, L. (1989). Comprehending sentences with long-distance dependencies In G. Carlson & M. Tanenhaus (Eds.), *Linguistic structure in language processing.* Dordrecht: Kluwer Academic Publishers.

Corver, N., & van Riemsdijk, H. (Eds.) (1994). *Studies on scrambling: Movement and non-movement approaches to free word-order phenomena.* New York, NY: Mouton de Gruyter.

Crocker, M. (1994). On the nature of the principle-based sentence processor. In C. Clifton, L. Frazier & K. Rayner (Eds.), *Perspectives on sentence processing* (pp. 245-266). New York: Erlbaum.

De Vincenzi, M. (1991). *Syntactic parsing strategies in Italian.* Dordrecht: Kluwer Academic Publishers.

Di Sciullo, A.M., & Williams, E. (1987). *On the definition of word.* Cambridge, MA: MIT Press.

Ferreira, F., & Henderson, J. (1990). Use of verb information in syntactic parsing: Evidence from eye-movements and word-by-word self-paced reading. *Journal of Experimental Psychology: Learning, Memory and Cognition, 30,* 555-568.

Fodor, J.A., Bever, T., & Garrett, M. (1974). *The psychology of language.* New York: McGraw Hill.

Fodor, J.D. (1978a). Parsing strategies and constraints on transformations. *Linguistic Inquiry, 9,* 427-474.

Fodor, J.D. (1978b). Superstrategy. In W. Cooper & E. Walker (Eds.), *Sentence processing: Psycholinguistic studies presented to Merrill Garrett.* Hillsdale, NJ: Erlbaum.

Fodor, J.D., & Frazier, L. (1980). Is the human sentence parsing mechanism an ATN? *Cognition, 8,* 417-459.

Frazier, L. (1993). Processing Dutch sentence structures. *Journal of Psycholinguistic Research, 22,* 85-108.

Frazier, L. (1989). Against lexical generation of syntax. In W. Marslen-Wilson (Ed.), *Lexical representation and process.* Cambridge, MA: MIT Press.

Frazier, L. (1978). *On comprehending sentences: Syntactic parsing strategies.* Unpublished Ph.D. dissertation, The University of Connecticut. Distributed by the Indiana University Linguistics Club.

Frazier, L., & Clifton, C. (1996). *Construal.* Cambridge, MA: MIT Press.

Frazier, L., & Clifton, C. (1989). Successive cyclicity in the grammar and the parser. *Language and Cognitive Processes, 4,* 93 -126.

Frazier, L., & Flores d'Arcais, G. (1989). Filler-driven parsing: A study of gap filling in Dutch. *Journal of Memory and Language, 28,* 331-344.

Frazier, L., & Fodor, J.D. (1978). The sausage machine: A new two-stage parsing model. *Cognition, 6,* 291-325.

Frazier, L., & Rayner, K. (1988). Parameterizing the language processing system: Left- versus right-branching within and across languages. In J. Hawkins (Ed.), *Explaining language universals* (pp. 247-279). Oxford: Basil Blackwell.

Friederici, A. (1995). The time course of syntactic activation during language processing: A model based on neuropsychological and neurophysiological data. *Brain and Language, 50*, 259-281.

Friederici, A., & Mecklinger, A. (1996). Syntactic parsing as revealed by brain responses: First-pass and second-pass processes. *Journal of Psycholinguistic Research, 25*, 157-176.

Friederici, A., Mecklinger, A., Steinhauer, K., & Meyer, M. (submitted). *Syntactic parsing preferences and their on-line revisions: Effects of case marking and number agreement.*

Gazdar, G. (1981). Unbounded dependencies and coordinate structure. *Linguistic Inquiry, 12*, 155-184.

Gazdar, G., Klein, E., Pullum, G., & Sag, I. (1985). *Generalized phrase structure grammar.* Oxford: Basil Blackwell.

Gibson, E., Hickok, G., & Schütze, C. (1994). Processing empty categories: A parallel approach. *Journal of Psycholinguistic Research, 23*, 381-405.

Gorrell, P. (in prep.). *The variable structure of German clauses.* Manuscript in preparation. Max Planck Institute for Cognitive Neuroscience, Leipzig.

Gorrell, P. (in press). Syntactic analysis and reanalysis in sentence processing. In J.D. Fodor & F. Ferreira (Eds.), *Reanalysis in sentence processing.* Dordrecht: Kluwer Academic Publishers.

Gorrell, P. (1996). Parsing theory and phrase-order variation in German V2 clauses. *Journal of Psycholinguistic Research, 25*, 135-156.

Gorrell, P. (1995a). *Syntax and parsing.* Cambridge: Cambridge University Press.

Gorrell, P. (1995b). Japanese trees and the garden path. In R. Mazuka & N. Nagai (Eds.), *Sentence processing.* Hillsdale, NJ: Erlbaum.

Gorrell, P. (1991). COMP in formal grammar. *The Oxford International Encyclopedia of Linguistics.* Oxford: Oxford University Press.

Gorrell, P. (1989). Establishing the loci of serial and parallel effects in syntactic processing. *Journal of Psycholinguistic Research, 18*, 61-73.

Gorrell, P. (1987). *Studies of human syntactic processing: Ranked-parallel versus serial models.* Unpublished doctoral dissertation, University of Connecticut.

Grimshaw, J. (1991). *Extended projections.* Unpublished manuscript. Brandeis University.

Grimshaw, J. (1993). *Minimal projection, heads, & optimality.* (Tech. Rep. No. 4). Piscataway, NJ: Rutgers University, Center for Cognitive Science.

Haegeman, L. (1991). *Introduction to government binding theory.* London: Basil Blackwell.

Haider, H. (1993). *Deutsche Syntax.* Tübingen: Gunter Narr Verlag.

Hemforth, B. (1993). *Kognitives Parsing: Repräsentation und Verarbeitung sprachlichen Wissens*. Sankt Augustin: Infix Verlag.

Henderson, J., & Ferreira, F. (1995). Eye movement control during reading: Fixation measures reflect foveal but not parafoveal processing difficulty. In J. Henderson, M. Singer & F. Ferreira (Eds.), *Reading and language processing* (pp. 73-93). Mahwah, NJ: Lawrence Erlbaum Associates.

Höhle, T. (1982). *Explikation für "normale Betonung" und "normale Wortstellung"*. In A. Werner (Ed.), *Satzglieder im Deutschen: Vorschläge zur syntaktischen, semantischen und pragmatischen Fundierung*. Tübingen: Gunter Narr Verlag.

Holmes, V., & O'Regan, J. (1981). Eye fixation patterns during the reading of relative-clause sentences. *Journal of Verbal Learning and Verbal Behavior, 20*, 417-430.

Inoue, A. (1991). *A comparative study of parsing in English and Japanese*. Unpublished doctoral dissertation, University of Connecticut.

Inoue, A., & Fodor, J.D. (1995). Information-paced parsing of Japanese. In R. Mazuka & N. Nagai (Eds.), *Japanese sentence processing*. Lawrence Erlbaum Associates: Hillsdale, NJ.

Jackendoff, R. (1972). *Semantic interpretation in generative grammar*. Cambridge, MA: MIT Press.

Jordens, P. (1991). Linguistic knowledge in second language acquisition. In L. Eubank (Ed.), *Point counterpoint: Universal grammar in the second language*. Philadelphia, PA: John Benjamins.

Kaan, E. (1996). *Processing subject-object ambiguities in Dutch*. Doctoral dissertation, University of Groningen.

Kluender, R., & Kutas, R. (1993). Subjacency as a processing phenomenon. *Language and Cognitive Processes, 8*, 573-633.

Konieczny, L. (1996). *Human sentence processing: A semantics-oriented approach*. Unpublished doctoral dissertation. University of Freiburg.

MacDonald, M., Pearlmutter, N., & Seidenberg, M. (1994). The lexical nature of syntactic ambiguity resolution. *Psychological Review, 101*, 676-703.

Mecklinger, A., Schriefers, H., Steinhauer, K., & Friederici, A. (1995). Processing relative clauses varying on syntactic and semantic dimensions: An analysis with event related brain potentials. *Memory and Cognition, 23*, 477-497.

Meng, M. (1996). *Processing wh-questions in German and Dutch: Differential effects of disambiguation and their interpretation*. Unpublished manuscript. Friedrich-Schiller-University, Jena.

Mitchell, D. (1989). Verb-guidance and other lexical effects in parsing. *Language and Cognitive Processes, 3/4*, 123-154.

Partee, B., ter Meulen, A., & Wall, R. E. (1993). *Mathematical methods in linguistics*. Dordrecht: Kluwer Academic Publishers.

Pollard, C., & Sag, I. (1994). *Head-driven phrase structure grammar*. Chicago, IL: University of Chicago Press.

Pritchett, B. (1992). *Grammatical competence and parsing performance*. Chicago, IL: University of Chicago Press.

Pritchett, B. (1991). Head position and parsing ambiguity. *Journal of Psycholinguistic Research, 20*, 251-270.

Pritchett, B. (1988). Garden path phenomena and the grammatical basis of language processing. *Language, 64*, 539 - 576.

Schlesewsky, M., Krems, I., Klingl, R., Fanselow, G., Druck, U., & Mackedan, K. (1996). *Syntaktisches Priming bei Subjekts- und Objekts-Fragesätzen*. Talk given at the Second Fachtagung der Gesellschaft für Kognitionswissenschaft, Hamburg, Germany.

Schriefers, H., Friederici, A., & Kühn, K. (1995). The processing of locally ambiguous relative clauses in German. *Journal of Memory and Language, 34*, 227-246.

Schwartz, B., & Vikner, S. (1989). All V-2 clauses are CPs. *Working Papers in Scandinavian Syntax, 43*, 27-50.

Stabler, E. (1994). The finite connectivity of linguistic structure. In C. Clifton, L. Frazier & K. Rayner (Eds.), *Perspectives on sentence processing* (pp. 303-336). New York: Erlbaum.

Swinney, D., & Zurif, E. (1995). Syntactic processing in aphasia. *Brain and Language, 50*, 225-239.

Thiersch, C. (1978). *Topics in German syntax*. Unpublished Ph.D. dissertation, Massachusetts Institute of Technology.

Travis, L. (1991). Parameters of phrase structure and verb-second phenomena. In R. Freidin (Ed.), *Principles and parameters in comparative grammar* (pp. 339-364). Cambridge, MA: MIT Press.

Travis, L. (1984). *Parameters and effects of word-order variation*. Unpublished Ph.D. dissertation, Massachusetts Institute of Technology.

Trueswell, J., Tanenhaus, M., & Kello, C. (1993). Verb-specific constraints in sentence processing: Separating effects of lexical preference from garden paths. *Journal of Experimental Psychology: Learning, Memory and Cognition, 19*, 528-553.

Weinberg, A. (1993). Parameters in the theory of sentence processing: Minimal commitment theory goes east. *Journal of Psycholinguistic Research, 22*, 339-364.

Zurif, E., Swinney, D., Prather, P., Solomon, J., & Bushnell, C. (1993). An on-line analysis of syntactic processing in Broca's and Wernicke's aphasia. *Brain and Language, 45*, 448-464.

THE SUBJECT PREFERENCE IN THE PROCESSING OF LOCALLY AMBIGUOUS WH-QUESTIONS IN GERMAN*

Matthias Schlesewsky, Gisbert Fanselow,
Reinhold Kliegl and Josef Krems
Innovationskolleg Formale Modelle kognitiver Komplexität
University of Potsdam

INTRODUCTORY REMARKS

The processing of locally ambiguous wh-phrases has received much attention in the last years, and experimental results reported in the literature converge in at least one respect: if a clause-initial NP is locally ambiguous between a subject and an object interpretation, the human parser strongly prefers the former reading. The present chapter constitutes no exception to this general picture.

Our focus therefore does not so much lie in the identification of surprising new data, but rather on establishing that the subject preference is an ubiquitous phenomenon in German, and in particular on showing that it is caused by a syntax-related aspect of sentence processing (and not, say, by tuning to frequencies, by semantic preferences, etc.). Another issue is the identification of the point of time in on-line processing at which the subject preference is established.

A series of four self-paced reading and two off-line studies investigating various types of German wh-questions will be presented, which strongly support a syntactic interpretation of the subject preference. We will discuss these results in the context of a broader framework covering the processing of unambiguous questions as well (cf. Schlesewsky, Fanselow, and Kliegl 1997a), which takes differences in memory load to be the crucial factor in the processing of wh-questions.

PREVIOUS STUDIES

German feminine, neuter, and plural noun phrases do not distinguish overtly between nominative and accusative case. If such a noun phrase is the initial

B. Hemforth and L. Konieczny (eds.), German Sentence Processing, 65-93.

constituent of a clause, there is a local ambiguity in on-line processing with respect to its grammatical function, which can (but need not) be resolved by the overt case marking of following noun phrases or by the agreement morphology of the verb. Experiments involving comparable structures in Dutch (Frazier & Flores d'Arcais 1989, Kaan 1997) and Italian (De Vincenzi 1991a, b) show that the human parser prefers a subject interpretation if there is a local ambiguity between a subject and an object reading, provided that no non-syntactic factor biases the structure towards an object reading[1]. One should expect that similar preferences can be observed for German.

A constant result of experiments involving German declarative and relative clauses is a subject preference for locally ambiguous phrases, but an account for this preference does not necessarily require a recourse to *syntactic* processing strategies. On the other hand, previous work failed to show that the processing of locally ambiguous wh-questions is characterized by a subject preference as well. These two observations constitute the major rationale for our own experiments described in this chapter.

Hemforth (1993) reported a number of experiments which established that there is a strong subject preference for declarative clauses in which the initial noun phrase shows the relevant local ambiguity with respect to the subject-object distinction. Experimental subjects are strongly garden-pathed with object-initial structures, a fact manifesting itself in a reading time difference of roughly one second between the a.- and b.- versions of (1) in an eye movement study (Hemforth, Konieczny, & Strube 1993).

(1)	a.	die Henne	sieht	den	Bussard
		the hen	sees	the_{acc}	buzzard
	b.	die Henne	sieht	der	Bussard
		the hen	sees	the_{nom}	buzzard
		"the buzzard sees the hen"			

Hemforth's findings allow an interpretation in terms of the Active Filler Hypothesis (2), which Frazier & Flores d'Arcais (1989) have explained comparable findings for Dutch with.

(2)   *Active Filler Hypothesis [AFH]*

When a filler of a category XP has been identified in a non-argument position, such as COMP[2], rank the option of assigning its corresponding gap to the sentence over the option of identifying a lexical phrase of category XP. [Clifton & Frazier 1989:292]

According to the standard view of German clause structure, the underlying structure of German shows subject-object-verb (SOV) order, a configuration that manifests itself in complementizer-introduced complement clauses such as (3). Main declarative clauses are derived from such an underlying SOV-configuration by the application of two transformations, one that fronts the finite verb, and one that places a single constituent in front of the preposed verb (cf. e.g. Thiersch 1978). A concrete way of spelling out this basic insight is to assume that the verb moves to the Comp position, and that the fronted constituent moves to the specifier position of the Comp-phrase (cf. (4)) - but such details are irrelevant for most of what follows.

(3)   dass   der Bussard   die Henne   sieht
             that   the buzzard   the hen   sees
             "that the buzzard sees the hen"

(4)   [$_{CP}$ XP COMP [$_{IP}$ subject [$_{VP}$ object (verbal cluster)]]]

Given that the subject precedes the object in the underlying structure, the AFH predicts that the parser will rank the option of placing a movement trace into the subject position higher than expecting lexical material for that position, that is, it predicts the subject preference uncovered by Hemforth.

It is important to note, however, that Hemforth's results are merely *compatible* with an AFH interpretation, they do not force it. The processing of declaratives is influenced by a variety of factors, which are hard to distinguish experimentally. Declarative clauses are, thus, not optimal for experiments focussing on syntactic parsing preferences.

First, strong frequency effects may exert an influence on the processing of declaratives. Subject-initial declaratives are much more frequent than object-initial ones. Table 1 summarizes the results of a corpus study[3] based on 2826 sentences randomly selected from a larger text corpus that show that more than 90 percent of noun phrase initial sentences begin with a subject. Concentrating on items used in the experimental studies, we also computed the frequencies of the nominative and accusative version of sentence-initial "*die* (the$_{fem\text{-}sg.}$) + animate noun" in a corpus of 460 sentences randomly selected from the IdS-Corpora[4] of spoken language (selected from 269,714 words). Only 20 of 460 sentences were object initial (=4.34%). Therefore, the results uncovered by Hemforth (1993) may also be explained /in the context of the tuning hypothesis (cf. e.g. Cuetos & Mitchell 1988), according to which parsing preferences reflect statistical biases in the linguistic input of speakers.

		Nominative Initial	Accusative Initial	Dative Initial	Else
Spoken language: 1670	Number	1034	98	15	523
	% of Total	61.9	5.9	0.9	31.1
	% of NP-Initial	90.15	8.54	1.31	
Non-fiction: 570	Number	306	13	?	240
	% of Total	53.7	2.3	0.3	43.7
	% of NP-Initial	95.33	4.05	0.62	
Fiction: 586	Number	354	25	5	202
	% of Total	60.4	4.3	0.8	34.5
	% of NP-Initial	92.19	6.51	1.30	

Table 1: Frequencies for Different Types of Topicalization

Furthermore, in spite of the freedom of word order, the "unmarked" constituent order of declaratives in German is subject before object (Lenerz 1977). Only clauses with unmarked constituent order can be used freely in null contexts, while marked accusative-initial declaratives presuppose a special information structure of the context of the utterance that is in line with the pragmatic topicalization of the object. The subject preference of declarative clauses may thus be (partially) due to the need of building up a context model compatible with the marked focus/context structure of object initial clauses, which may be difficult to do in the null context of an experimental situation.

We therefore cannot be sure that the subject preference in declaratives has a syntactic cause at all - it could reflect clause type frequencies, or be a consequence of the fact that object before subject order pragmatically presupposes some special utterance context.[5]

It is therefore difficult if not impossible to find a clear interpretation for the subject preference of declaratives. Bader (1990), Kühn (1993), and Schriefers, Friederici, and Kühn (1993) investigated the processing of relative clauses with a case ambiguous relative pronoun, and reported a preference for the subject reading as well. Some of the problems discussed above do not affect the processing of relative clauses. Thus, pragmatic preferences are not likely to influence the choice of the grammatical function for the relative pronoun.

However, a different factor creates a considerable problem in the interpretation of preference data for relative pronouns. A series of self paced reading studies (Schlesewsky 1996) showed that the human parser prefers an analysis in which the case assigned to a locally ambiguous relative pronoun matches the case borne by the noun phrase which the relative clause modifies. Thus, if the syntactic context makes it clear that a noun phrase is an accusative object, a case ambiguous relative pronoun linked to this noun phrase shows an object (=accusative) preference. Note that all (Kühn 1993) or most (Bader 1990) noun phrases used in the experiments just mentioned involved structures which forced a nominative interpretation of the noun phrase linked to the relative clause. Thus, it is not at all clear that the experimental results reflect a general subject preference for ambiguous relative pronouns - they may be simply due to the case matching effect.

We are thus left with locally ambiguous wh-questions as a testing ground for the claim that there are subject preferences in German that need to be interpreted in terms of parsing strategies such as the AFH: Wh-questions are unaffected by pragmatic preferences (whatever is questioned is automatically in focus), they have a common syntactic representation, and case transfer effects can be excluded at least for initial ambiguous wh-phrases.

Furthermore, it is not likely that tuning to frequencies in the linguistic input (cf. Cuetos & Mitchell 1988) shapes the processing of wh-questions in a significant way. Table 2 summarizes the results of a pilot corpus study in which we considered the frequency of subject-, object- and adverb/PP-initial matrix questions in plays and newspaper and journal texts. Noun phrase initial questions turn out to be more or less equally distributed between subject- and object-initial structures. Meng (1995) found subject initial structures to be significantly more frequent than object initial questions in the IdS-*Spiegel* corpus (53%:47%). Even if Meng's figures come closer to the distribution of subject- and object questions in the speakers' input than ours, the subject bias in Meng's corpus is much smaller than what one would assume to be necessary for the triggering of a tuning effect.[6] In any event, we can be sure that wh-questions are the least problematic items.

	Subject-Initial			Object-Initial			Else	
	Total	% of Total	% NP-Initial	Total	% of Total	% NP-Initial	Total	% of Total.
Plays	63	21.3	39.4	97	32.8	60.6	136	45.9
Interviews	82	22.2	47.1	92	24.9	52.9	195	52.9
Articles	56	34.1	59.6	30	23.1	40.4	70	42.7

Table 2: Corpus Study for Wh-Questions.

The behavior of locally ambiguous wh-phrases may thus be considered to be crucial for the viability of syntactic explanations of subject preferences in German. Farke (1994) reported a self paced reading study concerning structures such as (5)-(6). Her results suggested that there is an *object* preference for the locally ambiguous wh-phrases in (6,6a) and no preference for either interpretation in (6b).

(5)   welche Frau   liebt   der/   den   Mann
           which   woman   loves   the$_{nom}$ /the$_{acc}$ man
           "which woman loves the man/which woman does the man love"

(6)   a.   welche Frau   glaubst Du liebt der/   den   Mann
           which   woman   believe you loves the$_{nom}$ /the$_{acc}$ man
           "which woman do you believe loves the man/the man loves"

       b.   welche Frau   hast Du   geglaubt   liebt der/den Mann
           which   woman   have you believed   loves the$_{nom/acc}$ man
           "which woman have you believed loves the man/the man loves"

(6) links to a structural representation such as (7), that is, they involve "long movement from V/2-complement clauses" in German (Haider 1986, Staudacher 1990): the wh-phrase originating in the complement clause is first moved to the specifier of this CP, leaving a trace there, and then continues to move to the specifier position of the matrix clause. Since Comp is not filled by a lexical complementizer in both CPs in question, the finite verbs of the matrix and the complement clause move to the pertinent Comp-positions as well.

(7)   a.   [$_{CP}$ welche Frau [$_{C'}$ hast [$_{IP}$ Du geglaubt [$_{CP}$ t liebt [$_{IP}$ t [$_{VP}$ den Mann]]]]]]

b.   [CP welche Frau [C' hast [IPDu geglaubt [CP t liebt [IP der
          Mann [VP t]]]]]]

Hildegard Farke kindly provided us with her experimental software and her experimental items. Unfortunately, we were not able to replicate her findings: no preference at all emanated from the reading times. A potential problem of her study may be the lack of control for the accuracy of parsing. The absence of any effect in our replication of Farke's experiment is in line with two self-paced reading studies reported in Meng (1995): There were no significant reading time differences between similar sentences disambiguated towards a subject or object interpretation of the initial wh-phrase.

ESTABLISHING A SUBJECT PREFERENCE

The AFH predicts a subject preference for locally ambiguous questions in German. The previous failure to identify this preference allows three interpretations:

- the methods used so far were not sensitive enough to detect the relevant distinctions
- there is a subject preference for locally ambiguous wh-questions in German as well, but reanalysis is either (close to being) cost free, or reanalysis costs do not show up for some reason.
- there are fundamental differences between the processing strategies of German on the one hand and Dutch and Italian on the other that imply that there is no *syntactic* subject preference in German.

As a first step towards a decision between these alternatives, a questionnaire study was designed that investigated off-line preferences for locally ambiguous questions of the kind exemplified in (6), that is, we concentrated on extractions from V/2-complements, because Farke's results suggested a potential difference in the processing of such structures depending on the tense of the matrix clause. The experimental items could thus have a simple (6a) or a periphrastic tense (6b).

Experiment 1
Questionnaire Study: Nominative vs. Accusative Wh-Questions

Method

Participants. Thirty-eight first term students of linguistics at the University of Potsdam participated in the experiment. They were in the second week of their syntax training, and not aware of the purpose of the study.

Procedure and Material. A questionnaire with 80 sentences was distributed in which exactly one word was left out. Subjects were instructed to insert a suitable word such that the result would be both well-formed and meaningful. They were asked to carry out the task as fast as possible. The questionnaire was given to the subjects at the end of their class time, so that 40 minutes were left for work on the questionnaire.

There were 40 distractor items and 40 experimental items with the structural properties described above, equally distributed between the two conditions "simple" and "periphrastic" matrix clause. The experimental items began with a case-ambiguous *welche*-"which" phrase in the singular that was extracted out of the verb-second complement clause. The inflected verb of the main clause could appear either in the plural or in second person singular form, so that verbal morphology made it clear that the *welche*-phrase was not the matrix subject. Furthermore, the matrix verbs used in the experimental items were either formally or semantically incompatible with *welche*+N being the matrix object. The noun phrase following the matrix clause was always composed of a masculine singular noun and a preceding blank space indicating a missing determiner/possessive pronoun, which had to be inserted by the participants of the study (cf. 8).[7] The morphology of the items inserted by the subjects (e.g. *der* vs. *den*, "the-nom vs. the-acc", *ein* vs. *einen* ("a-nom vs. a-acc"), or *ihr* vs. *ihren* "her-nom vs. her-acc") indicates which grammatical function they assigned to the case ambiguous wh-phrase. Distractors were sentences of different types in which also exactly one word was left out.

(8)   welche Frau glaubst Du liebt ____ Mann
            which woman believe you loves ____ man

Results and Discussion

The data from eight subjects were excluded from the analysis.[8] Therefore, 30 x 20 = 600 answers per condition were analyzed for the grammatical function assigned by the subjects to the initial wh-phrase as evidenced by the words they had inserted. Table 3 summarizes the results of the study. Note the baseline is 50% for subject initial wh-phrases. A repeated measures analysis of variance of subject initial preferences showed these values to be significantly different from the baseline, $F(1,29)=93.22$, $MSe=17.85$, $p< .01$. In addition, the difference between simple and periphrastic clause was significant, $F(1,29)=5.78$, $MSe=3.74$, $p< .05$.

Frequencies	simple matrix clause	periphrastic clause
1stNP = SU	476 = 79.3%	441 = 73.5%

Table 3: Frequency of Grammatical Functions in Experiment 1

Experiment 1 indicates that there is a preference for interpreting locally ambiguous initial wh-phrases as subjects. This is true both for simple and periphrastic matrix clauses. The results are in line with the findings of a contrast manipulation study using a slightly modified set of experimental items (Fanselow, Kliegl, & Schlesewsky, 1997) that yielded a 63:37 bias in favor of the subject interpretation of an initial case-ambiguous wh-phrase. We can therefore be sure that German does not differ from Dutch and other languages with respect to the strategies for computing initial analyses in the case of local ambiguities.

Given the positive results of the two off-line studies, we designed a series of self-paced reading experiments that tried to make the subject preference visible in on-line data as well. Here, we will report two studies involving disambiguation by verbal agreement.

Experiment 2:
Simple locally ambiguous wh-questions

Method

Participants. Twenty-nine students of the University of Potsdam participated in the experiment. None of them was familiar with the purpose of the study. They were paid for participation or received course credits.

Procedure. Subjects read 12 experimental items (4 per condition) and 108 distractor sentences in a self-paced reading task with non-stationary presentation on a computer screen and phrase-wise presentation. Accuracy of comprehension was controlled by a sentence matching task following each sentence.

By pressing a "Yes"- or a "No"-button, subjects had to decide whether the control sentence was a verbatim repetition of the preceding sentence.

Experimental items were locally ambiguous wh-questions of the type exemplified in (9), in which the initial singular wh-phrase either allowed a subject or an object reading. We used two different ways of disambiguation in the experiment, number and case. In the plural condition, the finite verb bore plural morphology, which excludes a subject analysis for the singular wh-phrase. If the verb was singular, the following noun phrase either bore overt nominative or overt accusative morphology, disambiguating the initial *welche*-phrase thereby. In the plural condition, the noun phrase following the verb was ⁴ ᵈᵉᶠⁱⁿⁱᵗᵉ plural noun phrase. These three experimental conditions are illustrated in (9), together with the segmentation for phrase-wise presentation.

(9) a.   welche Frau | sah | der Mann | am Freitag | ?
           which woman   saw_{sg} the_{nom} man   on Friday
           "which woman did the man see on Friday?"(SG, WH=ACC)

     b.   welche Frau | sah | den Mann | am Freitag | ?
           which woman   saw_{sg} the_{acc} man   on Friday
           "which woman saw the man on Friday?"(SG, WH=NOM)

     c.   welche Frau | sahen | die Männer | am Freitag | ?
           which woman   saw_{pl} the_{nom} men   on Friday
           "which woman did the men see on Friday?"(PLURAL)

     Region: 1   2   3   4   5

Results and Discussion

The data from one subject were excluded, because there were too few data points for at least one condition. Less than 1% of the data did not enter the analysis, either because the reading time for region 1 was below 100ms or because the total reading time surpassed 20 secs. There was a significantly lower accuracy in the plural condition relative to the mean of the two single conditions, $F(1,27) = 10.77$, MSe = 0.3, $p < .01$. Table 4 summarizes mean reading times in ms for the segments indicated in (9). The area showing a significant difference is set in italics.

Segment	1	2	3	4	5	% accuracy
	which NP_{sg}	$V_{sg/pl}$	$NP2_{nom/acc}$	PP	?	
SG, wh=nom	1090	*634*	822	993	*824*	93.5
SG, wh=acc	1014	*661*	881	943	*1003*	89.0
PL, wh=acc	941	*876*	923	907	*876*	78.6

Table 4: Mean reading times and Accuracy of comprehension in Exp. 1

In a repeated measures ANOVA of reading times, contrasts were specified for the differences between the first segment and each of the following segments of the clause (Segments 2 to 5). Two contrasts were also specified for sentence type (Singular vs. Plural and $Singular_{ACC}$ vs. $Singular_{NOM}$). A significant interaction was obtained for the contrast for the matrix verb (Segment 2) and the contrast for the singular-plural distinction, $F1(1,27) = 19.26$, $MSe = 669897$, $p < 0.01$; $F2(1,11) = 46,93$, $MSe = 108077$, $p < .01$. A similar result was obtained for the interaction of the second NP-contrast and the singular-plural-condition, $F1(1,27) = 5.69$, $MSe = 48787$, $p < 0.05$; $F2(1,11) = 3,70$, $MSe = 323202$, $p < 0.1$. A significant interaction was further found for the contrast for the last position of the sentence and the contrast "$Singular_{ACC}$ vs. $Singular_{NOM}$", $F1(1,27) = 5.52$, $MSe = 99214$, $p < .05$; $F2(1,11) = 5,50$, $MSe = 75894$, $p < 0.05$. As shown in Table 4 and verified by tests of simple effects the verb was read significantly slower in the plural conditions relative to the mean of the two single conditions, $F1(1,27) = 23.35$, $MSe = 41693$, $p < .01$; $F2(1,11) = 23.49$, $MSe = 15999$, $p < .01$. No other effects reached the level of significance.

The results of Experiment 2 show that the subject preference for locally ambiguous wh-phrases that was visible in the off-line study leads to a significant reanalysis effect at the point of disambiguation when the disambiguating item forces an object reading for the wh-phrase: the subject preference showed up clearly in the higher reading times for segment 2 (the verb) in structures beginning with a singular wh-phrase followed by a plural verb. The latter excludes the subject analysis for the initial wh-phrase due to number mismatch, while singular verbs are of course compatible with the assumption that the initial singular wh-phrase is a subject. Higher reading times of plural verbs can thus be assumed to be caused by the reanalysis necessary for the interpretation of the wh-phrase. German thus turns out to be in line with theoretical expectations derivable from the AFH even in those contexts for which neither frequency nor pragmatics are very likely to influence processing.

The initial subject preference also manifests itself in the higher reading times for segment 5 (=punctuation mark) in the singular object initial condition as compared to the singular subject initial condition. Note that this increase in reading times does not show up on the disambiguating segment itself, but only two regions later in the clause. This finding is reminiscent of results in other experiments working with case rather than number disambiguation: the reanalysis effect either becomes visible very late only, or is never visible at all. Apparently, case information has a different disambiguating effect for locally ambiguous initial wh-phrases than number agreement. See Schlesewsky (in prep.) for a discussion of this observation.

One might be unhappy with our argument involving the reading time difference on the verb (Barbara Hemforth, p.c.) because of a length difference between singular and plural forms of the verbs: in German, third person plural verb forms are longer than third person singular forms by one or two letters, so that the reading time difference between the plural and the singular conditions could also be a trivial consequence of this rather uninteresting dimension rather than follow from a reanalysis effect. This potential problem is easy to solve, however: If the reading time advantage of singular verbs in Experiment 2 is due to the subject preference, we expect the very same effect to show up with singular verbs when the initial wh-phrase is a plural noun phrase. Recall on the other hand that singular verbs are shorter than plural ones. If the results of Experiment 2 are caused by a length difference, one would expect that singular verbs are read faster than plural verbs even when they are preceded by plural wh-phrases. A decision between the two hypothesis can thus be arrived at by a simple modification of the design of Experiment 2.

Experiment 2a: Simple locally ambiguous wh-questions

Method

Participants. Twenty-two students of the University of Potsdam participated in the experiment. None of them was familiar with the purpose of the study. They were paid for participation or received course credits.

Procedure. Method and material employed in this experiment were identical to the ones used in Experiment 2, except that the initial wh-phrase had overt plural marking. From the perspective of the AFH, this initial wh-phrase should preferentially be interpreted as the clause's subject, an analysis that is refuted by the singular rather than the plural verb, in contrast to Experiment 2.

Plural noun phrases never distinguish nominative and accusative case overtly. Thus, Experiment 2a had two experimental conditions only (singular vs. plural verb), because case-disambiguation by a noun phrase is impossible in the plural condition. There were 7 experimental items per condition, and 92 distractor sentences. (10) illustrates the structures used in Experiment 2a, and indicates the segmentation for phrasewise retrieval.

(10) a. welche Frauen | sah | der Mann | am Freitag | ?
         which woman$_{Pl}$ saw$_{sg}$ the$_{nom}$ man   on Friday
         "which woman did the man see on Friday?" (WH=ACC)

    b. welche Frauen | sahen | den Mann | am Freitag | ?
         which woman$_{Pl}$ saw$_{Pl}$ the$_{acc}$ man   on Friday
         "which woman saw the man on Friday?" (WH=NOM)

Region: 1   2   3   4   5

Results and Discussion

Table 5 summarizes mean reading times in ms for the segments indicated in (11).

Segment	1	2	3	4	5	% accurate
	which NP$_{pl}$	V$_{sg/pl}$	NP2	PP	?	
verb=sg. Wh=acc	987	845	805	973	811	67.0
verb=pl Wh=nom	1015	650	751	943	752	83.1

Table 5: Mean reading times and accuracy of comprehension in Exp. 2a

In a repeated measures ANOVA of reading times, contrasts were specified for the differences between the first segment and each of the following segments of the clause (Segments 2 to 5). A significant interaction was obtained for the contrast for matrix verb (Segment 2) and the contrast for the singular-plural distinction, $F1(1,21) = 6.17$, MSe = 148754, $p < 0.05$; $F2(1,11) = 5.33$, MSe = 63596, $p < 0.05$. As shown in table 5 and verified by a simple test of simple effects, the verb was read significantly slower in the singular condition, F1(1,21) = 16.43, MSe = 20546, p < . 001, F2(1,11) = 4.98, MSe = 28470, p < . 05. No other effects were significant.

The result obtained in Experiment 2a is identical with the one found in Experiment 2. Verbs following an initial wh-phrase are read more slowly when their number marking is incompatible with a subject analysis of the wh-phrase, irrespective of the length of the singular and plural forms in terms of number of letters. This array of data is in line with the predictions of the AFH, but incompatible with the view that the number of letters of a verbal form is responsible for the reading time effect in experiment 2.

Since, as argued above, results for wh-questions are not likely to be caused by frequency effects, pragmatic biases or by word length, we can be sure that fundamental aspects of parsing independent of these factors cause the subject preference for the wh-phrase. It would be premature, however, to conclude that this property of the initial analysis is shaped by a formal parsing strategy such as the AFH. A semantic interpretation must also be considered.

THE SYNTACTIC NATURE OF THE SUBJECT PREFERENCE

MacWhinney, Bates, and Kliegl (1984) assessed the relative strength of formal and semantic cues for the subject function in a number of languages. For German, they established that animacy is a stronger cue for subjecthood than order and agreement. Note that the target items of our experiments were constructed such that the wh-phrase and the disambiguating DP did not differ with respect to animacy, that is, both DPs were either [+animate] or [-animate], in order to avoid a semantic bias. However, only very few items were constructed with pairs of inanimate DPs. Although the inanimate items did not behave differently, one could argue that the subject preference was due to the fact that subjects made use of the animacy cue (in combination with order) in assigning grammatical functions.

We therefore designed a second off-line experiment using [-animate] *was* "what, nom or acc" as the clause initial item. If animacy is the cue responsible for the subject preference in the preceding experiments, one expects to find an object preference for *was*. If, on the other hand, there is a strong formal factor biasing experimental participants towards the nominative interpretation of the case ambiguous item, an experiment with *was* should yield results qualitatively similar to the previous experiments.

An analysis of 480 items randomly selected from the Freiburg Corpus, yielded a slight but significant frequency bias for the object-interpretation of *was* as a first item of a matrix question (208 occurrences of nominative *was*, 253 of accusative *was*, and 19 cases in which a CP-interpretation of *was* cannot be excluded (alternative interpretation: accusative DP). A conservative interpretation thus assesses the frequency of the accusative interpretation of *was* among noun phrase initial questions at 55%). If tuning effects are sensitive to rather low frequency differences, an object preference could be expected in the results of relevant experiments as well.

Pretest: Questionnaire study "*was*-questions"

Method

Participants. Fifty high school students with a minimum age of 18 years volunteered to participate in the experiment. They were not aware of the purpose of the study.

Procedure and Material. Subjects had to insert a missing phrase into 42 incomplete sentences. They were told that exactly one phrase was missing, and were asked to insert exactly one completion for the sentence, so that the result was grammatical and made sense. There were 28 distractors and 16 experimental items, which could appear in either of the two following forms (11a,b). The initial wh-phrase could be either the subject or the object of the question. Verbs for experimental items were selected such that they allow both animate and inanimate subjects, and such that the noun phrase to be filled in could be animate or inanimate both as a subject.

(11) a.   was bewies   _____?
              what proved
              "what proved XP?" "what did XP prove?"

      b.   was hat   _____   ermöglicht?
              what has   made possible
              "what made X possible?" "what did X make possible?"

Results and Discussion

The data from 31 subjects entered the analysis. The questionnaires of the other participants were excluded because they had not completed the questionnaire.

	Absolute number	% of Total	% of Unambiguous
Was Interpreted as Subject	298	60.1	68.3
Was Interpreted as Object	138	27.8	31.7
Ambiguous Answer[9]	60	12.1	-

Table 6: Frequencies for Subject and Object Interpretation of *Was* in Exp. 3

An analysis of the preferences of individual subjects showed a significant bias to interpret *was* as a subject, $F1(1,30)=61.03$, MSe = .01, p < .001. The answers of five participants indicate a preference for an object reading of *was*. Twenty-four subjects showed a tendency for inserting animate subjects into sentences in which they assigned to *was* the grammatical function object. The reverse was true for five subjects. Two of the five subjects showing an object preference belong to the latter group.

The results of this pretest were qualitatively similar to the results of Experiment 1. The preference for interpreting initial ambiguous wh-phrases as nominatives/subjects is stable and independent of the semantic class to which the wh-phrase belongs. Since animacy could not cue subjects for the nominative interpretation, the results corroborate the view that the subject preference is caused by a formal factor.

If the cueing force of animacy is of a purely relational nature, there is no conflict between our findings and those of MacWhinney, Bates and Kliegl (1984). In the latter study, subjects were presented with complete sentences containing a pair of noun phrases and had to decide which noun phrase was the subject. Animacy was able to override word order and agreement information in this situation. In our study, subjects had to provide the second noun phrase themselves. Their answers indicated that, in the absence of information concerning the relative degree of animacy of the two verbal arguments, a formal parsing strategy biased subjects towards the nominative interpretation of *was*. The responses which interpret *was* as an object reflect, on the other hand, the influence of a semantic strategy because the second noun phrase tends to be animate in this case. Given that the experimental items of Experiment 1 were constructed such that the two noun phrases in question agreed with respect to animacy, there is little reason to assume that the results of our studies were determined by the animacy cue.

In the present experiment, there was no tuning effect visible in subjects' responses. A plausible interpretation is that frequency differences of around

10% do not suffice to influence initial analyses. This finding is of importance for the processing of wh-structures in general, because the frequency difference between subject and object initial wh-questions in Meng's (1995) corpus is not bigger than the (reverse) frequency difference we have found for *was*.

Finally, individual differences between subjects suggest that processing strategies may differ among speakers. The object preference visible in the answers of five subjects is compatible with the view that speakers attribute different weights to formal syntax based strategies, semantic information, and/or frequency effects.

In the following experiment, we subjected the items of the off-line study to an on-line reading time experiment.

Experiment 3: On-line study *"was-*questions"

Method

Participants. Twenty-nine students of the University of Potsdam participated in the experiment. They were not aware of the purpose of the study. They were paid for participation or received course credits.

Procedure and Material. The material of Experiment 3 was constructed on the basis of the material of the pretest by adding the disambiguating noun phrase to the sentences used in the questionnaire. All items involved simple past tense, disambiguating noun phrases could be either animate or inanimate. There were six experimental items that appeared in the *was*=nom and in the *was*=acc condition, and 108 distractor sentences. The method employed was identical to the one used in Experiments 2 and 2a. (12) represents the structure and partitioning of the experimental items for phrase-wise presentation.

(12) a.   was | erforderte | den Einbruch | in die Nationalbank | ?
was= nom
what   required   the$_{acc}$ break-in into the national bank
"what made breaking in into the national bank necessary?"

          1   2   3   4   5

b.   was | erforderte | der Einbruch | in die Nationalbank | ?
        was=acc
        what   required   the$_{nom}$ break-in into the national bank
        "what did the break in into the national bank require?"

             1   2   3   4   5

Results and Discussion

The data of one subject had to be eliminated from the analysis, because there were too many missing data points for one condition. There was no significant difference in accuracy: 79.9% of control questions for the nominative initial condition and 86.0% for the accusative initial condition were answered correctly.

	1	2	3	4	5
was=Subject	801	576	790	807	706
was=Object	787	615	808	946	762

Table 7: Mean Reading Times (ms) in Experiment 3

A repeated measures ANOVA for reading times with planned comparisons shows that the interaction for the contrast "Position vs. Subject/Object" was significant for the PP (=segment 4), F1(1,26)=7.98, MSe=348202, p< .01, F2 (1,11) = 3.27, MSe = 223514, p< .1 and for segment 5 (EOC), F1(1,27)=5,25,MSe=125683, p< .05, in so far as the PP is read faster in the nominative condition than in the accusative condition. A simple analysis of variance showed a significant reading time difference on position 4 (F1(1,26) = 7.99, MSe = 37150, p < .01, F2 (1,11) = 3.63, MSe = 29561, p > .1. No other effects were significant.

Experiment 3 supports the view that the cognitive advantage of subject initial questions is not caused by a simple semantic cue such as animacy. Even when the second noun phrase is animate in a substantial number of cases, subjects prefer to analyze *was* as a nominative noun phrase. We are therefore convinced that the subject bias is due to a formal parsing property.

Experiment 4: Simple locally ambiguous wh-questions

Inanimate wh-phrases

In order to replicate this finding with *which*-phrases, we designed a final experiment in which the initial segment of the question was a which phrase with an inanimate head noun such as *Skulptur* "sculpture". In all other respects, the experiment shared the design of Experiment 2, that is, the structures were disambiguated towards the object or subject interpretation of the initial wh-phrase by the agreement morphology of the verb immediately following the wh-phrase. If the subject preference is indeed of a truly formal nature, we should see cost of reanalysis on this verb if its agreement morphology is incompatible with a subject analysis of the wh-phrase. On the other hand, if semantic factors such as animacy play a role in determining the grammatical function of locally ambiguous phrases, no such reanalysis should show up, because there should be a tendency to interpret inanimate phrases as objects.

Method

Participants. 24 students of the University of Potsdam participated in the experiment. None of them was familiar with the purpose of the study. They were paid for participation or received course credits.

Procedure. Method and material employed in this experiment were identical to the ones used in Experiment 2, except that the initial wh-phrase had an inanimate head noun. From the perspective of the AFH, this initial wh-phrase should preferentially be interpreted as the clause's subject, an analysis that is refuted by a verb with plural morphology. There were 7 experimental items per condition, and 92 distractor sentences. (13) illustrates the structures used in Experiment 4, and indicates the segmentation for phrasewise retrieval.

(13) a.   welches System | unterstützt | die Programme | auf dem
             Computer | ?
             which system$_{sg}$ supports$_{sg}$ the$_{pl}$ programs on the
             computer
             "which system supports the programs on the computer?"
             (WH=nom)

      b.   welches System | unterstützten | die Programme | auf dem
             Computer | ?
             which system$_{sg}$ support$_{pl}$ the$_{pl}$ programs on the
             computer
             "which system do the programs on the computer support?"
             (WH=acc)

Region: 1   2   3   4

Results and Discussion

Table 8 summarizes mean reading times in ms for the segments indicated in
(11).

Segment	1	2	3	4	5	% accurate
	which NP$_{sg}$	V$_{sg/pl}$	NP2	PP/NP	?	
verb=sg, wh = nom	843	674	685	818	722	84.8
verb=pl, wh= acc	956	901	904	1019	939	89.9

Table 8: Mean reading times and Accuracy of comprehension in Exp. 4

In a one way ANOVA, we found significant reading time differences
between the subject- and object initial conditions with lower reading times for
the former at the following positions: Segment 2; F1(1,23)= 6.91, MSe =
310162.9, p< .05, F2(1,6)= 19.93, MSe=5754.3, p< .01; Segment 3; F1(1,23)
= 9.49, MSe= 287764.4, p< .01, F2(1,6)= 24.1, MSe= 5682.1, p< .001,
Segment 4; F1(1,23) = 4.86, MSe= 243298.6, p< .05, F2(1,6)= 15.7, MSe=
6520.4, p< .01, Segment 5; F1(1,23) = 3.23, MSe= 283585.3, p< .1, F2(1,6) =
7.21, MSe= 16296.2, p< .05. In other words, the reading time advantage for
subject-initial interpretation is visible from the position of the finite verb to
the final position of the clause.

Experiment 4 corroborates the findings of Experiment 3 and the off-line pretest. The subject preference for initial locally ambiguous wh-phrases is a stable phenomenon, and independent of the semantic properties of the clause-initial phrase. Therefore, the subject preference must be caused by a formal aspect of parsing.

THE STABILITY OF THE SUBJECT PREFERENCE: OTHER STUDIES

The results of our experiments, two off-line studies and four on-line studies, strongly support the view that the human parser initially assigns the subject role to a locally ambiguous wh-phrase. These results are in harmony with the findings for declaratives and relative clauses discussed above (although the latter processing facts must be interpreted with care, as we have seen). We were also able to establish (cf. Schlesewsky, in prep.) the same subject advantage for *wieviele* "how many" + *noun*-questions, and for constructions such as (14) involving long movement out of verb second complement clauses (see above)

(14)	welche Frau	glaubst Du	sahen	die Männer
	am Freitag	im Park?		
	which woman	believe you	saw_{pl}	the_{nom} man
	on Friday	in the park		

"which woman do you believe the man saw in the park on Friday?"

Further evidence comes from a reading time study carried out at the University of Regensburg in the context of our syntactic priming studies (Schlesewsky, Fanselow, & Kliegl 1997b). In contrast to what holds for North German dialects, speakers of South German (Bavarian) dialects tolerate the extraction of a wh-phrase out of a finite complementizer-introduced complement clause. In contrast to what Frazier found for Dutch, Brueck (1996) and Macketanz (1996) report the results of a self paced reading study in which they found a significant reanalysis effect on the position of the determiner of the second noun phrase in (15a), that is, they uncovered a subject preference for wh-phrases extracted out of *dass*/"that"-clauses as well.

(15) a.   welche Lehrerin glaubst du   daß der Schüler bewundert?
                which teacher-fem think you   that the$_{nom}$ pupil admires
                "which (female) teacher do you believe that the pupil ad-
                mires"?

       b.   welche Lehrerin glaubst du   daß den Schüler bewundert?
                which teacher-fem think you   that the$_{acc}$ pupil admires
                "which (female) teacher do you believe admires the pupil?"

The subject preference for locally ambiguous clause initial noun phrase is
therefore independent of semantics, frequency, operator type and the short vs.
long movement distinction. Such results contrast with experiments that fail to
show any preference at all, cf. Schlesewsky (in prep.) for an attention driven
model of parsing that explains the failure of the subject preference to show up
in a number of well-defined contexts.

WHEN ARE SUBJECT PREFERENCES ESTABLISHED (AND HOW)?

The six experiments reported above and the other studies mentioned in the
preceding section show that locally ambiguous noun phrases are preferentially
processed as syntactic subjects by the human parser. We have also seen that
the reanalysis which is necessary if the local ambiguity is later resolved for
the object interpretation is far from being cost-free: it causes significant differences in reading times on the disambiguating item, or immediately after it.
That this should be so is to be expected if one takes into account similar
results obtained for other languages, but it is worth while to point out that
German differs from Dutch or Italian in a number of respects that makes the
parallelism interesting: German is a free constituent order language, and
object before subject order is possible for wh-phrases in multiple questions, as
(16) illustrates:

(16)   warum hat   eigentlich   was   welcher Profes-
            sor   behauptet?
            why has   prt.   what   which   profes-
            sor   claimed?
            "which professor has claimed what, and why?"

Given this flexibility of word order even for question phrases, an application of the AFH to German presupposes that it is applied to the unmarked
canonical order: the fact that OSV order is also possible appears to be irrelevant for the computation of preferences for grammatical functions on the basis

of the AFH. Whether this reflects a syntactic property of German (as would follow from the approach to free constituent order proposed by Müller & Sternefeld 1993), or whether it is due to another parsing principle has to be left open here.

Notice that the original formulation of the AFH implies a somewhat passive role for the wh-phrase in establishing the subject preference. According to (2), repeated here as (17), AFH-preferences are established when the parser reaches a point in the input string that allows either the postulation of a gap position corresponding to the stored wh-phrase, or the expectation of lexical material filling the structural slot in question.

(17)   Active Filler Hypothesis [AFH]

              When a filler of a category XP has been identified in a non-argument position, such as COMP, rank the option of assigning its corresponding gap to the sentence over the option of identifying a lexical phrase of category XP. [Clifton & Frazier 1989:292]

Thus, in the light of the structural representation (18) for German matrix questions, (17) leads one to expect that the subject preference is established only *after* the finite verb moved to Comp has been read: it is only after the position of the preposed verb that the subject position can first be filled, either by a gap (the preferred alternative, according to the AFH), or by a lexical subject (in which case the preposed phrase would have to be e.g. an object).

(18) $[_{CP}$ WH-phrase $[_{Comp}$ verb$][_{IP}$ subject position $[_{VP}$ object position verb$]]]$

The results of experiments 2, 2a, and 4 do not support that view. If the subject preference cannot be established before the point in on-line parsing at which a lexical subject might first appear, it should not show up at the point when the finite verb is read. The significant reading time disadvantage of verb forms which are incompatible with the subject interpretation of the initial wh-phrase shows that the parser has formulated the subject preference *before* it has parsed that verb, that is, the subject preference must have come into being immediately during the processing of the wh-phrase.

How can this fact be understood? We believe that the instantaneous presence of the subject preference must be interpreted in the light of results concerning the processing of unambiguous wh-phrases in German. We were able to identify a subject advantage in the processing of non-ambiguous questions as well (Schlesewsky, Fanselow, and Kliegl, 1997a): In the nominative singular paradigm, nominative and accusative noun phrases can be distinguished on the basis of their overt morphology. Unambiguous object initial questions show higher reading times than subject initial questions, an effect that is visible on the wh-phrase itself and on various other parts of the clause.

What is responsible for this cognitive advantage of subject-initial structures? It is an established fact that the amount of structure/nodes that need to be kept in syntactic short term memory has a strong influence on the ease of parsing. This has been established for nested vs. crossed dependencies in Dutch and German (Bach, Brown & Marslen-Wilson 1986) and for relative clauses (Blaubergs & Braine 1974), cf. also Lewis (1993), Stabler (1994). Schlesewsky et al. (1997a) argue that the amount of structure that needs to be kept in memory influences parsing times for filler gap dependencies in a similar fashion. Consider again the abstract structural representation of a German clause:

(19) $[_{CP} \alpha \text{ COMP } [_{IP} \beta [_{VP} \gamma \text{ verb}]]]$

Let us assume that a category Σ can be recognized as soon as its specifier (or head) has been parsed. A category Σ can furthermore be integrated into a parse tree only if it is a daughter of a node already present in the parse tree Since α is the specifier of CP in (19), a CP node will be predicted ($[_{CP} \alpha [_{C'} $ Comp ..]]) as soon as α has been parsed.[10] If α bears overt nominative morphology, it can be recognized as the specifier of IP, so that IP is recognized as well if α is recognized as the subject (e.g. by case information). Therefore, the immediate construction of $[_{CP} \alpha [_{C'} $ Comp $[_{IP} .. $ Infl ..] is possible when α with an overt nominative morphology has been read, because IP is the daughter of C'. Continuous tree construction is therefore possible. Finally, α can be linked to Spec,IP, where β is set to trace of α. The structure constructible out of $\alpha =$ subject alone is therefore $[_{CP} \alpha [_{C'} $ Comp $[_{IP} t_{\alpha} $ Infl ..]. Nothing is left on the memory stack.

If, on the other hand, α bears overt object morphology, CP can again be predicted. In classical GB-Theory (Chomsky 1981), the object is the complement of VP. Therefore, no other categories are recognized, in particular, no information concerning IP can be constructed out of an object wh-phrase α. α therefore needs to be kept on the memory stack: IP has not been recognized so far, so that the parse cannot proceed beyond $[_{CP} \alpha [_{C'} $ Comp ..]]. Consequently, the processing of object-initial structures implies the presence of at least one item more in short term memory than the processing of structures beginning with the subject.

If memory load interferes with parsing, we predict that unambiguous structures beginning with a subject α should be read faster than object initial ones at the initial segment α itself (which is correct, cf. Schlesewsky et al. 1997a) and at other segments. For ambiguous structures, we propose that they show a subject preference because the subject alternative can be pursued faster and will therefore block its alternatives. Our view thus comes close to the following position: At the ambiguous point, both possibilities are considered and the pertinent substructures are built up. The syntactic analyses are immediately communicated to the semantic system, which constructs a single semantic representation. If two syntactic analyses are possible, only the one reaching semantics first is going to be integrated in the semantic representation. The two systems interact, so that the slower syntactic alternative is blocked by the faster one (cf. also Gorrell 1987 for a similar position). Since subject-initial structures can be processed faster than object-initial ones, an overall subject preference for locally ambiguous structures will thus be predicted.

ACKNOWLEDGMENTS

For helpful suggestions and useful comments, we would like to thank Markus Bader, Josef Bayer, Lyn Frazier, Susan Kemper, Michael Meng, Jens Michaelis, Ralf Krampe, Peter Staudacher, Gerhard Strube, and Christian Wartena. We are especially indebted to Barbara Hemforth for her critical remarks on an earlier version of this chapter, which helped to improve it substantially. For technical assistance, we would like to thank Hannelore Gensel, Petra Gröttner, and also Eva Brehm, Anja Meinke, Antje Lorenz, Anke Schulz, Carola Steffen, Alexandra Wendeler.

NOTES

[1] We add this proviso concerning the effect of non-syntactic factors mainly in the interest of faithful citation. We do not necessarily subscribe to the view that non-syntactic factors may change processing preferences in the domain of grammatical function assignment.

[2] That is, the specifier of the Comp phrase in more recent approaches to syntax.

[3] Our corpus analyses were carried out by Carola Steffen.

[4] The Freiburg corpus and the Diskurs corpus.

[5] Even if we establish that the subject preference of declaratives is syntax based, that finding would not imply that it is due to the particular way the

human parser handles movement dependencies (which the AFH tries to characterize). Based on an approach first proposed by Travis (1984), there is a (non-mainstream) tradition of analyzing German declarative clauses according to which the structures of subject and object initial declaratives differ fundamentally. For example, Zwart (1993) proposed that subject initial declaratives are simple inflection phrases (IP), (that is, that they have the same status as English declaratives), while object initial clauses involve left dislocation, such that the structure of (1b) would be (roughly) similar to the one of (i). Thus, the subject preference might be due to a strategy of not postulating a left dislocation analysis without good evidence for it (cf. Gorrell in press for an approach linked to such considerations) - the preference would thus be completely unrelated to the AFH.

(i) the hen, the buzzard sees it

[6] There are no accepted standards for the necessary size of frequency differences triggering tuning effects, so the claim made above may have to be modified. A further difficulty lies in the fact that there is no general consensus concerning the level of analysis at which tuning applies.

[7] In three of the items, we had used *wessen* "whose" instead of *which*. An elimination of these items from the analysis does not affect the results of the study.

[8] In one case, the participant's data were not included because she was bilingual, in the other cases, the subjects had not provided the disambiguating word for at least one experimental item, or had provided more than one option for a target item, or had provided a word that made a target item ungrammatical or gave an interpretation different from the intended one.

[9] Data were assigned to this category if an unambiguous identification of the grammatical function of the phrase inserted by the subjects was not possible on formal grounds.

[10] α = specifier of CP is of course not the only possible analysis for the initial maximal projection of a clause. α could be more deeply embedded in Spec,CP. Minimal attachment thus predicts that α = Spec,CP

REFERENCES

Bach, E., Brown, C., & Marslen-Wilson, W. (1986). Crossed and nested dependencies in German and Dutch: A psycholinguistic study. *Language and Cognitive Processes*, 1, 249-262.

Bader, M. (1990). *Syntaktische Prozesse beim Sprachverstehen: Theoretische Überlegungen und experimentelle Untersuchungen*. Unpublished Master's Thesis, University of Freiburg.

Blaubergs, M.S., & Braine, M.D. (1974). Short term memory limitations on decoding self-embedded sentences. *Journal of Experimental Psychology, 102*, 745-748.

Brueck, U. (1996). *Auswirkungen erwartungsgeleiteter syntaktischer Verarbeitung bei Interrogativsätzen mit ambigen wh-Strukturen*. Diploma Thesis, University of Regensburg.

Chomsky, N. (1981). *Lectures on Government and Binding*. Dordrecht: Foris.

Clifton, C., & Frazier, L. (1989). Comprehending sentences with long distance dependencies. In G. Carlson & M. Tanenhaus (Eds.), *Linguistic structure in language processing* (pp. 273-317). Dordrecht: Kluwer.

Cuetos, F., & Mitchell, D.C. (1988). Cross-linguistic differences in parsing: Restrictions on the use of the Late Closure strategy in Spanish. *Cognition, 30*, 73-105.

De Vincenzi, M. (1991a). *Syntactic parsing strategies in Italian*. Dordrecht: Kluwer.

De Vincenzi, M. (1991b). Filler-gap dependencies in a null subject language: Referential and nonreferential WHs. *Journal of Psycholinguistic Research, 20*, 197-213.

Fanselow, G., Kliegl, R., & Schlesewsky, M. (1997). *Variation von experimentellen Methoden zur Untersuchung von Subjekt-Objekt-Asymmetrien*. Unpublished manuscript.

Farke, H. (1994). *Grammatik und Sprachverarbeitung*. Opladen: Westdeutscher Verlag.

Frazier, L., & Flores d' Arcais, G. (1989). Filler-driven parsing: A study of gap filling in Dutch. *Journal of Memory and Language, 28*, 331-344.

Gorrell, P., 1987. *Studies of human processing: Ranked parallel versus serial models*. Unpublished doctoral dissertation, University of Connecticut, Storrs.

Gorrell, P. (in press). Parsing theory and phrase-order variation in German V2-clauses. *Journal of Psycholinguistic Research*.

Haider, H. (1986). Affect α: A reply to Lasnik and Saito. *Linguistic Inquiry 17*, 113-126.

Hemforth, B. (1993). *Kognitives Parsing: Repräsentation und Verarbeitung sprachlichen Wissens*. Sankt Augustin: Infix.

Hemforth, B., Konieczny, L., & Strube, G. (1993). Incremental syntax processing and parsing strategies. *Proceedings of the 15th Annual Conference of the Cognitive Science Society*. Hillsdale, NJ: LEA. 539-545.

Kaan, E. (1997). *Processing subject-object ambiguities in Dutch*. Doctoral dissertation, Rijksuniversiteit Groningen.

Konieczny, L., Scheepers, C., Hemforth, B., & Strube, G. (1994). Semantik-orientierte Syntaxverarbeitung. In Felix, S., Habel, C., & Rickheit, G., (Eds.), *Kognitive Linguistik: Repräsentationen und Prozesse*. Opladen: Westdeutscher Verlag.

Kühn, K. (1993). *Syntaktische Prozesse beim Sprachverstehen: Eine empirische Studie zur Verarbeitung lokal ambiger Relativsätze im Deutschen*. Unpublished Master's thesis, Free University of Berlin.

Lenerz, J., (1977). *Zur Abfolge nominaler Satzglieder im Deutschen*. Tübingen: Narr.

Lewis, R. (1993). *An architecturally-based theory of human sentence comprehension*. Unpublished doctoral dissertation, Carnegie Mellon University, Pittsburgh.

MacWhinney, B., Bates, L., & Kliegl, R. (1984). Cue validity and sentence interpretation in English, German, and Italian. *Journal of Verbal Learning and Verbal Behavior, 23*, 127-150.

Macketanz, K. (1996). *Gibt es Primingeffekte bei der Verarbeitung ambiger Fragesätze?* Diploma Thesis, University of Regensburg.

Meng, M. (1995). *Processing wh-questions in German and Dutch: Differential effects of disambiguation and their interpretation*. Manuscript., University of Jena.

Müller, G., & Sternefeld, W. (1993). Improper movement and unambiguous binding. *Linguistic Inquiry, 24*, 461-507.

Schlesewsky, M. (1996). *Kasusphänomene in der Sprachverarbeitung*. Doctoral dissertation, University of Potsdam.

Schlesewsky., M. (in prep.). *The nature of case reanalysis: Evidence for an attention-driven model*.

Schlesewsky, M., Fanselow, G., & Kliegl, R. (1997a). The costs of wh-movement in German. Manuscript submitted for publication.

Schlesewsky, M., Fanselow, G., & Kliegl, R. (1997b). *Extraktionen aus daß-Strukturen - eine Pilotstudie zum Priming von Objekt-Erst-Strukturen*. Manuscript. University of Potsdam.

Schriefers, H., Friederici, A., & Kühn, K. (1995). The processing of locally ambiguous relative clauses in German. *Journal of Memory and Language, 34*, 499-520.

Stabler, E. (1994). The finite connectivity of linguistic structure. In C. Clifton, L. Frazier & K. Rayner (Eds.), *Perspectives on sentence processing* (pp. 303-336). Hillsdale, NJ: LEA.

Staudacher, P. (1990). Long movement from verb second complements in German. In G. Grewendorf & W. Sternefeld (Eds.), *Scrambling and barriers* (pp. 319-339). Amsterdam: Benjamins.

Thiersch, C. (1978). *Topics in German syntax.* Umpublished doctoral dissertation, MIT, Cambridge, Mass.

Travis, L. (1984). *Parameters and effects of word order variation.* Unpublished doctoral dissertation, MIT, Cambridge, Mass.

Zwart, J.W. (1993). *Dutch syntax. A minimalist approach.* Groningen Dissertations in Linguistics, Groningen.

LINKING SYNTACTIC FUNCTIONS WITH THEMATIC ROLES: PSYCH-VERBS AND THE RESOLUTION OF SUBJECT-OBJECT AMBIGUITY

Christoph Scheepers*, Barbara Hemforth+ and Lars Konieczny#

*University of Glasgow
+University of Freiburg
#Saarland University

INTRODUCTION

Subject-object ambiguities like in (1a-d), where the first NP can either be interpreted as the subject or as the direct object of the sentence, are one of the most intensively studied phenomena of German sentence processing, as is reflected by the number of contributions on this topic in the current volume (cf. the chapters of Markus Bader, Paul Gorrell, Lars Konieczny et al., and Matthias Schlesewsky et al.).

(1) a. Welche Nachbarin kannte die Frau?

[Which neighbor]$_{[fem, \{nom, acc\}]}$ knew [the woman]$_{[fem, \{nom, acc\}]}$?

b. Die Nachbarin, die die Frau kannte, ...

[The neighbor]$_{[fem, \{nom, acc\}]}$, who [the woman]$_{[fem, \{nom, acc\}]}$ knew, ...

c. Die Nachbarin kannte die Frau.

[The neighbor]$_{[fem, \{nom, acc\}]}$ knew [the woman]$_{[fem, \{nom, acc\}]}$.

d. Daß die Nachbarin die Frau kannte, ...

That [the neighbor]$_{[fem, \{nom, acc\}]}$ [the woman]$_{[fem, \{nom, acc\}]}$ knew, ...

B. Hemforth and L. Konieczny (eds.), German Sentence Processing, 95-135.

Although the point of error detection as well as the strength of observable garden-path effects vary considerably with respect to the kind of structure under investigation, a robust preference in favor of the subject-before-object linearization, i.e. a preference to interpret the first NP as the subject of the sentence, has been observed in an impressive number of studies using various experimental techniques (for wh-questions like 1a see, e.g., Meng, 1996; Schlesewsky et al., this volume; for relative clauses like 1b see, e.g., Mecklinger, Schriefers, Steinhauer and Friederici, 1995; for main clauses like 1c see, e.g., Hemforth, 1993; Konieczny, 1996; Scheepers, 1996; and for complement clauses like 1d see, e.g., Bader and Lasser, 1994; Bader, Bayer, Hopf and Meng 1996; Scheepers, 1996).

Several principle based models have been developed to explain this and other constituent ordering preferences in German (and other languages as well). These principles refer to various aspects of sentence processing, like filler-gap dependencies (i.e. assuming that the parser always postulates the fewest number of chain members possible, e.g. De Vincenzi, 1991; Crocker, 1993), structural parsimony (cf. *Simplicity*; Gorrell, this volume), case marking (cf. Bader, this volume), or memory load associated with structure building (cf. Schlesewsky et al., this volume). What all these proposals have in common is that they strongly rely on syntactic information to explain the observed preferences. A further commonality is that all of these models take a derivational grammar theory as a basis for syntactic representation, thereby assuming that derived structures (implying *wh-movement* or *scrambling*) require some extra processing compared to non-derived (i.e. "close to base-generated") orderings.

Although none of these models explicitly denies an influence of verb-specific information on constituent ordering preferences, only little work has been carried out on this topic so far.[1] This is quite surprising, given the fact that with the development of lexically oriented grammar theories the role of verb-argument structure and thematic information has inspired various sentence processing models which more or less share the assumption that the subcategorization properties of the verb (and sometimes even their thematic properties) guide initial parsing decisions (e.g. Abney, 1989; Gibson, 1991; Frazier and Clifton, 1996; Konieczny, 1996; Konieczny, Hemforth, Scheepers and Strube, 1997; MacDonald et al., 1994; Pritchett, 1992; Stevenson, 1993).

The present chapter primarily addresses the relationship between syntactic processing and thematic interpretation in the context of subject-object ambiguity resolution in German. We will focus on the question of whether observable subject-object asymmetries can be reduced to a constituent ordering principle which places the more prominent thematic roles of a verb before the less prominent ones in d-structure (cf. Grimshaw, 1990; 1991; 1993; Haider, 1993; Gorrell, this volume), as opposed to the more "traditional" proposal that the subject and the object(s) occupy fixed positions in the canonical sentence structure, producing a standard functional linearization independent of the main verb in the sentence.

We will present two questionnaire studies and an eye-tracking experiment which were designed to test the predictions derivable from these proposals. In these experiments, we varied the linking between syntactic functions (subject and object) and thematic roles (*experiencer* and *theme*) by using a systematic alternation observable for certain psychological verbs (the "fear/frighten" alternation). Before we turn to these experiments, we want to discuss in some more detail the representational issues of the structures under investigation.

DEFINING "SUBJECT" AND "OBJECT"

The configurational account

In standard GB-oriented analyses of German (e.g. Stechow and Sternefeld, 1988), the subject and the object(s) are conceptualized as occupying fixed positions in the canonical (i.e. base-generated) sentence structure, so that they occur in a particular configurational relation to each other (p1): the subject, which is assumed to receive its case (nominative) from the SpecIP (or SpecVP)[2] position, c-commands the object(s) in d-structure; the indirect object (typically a dative-NP) c-commands the direct object (an accusative-NP) which in turn c-commands the oblique object (typically a PP) (see Figure 1). Example (2) therefore shows a base-generated (or "canonical") ordering of the verbal arguments.

(p1)   c-command (informally):

node A c-commands node B, iff A does not dominate B and every node C that dominates A dominates B.

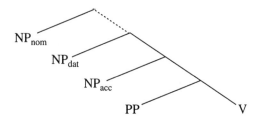

Figure 1: Functional configuration

(2)   Ich sah, wie der Junge seinem Freund den Brief in die
             Tasche steckte.

             I saw, how the boy$_{nom}$ his friend$_{dat}$ the letter$_{acc}$ into the bag
             put.

To generate an object-before-subject linearization at the sentence surface,
movement of the corresponding object-NP into a position before the subject is
required (i.e. either movement of the object-NP into an already existing
"topic"-position [SpecCP], or *scrambling*, i.e. adjoining the object-NP to a
pre-subject position which has to be generated particularly for that purpose).
Thereby a chain is formed between the lexical filler (i.e. the moved object-NP)
and its corresponding trace in the d-structural object-position (2').

(2`)   Ich sah, wie [den Brief]$_i$ der Junge seinem Freund t$_i$ in die
             Tasche steckte.

             I saw, how [the letter$_{acc}$]$_i$ the boy$_{nom}$ his friend$_{dat}$ t$_i$ into the
             bag put.

Most of the current sentence comprehension models agree in the assumption that the parser, if possible, avoids postulating a derived, "non-canonical"
structure, because such a structure would imply higher memory load in terms
of chain formation (cf. the *Minimal Chain Principle*; De Vincenzi, 1991), and
processing load associated with structure building (cf. *Simplicity*, Gorrell,
1995; this volume), respectively. Taking a configurational definition of syntactic function as a basis, the processing models would predict a general, item-
independent preference to interpret the first NP in a sentence as the subject if
this NP is ambiguous between a subject-or an object-reading, as in (1a-d).

A non-configurational account: thematic prominence

For German, it has been proposed that, instead of a general configurational restriction on argument ordering, the d-structural linearization of syntactic functions is open to lexical variation (Haider, 1993; cf. Bader, this volume). The motivation for this assumption stems from the observation that at least some verbs (e.g. *auffallen*, to strike somebody) intuitively favor the object (NP_{dat})-before-subject (NP_{nom}) ordering (3b) (or at least this ordering is not very problematic with these verbs), while the majority of other transitive verbs in German (e.g. *zuhören*, to listen to) take subject-before-object (3a) as the unmarked order:[3]

> (3)   a.   daß der Schüler dem Lehrer {?auffiel / zuhörte}
>   (subject < object)
>
>   that the pupil_nom the teacher_dat {?struck / listened to}
>
>   b.   daß dem Lehrer der Schüler {auffiel / ?zuhörte}
>   (object < subject)
>
>   that the teacher_dat the pupil_nom {struck / ?listened to}

Verb-dependent contrasts like these led Haider (1993) to conclude that syntactic functions cannot be determined configurationally, as this would imply the same basic argument order for each verb. Instead, he defines syntactic functions by lexical designation: the "subject" of the sentence is roughly defined as "the NP receiving nominative case", the direct object as "the NP receiving accusative case" etc. (where case is not provided by particular positions in d-structure, but by the lexical frame of the verb)[4], so that all verbal arguments are already specified with respect to case-marking when they enter the d-structural projection(s) of the verb.

Since all of the examples discussed so far indicate, to a greater or lesser degree, clear functional ordering preferences, the question arises which principles actually determine the linear order of the arguments in the canonical sentence structure. Several authors who adopt a non-configurational definition of syntactic function—including Haider (1993)—suggest that functional order results from a general constraint holding between the *thematic roles* of a verb, as expressed by the following hierarchical relation (cf. Grimshaw, 1990; 1991; 1993; Uszkoreit, 1986; Pechmann et al., 1994):[5]

> (p2)   agent > experiencer > goal/source/location > theme

(p2) ranks the *agent*-role of a predicate as more prominent than an *experiencer* which is, in turn, more prominent than *goal* (or *source*, or *location*) which is more prominent than *theme*. Presuming that the prominence relations in (p2) determine the linear precedence relations that must hold between the functional arguments in the d-structural projection(s) of the verb (cf. Grimshaw, 1991; 1993; Gorrell, this volume), a non-configurational account predicts that the base-generated order of syntactic functions is affected by item-dependent variation (at least to a certain extent): a verb like *auffallen* (to strike somebody) links its thematically more prominent role (*experiencer*) with the object function (i.e. dative case) and the less prominent role (*theme*) with the subject function (i.e. nominative case), so that, following (p2), object-before-subject (i.e. dative-before-nominative) results as the base-generated order. A verb like *zuhören* (to listen to), on the other hand, links its more prominent role (*agent*, presuming that the verb is interpreted as an intentional event) with the subject and the less prominent *theme*-role with the object function, generating subject-before-object as canonical order. Thus, thematic prominence is able to explain the contrast in (3).

An important point to note here is: originally, the thematic hierarchy in (p2) was proposed to be a universal principle of *subject selection*, presuming that the thematically most prominent argument in the set of argument positions provided by a verb is typically designated as the subject. In fact, this is true for a majority of verbs like, e.g., agentive predicates (*John listens to Mary*), stative predicates (*John owns a house*), or process predicates (*John runs*). But a particular subsets of verbs, i.e. ergatives and certain psychological verbs (e.g. *auffallen*, to strike somebody), deviate from this default. Grimshaw (1990) argues that these deviations are not arbitrary, as they follow from additional conceptual properties of the particular verbs. In Grimshaws theory, verbal predicates are not only analyzed along a thematic dimension but also with respect to their causal event structure, i.e. along an *aspectual* dimension which is—under certain circumstances—able to override the thematic constraint (p2) on subject selection: the entity which causally initiates an event (i.e., the argument receiving the aspectual *cause* role) is marked as the most prominent argument on the aspectual dimension. If this (*cause-*)argument, however, is not denoted as the most prominent one on the thematic dimension, an incongruity emerges.

With respect to subject selection, such an incongruity is obviously resolved in favor of aspectual prominence, as can be demonstrated by a verb like *auffallen* (to strike somebody), a so-called *psychological causative* (P-causative) predicate: this verb provides two thematic roles, namely *experiencer* (i.e. an entity involved in perception) and *theme* (i.e. the perceived entity). The particular point about *auffallen* is that the argument which is identified with the thematically less prominent (*theme*) role receives the most prominent (*cause*) role on the aspectual dimension, i.e. the perceived entity is analyzed as having certain properties or characteristics which are causally responsible for perceiving the entity (this is exactly what differentiates a predicate like *to strike somebody* from simple *perception of something*).[6] The syntactic function of the subject (i.e. nominative case) is assigned to the aspectually more prominent argument, not to the thematically more prominent one. The canonical functional ordering, however, is not influenced by aspectual prominence, since it follows (p2), as already discussed above.

For the majority of verbal predicates (e.g. agentive, stative, and process verbs) thematic and aspectual prominence do not compete with each other: the *agent* of an intentional predicate is necessarily identified with the *cause* role, and for the thematically most prominent argument of a stative predicate there is no competitor (*cause*) on the aspectual dimension.

To conclude, for most of the verbs in German the non-configurational thematic hierarchy approach sketched here generates the same canonical functional ordering as the configurational approach, namely subject-before-object. For a subset of verbs, however, thematic prominence predicts the object-before-subject linearization to be preferred. This subset of verbs is characterized by a thematic-aspectual incongruity concerning the prominence of their arguments.

Psychological verbs

In the following experiments, we will use psychological verbs like *fürchten* (to fear) and *ängstigen* (to frighten) as empirical test-cases for the two accounts on syntactic function definition. All of these verbs describe a mental state (or a change of mental state) of an *experiencer* towards a perceived entity (a *theme*). Two subclasses of psychological verbs can be identified: verbs like *fürchten* (to fear) belong to the class of *psychological statives* (P-statives) which realize their thematically most prominent *experiencer* role as the subject (i.e. as nominative-NP) and their *theme* as accusative-object. *Psychological causatives* (P-causatives), like *ängstigen* (to frighten) (cf. *auffallen*, to strike somebody),[7] on the other hand, show exactly the opposite role-function mapping when compared to their stative counterparts (presumably because of thematic-aspectual incongruence, as discussed above). Since P-causatives select their thematically less prominent *themes* as subjects, they belong to the subset of verbs for which the non-configurational thematic hierarchy account predicts a preference in favor of the object-before-subject-preference (cf. Haider, 1993:117).

In the following sections, we will describe three experiments: Experiments 1 and 2 were acceptability judgement questionnaires designed to examine the influence of role-function linking (varied by the type of psychological predicate) on functional ordering preferences. Experiment 3 is an eye-tracking study focusing primarily on the time course of forming thematic-functional links during subject-object-ambiguity resolution.

EXPERIMENT 1

The first experiment was a questionnaire study designed to test the influence of three orthogonally varied factors on sentence acceptability (cf. Table 2): firstly, the position of the verb (factor *verb position*) which either preceded (V-Args) or followed (Args-V) its arguments; secondly, the surface linearization of subject and direct object (factor *functional order*: all sentences introduced a syntactic function ambiguity at the—always feminine—first argument-NP which was disambiguated by the case morphology of the—always masculine—second NP, yielding either *subject-before-object* (S-O) or *object-before-subject* (O-S) as functional order); thirdly, the type of verb was varied (factor *verb type*) by pairing *P-stative* verbs with semantically similar *P-causative* verbs, in order to produce inverse functional realizations of the thematic roles *experiencer* and *theme*. Most of the verbs were translations of the psychological predicates given in Grimshaw (1990:175).[8]

			V-Args (main clauses)
S-O	P-stative	i	Vielleicht fürchtete die stille Schülerin den strengen Lehrer ein wenig, so wurde vermutet. "Perhaps feared [the quiet pupil]$_{[fem, \{nom, acc\}]}$ [the strict teacher]$_{[masc, acc]}$ a bit, as was supposed."
	P-causative	ii	Vielleicht ängstigte die strenge Lehrerin den stillen Schüler ein wenig, so wurde vermutet. "Perhaps frightened [the strict teacher]$_{[fem, \{nom, acc\}]}$ [the quiet pupil]$_{[masc, acc]}$ a bit, as was supposed."

Table 1: Materials of Experiment 1

| O-S | P-stative | iii | Vielleicht fürchtete die strenge Lehrerin der stille Schüler ein wenig, so wurde vermutet. "Perhaps feared [the strict teacher]$_{[fem, \{nom, acc\}]}$ [the quiet pupil]$_{[masc, nom]}$ a bit, as was supposed." |
| | P-causative | iv | Vielleicht ängstigte die stille Schülerin der strenge Lehrer ein wenig, so wurde vermutet. "Perhaps frightened [the quiet pupil]$_{[fem, \{nom, acc\}]}$ [the strict teacher]$_{[masc, nom]}$ a bit, as was supposed." |

Args-V (complement clauses)

S-O	P-stative	v	Man vermutete, daß die stille Schülerin den strengen Lehrer ein wenig fürchtete. "It was supposed, that [the quiet pupil]$_{[fem, \{nom, acc\}]}$ [the strict teacher]$_{[masc, acc]}$ a bit feared."
	P-causative	vi	Man vermutete, daß die strenge Lehrerin den stillen Schüler ein wenig ängstigte. "It was supposed, that [the strict teacher]$_{[fem, \{nom, acc\}]}$ [the quiet pupil]$_{[masc, acc]}$ a bit frightened."
O-S	P-stative	vii	Man vermutete, daß die strenge Lehrerin der stille Schüler ein wenig fürchtete. "It was supposed, that [the strict teacher]$_{[fem, \{nom, acc\}]}$ [the quiet pupil]$_{[masc, nom]}$ a bit feared."
	P-causative	viii	Man vermutete, daß die stille Schülerin der strenge Lehrer ein wenig ängstigte. "It was supposed, that [the quiet pupil]$_{[fem, \{nom, acc\}]}$ [the strict teacher]$_{[masc, nom]}$ a bit frightened."

Table 1: Materials of Experiment 1

Note that the instantiations of the thematic roles were held constant across conditions (in i.-viii., for example, the *experiencer* is always instantiated by "the quiet pupil" and the *theme* by "the strict teacher"), so that all factor combinations were as parallel as possible with respect to meaning. Consequently, any plausibility differences between conditions—as to whether the participants are "good" or "bad" instantiations of the respective roles in the given situation—were eliminated.

16 items were constructed, yielding a pool of 16(items)*8(conditions)=128 sentences. Eight material sets with different factor-item-combinations were created. The factors were manipulated *within subjects*, so that each set of materials contained two items per condition. Additionally, 20 distractor sentences were included in each material set which differed structurally from the test items in that the so-called *Vorfeld*-position was always occupied by an argument (see below). Half of the fillers were grammatically well-formed, the other half either contained a syntactic violation, as in (4) where two NPs bear the same (unambiguous) case marking, or a lexical/semantic violation, as in (5) where neither of the two (case-ambiguous) NPs fulfills the requirement for a propositional *theme* in the transitive reading of the verb.

(4)   *Der hungrige Fuchs bemerkte der fette Hahn offenbar nicht, ...

"[The hungry fox]$_{[masc, nom]}$ noticed [the fat rooster]$_{[masc, nom]}$ obviously not, ..."

(5)   #Die befragte Zeugin erzählte die mutmaßliche Täterin, ...

"[The interrogated witness]$_{[fem, \{nom, acc\}]}$ told [the presumed culprit]$_{[fem, \{nom, acc\}]}$"

For each material set, four different quasi-random sequences of sentences were generated. We used an algorithm that minimizes the chance of two sentences of the same condition appearing in immediate succession. Additionally, the procedure was restricted to generate lists beginning with at least four distractor sentences.

The resulting 32 questionnaire lists were randomly distributed among 32 subjects. All of them were native speakers of German and they were naive concerning the problem under investigation. Subjects were asked to rate the acceptability of each sentence in the questionnaire using a four-point rating scale labelled with "gar nicht akzeptabel" (*not acceptable at all*), "eher nicht akzeptabel" (*fairly unacceptable*), "eher akzeptabel" (*fairly acceptable*), and "völlig akzeptabel" (*completely acceptable*). For later data analysis, these labels were scored as 1, 2, 3, and 4, respectively.

Hypotheses

Verb position

It has been demonstrated that the difficulty of the non-canonical functional order strongly interacts with the type of sentence involved. For example, the garden-pathing O-S-linearization is much harder to process in complement clauses (9) than in main clauses (6) (Scheepers, 1996; Scheepers, Konieczny and Hemforth, 1997).

(6)   Die kleine Nichte besuchte der nette Onkel, ...

           "[The little niece]$_{[fem, \{nom, acc\}]}$ visited [the nice uncle]$_{[masc, nom]}$, ..."

(7)   Als die kleine Nichte der nette Onkel besuchte, ...

           "When [the little niece]$_{[fem, \{nom, acc\}]}$ [the nice uncle]$_{[masc, nom]}$ visited, ..."

(8)   Die kleine Nichte besuchte den netten Onkel, ...

           "[The little niece]$_{[fem, \{nom, acc\}]}$ visited [the nice uncle]$_{[masc, acc]}$, ..."

(9)   Als die kleine Nichte den netten Onkel besuchte, ...

           "When [the little niece]$_{[fem, \{nom, acc\}]}$ [the nice uncle]$_{[masc, acc]}$ visited, ..."

The greater difficulties with (9) compared to (6) cannot be due to just the position of the verb, since in structures with canonical S-O-order (cf. 6 vs. 9) no penalty for complement clauses was observed. Instead, what makes (9) harder than (6) seems to be a difference in structural complexity: (6) simply requires topicalization, i.e. movement of the object-NP into the so-called *Vorfeld*-position (cf. 6'). In (9), however, both arguments remain within the *Mittelfeld* whose base form does not provide any position for fronting an argument. Since constructions like (9) are not ungrammatical per se, it is assumed that the *Mittelfeld* is augmented by an additional projection which functions as the final host of the moved NP (*scrambling*) (cf. 9'). The higher complexity of scrambling compared to topicalization might be responsible for the additional processing cost in structures like (9).

(6')[$_{CP}$ [Die kleine Nichte]$_i$ [$_{C1}$ besuchte$_j$ [der nette Onkel t$_i$ t$_j$]]]

(9')[$_{CP}$ [$_{C1}$ Als [[die kleine Nichte]$_i$ [der nette Onkel t$_i$ besuchte]]]]

If this explanation of the earlier findings is correct, we should expect no acceptability differences between the *verb-position* variants examined in the current experiment, since both of them—the complement clauses in the Args-V condition as well as the main clauses in the V-Args condition—imply each functional ordering to be realized within the *Mittelfeld*. Scrambling is required in both cases to generate the non-canonical functional order, as exemplified in (iii'.) and (vii'.). The verb-placement variants examined here are therefore parallel with respect to structural complexity.

iii'.[$_{CP}$ ... [$_{Cl}$ fürchtetej [[die strenge Lehrerin]$_i$ [der schweigsame Schüler t$_i$ t$_j$]]]]

vii'.[$_{CP}$ [$_{Cl}$ daß [[die strenge Lehrerin]$_i$ [der schweigsame Schüler t$_i$ fürchtctc]]]]

Verb type and functional order

Although there are gross differences in their underlying explanatory mechanisms, most of the current processing models (e.g. De Vincenzi, 1991; Gorrell, 1995; this volume) widely agree in their predictions concerning the structures considered here. Generally speaking, a preference in favor of base-generated linearizations is predicted, as opposed to derived functional orderings (i.e. structures implying argument-fronting by movement or scrambling, respectively). Whether or not the type of verb should have an impact on the preferred functional sequence strongly depends on the conceptualization of syntactic functions in d-structure projection.

We identified a *configurational* approach in which syntactic functions are defined by fixed d-structural positions, with the subject standing in a c-command relation to the object. In this account, the subject *per definition* precedes the object in the base-generated structure, and so a general preference in favor of the S-O-linearization is predicted, regardless of the main verb in the sentence. We will refer to this account as the *functional linearization* hypothesis, emphasizing the fact that the unmarked order emerges from the definition of syntactic function.

On the other hand, we considered a designatory approach of syntactic function definition (as proposed, e.g., by Haider,1993), which generates different base orders of subject and object, depending on the thematic properties of the verb: for P-stative verbs like *fürchten* ("to fear") whose subject corresponds to the thematically more prominent *experiencer* role, S-O is generated as canonical order. For P-causative verbs like *ängstigen* ("to frighten") which realize their less prominent *theme* role as subject, O-S is the unmarked linearization.

This approach will further be referred to as the *thematic linearization* hypothesis.

To summarize, the first approach predicts a main effect of *functional order* with the O-S-linearization being generally less acceptable than the S-O ordering. According to *thematic linearization*, however, (at least in its strongest form) a disordinal interaction between *verb type* and *functional order* should be obtained which nullifies any general bias in favor of a particular functional order: S-O should be preferred in P-stative sentences, whereas O-S should be preferred in P-causative sentences.

Results

Because the collected rating data hardly fulfill the requirements for parametric testing, statistical analyses were exclusively based on the *Wilcoxon Signed-Ranks Test* for dependent measures which is appropriate for any data distribution obtained on (at least) an ordered metric scale. In order to test statistical interactions between two or more factors, the particular *differences* between aggregated design cells were submitted to this nonparametric test. For each effect, two different test-statistics (and their particular two-tailed probabilities) will be reported, one of which refers to analyses of data collapsed across subjects (Z1 with N – 32), while the other stems from analyses across items (Z2 with N = 16), respectively.

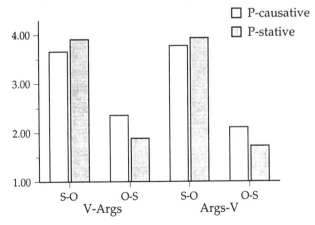

Figure 2: Results of Experiment 1. Mean acceptability scores.

Figure 2 shows the mean acceptability ratings in each factor combination of *verb position* (V-Args vs. Args-V), *functional order* (S-O vs. O-S), and *verb type* (P-causative vs. P-stative). As predicted by the *functional lineariza-tion* approach, a reliable overall main effect of *functional order* was obtained, with S-O-linearizations being more acceptable than O-S-linearizations (3.82 vs. 2.02: $Z1 = -4.92$; $p < .001$; $Z2 = -3.52$; $p < .001$). However, also the *verb type * functional order* interaction was significant ($Z1 = -4.07$; $p < .001$; $Z2 = -3.15$; $p < .002$). The *verb type* simple contrasts are consistent with the predic-tions of thematic prominence: the S-O-linearization is slightly more accept-able for P-stative verbs than for P-causatives (3.93 vs. 3.72: $Z1 = -2.52$; $p < .02$; $Z2 = -2.16$; $p < .04$), whereas the reverse is true for the O-S-ordering which is reliably more acceptable in P-causative sentences than in P-stative sentences (2.24 vs. 1.81: $Z1 = -3.30$; $p < .001$; $Z2 = -3.18$; $p < .002$). Contrary to the strong *thematic linearization* hypothesis, however, the main effect of *functional order* was not overridden by *verb type* effects, since for each type of verb, there was a clear preference in favor of the S-O-linearization (P-stat-ive, S-O = 3.93 vs. P-stative, O-S = 1.81: $Z1 = -4.94$; $p < .001$; -3.52; $p < .001$; P-causative, S-O = 3.72 vs. P-causative, OS = 2.24: $Z1 = -4.86$; $p < .001$; $Z2 = -3.52$; $p < .001$).

No other effects were significant. In particular, there were no differential influences of *verb position* (all $|Z| < 1.5$). This indirectly confirms the interpre-tation of earlier results (Scheepers, 1996; Scheepers et al., 1997) that not verb position "per se", but the underlying complexity of argument fronting—which was the same across the *verb position* variants of the current experiment—contributes to processing difficulty.

Discussion

At first glance, the robustness of the obtained S-O-preference can be regarded as evidence supporting the *functional linearization* hypothesis. However, there was a modulating effect of *verb type*—though not fully compatible with the strong version of *thematic linearization*—which reflects a residual influence of thematic prominence on sentence acceptability: a functional order that conflicts with thematic hierarchy (p2) is less acceptable than a functional order that agrees with it. Consequently, although an overall S-O-preference was observed, we cannot rule out *thematic linearization* with certainty, as will become particularly evident in the next section.

Agentivity

There is an alternative explanation for why *verb type* might not have been able to eliminate the general S-O-preference: P-causative verbs like "to frighten" are, in principal, thematically ambiguous between a non-intentional reading on the one hand, and an intentional (*agentive*) reading on the other hand. In our considerations so far, we assumed the subject of a P-causative verb to be interpreted as *theme* and the object as *experiencer*, so that—according to the *thematic linearization* approach— thematic prominence generates O-S as base order. The intentional interpretation of a P-causative, however, implies the subject to be interpreted as *agent* and the object as (less prominent) affected *theme* or patient. Consequently, the same d-structural argument order should emerge for agentively interpreted P-causatives as for P-statives, namely S-O.

Given that the observed interaction between *verb type* and *functional order* was reliable even across items, it is unlikely that a *predominant* proportion of the P-causatives was interpreted as agentive predicates. However, since *agent* and *theme* contrast more sharply in thematic prominence than *experiencer* and *theme* (cf. p2), it could well be that P-causatives interpreted as agentive predicates produced a *stronger* linearization preference (favoring S-O) than non-agentive P-causatives (favoring O-S), yielding an overall S-O-preference in P-causative sentences which is still somewhat weaker than in P-stative sentences.[9] The obtained data therefore easily fit with a *thematic linearization* account which is tuned by the interpretation of the verb and the corresponding "strength" of the contrast in thematic prominence (henceforth *thematic linearization*±).

The critical factor promoting an agentive interpretation of the P-causative verbs in the present experiment was certainly the fact that the subject was always animate (cf. Table 2). With an inanimate subject, however, the agentive reading of a P-causative is very unlikely to be considered, as can be demonstrated by the following contrast (10).

(10) a.   Peter frightened the children just for fun.

b.   #Peter's face frightened the children just for fun.

Presuming that *thematic linearization*± is right, a general O-S-preference should emerge for P-causative sentences if their agentive interpretation is blocked by an inanimate subject, whereas, parallel to Experiment 1, an S-O-preference should be obtained in P-causative sentences with animate subjects. The following experiment was designed to evaluate these predictions.

EXPERIMENT 2

The P-causative items of Experiment 1 were modified in order to manipulate two experimental factors (cf. Table 2). As in Experiment 1, we varied the *functional order* of the arguments: the first (feminine) NP was always ambiguous with respect to case marking. The second (masculine) NP was either overtly marked in the accusative case, yielding the S-O functional order, or in the nominative case, producing the O-S linearization. Secondly, we manipulated the *animateness* of the subject-NP which was either animate (like in Experiment 1) or inanimate, respectively. To keep the items semantically parallel, the instantiations of the thematic roles were held constant across the *functional order* conditions (as in the first experiment), and the head of the *animate* subject NP always appeared as genitive-modifier of the respective *inanimate* counterpart. Only main clauses with both arguments in the *Mittelfeld* were constructed.

S-O	animate subject	ix	Vielleicht ängstigte die grimmige Lehrerin den stillen Schüler ein wenig, so wurde vermutet. "Perhaps frightened [the grumpy teacher]$_{[fem, \{nom, acc\}]}$ [the quiet pupil]$_{[masc, acc]}$ a bit, as was supposed."
	inanimate subject	x	Vielleicht ängstigte die Miene der Lehrerin den stillen Schüler ein wenig, so wurde vermutet. "Perhaps frightened [the face-expression of the teacher]$_{[fem, \{nom, acc\}]}$ [the quiet pupil]$_{[masc, acc]}$ a bit, as was supposed."
O-S	animate subject	xi	Vielleicht ängstigte die stille Schülerin der grimmige Lehrer ein wenig, so wurde vermutet. "Perhaps frightened [the quiet pupil]$_{[fem, \{nom, acc\}]}$ [the grumpy teacher]$_{[masc, nom]}$ a bit, as was supposed."

Table 2: Materials of Experiment 2

inanimate subject	xii	Vielleicht ängstigte die stille Schülerin der Gesichtsausdruck des Lehrers ein wenig, so wurde vermutet. "Perhaps frightened [the quiet pupil]$_{[fem, \{nom, acc\}]}$ [the face-expression of the teacher]$_{[masc, nom]}$ a bit, as was supposed."

Table 2: Materials of Experiment 2

The 16(items)*4(conditions) = 64 sentences were divided among four material sets with different factor-item-combinations. Each set contained four items per condition. Additionally, 54 distractors with various syntactic structures were included in each set, most of which were sentences from experiments unrelated to the questions under investigation. Six different randomizations per set were generated according to the same procedure as in Experiment 1.

The questionnaires were randomly distributed among 24 subjects who were native speakers of German, and who were unaware of the purpose of the study. None of them participated in any other experiment described in this chapter. Subjects were asked to rate the acceptability of each sentence in the questionnaire on a seven-point rating scale (scored from 1 to 7) with the left extreme labeled as "gar nicht akzeptabel" (*not acceptable at all*), and the right extreme labeled as "völlig akzeptabel" (*completely acceptable*).[10]

Hypotheses

For the P-causative items examined here, *thematic linearization*$^{\pm}$ predicts a compensatory interaction between *animateness of the subject* and *functional order*: in accordance with the earlier results, an S-O-preference is expected for sentences with animate subjects, because at least a sub-proportion of these items is interpreted as agentive predicates. With an inanimate subject, however, a preference in favor of the O-S-linearization should show up, since an agentive interpretation is ruled out, so that the object receives a more prominent thematic role than the subject.

The *functional linearization* hypothesis, on the other hand, predicts an overall S-O-preference which cannot be overridden by the *animateness* manipulation. In particular, an S-O-preference should show up even in the inanimate-subject condition.

Results

As in the former experiment, the rating data were submitted to the *Wilcoxon Signed-Ranks Test* after summarizing them across subjects (Z1 with N = 24), and across items (Z2 with N = 16), respectively. For each effect, two-tailed probabilities are reported.

As the descriptive data in Figure 3 suggest, there was a significant main effect of *functional order* in form of a general S-O-preference (S-O = 6.34 vs. O-S = 5.05; Z1 = –4.20; p < .001; Z2 = –3.52; p < .001). Also, the *animateness * functional order* interaction was significant (Z1 = –3.48; p < .001; Z2 = –2.95; p < .003). Planned comparisons revealed a significant contrast in the O S-condition, with inanimate subjects being more acceptable than animate subjects (Z1 = –3.82; p < .001; Z2 = –3.35; p < .001). As a by-product of this contrast, the main effect of *animateness* was reliable as well (Animate Subject: 5.41 vs. Inanimate Subject: 5.98; Z1 = –3.51; p < .001; Z2 = –3.25; p < .002). In the preferred S-O-linearization condition, the difference between animate and inanimate subjects was far from being significant (| Z1, Z2 | < 0.5). Most importantly, separate comparisons for each of the *animateness* conditions revealed a reliable S-O-linearization preference for sentences with animate subjects (Z1 = –4.20; p < .001; Z2 = –3.52; p < .001) as well as for sentences with inanimate subjects (Z1 = –3.21; p < .002; Z2 = –3.04; p < .003).

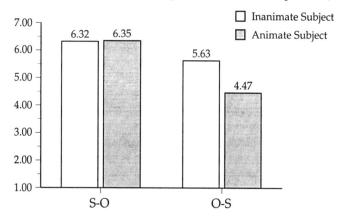

Figure 3: Results of Experiment 2. Mean acceptability scores.

Discussion

The data of this experiment clearly favor the functional account on subject-object-linearization: contrary to the *thematic linearization*$^{\pm}$ hypothesis, P-causative sentences were generally more acceptable when the subject preceded the direct object. Since this S-O-preference was observed even in sentences with inanimate subjects, it is rather unlikely to result from an agentive bias.

Though this result is clearly incompatible with *thematic linearization*, the interaction between *animateness* and *functional order* nevertheless points to a modulating influence of thematic prominence on the acceptability of the dispreferred linearization: placing the object before the subject is more acceptable when it receives the less prominent *theme* role (inanimate-subject condition) than when it receives the thematically more prominent *agent* role which (at least sometimes) is the case in the animate-subject condition.[11]

One might consider the general S-O-preference to result from the aspectual properties of the verbs. In the same way in which aspectual prominence overrides thematic hierarchy constraints in subject-designation (cf. Grimshaw, 1990; Haider, 1993), it could also determine the linear ordering of subject and object in d-structure: the thematically less prominent subject of a P-causative verb receives the most prominent *cause* role in the aspectual decomposition of the predicate, and so—given that linear order is determined aspectually—S-O should be base-generated even with these verbs. Such a proposal, however, predicts that thematic prominence should produce no reliable effects at all, as it should be completely suppressed by aspectual prominence.

THE TIME COURSE OF FUNCTIONAL AND THEMATIC CONSTRAINTS

Taking together the results from both questionnaire studies, two types of grammatical constraints can be identified which contribute to the acceptability of subject-object-linearization alternatives. The first one is a general restriction on functional order according to which the subject precedes the direct object in the base-generated structure. A deviation from this canonical (S-O) sequence is accompanied with a general decrease in acceptability. The other constraint is thematic prominence: whenever an argument ordering conflicts with the prominence relation specified in the thematic hierarchy (p2), it becomes less acceptable.

Thus, although the general functional restriction is clearly dominant, it does not completely eliminate the influence of thematic prominence, suggesting that the two different constraints must *compete* at some stage during sentence processing.[12] Hence, the question arises of how these constraints interact on-line, most importantly, whether they compete immediately during subject-object ambiguity resolution (i.e. at an "early" stage of processing) or not. The following eye-tracking experiment attempts to answer this question.

EXPERIMENT 3

In this experiment, we used basically the same sets of materials as in Experiment 1 (cf. Table 2) with the factors *verb position* (V-Args vs. Args-V), *functional order* (S-O vs. O-S), and *verb type* (D accusative vs. Dative) manipulated according to a 2*2*2 within subjects design. As demonstrated in the example below (Table 3), the complement clauses in the Args-V condition were modified so that they appeared before their corresponding matrix clauses. This was done in order to place all critical regions in the first line of the sentence (parallel to the main clauses).

In contrast to the questionnaire experiments, all target sentences were embedded in small texts in order to induce a more natural, fluent reading behavior. To construct coherent contexts, the non-critical clauses of some target items were slightly modified. Each text consisted of three segments which were presented separately in succession (cf. Table 3).

segment 1	Der Schulpsychologe diskutierte mit der Direktorin über die Sorgen, die ihm {ein ungewöhnlich introvertierter Schüler und eine ziemlich rigide Lehrerin / eine ziemlich rigide Lehrerin und ein ungewöhnlich introvertierter Schüler} bereiteten. "The school-psychologist discussed with the headmistress about the worries which {an unusually introverted pupil and a quite rigid teacher / a quite rigid teacher and an unusually introverted pupil} caused him to have."
segment 2	Daß die strenge Lehrerin den stillen Schüler ein wenig ängstigte, hatte der Psychologe von einigen Klassenkameraden erfahren. "That the strict teacher frightened the quiet pupil a bit, the psychologist had been told by some class-mates."
segment 3	Die Direktorin schlug vor, auch mit den Eltern darüber zu sprechen. "The headmaster suggested to talk about it with the parents as well."

Table 3: Text example for Experiment 3

The first segment was a preparative context containing one sentence (sometimes two sentences) which introduced the critical protagonists of the test sentence within a coordinative phrase in subject position. The surface order of the conjuncts was counterbalanced across all experimental conditions, so that for half of the items the *experiencer* and for the other half the *theme* of the test sentence appeared as the first conjunct. In the second segment, the target sentence was presented with the critical clause always being in the first line and the other clause always following a line break. The last segment contained a follow-up sentence which was identical across all conditions.

After line breaks, two additional returns were inserted so that fixations slightly below or above a line could unambiguously be related to the respective text-positions.

The eight material sets constructed for the current experiment included not only the 16 test-items (with two texts per condition), but also a sample of 76 texts designed for experiments with different purposes (the text-segment containing the "critical" sentence was different between experiments). 10 additional texts were included which functioned as pure fillers for initiating new experimental blocks.

Procedure

Prior to the experiment, the subject was fitted to a headrest to prevent head movements during reading. This was followed by a brief calibration procedure and a warming-up block consisting of two distractor texts. Then the experiment, which was built up of eight experimental blocks, began. Each block was initiated by a brief calibration procedure and a filler text. After the filler, 12 texts randomly taken from the full set of experimental items were presented in random succession (the last experimental block was made up of one filler and eight experimental texts). Between the blocks, subjects were given the opportunity to have a short break.

The presentation of the particular text-segments was subject-paced: presentation was initiated as soon as the subject fixated a cross on the screen, which indicated the start-position (i.e. the first character) of the text-segment. When subjects had finished reading the segment, they pressed a button, thereby erasing the segment from the screen. The presentation of the following text-segment again started with the fixation of a cross (which was five lines below the preceding cross), etc. After the last text-segment was read, a question was presented which focussed on some interpretational aspect of the preceding text. In the current experiment, the question always addressed the thematic interpretation of the syntactic functions (e.g. *Was the [pupil / teacher] frightened?*). After subjects answered the question by pressing a "yes"- or "no"-button, respectively, the presentation of a new text was announced by a special message on the screen.

Subjects

Twenty-four undergraduate students (native speakers of German) from the University of Freiburg were paid to participate in the study. All of them had normal, uncorrected vision. During an experimental session of about 90 minutes at the Institute of Computer Science and Social Research in Freiburg, subjects had to read 102 texts while their eye movements were monitored. Subjects were told to read normally, and that the purpose of the study was to determine where people look during reading.

Apparatus

The subjects' eye movements were monitored by a Generation 5.5 Dual Purkinje Image eye-tracker, which has a resolution of less than 5 minutes of arc. Viewing was binocular, but eye movements were recorded only from the right eye. The eye-tracker was connected to an AT 386 computer which controlled the stimulus-presentation and stored the output from the eye-tracker for data analysis. The time sampling rate was 1 KHz. The sentences were presented on a 20-inch color monitor, beginning at the 1st column of the character matrix. The subject was seated about 80 centimeters from the face of the screen, so that 3 letters roughly equaled 1 degree of visual angle. To prevent disturbing light reflections, the monitor was surrounded by a black carton and the room was slightly dimmed.

Reading time measures

First pass reading times and *regression-path durations* were calculated for four scoring regions as indicated by labeled slashes in the examples below: the first NP which was ambiguous with respect to case marking, the disambiguating second NP (which was unambiguously marked as accusative [S-O-condition], or as nominative [O-S-condition]), the adverbial, and the verb.

Offenbar /$_{Verb}$ ängstigte /$_{NP1}$ die strenge Lehrerin /$_{NP2}$ den stillen Schüler /$_{ADV}$ ein wenig, /...
"Obviously / frightened / the strict teacher / the quiet pupil / a bit, /..."

Daß /$_{NP1}$ die strenge Lehrerin /$_{NP2}$ den stillen Schüler /$_{ADV}$ ein wenig /Verb ängstigte, / ...
"That / the strict teacher / the quiet pupil / a bit / frightened, /..."

The *first pass reading time* (FPRT) measure accumulates the durations of all fixations beginning after a region is entered from the left for the first time until there is a saccade to another region. If the considered region is skipped during the first pass, its FPRT is scored as *missing value*. Effects in FPRTs have often been interpreted as an indicator for garden-pathing, presuming that longer FPRTs reflect processes of error detection and recovery. This assumption implies that FPRTs collect the processing durations of both the first and the second (nth) analysis in the parser. However, readers do not always remain within a region to find a consistent analysis after encountering an inconsistency on that region. It happens quite often that subjects look back to earlier portions of the sentence in order to read them again. In these cases, FPRTs will not reflect all processes induced by an inconsistency, i.e. pursuing a second analysis and its final semantic evaluation.

Regression-path durations (RPDs) (cf. Konieczny et al., this volume) are suited to overcome the shortcomings of *first pass reading times*. RPDs accumulate the durations of all fixations in the *regression path*, i.e. the stream of fixations starting as soon as a region is entered for the first time with a progressive saccade, and ending when the region is left (or skipped) with a progressive saccade. The RPD measure unifies the standard FPRT with the time needed to re-read previous passages if the critical region is left with a regressive saccade after first-pass reading. RPDs are therefore particularly sensitive not only to the point of error detection, but also to the difficulty of recovery, i.e. the strength of a garden path effect.

Extreme values and length correction

Reading times of less than 100ms were deleted from the analyses. For the deletion of further extreme values, we calculated linear regression equations—across all scoring regions and separately for each subject—with region length (in number of characters) as the predictor and *first pass reading time* as the dependent variable.[13] FPRTs being more than three standard deviations above or below a subject's regression line were treated as missings (the corresponding RPDs were deleted as well). In sum, about 3% of the data points in each measure (distributed over different scoring regions) were excluded from the analyses. Additional five data points in the RPDs were deleted which had values greater than 6000ms.

Following the proposal of Trueswell, Tanenhaus and Garnsey (1994; cf. Ferreira and Clifton, 1986), regression analyses were also used to control the influence of region length on the obtained reading time data: based on the subject-specific best linear fits for *first pass reading time* as a function of region length (determined across all regions and with extremes excluded), *predicted FPRTs* (varying across subjects) were computed which finally were subtracted from the actual reading times (i.e. the actual FPRTs, and RPDs, respectively).[14] The resulting *residual reading times* therefore reflect the deviations of the actual reading times from the FPRTs predicted by the length of the corresponding regions. Negative values indicate the raw reading times being faster, positive values indicate the raw reading times being slower than predicted by length. The general first-pass reading rate (averaged across subjects) was 110ms + 26ms * length (in number of characters).

Hypotheses

As the previous questionnaire studies already suggest, there is an item-independent ordering principle favoring S-O. Hence we expect that the first (case-ambiguous) NP is preferredly interpreted as the subject rather than the object of the sentence when it is encountered. Earlier on-line experiments (e.g. Bader and Lasser, 1994; Konieczny, 1996; Scheepers, 1996) have shown that the corresponding processing difficulties for the O-S linearization show up as soon as case-marking information disambiguates the structure, even before the licensing head of the sentence (i.e. the main verb) has been read. Thus we expect immediate case-marking effects on the disambiguating region, regardless of verb placement: a second NP unambiguously marked as nominative (condition O-S) should be more difficult to process than a second NP marked as accusative (condition S-O).

The *verb-placement* variation in this experiment does not imply any differences in syntactic complexity, as was (more or less indirectly) confirmed by Experiment 1. In the context of the current eye-tracking experiment, however, the position of the verb is crucial to modify the point in time where critical lexical information, i.e. the role-function-linkings necessary to determine thematic prominence relations between the arguments, becomes available.

In verb-final sentences (condition Args-V) the subject-object ambiguity is encountered (and possibly even resolved) before the lexical properties of the verb are known to the sentence processor. The earliest point where thematic prominence effects can show up in these structures is at the clause-final verb itself which provides the critical information about the role-function correspondences.

In verb-second main clauses (condition V-Args), however, thematic prominence can, in principle, already influence the resolution of the subject-object ambiguity when it is encountered, and so it might reveal an effect on processing the critical disambiguating second NP in these structures: a second NP disambiguating the structure as O-S (i.e. a nominative case second NP) should evoke a less severe garden-path effect after having read a P-causative verb than after having read a P-stative. A second NP consistent with the preferred S-O ordering (i.e. marked in nominative case) should, in contrast, be somewhat easier after having read a P-stative than after a having read a P-causative verb (cf. Experiment 1). Such a pattern of results would support "early competition" between functional and thematic constraints.[15]

Results

Since we are primarily interested in qualitative processing differences caused
by different placements of the verb, we will report results from separate analyses of variance for the different *verb position* conditions. For each scoring
region in each type of sentence, the residual FPRTs and RPDs were submitted
to two-factorial analyses of variance with *functional order* (S-O vs. O-S) and
verb type (P-causative vs. P-stative) as *repeated measures* factors. The data
were collapsed across subjects (F1) and across items (F2), respectively.
Answering accuracy was analyzed by testing hierarchical loglinear models
with the factors *verb position, functional order*, and *verb type*.

First pass reading times

As can be seen from the descriptive FPRT-data in Figure 4, the functional
order O-S caused processing difficulties at the disambiguating second NP. The
corresponding main effect of *functional order* was significant in main clauses
(V-Args) (S-O: −19ms vs. O-S: +123ms; $F1_{1,23} = 24.88$; $p < .001$; $F2_{1,15} =$
13.58; $p < .002$). In complement clauses (Args-V), however, this effect was
only marginal across subjects and not reliable across items (S-O: −46ms vs.
O-S: +60ms; $F1_{1,23} = 3.28$; $p < .09$; $F2_{1,15} < 1.5$; n.s.).

Quite surprisingly, a reliable main effect of *verb type* was established for
the FPRTs on the verb in main clauses (V-Args), with P-causative verbs being
easier to process than P-statives (−77ms vs. 0ms; $F1_{1,23} = 20.05$; $p < .001$;
$F2_{1,15} = 13.39$; $p < .003$). No other effects showed up in the FPRTs. In particular, the interactions between *verb type* and *functional order* were far from
being significant (all $F < 1.5$).

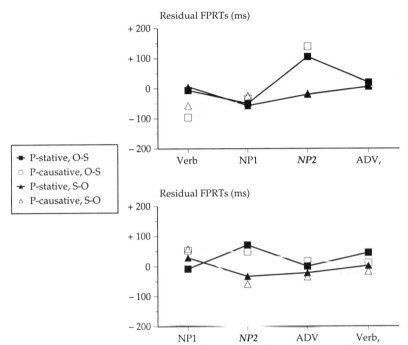

Figure 4: Residual first pass reading times on the four scoring regions in main clauses (V-Args, upper graph) and complement clauses (Args-V, lower graph).

Regression path durations

The mean residual RPDs in each condition are plotted in Figure 5. At the verb in main clauses, the *verb type* main effect was still reliable, though a bit less pronounced than in the corresponding FPRTs (P-causative: –44ms vs. P-stative: +18ms; $F1_{1,23} = 9.13$; $p < .01$; $F2_{1,15} = 5.87$; $p < .03$).

Reliable main effects of *functional order* were obtained as soon as the disambiguating second NP was read. In main clauses (V-Args), the O-S-linearization led to a significant garden path effect at the second NP (S-O: 55ms vs. O-S: 184ms; $F1_{1, 23} = 7.64$; $p < .02$; $F2_{1,15} = 9.90$; $p < .01$) as well as at the clause final adverbial (S-O: 339ms vs. O-S: 1198ms; $F1_{1,23} = 24.39$; $p < .001$; $F2_{1,15} = 29.63$; $p < .001$). In complement clauses (Args-V), a reliable O-S-penalty was established for the second NP (S-O: 30ms vs. O-S: 259ms; $F1_{1,23}$

$= 9.13; p < .01; F2_{1,15} = 10.50; p < .01$), for the adverbial (S-O: 40ms vs. O-S: 194ms; $F1_{1,23} = 4.28; p < .05; F2_{1,15} = 11.19; p < .005$), and for the clause final verb (S-O: 292ms vs. O-S: 997ms; $F1_{1,23} = 18.05; p < .001; F2_{1,15} = 22.70; p < .001$).

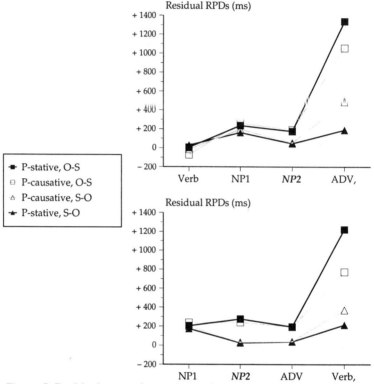

Figure 5: Residual regression path durations on the four scoring regions in main clauses (V-Args, upper graph) and complement clauses (Args-V, lower graph).

The expected *verb type * functional order* interaction became manifest only at clause final positions, i.e. at the adverbial in main clauses (V-Args) ($F1_{1,23} = 3.76; p < .08; F2_{1,15} = 5.31; p < .04$) and at the verb in complement clauses (Args-V) ($F1_{1,23} = 7.12; p < .02; F2_{1,15} = 6.57; p < .03$).[16] For all other scoring regions, no reliable interactions between the two factors were obtained (all F < 1.5).

Planned comparisons for the interaction at the clause-final adverbial in main clauses (V-Args) revealed a reliable *verb type* effect—though only by subjects—in the preferred S-O-linearization condition, with higher RPDs in

P-causative sentences (487ms) than in P-stative sentences (190ms) ($F1_{1,23}$ = 6.99; p < .02; $F2_{1,15}$ = 3.47; p < .09). For the O-S-linearization condition, the opposite effect—with greater difficulties in P-stative sentences (1338ms) than in P-causative sentences (1057ms)—was reliable across items ($F1_{1,23}$ = 1.98; n.s.; $F2_{1,15}$ = 5.30; p < .05). The simple effect of *functional order* at the clause final adverbial was reliable in P-stative sentences, showing an O-S-penalty of +1148ms ($F1_{1,23}$ = 23.70; p < .001; $F2_{1,15}$ = 21.16; p < .001). In P-causative sentences, the obtained O-S-penalty was considerably weaker (+570ms), producing a significant simple effect of *functional order* only across items ($F1_{1,23}$ = 3.45; p < .08; $F2_{1,15}$ = 9.85; p < .01).

The simple contrasts for the interaction at the clause-final verb in complement clauses (Args-V) revealed a quite similar pattern: In the preferred S-O-linearization condition, P-causatives (370ms) exhibited numerically higher RPDs than P-statives (214ms). This difference, however, was only marginal across subjects ($F1_{1,23}$ = 3.03; p < .10; $F2_{1,15}$ < 1.0; n.s.). In the garden pathing O-S-condition, the reverse contrast—with P-causatives (773ms) being less difficult than P-statives (1221ms)—was significant across items ($F1_{1,23}$ = 3.60; p < .08; $F2_{1,15}$ = 6.59; p < .03). Again, the simple effect of *functional order* was reliable in both *verb type* conditions, with the O-S-penalty being weaker for P-causatives (+403ms) ($F1_{1,23}$ = 5.86; p < .03; $F2_{1,15}$ = 6.28; p < .03) than for P-statives (+1007ms) ($F1_{1,23}$ = 17.01; p < .001; $F2_{1,15}$ = 30.54; p < .001).

Accuracy

Table 4 shows the relative frequencies of correct answers in each factor combination of *verb type* and *functional order*. The obtained two-way interaction is due to the following contrasts: with P-stative verbs, reliably more interpretation errors occurred in the O-S-condition than in the S-O-condition (LRCSC = 6.841, df = 1; p < .01), whereas no significant simple effect of *functional order* was obtained in P-causative sentences (LRCSC < 1.0). There was a reliable *verb type* contrast in the O-S-condition which is interpreted more accurately in combination with P-causative verbs than in combination with P-statives (LRCSC = 4.461, df = 1; p < .04). Numerically the opposite holds for sentences with S-O-linearization, but the corresponding simple effect of *verb type* is not significant (LRCSC < 1.0). The main effect of *functional order* showed up as a tendency (S-O: 85% O-S: 78%; LRCSC = 2.675;

df = 1; p < .11), and there were no significant influences of *verb position* on answering accuracy.

	P-causative	P-stative	LRCSC	df	p <
S-O	82%	87%			
O-S	85%	70%	4.601	1	.04

Table 4: Relative frequencies of correct answers in each combination of *functional order (S-O vs. O-S)* and *verb type (P-causative vs. P-stative)*. The *Likelihood Ratio Chi Square Change (LRCSC)* refers to the interaction between the two factors.

Discussion

Consistent with the results of Experiments 1 and 2, we found a dominant subject-before-object (S-O) preference in the reading time data, indicated by reliably prolonged reading times for the O-S condition as soon as case information of the second NP had disambiguated the structure. More than that, the eye-tracking study revealed additional support for the functional ordering preference being verb-independent: firstly, it was observed even before a licensing verb had been read (Args-V condition); secondly, it was not overridden by verb-type information (parallel to the results of the questionnaire studies).

Nevertheless, the modulating interaction between *verb-type* and *functional order* was replicated as well: the dispreferred O-S linearization was found to be somewhat easier to process in sentences with P-causative verbs than in sentences with P-statives. The opposite was found (at least as a statistical trend) for the preferred S-O condition, which is somewhat less difficult with P-statives than with P-causatives. This interaction can be interpreted in terms of a modulating influence of thematic prominence on the difficulty of functional linearization alternatives: functional orderings preserving the thematic prominence relation (p2) are less difficult to process than functional orderings which do not preserve this relation.

Not surprisingly, the thematic prominence effect is reflected in regressions from the clause-final region when the verb is placed at the end of a complement clause (condition Args-V), since this is the point where lexical information specifying the relevant role-function-linkings is encountered.

The pattern of results in verb-second main clauses (V-Args condition), however, is quite striking, as it indicates a substantial asynchrony regarding the impact of functional and thematic constraints on argument ordering: although the verb was available before the subject-object ambiguity was encountered, and although the point of disambiguation came rather late, the thematic prominence effect was delayed until the clause-final position (i.e. until the clause final adverbial had been read). In contrast, the functional linearization preference (generally favoring S-O) had already been obtained at critical second NP.

How can this delay of thematic prominence effects (which certainly does not support immediate competition between functional and thematic constraints) be explained? One possible way would be to claim that the role-function-linkings provided by the verb are completely ignored up to the clause boundary. This would be equivalent to saying that thematic or aspectual roles are not assigned before the end of the clause is reached. Such an assumption seems reasonable for complement clauses (Args-V) where the thematic assigner, the verb, is placed at the clause-final position.[17] In verb-second main clauses (V-Args condition), however, such a delay of thematic assignment does not seem very plausible, since there is a large number of studies (mainly in English) indicating that, if the verb is placed at a non-final position of the clause, thematic roles are assigned much earlier (e.g. Taraban and McClelland, 1988; Tanenhaus et al., 1989; 1990; 1993; Trueswell et al., 1994).

Another, perhaps more plausible explanation, would be that thematic prominence does not contribute to the process of syntactic (re-)analysis (as stated by modular accounts of syntax processing), but to an additional stage of sentence processing (i.e. some kind of "pragmatic rechecking") where the final interpretation of the sentence and maybe its focus structure[18] is determined. Note that, unlike the main effect of functional order, an effect of thematic prominence—i.e. an interaction between *verb-type* and *functional order*—was still present in answering accuracy. This is quite remarkable, since we kept the instantiations of the thematic roles—which were rather stereotypical in most of the cases—constant across all experimental conditions (cf. Table 2 and 3), and so the items were fairly biased in plausibility towards the *correct* role assignments. This may be taken as evidence for the substantial role which thematic prominence plays in the final interpretation of the sentence. Little is known, however, about how the final interpretation/integration-process operates. More importantly, the claim that the computation of focus structure is delayed certainly requires some additional empirical and theoretical foundation, given the highly incremental characteristic of natural language processing in general.

A third account we want to propose here focuses on thematic verb-frame selection during sentence comprehension. Before we discuss this proposal in detail, a few notes on the constraints governing the general S-O preference should be made.

Configuration vs. designation

So far, we have discussed the overall S-O-preference mainly in the context of a configurational treatment of subject and object. It is important to note, however, that our data do not rule out a lexical treatment of syntactic function "per se". Although non-configurational theories have the potential to treat linear order independently from functional designation (as the theories discussed so far presuppose, more or less explicitly) they are not restrained to do so. There are non-configurational grammar theories (like, e.g., HPSG, Pollard and Sag, 1987; 1994) which consider linear precedence and functional designation as being subject to identical lexical constraints, thereby generating predictions equivalent to those of configurational theories—even for fixed-order languages.[19] Thus, the configurational approach has to be regarded as one out of many different possibilities to explain the general S-O preference obtained in our experiments.

Multiple thematic frames

Let us, therefore, still keep a designatory approach on syntactic function definition (roughly in the sense of Haider, 1993). But let us further assume—in contrast to a "strong" thematic linearization hypothesis—that linear precedence of verbal arguments is restricted by two different types of constraints: a general (i.e. basically verb-independent) restriction, according to which subjects (i.e. nominative NPs) are *per default* placed before objects; and a verb-specific constraint by which the arguments of the verb are ordered according to the relative prominence (p2) of the respective roles in the thematic frame of the verb.

If we further assume that lexical information is projected into structure as soon as it is available, it follows that in the absence of contradicting verb-specific information (e.g. in verb-final structures, or if an agentive, or a stative predicate has already been read), S-O is initially selected by the parser. This implies that a syntactically and presuppositionally more complex, *marked* linearization has to be computed if the structure is eventually disambiguated as O-S.

But what happens if a P-causative verb is read before its arguments? Remember that this class of verbs is lexically/semantically ambiguous, since it can suggest either an agentive reading (selecting S-O as canonical order, according to p2) or a non-agentive reading (selecting O-S). Therefore not only a subject-object ambiguity (encountered at the first NP) has to be resolved in these cases, but also a lexical ambiguity due to multiple thematic frames of the verb.

Which reading of the verb does the parser choose in the first pass? Since there is an item-independent S-O ordering principle, it seems plausible that it initially selects a lexical entry which is consistent with this principle rather than a lexical entry which is not. Consequently the parser (temporarily) prefers the agentive reading to the non-agentive reading of a P-causative verb, provided that there is no explicit infomation against an agentive interpretation. If the sentence is finally disambiguated for O-S, an alternative O-S-compatible verb-frame is available, the access of which should be less difficult than computing a marked ordering. Thus, O-S is somewhat easier with P-causatives than with P-statives (which completely lack an O-S-compatible lexical entry).[20]

If, on the other hand, the sentence is disambiguated for S-O, but pragmatic considerations (presumably evaluated clause-finally) render the agentive reading of the P-causative verb implausible, processing should be more difficult than with a P-stative.

The multiple frame account sketched here bears some important implications for further empirical research, as it suggests, for example, that O-S should be easy for P-causatives without an alternative agentive reading (e.g. *auffallen*, to strike somebody), and also should be easy for cases where the agentive reading of a P-causative like *ängstigen* (to frighten) is not considered at all.[21]

SUMMARY AND CONCLUSION

As our experiments have demonstrated, linearization preferences governing subject-object ambiguity resolution in German are hardly reducible to thematic hierarchy constraints, as claimed by some linguistic theories. Instead, our data indicate a dominating tendency to place the subject before the object, irrespective of the thematic roles each argument receives from the verb. Nevertheless, our experiments showed reliable, though only modulating influences of thematic hierarchy, in the sense that functional linearizations which preserve the prominence relations specified in the hierarchy are more acceptable and easier to comprehend than functional linearizations which do not. Furthermore, thematic prominence effects showed up with quite a delay during sentence processing (i.e. during regressions from clause-final regions), whereas verb-independent constraints (generally favoring subject-before-object) had a much earlier impact.

We suggested two possible explanations of our findings, one of which merely states that thematic prominence is irrelevant to syntactic processing, but has an impact on final pragmatic evaluation (possibly to determine the sentence's focus structure). The second proposal is that whenever there are alternative lexical/thematic entries of a verb, the parser will prefer an entry which is compatible with the item-independent subject-before-object restriction, but lexical alternatives which favor an object-before-subject linearization may help to guide a more efficient reanalysis. Further empirical research will hopefully clarify which one of these accounts is the more appropriate.

ACKNOWLEDGEMENTS

This paper is based on the first author's Ph.D. thesis (*Menschliche Satzverarbeitung: Syntaktische und thematische Aspekte der Wortstellung im Deutschen*), submitted at the University of Freiburg in September 1996. We want to thank the supervisors, Gerhard Strube and Jürgen Dittmann, for various fruitful comments. Also, we would like to thank Markus Bader, Josef Bayer, Chuck Clifton, Lyn Frazier, Gisbert Fanselow, Paul Gorrell, Yuki Kamide, Michael Meng, Don C. Mitchell, Matthias Schlesewsky, and Marica de Vincenzi for helpful discussions on this and related topics. Special thanks to Judas Robinson who corrected the English manuscript.

NOTES

[1] However, the chapters of Markus Bader and Paul Gorrell bear some interesting implications on the issue, some of which we will address in the current paper as well.

[2] Whether or not the subject in German is separated from the objects by an additional projection level (SpecIP, as in English) is still a matter of debate. Haider (1993) and Frey (1993), for example, deny the existence of an IP projection in German and analyze all verbal arguments including the subject VP-internally. Since this issue is only secondary to our current considerations, we keep it underspecified, as indicated by the dashed lines in Figure 1.

[3] The contrasts in (3) are confirmed by differences in the respective focus structures: with a verb like *zuhören* (to listen to) the object-before-subject

order (3b) implies only the phrase *der Schüler* (the pupil) to be in focus, while the subject-before-object linearization (3a) has a greater focus-potential, i.e. it sounds natural as answer to questions like *What happened?*, *Who listened to the teacher?*, *Who did the pupil listen to?*. The reverse seems to be true for a verb like *auffallen* (to strike somebody) where the subject-before-object order intuitively has a smaller focus-potential than the object-before-subject order.

[4] In this respect, Haider's (1993) account is similar to monostratal, non-derivational grammar theories such as HPSG (Pollard and Sag, 1987; 1994). Note, however, that Haider still presupposes a distinction between (base-generated) d-structure and (derived) s-structure which classifies his account as a variant of GB (e.g. Chomsky, 1981).

[5] Haider's (1993) formal conceptualization of thematic relations differs from more traditional, feature-based analyses (e.g. Fillmore, 1968) in that he considers thematic roles as generalized positions in so-called *conceptual structures* of verbal predicates (similar to the conceptual configurations in Jackendoff, 1987) by which he is able to generate the same predictions as (p2) without explicitly referring to such a hierarchy. Thematic hierarchies like (p2) are certainly quite unsatisfactory from a theoretical point of view, since they merely restate the facts that are to be explained in more general terms rather than providing an independent *explanation* of these facts. But the *conceptual structure* approach is by no means superior as long as it lacks a theoretical motivation for the structural properties of the concepts used to explain the observed data. We will omit a detailed description of Haider's proposal, because—at least with respect to the phenomena under investigation—it appears to be theoretically and empirically equivalent to the thematic hierarchy approach (and its aspectual extension described later).

[6] In Haider's (1993) terms, this difference is expressed by the complexity of the respective conceptual structures: a verb of perception is represented by a simple two-place predicate like (a). P-causative verbs, however, are analyzed as complex predicates where one variable (y) is bound by two argument-positions (b).

a.   [*x PERCEIVES y]

b.   [*y CAUSES [x PERCEIVES *y]]

According to Haider, subject designation follows the "leftmost" occurrence of a variable (as indicated by asterisks), whereas the base-generated order of the arguments follows the order marked by the "innermost" predicate.

[7] Intransitive P-causatives like *auffallen* were actually not considered in our experiments, since we restricted our materials to verbs subcategorizing for accusative objects.

[8] Materials of this and the following experiments are available from the first author.

[9] In a similar way, Kurtzman and MacDonald (1993) considered the relative "strength" of a thematic prominence contrast as explanation for verb-dependent variations in the resolution of quantifier-scope ambiguities.

[10] This finer-grained scaling was motivated by the higher variability of the sentences as a consequence of the fact that materials of several unrelated experiments were examined in this questionnaire.

[11] A confounding factor could be that inanimate subject-NPs were always one word longer than animate subject-NPs. According to the proposal that longer constituents tend to be postponed (Hawkins, 1990), the weaker S-O-preference for inanimate subjects may reflect a heavy-NP shift rather than an influence of thematic prominence, or a combined effect of a heavy NP-shift and thematic prominence, respectively. Certainly, we cannot rule out this possibility on the basis of the present data. However, the S-O linearization preference is still present although both thematic prominence *and* (presumably) length operate against it.

[12] With respect to the *preferred* (S-O) linearization condition, the two rating studies revealed somewhat different results, in that only Experiment 1 could establish a reliable thematic prominence contrast with S-O ordering. In the garden-pathing O-S-condition, however, both experiments showed a significant influence of thematic hierarchy. Thus, although the thematic influences are obviously stronger in the non-preferred linearization condition, they also have a certain impact on the preferred functional order condition.

[13] For each of the twenty-four subjects, a reliable positive correlation between region length and FPRT was obtained, ranging from $R = +.32$; $p < .03$ to $R = +.77$; $p < .001$.

[14] We assume only the FPRT-component of the RPDs to be influenced by the length of the considered region. The component resulting from a re-inspection of earlier text-portions (whose basic lexical processing is presumably being completed during first-pass reading of these regions) is considered as being unrelated to the length of the particular region of interest. Consequently, the

residual reading times were determined exclusively on the basis of linear regressions with FPRTs as dependent variable.

[15] Modulating influences of verb type—provided that they really show up on the disambiguating region—could not only be due to lexical/thematic expectations guiding the sentence processor, as suggested by multiple constraint architectures (e.g. MacDonald et al., 1994; Tanenhaus et al., 1991) or parsing models emphasizing the role of argument-structure information in structure building (e.g. Abney, 1989; Ford et al., 1982; Gibson, 1991; Konieczny, 1996; Konieczny et al., 1997; Pritchett, 1992). A modular syntax-first account like the garden-path model (e.g. Frazier, 1987; 1990) generates very similar predictions by stating that reanalysis of the (generally dispreferred) O-S ordering condition is more efficient when it agrees with thematic hierarchy (p2) than when it does not. Note, however, that such a modular account does not offer a straightforward explanation for thematic prominence effects in the S-O ordering condition where no garden-path effect (i.e. no reanalysis) should occur.

[16] Due to the differential effects of *verb position* on the *verb type * functional order* interaction in the respective scoring regions, the particular three-way (*verb position * verb type * functional order*) interactions were reliable as well (verb: $F1_{1,23} = 6.99$; $p < .02$; $F2_{1,15} = 4.85$; $p < .05$; adverbial: $F1_{1,23} = 3.76$; $p < .08$; $F2_{1,15} = 5.31$; $p < .04$).

[17] Bader (this volume), for example, has demonstrated that verb-final *recipient passives* like a. do not provoke any garden-path effects compared to active sentences like b..

   a.   Jemand hat behauptet, daß Peter Postkarten geschickt bekam.
           "Somebody has claimed, that Peter$_{nom}$ postcards$_{acc}$ sent got."

   b.   Jemand hat behauptet, daß Peter Postkarten geschickt hat.
           "Somebody has claimed, that Peter$_{nom}$ postcards$_{acc}$ sent has."

In b. the first NP (*Peter*) is interpreted as the *agent/cause* of the predicate *schicken* (to send). With the quasi-auxiliary *bekam* (got) in a., however, *Peter* has to be analyzed as the *goal* (or *recipient*) of *schicken*. Bader found no indication of a thematic revision (both constructions are equally easy to process). Thus, there is no reason to assume that NPs receive canonical "default roles" before the verb has been read. The result may be somewhat problematic for multiple constraint models like, e.g., MacDonald et al.'s (1994).

[18] As we have mentioned earlier (see footnote 3) the primary data on which the thematic linearization account has been grounded (cf. Haider, 1993; Frey, 1993) are contrasts in the focus potential of different orderings dependent on different verbs. One could argue that these focus potential differences merely indicate constraints on pragmatics which are basically independent from syntactic analysis.

[19] In the standard HPSG analysis of English, for example, syntactic functions are defined by the position of elements on the subcategorization list of the verb, so that the first element is the "subject", the second the "object", etc. The order of the elements in the subcat list (which follows from a general *obliqueness hierarchy*, cf. Keenan and Comrie, 1977) also determines the order of the functions in the verbal projections, so that the subject per default precedes all other arguments.

[20] We admit that this explanation still lacks a motivation for why there is such a profound delay in reconsidering the alternative lexical entry.

[21] Note, that Experiment 2 still indicated a moderate O-S-penalty for constructions where the agentive reading of a verb like *ängstigen* (to frighten) is more or less blocked (cf. example xii. in Table 2). The lexical preference account can easily cope with this finding, since the animateness-features which render the agentive reading implausible become available *after* the agentive reading of the verb has been chosen.

REFERENCES

Abney, S. (1989). A computational model of human parsing. *Journal of Psycholinguistic Research, 18* (1), 129-144.

Bader, M., Bayer, J., Hopf, J.-M., & Meng, M. (1996). Case-assignment in processing German verb-final clauses. *Proceedings of the NELS Workshop on Sentence Processing* (Occasional papers in linguistics, Vol. 9). Cambridge: MIT Press, 1-25.

Bader, M., & Lasser, I. (1994). German verb-final clauses and sentence processing: Evidence for immediate attachment. In C. Clifton, L. Frazier & K. Rayner (Eds.), *Perspectives in sentence processing* (pp. 225-242). Hillsdale, NJ: Lawrence Erlbaum.

Chomsky, N. (1981). *Lectures on government and binding.* Dordrecht: Foris.

Crocker, M. (1993). Properties of the principle-based sentence processor. *Proceedings of the Fifteenth Annual Conference of the Cognitive Science Society, June, 18-21, 1993.* Hillsdale, NJ: Erlbaum, 371-376.

De Vincenzi, M. (1991). *Syntactic parsing strategies in Italian: The minimal chain principle* (Studies in theoretical psycholinguistics, Vol. 12). Dordrecht, NL: Kluwer Academic Publishers.

Ferreira, F., & Clifton, C. (1986). The independence of syntactic processing. *Journal of Memory and Language, 25,* 348-368.

Ford, M., Bresnan, J., & Kaplan, R. M. (1982). A competence-based theory of syntactic closure. In J. Bresnan (Ed.), *The mental representation of grammatical relations* (pp. 727-796). Cambridge, MA: MIT Press.

Frazier, L. (1987a). Sentence processing: A tutorial review. In M. Coltheart (Ed.), *The psychology of reading* (pp. 559-586). Hove: Lawrence Erlbaum Associates.

Frazier, L. (1987c). Theories of sentence processing. In J. Garfield (Ed.), *Modularity in knowledge representation and natural-language understanding* (pp. 291-308). Cambridge, MA: MIT Press.

Frazier, L. (1990). Exploring the architecture of the language processing system. In Gerry T.M. Altmann (Ed.), *Cognitive models of speech processing* (pp. 409-433). Cambridge, MA: MIT Press.

Frazier, L., & Clifton, C. (1996). *Construal.* Cambridge, MA: MIT Press.

Frey, W. (1993). *Syntaktische Bedingungen für die semantische Interpretation: Über Bindung, implizite Argumente und Skopus.* Berlin: Akademie Verlag.

Gibson, E. (1991). A computational theory of human linguistic processing: memory limitations and processing breakdown. Unpublished doctoral dissertation, Carnegie Mellon University, Pittsburgh, Pennsylvania.

Gorrell, P. (1995). *Syntax and parsing.* Cambridge: Cambridge University Press.

Grimshaw, J. (1990). *Argument structure.* Cambridge, MA: MIT Press.

Grimshaw, J. (1991). *Extended projections.* Unpublished manuscript, Brandeis University.

Grimshaw, J. (1993). *Minimal projection, heads, and optimality* (Tech. Rep. No. 4). Piscataway, NJ: Rutgers University, Center for Cognitive Science.

Haider, H. (1993). *Deutsche Syntax - generativ: Vorstudien zur Theorie einer projektiven Grammatik.* Tübingen: Narr.

Hawkins, J. A. (1990). A parsing theory of word order universals. *Linguistic Inquiry, 21,* 223-261.

Hemforth, B. (1993). *Kognitives Parsing: Repräsentation und Verarbeitung sprachlichen Wissens.* Sankt Augustin: Infix.

Keenan, E., & Comrie, B. (1977). Noun phrase accessibility and universal grammar. *Linguistic Inquiry, 8,* 63-99.

Konieczny, L. (1996). *Human sentence processing: A semantics-oriented parsing approach* (IIG-Bericht Nr. 3/96). Freiburg: Universität Freiburg, Institut für Informatik und Gesellschaft.

Konieczny, L., & Hemforth, B., Scheepers, C., & Strube, G. (1997). The role of lexical heads in parsing: Evidence from German. *Language and Cognitive Processes, 12*, 307-348.

Kurtzman, H. S., & MacDonald, M. C. (1993). Resolution of quantifier scope ambiguities. *Cognition, 48*, 243-279.

MacDonald, M., Pearlmutter, N., & Seidenberg, M.S. (1994). The lexical nature of syntactic ambiguity resolution. *Psychological Review, 101* (4), 676-703.

Mecklinger, A., Schriefers, H., Steinhauer, K., & Friederici, A. (1995). Processing relative clauses varying on syntactic and semantic dimensions: An analysis with event-related potentials. *Memory and Cognition, 23*, 477-494.

Meng, M.(1996). Processing wh-questions in German and Dutch: Differential effects of disambiguation and their interpretation. Unpublished manuscript, Friedrich-Schiller Universität, at Jena.

Pechmann, T., Uszkoreit, H., Engelkamp, J., & Zerbst, D. (1994). *Word order in the German middle field: Linguistic theory and psycholinguistic evidence* (Report No. 43). Saarbrücken: Universität des Saarlandes.

Pollard, C., & Sag, I. A. (1987). *Information-based syntax and semantics. Vol. 1* (CSLI Lecture Notes No. 13). Stanford: Center for the Study of Language and Information.

Pollard, C., & Sag, I. A. (1994). *Head-driven phrase structure grammar.* Chicago, London: University of Chicago Press and CSLI Publications.

Pritchett, B. (1992). *Grammatical competence and parsing performance.* Chicago: University of Chicago Press.

Scheepers, C. (1996). *Menschliche Satzverarbeitung: Syntaktische und thematische Aspekte der Wortstellung im Deutschen.* Unpublished doctoral dissertation, University of Freiburg, Germany.

Scheepers, C., Konieczny, L., & Hemforth, B. (1997, March). *The influence of sentence type and constituent order on parsing difficulty in German.* Poster presented at the 10th Annual CUNY-Conference on Human Sentence Processing, Los Angeles, California.

Stechow, A. von, & Sternefeld, W. (1988). *Bausteine syntaktischen Wissens.* Opladen: Westdeutscher Verlag.

Stevenson, S. (1993). *A constrained active attachment model for resolving syntactic ambiguities in natural language parsing.* Unpublished doctoral dissertation, University of Maryland.

Tanenhaus, M., Carlson, G., & Trueswell, J. C. (1989). The role of thematic structures in interpretation and parsing. *Language and Cognitive Processes, 4,* 211-234.

Tanenhaus, M. K., Boland, J., Mauner, G., & Carlson, G. (1993). More on combinatory lexical information: thematic structure in parsing and interpretation. In G. T. M. Altmann & R. Shillcock (Eds.), *Cognitive models of speech processing: The Second Sperlonga Meeting* (pp. 297-319). Hove: Lawrence Erlbaum Associates.

Tanenhaus, M. K., Garnsey, S. M., & Boland, J. (1990). Combinatory lexical information and language comprehension. In G. T. M. Altmann (Ed.), *Cognitive models of speech processing: Psycholinguistic and computational perspectives* (pp. 383-408). Cambridge, MA: MIT Press.

Taraban, R., & McClelland, J. L. (1988). Constituent attachment and thematic role assignment in sentence processing: Influence of content-based expectations. *Journal of Memory and Language, 27,* 597-632.

Trueswell, J.C., Tanenhaus, M.K., & Garnsey, S.M. (1994). Semantic influences on parsing: Use of thematic role information in syntactic ambiguity resolution. *Journal of Memory and Language, 33,* 285-318.

Uszkoreit, H. (1986). Constraints on order. *Linguistics, 24,* 883-906.

REFERENTIAL BIASES IN SYNTACTIC ATTACHMENT

Lars Konieczny and Nicole Völker
University of Freiburg

SUMMARY

This chapter tackles the question of whether contextual constraints can override the syntactic and thematic preferences established in Konieczny et al. (1997). We present eye-movement data on participants reading German verb-second and verb-final sentences containing a PP attachment ambiguity, embedded in short biasing contexts. For isolated sentences, Konieczny et al. (1997) established a non-minimal attachment preference for verb-final constructions, whereas verb-second constructions exhibited a verb-specific lexical or thematic preference. In the present paper, target sentences are embedded in short contexts manipulating the referential success (Crain and Steedman, 1985) of the potential NP host. The results suggest that inital parsing decisions are made independent of the contextual bias.

INTRODUCTION

In a former series of experiments, PP-attachment preferences in sentences like (1a,b, 2a,b) were demonstrated to depend a. on the availability of lexical heads during processing and b. on their lexical properties (Konieczny et al., 1997).

(1) a. Marion beobachtete/erblickte das Pferd mit dem neuen Fernglas.

 Marion watched/caught sight of the horse with the new binoculars.

 b. Marion beobachtete/erblickte das Pferd mit dem weißen Fleck.

 Marion watched/caught sight of the horse with the white patch.

B. Hemforth and L. Konieczny (eds.), German Sentence Processing, 137-160.

(2) a.   Daß Marion das Pferd mit dem neuen Fernglas beobachtete/
              erblickte, ...

              That Marion the horse with the new binoculars watched/
              caught sight of...

      b.   Daß Marion das Pferd mit dem weißen Fleck beobachtete/
              erblickte, ...

              That Marion the horse with the white patch watched/caught
              sight of, ...

In these experiments, attachment preferences in verb second sentences
depended on the particular properties of the respective preceding heads. For
sentences with verbs like *beobachten* (watch), for which a preference for an
instrumental PP was established in pre-studies, the authors found a preference
to attach the PP to the verb. On the other hand, in sentences with verbs like
erblicken (to catch sight of), which did not show a preference for an instrumental PP in the pre-studies, a preference to attach the PP to the preceding NP
showed up in the experiments. In verb final constructions, we established a
preference to attach a structurally ambiguous PP nonminimally to the preceding NP.

Konieczny, Scheepers, Hemforth, & Strube (1994; 1997; see also
Konieczny, Hemforth, & Strube, 1991) proposed the *parametrized head
attachment* (PHA) principle to account for a variety of initial analysis
phenomena. PHA is assumed to guide syntactic analyses in a serial first analysis model (i.e., a garden path model) pursuing only one analysis in the case
of a structural ambiguity. The first syntactic analysis is assumed to be determined by three sub-principles (p1-3) referring to the linear ordering of lexical
heads and their lexical properties, in particular their thematic preferences.
PHA is a serial garden-path variant of lexicalist models.

Parametrized head attachment

(p1)   *head attachment*, HA (Konieczny, Hemforth & Strube,
              1991)

              if possible, attach a constituent to a phrase whose lexical
              head has already been encountered.

If further attachment possibilities exist, then

(p2)   *preferred role attachment*

attach constituent *i* to a phrase within the current clause
whose head highlights a theta-role for *i*.

If further attachment possibilities exist for the constituent, then

(p3)   *recent head attachment*

attach the constituent to the phrase whose head was encountered most recently.

Head attachment (p1) predicts an inital PP-to-NP attachment preference in
verb-final constructions (2). For the verb-second construtions (1), preferred-
role attachment (p2) predicts the attachment to the VP, if the verb (such as
"observe") highlights the INSTRUMENT role for the PP. If the role is not
highlighted, as in "notice", recent head attachment (p3) predicts the attachment of the PP to the preceding NP.

The basic idea underlying *parametrized head attachment* is that the parser
initially builds syntactic structures which can be evaluated semantically as
quickly as possible. Processing is assumed to be *semantics oriented* (see also
immediate semantic integration, Konieczny et al., 1991, and the *principle of
incremental interpretation*, Crocker, 1992). In the first analysis, the parser is
forced to attach an ambiguous constituent to the phrase whose semantically
most relevant constituent, the lexical head, has already been encountered (p1).
In this way, the discourse entity introduced by the ambiguous phrase can be
related to other entities that already exist in the discourse model. *Parameterized head attachment* therefore forces the parser to avoid unconnected discourse elements. *Parameterized head attachment* has been shown to account
for a broad variety of ambiguities (Konieczny, 1996).

Attachment preferences in referentially biasing contexts

Models of the garden-path family where initial parsing decisions are only
based on syntactic and lexical information have been questioned by, among
others, Crain and Steedman (1985) as well as Altmann and Steedman (1988).
They assume that some aspects of meaning and pragmatics can guide parsing
in an – at least weakly – interactive manner. In their weakly interactive parallel model, all syntactically possible analyses at an ambiguous position in a
sentence are carried out in parallel without restricting preferences occurring at
the syntactic level. Pragmatic information is used immediately to choose the
most plausible analysis. According to the principle of *Referential Support* (p4,

Altmann & Steedman, 1988), potentially noun-modifying constituents following a definite NP should not be attached to the NP, if the simple NP already provides sufficient information to identify a unique referent in the discourse model.

(p4)   *The Principle of Referential Support*

An NP analysis which is referentially supported will be favored over one that is not. (Altmann & Steedman, 1988, p. 201)

This hypothesis was substantiated by a series of experiments where structurally ambiguous sentences were presented in pragmatically biasing contexts. In an experiment reported in Altmann & Steedman (1988), sentences with a semantically disambiguated PP-attachment ambiguity (a:NP-attached, b:VP-attached) were preceded by an NP-attachment biasing context (3) or a VP-attachment biasing context (4). In the NP-attachment biasing context, there were two potential referents for the object NP (*the safe*), so a modifier was needed to provide enough information to unambiguously identify a referent. In the VP-biasing context, on the other hand, only one potential referent was introduced, therefore the simple (non-modified) object NP sufficed to establish reference.

(3)   NP-supporting context

A burglar broke into a bank carrying some dynamite. He planned to blow open a safe. Once inside he saw that there was a safe with a new lock and a safe with an old lock.

(4)   VP-supporting context

A burglar broke into a bank carrying some dynamite. He planned to blow open a safe. Once inside he saw that there was a safe with a new lock and a strongbox with an old lock.

    a.   NP-attached target

The burglar blew open the safe with the new lock and made off with the loot.

    b.   VP-attached target

The burglar blew open the safe with the dynamite and made off with the loot.

Without an explicit context, no reference-based preference can be derived straight-forwardly. However, as Crain and Steedman (1985) point out, isolated sentences carry their presuppositions as to pragmatic requirements which have to be fulfilled to render the respective sentence plausible. According to the principle of *Parsimony*, readers avoid interpretations with too many unsupported presuppositions.

(p5)   *The Principle of Parsimony*

A reading which carries fewer unsupported presuppositions will be favored over one that carries more.

For modified NPs in isolated sentences, a set of entities has to be presupposed in the universe of discourse so that the modifier is needed to uniquely identify one of them. A simple NP does not carry any such presuppositions. With respect to PP-attachment phenomena, the principle of *Parsimony* therefore predicts attachment to the VP irrespective of verb placement, when the sentences are read without a surrounding context. Although these predictions for sentences presented in the "null context" contradict the findings from experiments on PP-attachment in neutral contexts (Konieczny et al., 1997), it has yet to be shown how verb-second and verb-final constructions are processed when presented in referentially biasing contexts.

The question of whether or not contextual influences can override preferences seemingly determined by syntactic or lexical principles has been heavily disputed in psycholinguistic literature. Crain and Steedman's (1985) evidence for the influence of pragmatically biasing contexts in sentential complement / relative clause ambiguities was soon argued to be irrelevant for initial parsing decisions because of the coarse experimental techniques used (sentence reading times and grammaticality judgements). In more sensitive self-paced reading and eye-tracking studies, Ferreira and Clifton (1986; Clifton & Ferreira, 1989) found a residual preference for the main verb (*"Minimal Attachment"*) reading in main verb / reduced relative ambiguities even in contexts biasing the reduced relative reading.

Altmann & Steedman (1988) criticized Ferreira and Clifton´s (1986) experiments for not including appropriate control conditions. In the experiment described above they claimed again that they had established an influence of context overriding any potential syntactic biases. Unfortunately, some inconsistencies in Altmann and Steedman´s results as well as some confoundations with the ordering of antecedents in the context (cf. Rayner et al., 1992; Britt, 1994) made these results look much less convincing. Furthermore, their findings have so far only been established in self-paced reading studies. Thus, the elimination of the residual effect might simply be due to decreased reading speed induced by this experimental technique. Altmann et al. (1992) argue, however, that the residual effects for syntactic attachment preferences in eye-tracking experiments can only be found in a minority of cases in a regression contingent measure.

A delayed influence of pragmatic biases was established by Rayner et al. (1992) as well as Mitchell et al. (1992). Most convincing is Mitchell et al.´s (1992) experiment, where sentences were disambiguated very early, so that the experiment really tapped into immediate influences on parsing decisions. Mitchell et al. investigated sentences like (5) which are ambiguous between a complement clause and a relative clause reading. In isolated sentences, the complement clause reading is preferred in this kind of structures. Half of the sentences were disambiguated early by omitting the pronoun *he* so that only the relative clause reading was syntactically possible. Mitchell et al. found a strong contextual effect, but only in the segment following the *had been* segment. When the sentence was only disambiguated towards one of the readings in this late segment (as is the case when the pronoun *he* is included), subjects spent longer reading this segment if the disambiguation was supported by the context. However, the context was not able to affect the complement preference in the early region, indicating that contextual biases are only effective in a later stage of processing.

(5)   a.   Don shouted to the assistant that (he) / had been / ...

      b.   Don forced the assistant that (he) / had been / ...

      c.   Don and the assistant that (he) / had been / ...

To account for the variation of results with respect to context effects, Britt, Gabrys, and Perfetti (1993; Britt, 1994) propose a somewhat different account on pragmatic effects on parsing decisions. In their *restrictive interactive model*, the influence of the *discourse model* is restricted to the attachment of optional verb-arguments. However, in the case where a PP fits a slot for an obligatory role of a verb, contextual information is ignored and the potential role-filler is initially attached to the VP by a subprocessor called *argument filler*. Low level phrasal units, such as PPs and NPs, are constructed autonomously by the so called *constituent builder*. This account is substantiated by self-paced reading studies, crossing referential biases with the optionality of the ambiguous constituent.

Summing up, the picture arises that context cannot override strong lexical or syntactic attachment preferences as they are modeled by the *principle of preferred role attachment*. However, it still remains to be investigated whether in cases where a syntactic preference has been established in the absence of a strong lexical preference (i.e. in head final sentences) a principle like *head attachment* can be overridden by referential biases. In the following sections, we will discuss data from an eye-tracking experiment where PP-attachment ambiguities in verb-second and verb-final sentences were presented in pragmatically biasing contexts.

THE EXPERIMENT

Materials and design

The experimental sentences were manipulated according to a 2*2*2 within-subjects design with the factors *verb placement* (*verb-final* (7, 9) vs. *verb-second* (6,8)), *semantic bias* (*VP-attachment biased* (6, 7) vs. *NP-attachment biased* (8, 9)) and *contextual bias* (*one possible referent* (10a, 11a) vs. *more than one possible referent* (10b, 11b)). The verbs used in the target sentences showed a preference to expect an instrumental PP, as established in pre-tests. For each experimental condition, one text was presented, resulting in eight texts per subject.[1] These eight texts were taken from a pool of 8 sets differing in content. The order of presentation was randomized. Every text was presented to an equal number of subjects. Additionally, 28 filler texts were included.

(6)   Volker [bastelte [den Rahmen] [mit der Laubsäge]], ...

        Volker made the frame with the fretsaw, ...

(7)   Daß Volker [[den Rahmen] [mit der Laubsäge] bastelte], ...

        That Volker the frame with the fretsaw made, ...
        "That Volker made the frame with the fretsaw, ..."

(8)   Volker [verpackte [die Werkzeugkiste mit der Laubsäge]], ...

        Volker wrapped up the tool-box with the fretsaw.

(9)   Daß Volker [[die Werkzeugkiste mit der Laubsäge] verpackte], ...

        That Volker the tool-box with the fretsaw wrapped up, ...
        "That Volker wrapped up the tool-box with the fretsaw, ..."

In each target sentence, the PP *mit der Laubsäge* (*with the fretsaw*) can be attached syntactically to the direct object-NP as an attribute (NP-attachment), or to the VP specifying the instrument of the action (VP-attachment). However, sentences (6-9) are semantically biased (indicated by "[]" brackets) in such a way that world knowledge strongly biases the VP-attached interpretation in sentences (6, 7) and the noun-modifying interpretation in (8, 9). The PP was not exchanged between the conditions in this experiment in order to provide maximally parallel material, at least at the critical point of interest. Instead, the verb and the object were replaced so that the same PP can be interpreted as an argument of the verb, as in (6, 7), or as a NP-modifier, as in (8, 9).

Each target sentence was presented within a short text (10, 11), which introduced either a single referent (a: R=1), or two possible referents (b: R>1) of the direct object in the target sentence (e.g. one or two frames for 6, 7 and one or two tool-boxes for 8, 9, respectively).

In order to achieve minimal contrasts between the pragmatic bias conditions, the context was designed in such a way for both target sentences to fit in easily. Since the targets contained different direct objects, both objects were introduced in both contexts (Thus, there was at least one frame and at least one tool-box in each of the contexts for the targets 6-9). The antecedent of the direct object was always introduced in the sentence immediately preceding the target sentence, in order to avoid a focus shift between antecedent and target (Rayner, Garrod, and Perfetti, 1992).

(10)   Volker kümmerte sich um das Weihnachtspaket für seinen Neffen. Er sollte eine Werkzeugkiste bekommen, die eine Laubsäge enthielt. / Aber es mußten noch andere Weihnachtsvorbereitungen getroffen werden. /

(Volker took care of the Christmas package for his nephew. He was supposed to receive a tool-box which contained a fretsaw. / But other preparations for Christmas also had to be made.)

a.   (R = 1): Volker fertigte das Weihnachtsgeschenk für seine Oma selbst. Sie sollte einen Bilderrahmen bekommen, der eine Einlegearbeit hatte./

(Volker made the Christmas present for his grandma himself. She was supposed to receive a picture-frame that had sections of inlaid work.)

b. (R > 1): Für seine beiden Omas fertigte Volker die Weihnachtsgeschenke selbst. Sie sollten beide jeweils einen Bilderrahmen bekommen, wovon der eine eine Einlegearbeit, der andere eine Blattgoldverzierung hatte. /

(For his two grandmas, Volker made the Christmas presents himself. Each of them was supposed to receive a pictureframe, one of which had sections of inlaid work, the other of which was decorated with gold leaf.

Target:

Volker bastelte den Rahmen mit der Laubsäge, bevor er sie einpackte. (Volker made the frame with the fretsaw before he wrapped it up)/ (6) or Volker sorgte dafür, daß er den Rahmen mit der Laubsäge bastelte, bevor er sie einpackte. (Volker made sure that he made the frame with the fretsaw before he wrapped it up /(7)

Er konnte seine eigene Laubsäge nicht finden.

(He could not find his own fretsaw.)

(11) Volker fertigte das Weihnachtsgeschenk für seine Oma selbst. Sie sollte einen Bilderrahmen bekommen, der eine Einlegearbeit hatte./ Aber es mußten noch andere Weihnachtsvorbereitungen getroffen werden.

(Volker made the Christmas present for his grandma himself. She was supposed to receive a picture-frame that had sections of inlaid work./ But other preparations for Christmas also had to be made)

a. (R = 1): Volker kümmerte sich um das Weihnachtspaket für seinen Neffen. Er sollte eine Werkzeugkiste bekommen, die eine Laubsäge enthielt./

(Volker took care of the Christmas package of his nephew. He was supposed to receive a tool-box which contained a fretsaw.)

b. (R > 1): Volker kümmerte sich um die Weihnachtspakete für seine beiden Neffen. Jeder sollte eine Werkzeugkiste bekommen, die im einen Fall eine Laubsäge, im anderen Fall eine Kombizange enthielt./

(Volker took care of the Christmas package of his two nephews. Each of them was supposed to receive a tool-box, one of which contained a fretsaw, the other a pair of pliers.)

Target:

Volker verpackte die Werkzeugkiste mit der Laubsäge, bevor er zur Post ging. (Volker wrapped up the tool-box with the fretsaw before he went to the post-office) / (8) or: Volker sorgte dafür, daß er die Werkzeugkiste mit der Laub säge verpackte, bevor er zur Post ging. (Volker made sure that he wrapped up the tool-box with the fretsaw, before he went to the post-office)/ (9)

Sie mußte unbedingt rechtzeitig ankommen./

(It absolutely had to arrive in time.)

Whenever a sentence had to be presented in more than one line, the lines were separated by two empty lines. This was done in order to be able to count fixations that were only slightly below or above the material as fixations on the text.

Method

Procedure

Prior to the experiment, the subject was fitted to a headrest to prevent head movements during reading. The experiment started with a warming-up block consisting of two texts. Then the experiment, which was built up of six blocks, began. Each block was initiated by a brief calibration procedure and contained six randomly mixed texts. The text was presented in five segments, indicated by a slash ("/") in (10, 11). Each text was followed by a simple yes/no-question, which the subject answered by pressing one of two buttons (left-hand button: "yes", right-hand button: "no"). They answered with a high degree of accuracy, which did not vary across conditions.

Apparatus

The subjects' eye movements were monitored by a Generation 5.5 Dual Purkinje Image Eyetracker. Viewing was binocular, but eye movements were recorded only from the right eye. The eyetracker was connected to an AT 386 computer which controlled the stimulus-presentation and stored the output from the eyetracker. The sampling rate for data collection was 1 KHz. The sentences were presented on a 20-inch color monitor, beginning at the 6th column of the character matrix. The subject was seated 83 cm from the face of the screen, so that 3 letters equaled 1 degree of visual angle. External distractions and light reflections were screened off by a black tube and the room was slightly darkened.

Subjects

Thirty-two undergraduate students (native speakers of German) from the University of Freiburg were paid to participate in the study. All of them had normal, uncorrected vision and they were all naive concerning the purpose of the study. During an experimental session of about 40 minutes, each of the subjects had to read 32 texts while their eye movements were monitored. Three subjects had to be excluded from the analyses because of inaccuracies or too many missing data.

Dependent variables and data analyses

For the statistical analyses, the data were summarized for each word, except for the NP licensed by the preposition *mit* (*with*), which was treated as a single region, yielding two dependent variables, namely *first pass reading times*, and *regression path durations*, RPDs. *First-pass reading time* is the amount of time a reader spends on a region (word) before moving on to another word; i.e. the sum of all fixations on a region excluding any that result from regressions to the word. *Regression-path durations* (RPDs) sum up all durations of fixations in the *regression path*, i.e. in the stream of fixations starting with the first fixation on a region and including all fixations up to the point when there is a forward saccade past the region under consideration (see Konieczny, Hemforth, & Scheepers, this volume, for more details).

Exclusion of data

First pass reading times and *regression path durations* smaller than 100 ms were excluded from the analysis. If the sum of durations of erroneous fixations[2] in a sentence exceeded 200 ms, the data for this sentence were also excluded.

Accounting for word length effects

Although the PPs did not vary across the conditions, word length had to be taken into account for two reasons. Firstly, we were also interested in positions other than the PP, such as the verb, which do not contain the same word in each condition. Secondly, even at the PP, some data had to be occasionally excluded from the analysis (see paragraph above). Word length was accounted for by *subtracting* 20 ms for each character from the *first pass reading times*, starting at the fourth character of each word (i.e., FPRT - ((world-length -4) * 20)).

Hypotheses

The locus of impact

Contextual bias. With respect to *referential support*, a preference for one of the alternative readings can be established immediately after the object-NP has been processed because a judgement can be made from the object-NP alone as to whether or not it successfully refers to a discourse referent. At this position, a preference for a modified NP must therefore have been established in multiple referent contexts, and a simple NP reading should be preferred in contexts introducing a unique antecedent.

Effects on reading times, however, may show up only when the referentially supported analysis fails for some reasons, such as its implausibility. It is therefore assumed that the earliest position at which the contextual bias may show its impact is a position where it conflicts with preferences imposed by other principles. In order to predict the position, we therefore have to identify the locus of impact of other constraining mechanisms, such as *parametrized head attachment* and *semantic bias*.[3]

Parametrized head attachment. The locus of impact of PHA differs between verb-final and verb-second constructions. In verb-final constructions, *head attachment* forces the PP to be attached to the preceding NP, *as soon as a PP is started* (see Konieczny et al., 1991; Konieczny et al., 1997). However, since short prepositions, such as "mit", are very often skipped, an effect might show up in the data only at the prepositional NP.

In verb-second constructions, however, the verb imposes its lexical expectations onto the parsing-process according to *preferred role attachment*, as soon as *the verb* is read. Subcategorization requirements or thematic role expectations are thus directly projected into the structure.

Instrumental-PPs are regarded as optional complements. In the model underlying our approach, they are predicted immediately when the corresponding subcategorizer, the verb, is processed if it carries a lexically preferred expectation of the complement.

Semantic bias. It is obvious that the semantic bias cannot show its impact before the content of the PP is established. The earliest position possible is therefore the PP-noun, the last word of the PP in our sentences.

Interactions

Verb-second constructions. Since the verbs in this experiment have a preference to bind possible instruments, the verb-bias should interact with the contextual and the semantic bias, such that increased reading times can be expected when the context introduces two potential referents and thus supports the NP-modifying attachment of the PP, or the semantic bias renders the VP attachment implausible. This effect might already occur on the direct-object NP if an optional instrumental PP has been predicted at the verb.

Verb-final constructions. If there is an initial analysis according to *head attachment*, reading times should be increased at the prepositional NP, when contextual and/or semantic bias force the simple NP-reading of the direct object.

An interaction of contextual and semantic bias can be expected, in such a way that an infelicitous combination, i.e. contextual and semantic bias forcing opposing interpretations, results in longer reading times than the felicitous combinations.

To sum up: if the contextual bias alone guides the initial parsing preferences, no interaction with the placement of the verb should be expected, even more so because the contextual influence is established at the end of the direct object NP, while *head attachment* is supposed to be effective only at a later position in the sentence, namely, at the PP.

Results

All reading time measures were submitted to a full factorial 2*2*2 analysis of variance for repeated measures including the factors *verb placement, contextual bias*, and *semantic bias*.

Effects at the prepositional NP

Table 4 shows the mean adjusted RPDs and first pass reading times (in parentheses) at the prepositional NP (determiner and noun).We will go into detail below.

	context: R = 1		context: R > 1	
	VP-attach.	NP-attach.	VP-attach.	NP-attach.
v-second	332 (278)	333 (312)	365 (293)	528 (369)
v-final	283 (236)	315 (223)	240 (205)	249 (212)

Table 1: Regression-path durations and first pass reading times (in parentheses) in ms at the prepositional NP by levels of *contextual bias* (R=1 vs. R>1), *semantic bias* (*VP-attachment bias* vs. *NP-attachment bias*), and *verb placement* (*verb-second* vs. *verb-final*)

Verb-placement. Not surprisingly, processing the PP took longer in verb-second sentences than in verb-final sentences (FPRT: $F1_{1,\,28} = 13.36$, p <.01. $F2_{1,\,7} = 15.22$, p <.01.; RPD: $F1_{1,\,28} = 13.90$, p <.01. $F2_{1,\,7} = 12.65$, p <.01.), which can be easily attributed to the clause-final wrap-up effect in verb-second sentences.

However, the interaction of verb-placement with the other factors is of special interest. With respect to this interaction, the following picture arises: differing from previous studies on isolated sentences, no reliable two way

interaction of semantic bias and verb-placement was found at the prepositional NP (Table 2).

	sem. bias: VP-attach	sem. bias: NP-attach
Verb-second	349 (285)	430 (341)
Verb-final	261 (221)	282 (217)

Table 2: Regression-path durations and first pass reading times (in
parentheses) in ms at the prepositional NP by levels of *semantic bias* (*VP-
attachment biased* vs. *NP-attachment biased*), and *verb placement* (*verb-
second* vs. *verb-final*).

As can be seen in Table 3, however, there was a significant two-way interaction of *verb placement* and *contextual bias* with respect to RPDs

	context: R = 1	context: R > 1	subject analyses	item analyses
Verb-second	333 (295)	446 (331)	$F1_{1, 28} = 8.88$, $p < .01$	$F2_{1, 7} = 21.35$, $p < .01$
Verb-final	299 (229)	244 (209)		

Table 3: Regression-path durations and first pass reading times (in
parentheses) in ms at the prepositional NP by levels of *contextual bias* (R=1
vs. R>1), and *verb placement* (*verb-second* vs. *verb-final*). The inferential
statistics refer to the two-way interaction with respect to RPDs.

Verb-second constructions. There was a reliable increase of the RPDs in
the R>1 context, compared to the R=1 context within the verb-second condi-
tion ($F1_{1, 28} = 6.99$, $p < .02$; $F2_{1, 7} = 37.17$, $p < .01$). Although no reliable interaction of verb-placement and semantic bias was established, first pass reading
times were reliably increased (only for the F1 analysis, however: $F1_{1, 28} =
4.42$, $p < .05$), and RPDs marginally so ($F1_{1, 28} = 3.46$, $p < .08$), when a noun-
modifying prepositional NP was read in a verb-second sentence (see Table 2)
compared to a verb-modifying PP. This contrast in the verb-second condition
further confirms the hypothesis that processing difficulties result, when the

R>1 context or the semantic bias support the complex-NP reading, which had been ruled out by the role-preferences of the verb.

However, Table 4 shows that increased reading times in the NP-attachment biased condition are mainly due to the cases where context and semantic bias both contradict the initial analysis, namely VP-attachment. In these cases, processing seems to be severely hampered, leading to a significant reanalysis of large parts of the entire sentence, which show up in increased RPDs (R>1 vs. R=1 / NP-attachment biased: $F1_{1, 28}$ =7.36, p<.02; $F2_{1, 7}$ = 7.30, p <.04), resulting in a reliable two-way interaction between contextual bias and semantic bias for subject analysis ($F1_{1, 28}$ =4.34, p<.05).

Verb-final constructions. There were no reliable effects with respect to either RPDs or *first pass reading times* in *verb-final* sentences. However, RPDs were increased in the R=1 condition (see Table 3; $F1_{1, 28}$ = 2.79, p <.11; $F2_{1, 7}$ = 3.49, p <.11). Though not reliable, this tendency is compatible with the assumption that NP-attachment was carried out first, according to *head attachment*, resulting in a conflict if the context supports the simple-NP reading (R=1).

Other positions

The words at positions other than the PP varied between the semantic conditions. We will therefore only consider the effects of contextual bias and verb-placement at the noun of the direct object and only for verb-final constructions at the verb.

Direct object NP. As can be seen in Table 4 there was a significant two-way interaction of *verb placement* and *contextual bias* with respect to RPDs, and a tendency for first pass reading times at the noun of the direct object.

	context: R = 1	context: R > 1	subject analyses	item analyses
Verb-second	204 (182)	280 (216)	$F1_{1,28}=7.96$, p<.01	$F2_{1,7}=7.13$, p<.04
Verb-final	231 (183)	233 (186)	$(F1_{1,28}=2.68$, p<.12)	$(F2_{1,7}= 3.97$, p <.09)

Table 4: Mean adjusted *regression-path durations* and mean adjusted *first pass reading times* (in parentheses) in ms at the noun of the direct object by levels of *contextual bias* (R=1 vs. R>1), and *verb placement* (*verb-second* vs. *verb-final*). The inferential statistics refer to the two-way interaction with respect to RPDs (statistics for FPRTs are given in brackets).

It is obvious that this interaction results from the reliable contrasts between the context conditions within the verb-second condition (RPDs: $F1_{1,28}= 20.22$, p <.01; $F2_{1,7} = 8.24$, p <.03; FPRTs: $F1_{1,28} = 8.02$, p <.01; $F2_{1,7} = 9.44$, p <.02). Thus, PHA and referential support show their impact as early as at the direct object in verb-second sentences. In verb-final sentences, however, the effect does not show up before the PP is processed.

The verb. It is hardly surprising that first pass reading times ($F1_{1,28} = 61.33$, p <.01. $F2_{1,7} = 25.53$, p <.01) and RPDs ($F1_{1,28} = 62.13$, p <.001. $F2_{1,7} = 63.71$, p <.001) were longer in verb-final sentences, due to the clause wrap-up effect. Since the verb in verb-second sentences is of no further interest, I have only presented the results for verb-final sentences (see Table 5).

	context: R = 1	context: R > 1	subject analyses	item analyses
verb-instr.	247 (238)	337 (245)	$F1_{1,28}=3.79$, $p<.07$	$F2_{1,7} = 2.13$, $p<.18$
noun-mod.	272 (218)	278 (238)		

Table 5: Mean adjusted *regression-path durations* and mean adjusted *first pass reading times* (in parentheses) in ms at the verb in verb final sentences by levels of *contextual bias* (R=1 vs. R>1), and *semantic bias* (*verbal instrument* vs. *noun modifier*). The inferential statistics refer to the simple contrast of contextual bias within the verb-instrument condition with respect to RPDs.

Although no reliable effects could be found at the verb in verb-final sentences, RPDS for R>1 condition were slightly increased ($F1_{1,\,28} = 2.87$, p <.11), which results from the marginally reliable simple contrast (R=1 vs. R>1) within the verb-modifying condition

This result might look a little puzzling at first glance, since it appears to go against the findings at the PP-position. In the following section, however, we will argue that it is fully compatible with our processing model.

Discussion

It might seem surprising, at least at first glance, that the semantic bias of the sentences did not have an effect on processing times at the prepositional NP in verb-final sentences that were given in contexts, as it did in isolated sentences. However, several explanations can be considered: since the overall sentence reading times are smaller in contextually embedded sentences, time consuming high level semantic processes, such as evaluation of plausibility at the level of general world knowledge, might have occurred a few words later than in isolated sentences, especially since interfering contextual (referential) processes might have slowed down conceptual evaluation.

If we take another look at the examples, a further reason suggests itself: NP-attachment violations, as in "*der Rahmen mit der Laubsäge*" (*the frame with the fretsaw*), might generally be "weaker" than VP-attachment violations, as in "*mit einer Laubsäge einpacken*" (*to wrap up with a fretsaw*). Nouns seem to impose much weaker constraints on their possible modifiers than verbs do. If so, semantic evaluation might have been delayed until the verb, at least in the case of verb-modifying semantic bias in the materials used in this experiment. Subjects might thus have behaved according to a "wait and see" strategy with respect to semantic evaluation in verb-final sentences.

Referential aspects are, however, inseparably tied to NPs, and in cases of explicit anaphora, such as in our experiments, they do not require any inferences at a general conceptual level. We therefore assume that referential aspects are evaluated immediately and before other aspects of plausibility enter the game. Since these referential processes are supposed to be time consuming, to a small but definite extent, semantic effects might have been delayed even further, presumably beyond the subclause boundary. Unfortunately, the continuation of the sentence was not properly controlled, i.e words after the comma differed across the conditions. Thus, we do not have access to the processing times beyond the subclause boundaries, where the semantics might have shown its effect.

Parametrized head attachment. If PHA, and in particular *head attachment* and *preferred role attachment,* had not guided the first analysis, the interaction of contextual bias and verb-placement would be hard to explain. However, the impact of preferred role attachment in verb-second sentences was much stronger than that of head attachment in verb-final sentences, which was only marginally reliable. A quite similar interaction was also found in verb-second sentences even at the noun of the direct object. If we assume that the beginning of the PP ("*mit*") had been pre-processed within the perceptual span at the object noun, referential failure of the object in the R>1 context might have produced a conflict with the expectation of an instrumental PP imposed by the verb in verb-second sentences. In verb-final sentences, however, pre-processing is probably not sufficient as a trigger for *head attachment,* where no such expectation of a PP is effective. Interestingly, contextual influences could not hinder the parser from adopting an analysis preferred by *head attachment.*

In verb-second sentences, increased reading times resulted at the object noun and during the PP when the contextual bias contradicted a preference imposed by *preferred role attachment.* At the PP, the highest penalty was observed when both contextual and semantic bias contradicted preferred role attachment. The highly increased regression path durations in these cases indicate an extensive reanalysis of the entire sentence.

In verb-final sentences, processing times were increased only at the PP if the contextual bias (R=1) contradicted the obvious *head attachment* of the PP to the preceding NP. However, processing difficulties were weaker than in verb-second sentences and only marginally reliable.

There are three possible reasons for this difference. Firstly, it might be due to the ease of recovery from an initial NP-attachment of the PP as a *modifier*, compared with recovering from the initial VP-attachment as a *complement*. Secondly, in verb-final constructions, a weak penalty might have resulted from a referentially *successful* object-NP (biasing the parser towards the non-preferred VP-attachment), whereas a referential *failure* in verb-second sentences (biasing the parser towards the non-preferred NP-attachment) might have caused a stronger penalty. Whereas the overall interpretation can be sufficiently established in the case of referential success of the simple NP, an interpretation has to be postponed in case of a referential failure.

Note also that a NP-modifier, such as a PP, can very easily be re-interpreted as non-restrictive, while it remains attached to the NP. In the case of an R=1 context in verb-final sentences it may have occurred that the PP was not reanalyzed as a complement of the verb at all, but re-interpreted as non-restrictive, still remaining a NP-modifier. This is likely to cause a much weaker penalty than in the case of a conflict in verb-second sentences, where the PP must be reanalyzed from a verb-complement to a restrictive modifier and thus be attached to a different host.

This interpretation is supported by the result that the highest processing times at the verb occurred in verb-final sentences, when the verb-modifying semantic bias forced the initially *head attached* PP, which was furthermore referentially supported by an R>1 context, to be reanalyzed as a complement of the verb. Whereas reversed, the noun-modifying semantic bias does not seem able to initialize a reanalysis when it should have conflicted with the R=1 context. So, again, it seems to be the case that the PP has only been interpreted as non-restrictive in the R=1 context, still remaining NP-modifying.

Implications for parsing models

In general, the data are incompatible with all models that do not predict differential parsing preferences for verb-placement variations.

The weakly interactive, parallel model of Altmann and Steedman (1988) does not assume initial *syntactic* preferences. In their model, the PP should have been attached according to referential support exclusively. Thus, the only type of interaction that should have occurred is one between contextual and semantic bias, in both verb-final sentences and verb-second sentences. In verb-second sentences, however, the most difficult condition is a "felicitous" one (Altmann, 1988), in which the context (R>1) and semantic bias (NP-modifying) both support the same attachment. Even more importantly, the interaction of contextual bias and verb-placement remains unexplained.

In Britt's model, it is not clear whether or not the discourse model is consulted in attaching the PP in verb-final sentences. If it is, predictions are the same as those of the Altmann & Steedman model and thus, false. If, however, the discourse model requires a call from the *argument filler* it is not consulted, since no verb, which could have activated the *argument filler*, has been read until the PP. Thus, only the *constituent builder* could carry out an attachment, i.e. an attachment to the preceding NP. In this case, the encountered preference towards the [NP PP] attachment would be explained in much the same way as it is by any other head-licensing model, such as Abney´s (1989) *licensing structure parser*. We have argued elsewhere (Hemforth, 1993, Hemforth, Konieczny, & Strube, 1993; Konieczny, 1996) that such models are inadequate because they require a licensing head in order to build structure at all (see also Gorrell, this volume; Schlesewsky et al., this volume). With respect to the verb-second sentences in our study, the model predicts an interaction of contextual and semantic bias at the PP, as the Altmann and Steedman model does, because the instrumental PPs were all optional arguments. Since the *argument filler* tries to match a preposition only against the obligatory slots of the verb, no attempt is made to attach the PP to the VP initially. Therefore, the initial attachment only depends on the discourse model and can later conflict with the semantic bias. Again, this prediction contradicts the result that a "felicitous" condition (R> 1/noun modifying) was the hardest to process. This can only be explained by a strong initial attachment to the VP, *before* contextual and semantic bias enter the game.

Optional verb-complements, such as the "*mit*"-PPs in this experiment, are thus initially attached to the VP if the verb that bears the corresponding lexical preference has already been processed. It is therefore insufficient to distinguish only between optional complements and obligatory complements, as the restricted interactive model of Britt et al. (1993) does. It remains to be seen whether the results of this research, especially the interaction of contextual bias and verb-placement, could be replicated if verbs without a preference for an instrumental PP were used. In any case, however, it was shown that even optional complements are initially attached to their subcategorizer. The PHA model therefore fits the data presented.

CONCLUSION

Parametrized head attachment was demonstrated to be effective even when the target sentences were presented in contexts. The results presented in this chapter strongly suggest that the syntax processor operates independent of higher level influences. Nevertheless, contextual influences were demonstrated to be effective fairly early and they seem to terminate before the conceptual evaluation of the proposed attachment. Therefore, a feedback channel between the syntactic processor and the higher level system must be assumed.

The architecture that emerges from this is illustrated in figure 1.

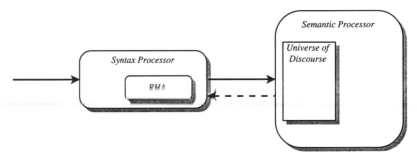

Figure 1: The architecture of the HSPM

The results are thus compatible with the view that the syntax processor operates as a *module* (Fodor, 1983) in that its initial operations are not influenced by processes of modules further downstream. Whether or not the higher level processes can *suggest* alternative analyses in case of a parsing failure, as proposed for the *thematic processor* (Frazier, 1987), remains an open question.

NOTES

[1] Admittedly, it would have been better to have more sentences per condition in particular for F2-analyses. Nevertheless, the data we will present cannot easily be attributed to single item artifacts because for the most relevant conditions of pragmatic bias and verb-placement the items differed only minimally between conditions.

[2] i.e. a fixation not at a word in the target sentence but somewhere else on the screen.

[3] We will only discuss potential pragmatic influences on parsing decisions with respect to the predictions which can be derived from parametrized head attachment in this chapter, but see Konieczny et al., 1997, for a comparison of PHA and other parsing models.

⁴ The preposition was excluded from the data analysis, since it was skipped in about 80% of the cases, which further supports the assumption, that it had often been pre-processed at the object-noun.

REFERENCES

Abney, S. (1989). A computational model of human parsing. *Journal of Psycholinguistic Research, 18(1)*, 129-144.

Altmann, G. (1988). Ambiguity, parsing strategies and computational models. *Language and Cognitive Processes, 3(2)*, 73-97.

Altmann, G., & Steedman, M. (1988). Interaction with context during human sentence processing. *Cognition, 30*, 191-238.

Altmann, G. T., Garnham, A., & Dennis, Y. (1992). Avoiding the garden path: Eye movements in context. *Journal of Memory and Language, 31*, 685-712.

Britt, M. A. (1994). The interaction of referential ambiguity and argument structure in the parsing of prepositional phrases. *Journal of Memory and Language, 33*, 251-283.

Britt, M. A., Gabrys, G., & Perfetti, C. A. (1993). A restrictive interactive model of parsing. In *Proceedings of the 15th Annual Conference of the Cognitive Science Society, Boulder, CO* (pp. 260-265). Hillsdale, NJ: Erlbaum.

Clifton, C., & Ferreira, F. (1989). Ambiguity in context. *Language and Cognitive Processes, 4*, 77-104.

Crain, S., & Steedman, M. (1985). On not being led up the garden path: The use of context by the psychological parser. In D. R. Dowty, L. Karttunen & A. Zwicky (Eds.), *Natural language parsing: Psychological, computational, and theoretical perspectives* (pp. 320-358). Cambridge: Cambridge University Press.

Crocker, M. (1992). *A logical model of competence and performance in the human sentence processor.* Unpublished doctoral dissertation, University of Edinburgh, Edinburgh, Scotland.

Ferreira, F., & Clifton, C. (1986). The independence of syntactic processing. *Journal of Memory and Language, 25*, 348-368.

Fodor, J. A. (1983). *The modularity of the mind.* Cambridge, MA: MIT Press.

Frazier, L. (1987). Sentence processing: A tutorial review. In M. Coltheart (Ed.), *The psychology of reading* (pp. 559-586). Hove/London/Hillsdale: Lawrence Erlbaum.

Hemforth, B. (1993). *Kognitives Parsing: Repräsentation und Verarbeitung sprachlichen Wissens.* Sankt Augustin: Infix.

Hemforth, B., Konieczny, L., Scheepers, C., & Strube, G. (1992, October). SOUL-Processing: Semantik-orientierte Prinzipien menschlicher Sprachverarbeitung. In G. Görz (Ed.), *KONVENS92* (pp. 198-208). Berlin: Springer.

Hemforth, B., Konieczny, L., & Strube, G. (1993). Incremental syntax processing and parsing strategies. In *Proceedings of the 15th Annual Conference of the Cognitive Science Society, July, 1993* (pp. 539-545). Hillsdale, NJ: Erlbaum.

Konieczny, L. (1996). *Human sentence processing: A semantics-oriented parsing approach* (IIG-Bericht Nr. 3/96). Freiburg: Universität Freiburg, Institut für Informatik und Gesellschaft.

Konieczny, L., Hemforth, B., Scheepers, C. & Strube, G. (1997). The role of lexical heads in parsing: Evidence from German. *Language and Cognitive Processes, 12,* 307-348.

Konieczny, L., Hemforth, B., & Strube, G. (1991). Psychologisch fundierte Prinzipien der Satzverarbeitung jenseits von Minimal Attachment. *Kognitionswissenschaft, 1*(1), 58-70.

Konieczny, L., Scheepers, C., Hemforth, B., & Strube, G. (1994). Semantikorientierte Syntaxverarbeitung. In S. Felix, C. Habel & G. Rickheit (Eds.), *Kognitive Linguistik: Repräsentationen und Prozesse.* Opladen: Westdeutscher Verlag.

Mitchell, D. C., Corley, M. M. B., & Garnham, A. (1992). Effects of context in human sentence parsing: Evidence against a discourse-based proposal mechanism. *Journal of Experimental Psychology: Learning Memory and Cognition., 18,* 69-88.

Rayner, K., Garrod, S., & Perfetti, C. A. (1992). Discourse influences during parsing are delayed. *Cognition, 45,* 109-139.

MODIFIER ATTACHMENT:
RELATIVE CLAUSES AND COORDINATIONS

Barbara Hemforth[*], Lars Konieczny[+] and Christoph Scheepers[#]
*University of Freiburg
+Saarland University
#University of Glasgow

SUMMARY

In this paper, we will discuss accounts of cross-linguistic differences in attachment preferences for relative clauses. In the first section, we will present an overview of data from two-site attachment ambiguities like (1). We will argue for a modular model of sentence processing where a discourse-based preference for a salient antecedent of the relative pronoun and a syntax-based recency preference contribute to empirically observable attachment preferences.

(1)   the daughter of the teacher who lived in France

In the second section, we will extend this account to three-site ambiguities like (13,3) which were first investigated by Gibson et al. (1996a, b), based on three German questionnaire experiments.

(2)   the lamp near the painting in the house that was damaged in the flood (Gibson et al., 1996a)

(3)   the customer with the child with the dirty face and
            - the wet diaper
            - the one with the wet diaper
            - the one with the baby with the wet diaper

For English and Spanish, Gibson et al. (1996a) found an NP3 over NP1 over NP2 attachment preferences for relative clauses which could also be established for English conjoined NPs. We will show that attachment preferences in comparable German constructions are highly similar to the preferences established for English (and Spanish where available). We will present evidence for a change in the preference pattern if the relative clause is extraposed leading

B. Hemforth and L. Konieczny (eds.), German Sentence Processing, 161-186.

INTRODUCTION

Most of the papers in this volume share a particular approach as to how psycholinguistic work in a particular language such as German may contribute to a crosslinguistic perspective on language processing: they all present constructions highly specific for German, use ways to disambiguate between structural alternatives which are highly specific for German, and, in this way, answer questions that could not have been tackled in many languages. However, as Mitchell (1996) pointed out, this is only one route to follow. To get closer to a universal theory of human sentence processing, we should not only look at the peculiarities of a particular language but we should also try to find constructions which are as similar as possible between languages and for which a universal sentence processing theory will predict comparable preference patterns.

The construction which fulfills this constraint and has been investigated most often in cross-linguistic studies so far involves relative clause modifiers as in (4).

(4)   Someone shot the daughter of the colonel who was on the
               balcony.

The relative clause in this kind of construction may be attached to either of the preceding two NPs, the head of the object noun phrase ("the daughter"; N1 or "high" attachment) or the modifying NP ("the colonel"; N2 or "low attachment"). Apart from English, this ambiguity also exists in a large number of highly variable languages. Following the seminal work of Cuetos and Mitchell (1988) who compared preference patterns for relative clause attachment in English and Spanish (see also Carreiras & Clifton, 1993; Gilboy, Sopena, Frazier, & Clifton, 1995), this construction was investigated in languages such as Italian (De Vincenzi & Job, 1995), French (Pynte & Zagar, in press), Japanese (Kamide & Mitchell, 1996), Dutch (Brysbaert & Mitchell, 1996), and German (Hemforth, Konieczny, & Scheepers, 1994, in press).

Two major outcomes from this comparative research are currently stimulating many theoretical considerations: firstly, the preference for relative clause attachment in these kinds of constructions appears to vary between languages. Whereas either no preference or a low (N2) attachment preference was found for English (e.g. Cuetos & Mitchell, 1988; Frazier & Clifton, 1996; Gilboy, Sopena, Frazier, & Clifton, 1995), in most other languages, the relative clause is preferentially attached high at least with respect to final interpretations.[1] Secondly, this high attachment preference contradicts a widely assumed and cognitively highly plausible preference for local attachments (e.g., *late clo-*

sure: Frazier, 1979; *recency*: Gibson, Pearlmutter, Canseco-Gonzalez, & Hickock, 1996; *most recent head attachment*: Konieczny, Hemforth, Scheepers, & Strube, 1997).

Locality

A preference for recent attachment sites is for example assumed to be responsible for garden-path effects found in sentences like (5a-c). In (5a), the adverb *yesterday* is preferentially attached to the most recent (but inconsistent) predicate *will arrive* (Fodor & Frazier, 1980; Wanner, 1980). In (5b), the NP *the wine* is preferentially attached to the more recent verb *drank* leaving the obligatorily ditransitive verb *gave* without its second argument (Kamide, Mitchell, & Scheepers, 1997). Finally, a preference to attach the NP *his car* in (5c) as the object of the preceding verb *repair* rather than as the subject of the following *was stolen* makes (5c) difficult to process.

(5) a.   Nick said his parents will arrive yesterday.

    b.   Yuki gave the man who drank the wine.

    c.   While Tom was repairing his car was stolen.

Apparently, recency does not work for relative clause attachment in Spanish, French, German, and many other languages. Several accounts were offered in the past few years to explain this phenomenon. One approach shared by several authors was to posit a competitive strategy counteracting a recency based attachment preference. According to this strategy, major discourse referents (Frazier & Clifton, 1996; Gilboy et al., 1995; Hemforth et al., in press) or arguments of the main predicate (Gibson et al., 1996a) attract modifiers such as relative clauses. In some languages this attraction may be stronger than any recency based preference. The theories differ with respect to the question of where, i.e., to which kinds of grammatical relations, this competitive strategy applies and where language specific differences come from.

Underspecification

One approach to explaining the preference patterns for relative clauses is to underspecify the syntactic attachment of relative clauses so that final attachments can be determined by non-syntactic (e.g., pragmatic or prosodic) principles. Construal theory (Frazier & Clifton, 1996; 1997) offers an account where underspecification is assumed for a restricted set of syntactic relations. Two kinds of syntactic relations are differentiated in Construal: primary and secondary relations. Primary relations are (roughly) argument relations of the main predicate and arguments of those arguments. A fully determinate syntactic analysis is computed for these relations by an economy oriented parser with a preference to build the least complex structure (minimal attachment) and to attach locally (late closure). For non-primary relations (roughly modifiers), only an underspecified representation is constructed during the first analysis: the modifier is associated with the most recent thematic processing domain without a commitment to a particular site within that domain (i.e., the extended maximal projection headed by the most recent thematic licenser). The final attachment of the modifier is determined by syntactic, semantic, prosodic, and pragmatic strategies. For relative clauses as in (4), the head of the complex NP is the most recent thematic licenser thus heading the most recent thematic processing domain. Within this domain, which includes both attachment sites, Gricean principles may, among others, affect attachment decisions. The high attachment preference found in many languages is assumed to be due to a preference to attach modifiers to main discourse referents following the principle of relevance. In English, this principle may be counteracted by the principle of clarity of expression: attachment to the head of the complex NP could in many cases be unambiguously expressed by a Saxon genitive ("the colonel´s daughter"). Therefore it might be assumed that the speaker or writer would have used this unambiguous construction if attachment to N1 had been intended. Note, that the preferences which were attributed to *late closure* in Garden-Path Theory (Frazier, 1987a,b) can still be derived from its successor Construal: the attachment ambiguities in (5b,c) involve primary relations, therefore late closure applies as before. In (5a) the adverb yesterday is associated to the most recent thematic processing domain which is headed by the verb of the sentential complement ("will arrive").

Competing principles

Whereas Construal restricts the influence of non-syntactic principles to a particular type of syntactic relation, Gibson et al. (1996a) present two competing strategies which operate in parallel: a preference to attach to recent heads (recency) and a preference to attach to heads close to the main predicate of the sentence (predicate proximity). The recency preference is assumed to be based on the general architecture of the human sentence processor and therefore its strength is presumably rather similar in different languages (modulo individual working memory differences). However, predicate proximity, i.e., the preference to attach a phrase close to the main predicate, may be stronger in languages where the distance between a predicate and its arguments may be rather large. This is surely the case in languages which allow scrambling such as German or Spanish. Hence, language specific differences may be explainable by differences in the strength of the principle of predicate proximity.

Relative pronoun resolution

In Hemforth et al. (in press), we present an account for relative clause attachment based on the fact that relative clauses in German and many other languages are headed by a relative pronoun. Binding this relative pronoun to its antecedent is an anaphoric process. Thus, finding the entity to be modified by a relative clause is not only a question of syntactic attachment but also one of anaphor resolution. What preferences do we expect and find for anaphoric pronouns in comparable constructions? Anaphors tend to go for salient, focused, main discourse entities (Sanford & Garrod; 1981; Garrod & Sanford, 1985) and not for modifiers. Accordingly, preferences found for relative clause attachment and anaphoric binding in constructions like (6a,b) go along the same lines for most languages (with the exception of English): a strong high attachment/binding preference can be established in both cases (Hemforth et al., in press).

(6)   a.   Jemand sah den Studenten des Professors, der im Labor war.

              Someone saw the student of the professor who was in the lab.

      b.   Jemand sah den Studenten des Professors, als er im Labor war.
              Someone saw the student of the professor when he was in the lab.

If ambiguity resolution involving relative clauses is determined by a combination of syntactic and anaphoric processes, this can explain why these constructions do not behave the way a purely syntax based mechanism would predict. Consequently, we propose a modular approach where each module works according to its own set of principles. Whichever module provides the first solution for an attachment or binding, respectively, determines the initial preference. Syntactic attachment is supposed to be recency-based (with certain exceptions, see Konieczny, Hemforth, Scheepers, & Strube, 1997). If, however, pronoun resolution is involved in disambiguation, a discourse-based preference for salient referents may be available as the first solution.

But why do we find language specific differences? The use of an overt relative pronoun in a language may influence the degree to which anaphoric processes determine the attachment preference. In English, relative pronouns may be omitted, resulting in constructions like (7a,b).

(7)   a.   the director of the movie (who was) accused of murder

        b.   the wife of the major (who was) wearing pink lipstick

The reduced reliability of anaphoric information in English may increase the role of syntactic attachment processes, thus leading to a low attachment preference even in cases where a pronoun is available.

Tuning

The theories discussed so far share the idea that the human sentence processor generally works according to a set of principles which are in some ways parameterized due to peculiarities found in individual languages. Mitchell, Cuetos, & Zagar (1990) pointed out that this approach may be the wrong way to go. It may be the case that principles such as *minimal attachment* and *late closure* or *recency* and *predicate proximity* are simply not valid as descriptions of how the human sentence processor generally works. Universality may not be based on such principles but on the way the human sentence processor learns from its individual experience with a particular language, how it generalizes from the input, and how it processes new input based on its experience. First corpus counts in English, Spanish, and French seemed to confirm this view. Whereas NP1-attachment in constructions like (4) was predominant in French and Spanish, more NP2-attachments were found in English corpora.

AN INTERMEDIATE EMPIRICAL EVALUATION

Before we extend the ideas presented to three-site ambiguities, we would like to evaluate the approaches discussed so far based on data from various experiments on relative clause attachment preferences in two-site ambiguities.

Different kinds of modifiers

In a series of experiments (Hemforth et al., 1994, in press), we tried to find out whether the attachment preferences found for relative clauses extend to modifiers in general. Therefore, we compared structurally and pragmatically similar relative clauses and prepositional phrases (8a,b).

(8)   a.   die Tochter der Lehrerin, die aus Deutschland kam,
                 the daughter of the teacher who was from Germany

        b.   die Tochter der Lehrerin aus Deutschland
                 the daughter of the teacher from Germany

An interaction between modifier type and attachment preference was established in on-line and off-line experiments in reading as well as listening. Whereas relative clauses were preferentially attached high, prepositional phrases showed a preference for low attachment. This modifier dependent preference shift was also found for English by Traxler, Pickering, & Clifton (1996). Prepositional phrases appear to be preferentially attached to the most recent head in English as well as in German (and as informants tell us, presumably also in Spanish, Italian, and French).

How can the different approaches cope with these results? A statistical account might be able to explain the preference patterns if compatible corpus counts at the correct grain size can be established. However, we are currently not aware of appropriate corpus counts.

The competitive strategies of predicate proximity and recency (Gibson et al., 1996a,b) do not differentiate between different kinds of phrases. They do not only apply to modifier attachment but to all kinds of attachment processes. Therefore, no differences between attachment preferences are predicted for relative clauses and PPs.

At least two explanations of the low attachment preference of PPs in a language where relative clauses are preferentially attached high have been presented within the Construal framework. Traxler, Pickering, and Clifton (1996) claim that prepositional phrases might not fall in the class of non-primary relations even if they occur in a syntactic environment where they can only be analyzed as modifiers. They advance the idea of generalized primary relations holding for types of phrases which can be arguments in some syntactic environments. Whereas relative clauses are always modifiers, prepositional phrases can also be verbal arguments, as in (9).

(9)   John put the book [PP on the shelf].

For such generalized primary relations, a fully determinate syntactic structure is assumed to be constructed, following the principles of *minimal attachment* and *late closure*.

The consequences of the concept of a generalized primary relation remain unclear, however. If a phrase that might be an argument in some constructions is always handled as such even if it is a modifier in the sentence under investigation, the range of constructions Construal applies to is considerably reduced. It might even be argued that relative clauses are obligatory in sentences like (10).

(10)   diejenige Tochter, die in Frankreich lebt
                the one of the daughters who lives in France

A presumably more viable approach can be developed within the Construal framework. prosodic (Schafer et al., 1996) and pragmatic differences between relative clauses and PPs may explain the different preference patterns. A clause boundary precedes a relative clause modifier whereas the PP is only preceded by a phrasal boundary. A full clause can be predicted to need a larger amount of processing and/or memory capacity than a PP. Therefore, it may be assumed that non-central discourse referents (such as modifiers) are deactivated at clause boundaries in order to free processing/memory capacity (Walter & Hemforth, 1997). Consequently, NP1 will be more accessible as an attachment site than NP2. Without this deactivation, more recent discourse referents are more active so that NP2-attachment is preferred after non-clausal phrase boundaries.

The difference between preferences in relative clause attachment and PP attachment is a natural consequence of the distinction between syntactic attachment and pronoun resolution (Hemforth et al., in press). Since PPs are not headed by any kind of pronoun, they are preferentially attached to the most recent head. Contrary to relative clause attachment, this attachment process cannot be outweighed by a preference for salient antecedents in pronoun resolution.

Thematic prepositions

The distribution of preferences across languages, as it was presented before, does not hold for relative clause attachment in general. A preference for NP1-attachment is found for Spanish, French, Italian, and German only if the modifying NP is not thematically licensed by a preposition (Gilboy et al., 1995; De Vincenzi & Job, 1995; Pynte & Frenck-Mestre, 1996; Hemforth et al., in press). This is the case if the modifying PP in English is headed by non-thematic "of" (11a), in Spanish and French by non-thematic "de" (11b), or, in German, if a genitive-marked NP modifies the head noun (11c).

(11) a.   the daughter of the actress

     b.   la fille de l'actrice

     c.   die Tochter der Schauspielerin.

If, however, a modifying PP is headed by a thematically licensing preposition, there is a consistent preference for NP2-attachment in all languages investigated so far.

(12) a.   the daughter with the actress

     b.   la fille avec l'actrice

     c.   die Tochter mit der Schauspielerin

This change in the distribution of preferences is clearly compatible with Construal. A thematically licensing preposition defines the most recent thematic processing domain. Hence, the relative clause is associated to a domain including only the preposition and NP2. NP1-attachment is not even considered during the first analysis.

Gibson et al. (1996a,b) do not discuss thematic prepositions. No reason is given for why the strength of predicate proximity or recency should be influenced by a thematic preposition. In a very recent paper, however, Gibson (1997) presents an account of this phenomenon. The cost of attaching a phrase to a distant head is assumed to increase with the number of intervening discourse entities and presumably also with the number of intervening thematic prepositions. Thus, a thematic preposition makes NP1-attachment harder.

How do thematic prepositions influence the salience of discourse referents? We suggest that it is not the thematic nature of this kind of prepositions that makes the difference but the way they affect the status of the modifier in the discourse representation. German genitive modifiers or "of"-PPs are very often used to identify the referent of the head noun without the modifier itself necessarily being a part of the current scenario. In an expression like "the daughter of the teacher", the daughter surely plays a role in the current scenario whereas this may or may not be the case for the teacher. In general, this is different for thematic prepositions. In an expression like "the girl with the nice dress" or "the door next to the window" the entities referred to by the modifiers are more likely than not part of the current scenario. Sanford and Garrod (1981) showed that being part of the current scenario makes a discourse entity more accessible for a referential expression. Hence, the discourse status of the modifier may change with a thematic preposition so that the advantage of the head noun disappears. We should hasten to add that we do not say that entities referred to by modifiers without thematic prepositions cannot be part of the current scenario or that entities referred to by modifiers with thematic prepositions always are. We only assume that the discourse models presented before are more likely. Analyses of text corpora will have to be carried out to substantiate this claim.

An experience-based approach can only account for the data if separate corpus counts for complex NPs with modifiers headed by thematic and non-thematic prepositions are compatible with the preference distributions. As yet, we are not aware of any hard data with respect to this question.

Intermediate conclusions

From what we have presented so far, we can conclude that any theory of modifier attachment will have to take the following phenomena into account: the language specific preference patterns of relative clause attachment, the modifier specific preference patterns, the anaphoric status of the relative pronoun, and the role of thematic prepositions. Whereas Construal (with some extensions beyond Frazier and Clifton, 1996) and the attachment/binding approach can explain most of the data, Gibson et al.´s (1996a,b) competitive principles fail to explain the modifier specificity of the preferences or the role of thematic prepositions. Whether or not Tuning can account for the data depends on the grain size of the counting procedure. Statistical explanations tend to be less viable in the case of the constructions to be discussed in the following sections: three-site ambiguities where a relative clause (or a conjoined NP in Experiment III) can be attached to either of three noun phrases.

THREE-SITE ATTACHMENTS

In the following sections, we will extend the discussion on relative clause attachment to include a construction that was investigated first by Gibson et al. (1996a).

In sentences like (13, repeated here as 13) the relative clause can be attached to either of the three preceding noun phrases (see Figure 1).

(13)   the lamp near the painting in the house that was damaged in the flood

In several experiments Gibson et al. (1996a) provided evidence for a N3 over N1 over N2 preference in English as well as in Spanish. We will postpone the discussion of how the different accounts explain the N3 over N1 over

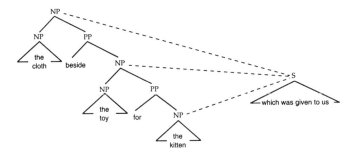

Figure 1: A three-site relative clause attachment

N2 preference for three-site ambiguities to the general discussion. First, we will present evidence from three questionnaire studies investigating three-site ambiguities in German. Experiment I and II were designed to test attachment preferences in relative clause attachment ambiguities like (13). In Experiment II, the three-site attachment ambiguities were additionally examined in a version where the relative clause was separated from the complex NP by extraposition. Moreover, relative clause attachment was compared to pronoun binding in a semantically similar adverbial clause. In Experiment III, we investigated conjoined NPs as in (3) which could be attached to either of three NPs.

Experiment I: Acceptability judgements

In the following experiment we wanted to find out whether the pattern of preferences for 3-site relative clause attachment ambiguities that was established for English and Spanish by Gibson et al. (1996) also holds for German.

In a questionnaire, the acceptability of the sentences (from 1 "not acceptable" to 7 "fully acceptable") had to be rated. Twelve sentences were constructed, each in a version with relative clause modifying NP1 (14a: "die Spieluhr"), NP2 (14b: "dem Ball"), or NP3 (14c: "das Kätzchen"). NP2 was constructed to most plausibly modify NP1, and NP3 to modify NP2. NP1, NP2, and NP3 differed in their respective gender marking. Disambiguation was realized by gender marking on the relative pronoun. Gender marking of the three NP-positions varied between items.[2] We prepared three lists with each list containing an equal number of each of the three experimental conditions but only one version of each sentence. From these three lists six lists were derived using two different randomizations for each one. The experimental items were embedded in a list of 57 fillers of various syntactic structures, partly from unrelated experiments. 12 of the fillers were the materials for

Experiment III. 19 students of the University of Freiburg (all native German speakers) were paid 5 DM for completing the questionnaire.

(14) a. Die Spieluhr neben dem Ball für das Kätzchen, die uns geschenkt wurde, war schnell kaputt.
         The musical clock [fem] next to the ball [masc] for the kitten [neuter] that [fem] was given to us was broken soon.

     b. Die Spieluhr neben dem Ball für das Kätzchen, der uns geschenkt wurde, war schnell kaputt.
         The musical clock [fem] next to the ball [masc] for the kitten [neuter] that [masc] was given to us was broken soon.

     c. Die Spieluhr neben dem Ball für das Kätzchen, das uns geschenkt wurde, war schnell kaputt.
         The musical clock [fem] next to the ball [masc] for the kitten [neuter] that [neuter] was given to us was broken soon.

Results

Table 1 shows the mean acceptability ratings for NP1, NP2, and NP3 attachment.[3] A reliable main effect of attachment site was established ($F1[2, 36]$: 6.23, p <.01; $F2[2, 22]$: 5.47, p <.02). While the acceptability of NP1 and NP3 attachment did not differ reliably (all Fs < 1), NP2 attachment was judged as less acceptable than NP1 attachment ($F1[1, 18]$: 6.62, p <.02; $F2[1, 11]$: 7.88, p <.02) and NP3 attachment ($F1[1, 18]$: 11,97, p < 0.01; $F2[1, 11]$: 9.16; p <.02).

NP1	NP2	NP3
4.79	3.70	4.88

Table 1: Three-site RC-attachment, mean acceptability judgements

Discussion

Although no clear NP3 over NP1 over NP2 preference was found in the acceptability judgements for German, the results are fairly compatible with English and Spanish with respect to the low acceptability of NP2 attachment. No simple algorithm walking up or down the tree within the complex NP can account for this pattern. However, if we assume competing strategies which either go for the most recent or the most salient referent, the data can be explained. The lack of a difference between NP3 and NP1 attachment may either be due to a stronger preference for salient referents in German as it is assumed for two-site ambiguities, or to the sensitivity of the experiment. The materials in the questionnaire included many rather complex constructions like the ones in this experiment and in Experiment III, as well as rather complex word order ambiguities. This may have reduced the sensitivity to only rather slight differences in acceptability. In the following experiment, we looked at three-site attachments with a different technique.

Experiment II: Anaphor resolution and relative clause attachment

In this questionnaire, the potential attachment sites did not differ in number and gender marking so that they were fully ambiguous (15, 16). Subjects were not only presented with a three-site NP with an adjacent relative clause (15a) but also with sentences containing an adverbial clause with a pronoun that could take either of the three NPs as its antecedent (15b). These two types of constructions were also presented in a version with the main verb intervening between the three-site NP and the relative clause (16a) or adverbial clause (16b) respectively. The relative clause in these examples is accordingly extraposed.

Sixteen experimental sentences were constructed, each in a version with a relative clause and a version with an adverbial clause either adjacent or non-adjacent to the complex NP. A sentence containing a gap in the subject position was presented after each item (17). Subjects were asked to complete the sentence to indicate their interpretation of the respective preceding item. We prepared four lists with each list containing an equal number of items per condition but only one version of each sentence. Each of these four lists was presented to eight subjects. The experimental items were randomly embedded in a list of 26 fillers of various syntactic structures. 32 students of the University of Freiburg (all native German speakers) were paid 5 DM for completing the questionnaire.

(15) a.   Jemand zerriß das Tuch neben dem Spielzeug für das Kätzchen, das uns geschenkt wurde.

Somebody tore up the cloth$_{[neut]}$ beside the toy$_{[neut]}$ for the kitten$_{[neut]}$ which$_{[neut]}$ was given to us.

b.   Jemand zerriß das Tuch neben dem Spielzeug für das Kätzchen, als es uns geschenkt wurde.

Somebody tore up the cloth$_{[neut]}$ beside the toy$_{[neut]}$ for the kitten$_{[neut]}$ when it$_{[neut]}$ was given to us.

(16) a.   Es war ärgerlich, daß jemand das Tuch neben dem Spielzeug für das Kätzchen zerriß, das uns geschenkt wurde.

Lit.: It was annoying that somebody the cloth$_{[neut]}$ beside the toy$_{[neut]}$ for the kitten$_{[neut]}$ tore up which$_{[neut]}$ was given to us.

It was annoying that somebody tore up the cloth$_{[neut]}$ beside the toy$_{[neut]}$ for the kitten$_{[neut]}$ which$_{[neut]}$ was given to us.

b.   Es war ärgerlich, daß jemand das Tuch neben dem Spielzeug für das Kätzchen zerriß, als es uns geschenkt wurde.

Lit.: It was annoying that somebody the cloth$_{[neut]}$ beside the toy$_{[neut]}$ for the kitten$_{[neut]}$ tore up when it$_{[neut]}$ was given to us.

It was annoying that somebody tore up the cloth$_{[neut]}$ beside the toy$_{[neut]}$ for the kitten$_{[neut]}$ when it$_{[neut]}$ was given to us.

(17)   Das _____ wurde uns geschenkt.

The _____ was given to us.

Results

Tables 2 and 3 show the mean numbers of attachment/binding decisions in percent. We found a three-way interaction of the experimental factors sentence type (relative clause vs. adverbial clause with ambiguous pronoun), position (adjacent vs. extraposed[4]), and attachment/binding site(NP1, NP2, NP3) ($F1[2, 62] = 3.79$, $p <.03$; $F2[2, 30] = 5.49$, $p <.01$). This three-way interaction is due to the fact that a two-way interaction of sentence type and attachment/binding site shows up for relative clauses adjacent to the complex NP and pronoun binding in the corresponding adverbial clauses (see Table 2, $F1[2. 62] = 6.01$, $p <.01$; $F2[2, 30] = 5.52$, $p <.01$) which could not be established for extraposed relative clauses and pronoun binding in the corresponding adverbial clauses (see Table 3, all Fs < 1).

	NP1	NP2	NP3
RC	29.95	16.67	53.39
pronoun	66.41	13.28	20.31

Table 2: Adjacent RCs, mean numbers of attachment/binding decisions

	NP1	NP2	NP3
RC	48.96	12.50	38.54
pronoun	64.58	13.28	22.14

Table 3: Extraposed RCs, mean numbers of attachment/binding decisions

For relative clauses adjacent to the complex NP, NP3 attachment is preferred to NP1 attachment ($F1[1, 31] = 4.24$, p <.05; $F2[1, 15] = 4.30$, p <.06) which in turn is preferred to NP2 attachment ($F1[1, 31] = 7.40$, p <.02; $F2[1, 15] = 3.96$, p <.07), though both only marginally so across items. If however the relative clause is extraposed, NP1 attachment is chosen most often numerically (though not reliably more often compared to NP3 attachment, all F's < 1.5). NP1 attachment and NP3 attachment are both strongly preferred to NP2 attachment (NP1 vs. NP2: $F1[1, 31] = 24.23$, p < 0.001; $F2[1, 15] = 25.63$, p <.001; NP3 vs. NP2: $F1[1, 31] = 19.55$, p < 0.001; $F2[1, 15] = 5.19$, p < 0.05). The pronoun in the adverbial clause is preferentially bound to NP1 irrespective of whether or not the main verb intervenes between the complex NP and the adverbial clause (adjacent, NP1 vs. NP2: $F1[1, 31] = 71.80$, p < 0.001; $F2[1, 15] = 28.27$, p <.001; NP1 vs. NP3: $F1[1, 31] = 30.72$, p < 0.001; $F2[1, 15] = 11.12$, p <.01; extraposed[5], NP1 vs. NP2: $F1[1, 31] = 68.08$, p <.001; $F2[1, 15] = 28.22$, p <.001; NP1 vs. NP3: $F1[1, 31] = 31.59$, p <.001; $F2[1, 15] = 9.28$, p <.01). Although there appears to be a slight advantage for NP3 binding over NP2 binding, this difference was not significant.

Discussion

The preference pattern found for relative clauses adjacent to a complex NP with three potential hosts is fully compatible with the evidence established for English and Spanish. Relative clause attachment in these constructions is obviously not just pronoun binding since the binding preferences for the pronouns in adverbial clauses are clearly different (N3 over N1 over N2 vs. N1 over N3 over/equal to N2). Most interestingly, the preference pattern of extraposed relative clauses differs considerably from adjacent relative clauses, becoming more similar to the pattern of pronoun binding.

Before wrapping all the evidence up in a general discussion of the different theories presented before, we will present evidence from one further construction which is distinct but related to the three-site ambiguities discussed so far.

Experiment III: Conjoined noun phrases

Gibson, Schütze, & Salomon (1996) present results from experiments and corpus counts for a construction that resembles relative clauses in an interesting way. In coordinations like (18) there is also a three-site attachment ambiguity involved when the head of the conjoined NP "and" is reached. It can be attached to the third or lowest NP "the dirty face" (18a), to the second or middle NP "the child" (18b) or to the first or highest NP "the customer" (18c) (see also Figure 2).

(18)   The salesman ignored the customer with the child with the dirty face

   a.   and the wet diaper [low].

   b.   and the one with the wet diaper [middle].

   c.   and the one with the baby with the wet diaper [high].

In their experiments Gibson et al. established a low over high over middle preference as was found for three-site relative clause attachment ambiguities before. In this section, we will present evidence from a questionnaire on comparable constructions in German.

Twelve sentences were constructed for this experiment, each in three versions: one version with a conjoined NP attached to the head of the object NP (NP1, high attachment), a second version with a conjoined NP attached to the modifier of NP1 (NP2, middle attachment), and a third version with a conjoined NP attached to the modifier of NP2 (NP3, low attachment). The materi-

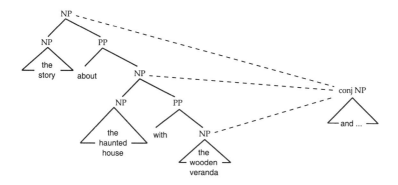

Figure 2: A three-site conjoined-NP attachment

als for this experiment served as fillers for Experiment I (and vice versa). Procedures and subjects were accordingly identical.

(19) a.   *high*
             Das Kindermagazin druckte eine Geschichte über ein Spukhaus mit einer Holzveranda und eine über eine alte Villa mit einem alten Garten, obwohl Weihnachten vor der Tür stand.
             The children´s magazine published a story about a haunted house with a wooden veranda and one about a villa with an old garden, although Christmas was just around the corner.

      b.   *middle*
             Das Kindermagazin druckte eine Geschichte über ein Spukhaus mit einer Holzveranda und eins mit einem alten Garten, obwohl Weihnachten vor der Tür stand.
             The children´s magazine published a story about a haunted house with a wooden veranda and one with an old garden, although Christmas was just around the corner.

      c.   *low*
             Das Kindermagazin druckte eine Geschichte über ein Spukhaus mit einer Holzveranda und einem alten Garten, obwohl Weihnachten vor der Tür stand.
             The children´s magazine published a story about a haunted house with a wooden veranda and an old garden, although Christmas was just around the corner.

Results

Acceptability judgements show a clear penalty for middle attachment of the conjoined NP (see Table 1).

NP1	NP2	NP3
4.79	3.70	4.88

Table 4: Three-site RC-attachment, mean acceptability judgements

The main effect of attachment site turned out significant ($F1[2, 36] = 4.33$, $p < .03$; $F2[2, 22] = 5.47$, $p < .02$). Whereas no reliable difference in acceptability was found for high and low attachment ($F1[1, 18] = 2.43$, ns; $F2[1, 11] = 1.10$, ns), high attachment was reliably judged as more acceptable than middle attachment ($F1[1, 18] = 8.47$, $p < .01$; $F2[1, 11] = 11.49$, $p < .01$). Middle and low attachment did not differ reliably ($F1[1, 18] = 2.15$, ns; $F2[1, 11] = 3.97$, $p < .08$).

Discussion

Although we did not find a low over high attachment preference for the conjoined NPs, attachment to the middle site seems to be the least acceptable choice as is the case for relative clause attachment. Explanations for this general difficulty in accessing the middle NP in three-site constructions will be presented in the general discussion.

General discussion

The N3 over N1 over N2 preference established for adjacent relative clauses in English, Spanish, and German can easily be explained by the competing principles of predicate proximity and recency. N2-attachment is particularly costly because it violates recency as well as predicate proximity. N1-attachment is more costly than N3-attachment because the cost of recency is assumed to increase with the distance from the phrase that has to be attached. Predicate proximity which is assumed to be a step function with some cost attributed to every phrase but the one closest to the main predicate cannot outweigh the increased cost of recency compared to N3.[6] This is obviously not only true for languages like English where predicate proximity is rather weak anyway but also for Spanish and German where predicate proximity is strong enough to yield a N1-attachment preference for two-site ambiguities. For German conjoined NPs, we did not find an N3 over N1 preference as it was established for English in Gibson et al. (1996b). This may be due to a stronger tendency to attach a phrase close to the main predicate.

Since relative clause attachment as well as conjoined NPs are non-primary relations in Construal, the N3-attachment preference found for these ambiguities can be explained if all PPs involve a thematic preposition. Then the only thematic processing domain initially considered is the last PP (in the house). No explicit account is presented, however, for the N1 over N2 preference. However, Gibson et al. (1997) showed that the preference pattern is not restricted to three-site ambiguities with thematic prepositions. They found the same preference pattern for complex NPs like (20).

(20)   the doctor of the daughter of the lawyer who ...

This pattern cannot be explained as straightforwardly as the one in (13). The current thematic processing domain in (20) is defined by the head of NP2 (daughter) which provides the thematic role for the following PP (of the lawyer). Reanalysis processes beyond the current thematic processing domain are assumed to be costly. Therefore it should be particularly difficult to attach the relative clause in (20) to N1 and not to N2.

Gibson et al. (1996a; see also Gibson et al., 1996b) compare the empirical preference patterns with extensive corpus counts on various grain sizes. They did not find any reflection of the N1 over N2 preference in the corpora, neither for relative clauses, nor for conjoined NPs. Whatever grain size they looked at, either N1- and N2-attachment frequencies did not differ, or N2-attachment was even more frequent than N1-attachment. Hence, given the corpus counts presented by Gibson et al. (1996a,b), the preference pattern cannot be predicted by a tuning account.[7]

What about the extraposed cases? Since the verb *zerriß* (tore up) is the most recent theta assigner, the whole sentence (as the extended projection if the VP) is the current thematic processing domain. Since N1 is the highest and most salient entity in this domain, the preference shift to N1 can be explained (Frazier & Clifton, 1997). If the extraposed relative clause is assumed to be attached to VP or IP, the predicate proximity / recency account may also predict a preference for N1, since there should not be any processing cost due to recency for N1. Both approaches, however, do not give an explicit account of why N3-attachment is nearly as frequent as N1-attachment, or why N2-attachment is still the least preferred reading, respectively.

How can we explain the preference patterns by a combination of syntactic and anaphoric processes? To do that, we have to have a closer look at the processes going on in the discourse model. We assume, that a discourse entity is attributed a certain amount of activity when it is first encountered. This activity decays with time (see Figure 3). Main discourse referents (arguments of the main predicate, in particular) are constantly provided with some additional activity because they are needed for major integration processes. Therefore they decay more slowly than other discourse entities.[8] With an activation pattern roughly like that illustrated in Figure 3, we are currently investigating two possible solutions for the distribution of preferences established for two- and three-site ambiguities.

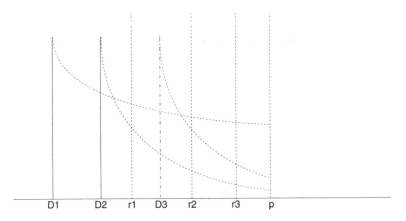

a.   ... die **Ärztin** der **Tochter die** in Frankreich lebte ...

b.   ... die **Ärztin** der **Tochter** der **Lehrerin die** in Frankreich lebte

c.   ... die **Ärztin** der **Tochter** der **Lehrerin** besuchte **die** in Frankreich lebte

d.   ... die **Ärztin** der **Tochter** der **Lehrerin** besuchte seitdem **sie** in Frankreich lebte

Figure 3: Activity of discourse referents

Both solutions rely on the idea that whenever anaphoric processes as well as syntactic attachment processes are involved in ambiguity resolution, each module tries to find a solution following its own set of principles as soon as possible. The initial preference will then be determined by the first available solution.

The success of a recency-based syntactic attachment process can be assumed to be determined by the distance between the phrase that has to be attached and the first potential attachment site. But what about the process of pronoun resolution? The speed of finding an appropriate antecedent for the relative pronoun may be influenced by its relative activation compared to potentially competing entities. In two-site cases (a), the distance in activation between the first discourse referent (D1) and the second (D2) is large enough to put out D1 as the best antecedent when the pronoun (r1) is encountered. In three-site cases like (b), however, D1 and D3 are very similar in their activation when the relative pronoun is read (r2) so that it may take longer to decide between them; therefore a recency-based attachment preference for D3 comes to a solution earlier. D1 is then chosen as the next best solution.

The preference pattern for adjacent relative clauses can also be explained if we assume that the speed of finding an appropriate antecedent for the relative pronoun directly depends on the absolute activation of the most active discourse referent. Since the activation of D1, which is the most active discourse referent in (a) and (b), decreases with time (or better with the number of intervening words, discourse entities etc.) processes take longer in the three-site cases (b) so that a recency-based attachment preference can take over.

Things are somewhat different for extraposed relative clauses. We will not discuss the debate on different potential analyses of extraposition here (but see e.g. Böring & Hartmann, 1995; Haider, 1995; Kayne, 1994; Müller, 1995; Wilder, 1995). However, it may be possible, that no syntactic attachment ambiguity is involved in the case of extraposed relative clauses. It may be the case that whatever the antecedent for the relative pronoun turns out to be in the end, the extraposed relative clause is always adjoined to VP or S (or better: IP). The head of the relative clause (i.e., the noun it modifies) may then be determined by coindexing the relative pronoun with its antecedent. Hence, a viable hypothesis would be that, in the case of extraposed relative clauses, only anaphoric processes are involved. What does the activation pattern in Figure 3 predict in this case? When the relative pronoun of the extraposed relative clause is encountered (example c in Figure 3), D1 is clearly more active than D3 which in turn is clearly more active than D2. A little further downstream, at the position of the pronoun in the adverbial clause, the distance between D1 and D3 is even more marked, and D3 is slightly more active than D2. This ordering of activations matches the preference pattern in Table 3.

What about conjoined NPs? N3-attachment of a conjoined NP should be easiest according to our account because this attachment takes place following a simple recency-based syntactic attachment preference. Since there is no anaphoric process involved in the case of low attachment, no conflict between preferences resulting from different modules can arise at any point. [9] Only in the cases of N1-attachment or N2-attachment discourse processes play a role because of the anaphoric expression "and *one* with ...". N1-attachment is preferred in these cases because D1 is the more active discourse referent.

CONCLUSIONS

In this chapter, we presented four theoretical accounts of modifier attachment: the purely experience-based account of Tuning, Construal theory as an under-specification account, the competing principles of predicate proximity and recency, and the combination of anaphoric binding and syntactic attachment processes. These theoretical approaches were discussed in the light of empir-ical phenomena on two-site attachment ambiguities involving relative clauses and prepositional phrases and on three site attachment ambiguities involving adjacent and extraposed relative clauses as well as conjoined NPs.

	Tuning	Con-strual	Predprox/ Recency	Attach/ Bind
language specific preferences	yes	yes	yes	yes
modifier specific preferences	?	?yes	no	yes
thematic prepositions	?	yes	no	yes
3-sites N3 > N1, N2	yes	?yes	yes	yes
3-sites N1 > N2	no	?	yes	yes
extrap. 3-sites, N1 pref	?	yes	yes	yes
extrap. 3-sites, N3 pref	?	?	?	yes
conjoined NP, N3 > N1, N2	yes	yes	yes	yes
conjoined NP, N1 > N2	no	?	yes	yes

Table 5: Who can explain what?

Table 5 gives an overview of the four approaches as well as the empirical phenomena. As Gibson et al. (1996a,b) have shown, statistical tuning cannot account for the N1 over N2 preference in three-site ambiguities. Construal does not give an explicit explanation for this preference. The N3 preference is only predicted for three-site cases with thematic prepositions. The competing principles of predicate proximity and recency provide no explanation for modifier specific preferences nor for the role of thematic prepositions.

As we have shown in this chapter, most of the phenomena can be explained if we acknowledge that whenever an anaphoric expression is involved in the process of ambiguity resolution, the outcome of the resolution is not only determined by syntactic attachment but also by principles governing pronoun resolution. These discourse based principles may conflict with syntactic attachment preferences. The outcome of the ambiguity resolution determining the initial preference depends on the speed of the respective processes. Whichever process comes to a solution first will provide the initial preference.

NOTES

[1] De Vincenzi & Job (1995) present evidence for an early low attachment preference in Italian that changes to a high attachment preference further downstream.

[2] The materials from all experiments are available from the first author.

[3] Data from all experiments was analyzed using analyses of variance. F1 statistics refer to analyses across subjects, F2 statistics refer to analyses across items.

[4] Of course, the adverbial clause following the verb final subclause is not extraposed. We will use this term, however, for the extraposed relative clause and the corresponding adverbial clause for ease of exposition.

[5] see Footnote 4

[6] See Gibson et al. (1996a) for the detailed functions.

[7] We are aware of the fact that there is a nearly infinite number of ways for counting, and counts always depend on the representativity of the corpus for the phenomena to be looked at. Therefore it is very difficult to exclude a tuning account in general.

[8] This idea is obviously similar to Gibson et al.´s principle of predicate proximity.

[9] We assume that whenever two processing modules provide conflicting solutions, a slight disruption of the process of interpretation may result at some point. This is compatible with Traxler et al.´s (1996) who showed that fully ambiguous two-site relative clause attachment ambiguities are less costly than constructions disambiguated for any of the two possible attachments.

REFERENCES

Brysbaert, M., & Mitchell, D. (1996, June). *Modifier attachment in Dutch: Deciding between garden-path, construal, and statistical tuning accounts of parsing*. Paper presented at the Workshop on Computational Psycholinguistics, Wassenaar, NL.

Brysbaert, M., & Mitchell, D. (1996). Modifier attachment in sentence parsing: evidence from Dutch. *Quarterly Journal of Experimental Psychology, 49A*, 664-695.

Böring, D., & Hartmann, K. (1995). All right! In U. Lutz & J. Pafel (Eds.), *On extraction and extraposition in German* (pp. 179-212). Amsterdam: John Benjamins Publishing Co.

Carreiras, M., & Clifton, Jr., C. (1993). Relative clause interpretation preferences in Spanish and English. *Language and Speech, 36*(4), 353-372.

Cuetos, F., & Mitchell, D. (1988). Cross linguistic differences in parsing: Restrictions on the issue of the late closure strategy in Spanish. *Cognition, 30*, 73-105.

De Vincenzi, M., & Job, R. (1995). An investigation of late closure: The role of syntax, thematic structure and pragmatics in initial and final interpretation. *Journal of Experimental Psychology: Learning, Memory, & Cognition, 21*(5), 1303-1321.

Fodor, J. D., & Frazier, L. (1980). Is the HSPM an ATN? *Cognition, 8*, 417-459.

Frazier, L. (1979). *On comprehending sentences: Syntactic parsing strategies*. Bloomington, IN: IULC.

Frazier, L. (1987). Sentence processing: A tutorial review. In M. Coltheart (Ed.), *The psychology of reading*. (Attention and Performance Vol. 12) (pp. 559-586). Hove/London/Hillsdale: Lawrence Erlbaum.

Frazier, L., & Clifton, C. (1996). *Construal*. Cambridge, MA: MIT Press.

Frazier, L., & Clifton, C. (1997). Construal: Overview, motivation, and some new evidence. *Journal of Psycholinguistic research, 26*(3), 277-296.

Garrod, S., & Sanford, A. J. (1985). On the real-time character of interpretation during reading. *Language and Cognitive Processes, 1*, 43-59.

Gibson, E. (1997). *Syntactic complexity: Locality of syntactic dependencies.* Unpublished manuscript, Massachusetts Institute of Technology.

Gibson, E., Pearlmutter, N., Canseco-Gonzalez, E., & Hickock, G. (1996). Recency preference in the human sentence processing mechanism. *Cognition, 59,* 23-59.

Gibson, E., Schütze, C. T., & Salomon, A. (1996). The relationship between the frequency and the processing complexity of linguistic structure. *Journal of Psycholinguistic Research, 25*(1), 59-92.

Gilboy, E., Sopena, J., Frazier, L., & Clifton, C. (1995). Argument structure and association preferences in Spanish and English complex NPs. *Cognition, 54,* 131-167.

Haider, H. (1995). Downright down to the right. In U. Lutz & J. Pafel (Eds.), *On extraction and extraposition in German* (pp. 245-272). Amsterdam: John Benjamins Publishing Co.

Hemforth, B., Konieczny, L., & Scheepers, C. (1994, October). Probabilistic or universal approaches to sentence processing: How universal is the human language processor? In H. Trost (Ed.), *KONVENS94* (pp. 161-170). Berlin: Springer.

Hemforth, B., Konieczny, L., & Scheepers, C. (in press). Syntactic attachment and anaphor resolution: Two sides of relative clause attachment. In M. Crocker, M. Pickering & C. Clifton, Jr. (Eds.), *Architectures and mechanisms for language processing.* Cambridge: Cambridge University Press.

Kamide, Y., & Mitchell, D. (1996, March). *Relative clause attachment: evidence from Japanese.* Poster presented at the 9th Annual CUNY Conference on Human Sentence Processing, New York.

Kamide, Y., Mitchell, D., & Scheepers, C. (1997, September). *Argument structure requirements and recency preference in the resolution of thematic attachment ambiguities.* Paper presented at the 3rd Conference on Architectures and Mechanisms of Language Processing (AMLaP), Edinburgh.

Kayne, R. (1994). *The antisymmetry of syntax.* Cambridge, MA: MIT Press.

Konieczny, L., Hemforth, B., Scheepers, C., & Strube, G. (1997). The role of lexical heads in parsing: Evidence from German. *Language and Cognitive Processes, 12,* 307-348.

Meng, M. (1997). *Die Verarbeitung von W-Fragen im Deutschen: Präferenzen und Reanalyseeffekte.* Unpublished doctoral dissertation, University of Jena.

Mitchell, D. C. (1996, June). *Empirical facts on human parsing: findings to be explained in viable models of the process.* Talk presented at the Workshop on Computational Psycholinguistics, NIAS, Wassenaar, Holland.

Mitchell, D. C., Cuetos, F., & Zagar, D. (1990). Reading in different languages: Is there a universal mechanism for parsing sentences? In D. Balota, G. B. Flores d'Arcais & K. Rayner (Eds.), *Comprehension processes in reading* (pp. 285-302). Hillsdale. NJ: Erlbaum.

Müller, G. (1995). On extraposition and successive cyclicity. In U. Lutz & J. Pafel (Eds.), *On extraction and extraposition in German* (pp. 213-244). Amsterdam: John Benjamins Publishing Co.

Pynte, J., & Frenck-Mestre, C. (1996, September). *Evidence for early-closure attachments on first-pass reading times in French: A replication.* Poster presented at the 2nd Conference on Architectures and Mechanisms for Language Processing in Turino, Italy.

Sanford, T., & Garrod, S. (1981). *Understanding written language.* Chicester: Wiley.

Schafer, A., Carter, J., Clifton, C., Jr, Frazier, L. (1996). Focus in relative clause construal. *Language and Cognitive Processes, 11,* 135-164.

Traxler, M. J., Pickering, M. J., & Clifton, C. (1996, September). *Architectures and mechanisms that process prepositional phrases and relative clauses.* Paper presented at the AMLaP-96 Conference, Turino, Italy.

Walter, M., & Hemforth, B. (1997, September). *Relative clause attachment and syntactic boundaries.* Paper presented at the 3rd Conference on Architectures and Mechanisms of Language Processing (AMLaP) in Edinburgh.

Wanner, E. (1980). The ATN and the sausage machine: Which one is baloney? *Cognition, 8,* 209-225.

Wilder, C. (1995). Rightward movement as leftward deletion. In U. Lutz & J. Pafel (Eds.), *On extraction and extraposition in German* (pp. 273-310). Amsterdam: John Benjamins Publishing Co.

ON REANALYIS: EVIDENCE FROM GERMAN

Markus Bader
Friedrich-Schiller-Universität Jena

INTRODUCTION

This paper will explore the question of how the phenomenon of variable garden-path strength might be modeled within a serial model of the human parsing mechanism. The basic property of a serial parser (cf. Frazier, 1979; Frazier
& Fodor, 1979) is that it always computes a single, fully specified syntactic
representation. This representation, which is called "current partial phrase
marker" (CPPM), is continuously updated as each word is read. Due to the
existence of local syntactic ambiguities, a serial parser will from time to time
compute syntactic structures that are contradicted by following material. In
such a situation, the original CPPM has to be revised in order to make it compatible with the current input. This paper will explore the question of what
determines whether recovery from a syntactic misanalysis is easy or difficult:
why do some misanalyses lead the parser down the garden-path while others
are easy to recover from?

Based on evidence from German, I will propose that current serial models
should be extended along two lines. The first extension concerns the relation
between syntactic and non-syntactic information sources as determinants of
the ease of reanalysis. In contrast to the common view - both within the framework of serial parsing and within competing frameworks like parallel or minimal commitment parsing (e.g. Gibson, 1991; Pritchett, 1992; Weinberg, 1993;
Fodor & Inoue, 1994; Gorrell, 1995) - that purely syntactic properties can
account for garden-path effects or the lack thereof, I will suggest that reanalysis, i.e. the recovery from a syntactic misanalysis, is a heterogeneous process
that cannot be explained by reference to a single level of linguistic representation. Instead, besides syntactic information, at least lexical-morphological and
prosodic information needs to be taken into account in order to explain the
whole range of garden-path phenomena.

Although it might seem to be more parsimonious to account for all kinds of
garden-path effects in syntactic terms, there is no a priori reason to favor a
homogeneous theory of reanalysis over a heterogeneous one. After all, parsing

187

B. Hemforth and L. Konieczny (eds.), German Sentence Processing, 187-246.
© 2000 Kluwer Academic Publishers. Printed in the Netherlands.

does not proceed in isolation, and the full process of understanding a sentence involves computing structures on various linguistic and non-linguistic levels of representation. Assuming a modular architecture of the human sentence processing mechanism (HSPM), understanding a sentence involves decisions within a range of different modules, and each revision of an initial decision bears the potential to make a sentence hard to process, independent from the module where this decision has been made.

Two modules apart from the parser will be shown to influence the ease with which the HSPM can recover from a misanalysis. Each of these two modules is needed to explain a specific type of ambiguity. The first one is the module responsible for *phonological coding*, i.e. for pairing written language with phonological representations. This module, which is only involved in reading comprehension, takes syntactic input in order to compute the prosodic properties of visually presented sentences. It will be shown in the next section that for certain phrase-structure ambiguities, revising the original CPPM in the case of a misanalysis is very easy, but if in addition to the phrase-structure reanalysis the associated prosodic structure computed via phonological coding has to be revised, a garden-path effect arises.

The second module that will be shown to be a determinant of reanalysis processes is the *lexical module*. Since this module provides the input that is needed by the parser to construct syntactic representations, it can influence the processing of syntactic ambiguities that are caused by lexical ambiguity. In German, a whole class of syntactic ambiguities is caused by the fact that many nouns and determiners are lexically ambiguous with respect to their case. A well-known example for this kind of ambiguity is given in (1). Both the relative pronoun *die* and the NP *das Kind* are case-ambiguous between nominative and accusative case. Therefore, the relative clause of (1) is globally ambiguous between a subject-before-object reading and an object-before-subject reading.

(1)   Das ist die Frau, die$_i$ (t$_i$) das Kind (t$_i$) besucht hat.
        This is the woman who   the child   visited has
        "This is the woman who has visited the child / who the child has visited."

Syntactic ambiguities that involve at least one NP that is locally or globally ambiguous with respect to its syntactic function will be called *syntactic function ambiguities*. The particular example in (1) involves an ambiguous filler-gap dependency because the relative pronoun is associated with a gap either in subject or in object position (cf. section *Linguistic Background* for details). This, however, is not true for every kind of syntactic function ambiguity. Certain syntactic function ambiguities do not involve any kind of ambiguous filler-gap dependency, nor any other kind of phrase-structure ambiguity, but only an ambiguity with respect to the assignment of case features. As will be shown, garden-path effects in sentences exhibiting such ambiguities cannot be explained by reference to syntactic processing alone but find a natural explanation if we take into account that they involve revising lexical decisions as to the case of a case-ambiguous noun.

An examination of different kind of syntactic function ambiguities will lead to the second extension of current serial models of the human parsing mechanism. This extension concerns the particular processes that occur during the processing of garden-path sentences. According to the basic assumption of serial parsing, the parser computes just a single syntactic structure. In the case of a garden-path sentence, this initial structure will lead to a mismatch with the input at some point of processing. It is this mismatch which triggers reanalysis. In serial models, the strength of garden-path effects is usually modelled exclusively in terms of the reanalysis processes that occur after the parser has detected a mismatch. However, the pattern of weak and strong garden-path effects in syntactic function ambiguities cannot be explained solely with reference to ease or difficulty of reanalysis. It is instead necessary to take a further option into account that the parser has after it has detected a mismatch between the initial syntactic structure and the current input, namely the option to judge a garden-path sentence as ungrammatical without an attempt at reanalysis. It will be shown that a serial model extended by this option provides a simple explanation of certain differences with respect to garden-path strength observed for syntactic-function ambiguities.

Explaining certain garden-path effects in non-syntactic terms does not mean that the role of syntactic parsing for human sentence understanding is diminished in any way. Quite to the contrary, the proposed influence of prosodic and lexical information on the ease of reanalysis is only possible due to the intimate connection of these non-syntactic information sources to syntactic representations. Therefore, a prerequisite of the approach pursued in this paper is an appropriate conception of the grammatical knowledge that underlies sentence comprehension. Such a conception is provided by the Principles- and Parameters Theory with its modular organization of the grammar. This theory will be assumed in its most general form, as outlined in Chomsky & Lasnik (1993). More specific grammatical assumptions will be introduced where needed.

Before beginning the discussion, we need to clarify how the term *garden-path* is used in this paper. In the literature, one finds basically two different uses. One position is closely connected to the notion of serial parsing. Faced by a local syntactic ambiguity, a serial parser always adopts a single structure. If this structure is contradicted by later input, a misanalysis has occurred. One way to use the term garden-path is to call every sentence that involves a misanalysis due to a local ambiguity a garden-path sentence. To illustrate by example, consider the well-known local ambiguities given in (2) and (3). (2a) and (3a) show the preferred structures that are easy to process. In (2b), the preferred main clause structure turns out to be false at the main verb *fell*. The reanalysis that becomes necessary at this point is very hard to accomplish. (3b) also involves a revision process, namely after encountering the verb *was*. However, in this case reanalysis is much easier than for (2b). If every sentence involving a misanalysis is called a garden-path sentence, then both (2b) and (3b) are garden-path sentences, and the difference between the two simply reduces to a difference in the ease with which the parser can recover from the misanalysis.

(2)   a.   The horse *raced past the barn* and fell.   (main clause)

        b.   The horse *raced past the barn* fell.   (reduced relative clause)

(3)   a.   Peter knew *the answer* immediately.   (object of main clause)

        b.   Peter knew *the answer* was false. (subject of embedded clause)

According to a second use of the term garden-path, only ambiguous sentences that elicit conscious processing difficulties at the point of disambiguation are called garden-path sentences. Sentence (2b) would be a garden-path sentence under this classification but sentence (3b) would not. This more restricted use of the term garden-path is closely linked to non-serial models of syntactic processing, as witnessed by such theories as Gibson (1991), Weinberg (1993) and Gorrell (1995). These theories see their main task in explaining why certain ambiguities lead to conscious processing difficulties whereas others do not.[1]

I will adopt the first use of the term garden-path in this paper, mainly because this use seems to be most suited to the present approach which is largely based on experimental evidence. The results of our usual experimental methods - like reading time measures or speeded-grammaticality judgments - do not give any direct indication of whether an observed increase in processing load at the point of disambiguation is due to conscious or unconscious reanalysis. Such results only show that certain disambiguations are harder to process than others or comparable non-ambiguous sentences. All ambiguity effects of this kind will be called garden-path effects in this paper. However, the intuition that lies behind the second use of the term garden-path will not be dismissed. If, as seems to be the case, certain garden-path sentences lead to conscious reanalysis processes, whereas others do not, then this is a fact in need of explanation. As will be shown below, the approach to reanalysis developed here can give at least a partial explanation of this fact.

The organization of this paper is as follows. In the next section, certain phrase-structure ambiguities will be discussed which make it necessary to introduce prosodic information as a determinant of the ease of reanalysis. The topic ofthe next section will be syntactic function ambiguities. It will be shown that garden-path effects can be caused by the need to revise lexical decisions. Furthermore, it will be proposed that certain subject-object ambiguities are difficult to reanalyze for purely syntactic reasons. The last section will contain a general discussion.

PHRASE-STRUCTURE AMBIGUITIES AND PROSODIC INFORMATION

This section will present the first case study of how non-syntactic information can influence the ease of reanalysis. It will be proposed that reanalysis is prosodically constrained. Prosodic information will thus play a crucial role in this section. Nonetheless, I will not have much to say about auditory language comprehension. Instead, reading comprehension will be the focus of the following - in accord with most other research on the human parsing mechanism, which either implicitly or explicitly has concentrated on the processing of written language. Prosody can play a role during reading because reading - which means silent reading here and throughout - is regularly accompanied by what is called *phonological coding*, by an inner voice we hear when reading something. Sometimes there are even muscle movements in the speech organs during reading; these are called *subvocalizations*. Phonological coding and subvocalization together make up the more general phenomenon of *inner speech*. Phonological coding seems to be an almost obligatory process during normal silent reading, while subvocalizations are optional (cf. Rayner and Pollatsek (1989), chapter 6). For this reason, I will only speak of phonological coding in the following, leaving open the relation between phonological coding and subvocalizations.[2]

As a result of phonological coding, readers do not only assign syntactic structures to the sentences they read but also prosodic structures. Since the mapping between syntactic and prosodic structure is not a one-to-one mapping (cf. Selkirk, 1984; 1986), the computation of both syntactic and prosodic structures can lead to two situations in case a sentence contains a local syntactic ambiguity: The two alternative syntactic structures are either associated with two different prosodic structures or they are associated with one and the same prosodic structure. In the former case, the prosodic structure will have to be revised if further input contradicts the syntactic structure initially chosen. In the latter case, where both syntactic structures are associated with one and the same prosodic structure, syntactic reanalysis will not require a revision of the prosodic structure. The hypothesis that syntactic reanalysis is prosodically constrained means that every revision of a syntactic structure requiring a revision of the associated prosodic structure leads to severe processing difficulties. Note that this does not entail that all revisions of the CPPM are easy as long as no additional prosodic revisions are involved. This holds only if no additional factors intervene that make reanalysis hard. Two such additional factors will be discussed in section *Syntactic Function Ambiguities* ....

Some Empirical Evidence

This section will discuss a particular ambiguity that is not only found in German but also in English. This is the ambiguity in English sentences like (4) (from Gibson, 1991) and German sentences like (5).

(4)   a.   I gave her earrings on her birthday.   dative

        b.   I gave her earrings to Sally.   possessive

(5)   a.   .. daß man ihr Vertrauen entgegengebracht hat. dative
            ...that one   her confidence shown has
            "... that one showed confidence in her"

        b.   ... daß man ihr Vertrauen mißbraucht hat. possessive
            ... that one   her confidence abused has
            "... that one abused her confidence"

As the English pronoun *her*, the German pronoun *ihr* is lexically ambiguous. It is either a dative pronoun (5a) or a possessive pronoun (5b). In (5), the actual status of *ihr* is determined by the lexical requirements of the respective verbs. The verb *entgegenbringen* in (5a) obligatorily subcategorizes for a dative and an accusative object; *ihr* is accordingly a dative pronoun and *Vertrauen* an accusative object. The verb *mißbrauchen* in (5b) subcategorizes for exactly one object, which has to bear accusative case; therefore, *ihr* must be a possessive pronoun and the whole NP *ihr Vertrauen* an accusative object. None of the four sentences in (4) and (5) causes conscious processing difficulties.

If one passivizes the sentences in (5), one gets the two sentences in (6) which are in the same way ambiguous as the sentences in (5). These sentences demonstrate a further syntactic difference between English and German. Sentence (6a) contains two arguments, the dative pronoun *ihr* and the nominative noun *Vertrauen* (*confidence*), which is the subject of the clause. (6a) shows that subjects may follow objects in German, which is the normal word order in passive clauses (cf. Lenerz, 1977; Höhle, 1982; and section *Linguistic Background*). Sentence (6b) contains just one argument, namely the NP *ihr Vertrauen* (*her confidence*), which is the subject of the clause. As with example (5), both disambiguations of the ambiguous sequence *ihr Vertrauen* are easy to process.

(6) a. ... daß ihr Vertrauen entgegengebracht wurde. dative
... that her confidence shown was
"... that confidence was shown in her."

b. ... daß ihr Vertrauen mißbraucht wurde. possessive
... that her confidence abused was
"... that her confidence was abused."

Intuitively, there is no clear initial preference in favor of one of the two possible structures. In a sentence completion study, sentences like (5) and (6) were presented to subjects with the main verb and the auxiliary deleted. Subjects gave a majority of completions with *ihr* functioning as possessive pronoun. If we make the assumption that results of sentence completion studies reflect on-line parsing preferences, then we must conclude that for sentences like (5) and (6) the possessive structure is the preferred structure.[3] This in turn means that reanalysis becomes necessary if a dative verb disambiguates in favor of the dative structure. As has been said already, this reanalysis is very easy and not consciously perceivable. However, not all sentences containing the *ihr*-ambiguity are easy to process. By simply introducing a focus particle like *nur (only)* or *sogar (even)*, the picture changes. The sentences in (7) are identical to the sentences in (6) besides containing the focus particle *nur* in front of the pronoun *ihr*. There is now a strong preference for analyzing *ihr* as a possessive pronoun modifying the noun *Vertrauen*. Furthermore, if the initially preferred structure has to be reanalyzed because of the lexical requirements of the clause final verb, conscious reanalysis becomes necessary.

(7)   a.   ... daß *nur* ihr Vertrauen entgegengebracht wurde.   dative
                 ... that only her confidence shown was
                 "... that confidence was only shown in her."

       b.   ... daß *nur* ihr Vertrauen mißbraucht wurde.   possessive
                 ... that only her confidence abused was
                 "... that only her confidence was abused."

The sharp contrast between locally ambiguous clauses with and without focus particles has been confirmed in a self-paced reading study. 32 sentences were created, with each sentence appearing in four versions: (i) dative structure without focus particle (6a); (ii) possessive structure without focus particle (6b); (iii) dative structure with focus particle (7a); (iv) possessive structure with focus particle (7b). All sentences were of the form main clause followed by subordinate clause. The crucial ambiguity was always part of the subordinate clause. Half of the subordinate clauses were active clauses (cf. (5)), the other half were passive clauses (cf. (6)). The experimental method was the moving-window condition described in Just, Carpenter & Wolley (1982), which is a word-by-word, non-cumulative, self-paced-reading procedure. 24 subjects participated in this experiment. Reading times for the sentence final auxiliary are shown in Figure 1 (cf. Bader, 1994a, for details).

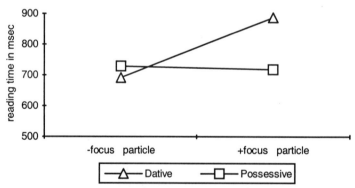

Figure 1: Reading times for sentences like (6) and (7)

As is evident from Figure 1, the introduction of a focus particle had virtually no influence on the processing of sentences where *ihr* functions as possessive pronoun, whereas for sentences with *ihr* as dative pronoun, reading times for sentences with focus particles were much longer than for sentences without focus particles. Furthermore, there is only a very small and non significant reading time difference between possessive sentences without focus particle and dative sentences without focus particle.[4] These results confirm the intuitions described above: for sentences without focus particles, both disambiguations are easy to process. For sentences with focus particles, the possessive structure is easy to process, whereas the dative structure induces a strong garden-path effect.

Focus and Prosody

What might be responsible for these results? Why is there a difference at the point of disambiguation between dative sentences with and without focus particles? If the phonological structure computed via phonological coding is taken into account, this question finds a simple and natural answer. In order to give this answer, some background information on prosody and focus has to be introduced. Let us begin by looking at the grammatical role of focus and focus particles (for comprehensive discussion cf. Selkirk, 1984; Rochemont, 1986; Stechow, 1991). Consider the two utterances in (8), which differ only in their intonational structure (capitals indicate the presence of a pitch accent). In (8a), the word *Mary*, which carries the pitch accent, is said to be focused. Focusing is indicated by the focus feature F subscripted to the focused constituent. In (8b), it is *Peter* which is focused.

(8)   a.   Peter kissed $\{_F \text{MARY}\}$.

       b. $\{_F \text{PETER}\}$ kissed Mary.

These two sentences have the same truth-conditional meaning but they are not equivalent. For example, (8a) could answer the question *Who did Peter kiss?* while (8b) could not. On the other hand,(8b) but not (8a) could answer the question *Who kissed Mary?* The reason for this difference lies in the following condition on question-answer pairs (from Rochemont & Culicover, 1990, p.18).

(9)   In a well-formed wh question/answer sequence, all and only the information requested in the question is focused in the response.

(8a.) cannot only answer the question *Who did Peter kiss?* but also the questions *What did Peter do?* and *What happened?*. According to the constraint in (18), this means that not only *MARY* can be focused in a) but also the VP [*kissed MARY*] or even the entire sentence [*Peter kissed MARY*]. The phenomenon that a given pitch accent can give rise to focused phrases of different sizes is called *focus projection*. Not every pitch accent licenses focus projection. b) is only an appropriate answer to *Who kissed Mary?*. With a pitch accent on the subject no other phrase can be focused than the subject itself[5]. Another case where focus projection is prohibited is exemplified in (10). While focus projection is possible from the head noun (cf. (10a)), a pitch accent on the possessive pronoun only licenses focus on the possessive pronoun (cf. (10b)), while focus on the whole NP is prohibited (cf. (10c)).

(10)   a.   The teacher lost {$_F$ his WALLET}.

       b.   The teacher lost {$_F$ HIS} wallet.

       c   *The teacher lost {$_F$ HIS wallet}

With the help of the notion of focus projection, it is possible to define the notion of an neutral or unmarked stress pattern. Such a definition is given in (11), adopted from Jacobs (1992).

(11)   A stress pattern a of a constituent X is neutral iff X can be a focus under a.

According to this definition, the neutral stress pattern for the NP *his wallet* is *his WALLET*, because accenting the noun allows focus projection up to the whole NP which therefore can be a focus under this stress pattern. The stress pattern *HIS wallet*, in contrast, is not a neutral one because it does not allow focus projection up to the whole NP. Only the stressed possessive pronoun can be a focus but not the NP of which it is a part. For the sentences in (8), the same reasoning shows that the stress pattern in (8a) is neutral whereas the stress pattern in (8b) is not. The notion of neutral stress pattern will become important later when we come to the question of which stress pattern readers assign to sentences they read.

(8) and (10) exemplify what is called *free focus*. A focus is free as long as it is not bound by a focus-sensitive operator. Standard examples of focus-sensitive operators are words like only or even. Consider the sentences in (12), where the respective foci are bound by the focus particle only.

(12)   a.   Peter only kissed {$_F$ MARY}.

       b.   Peter only {$_F$ KISSED} Mary.

Solely due to the different positions of the pitch accents, (12a) and (12b) differ in truth-conditional meaning. Whereas (12a) means that Peter kissed no one else but Mary, (12b) means that Peter did nothing else to Mary than kiss her. There are competing analyses for deriving the meaning contrasts in sentences like (12a) and (12b) which do not need to concern us here (cf. Stechow,

1991; Bayer, 1996). For our purposes, more important than the semantic impact of focus particles is the fact that a focus particle must be associated with a focus and that the structural relation between focus and focus particle underlies certain grammatical restrictions. An example of such a restriction is illustrated in (13) (from Jackendoff, 1972). While the head noun of the second object can associate with *only* when *only* is located in front of the verb (cf. (13a)), this association is barred if *only* is located between the verb and the first object (cf. (13b)). Descriptively stated, the following constraint holds for (13b): the focus associated to *only* must either be the phrase adjacent to only or be contained within this phrase (cf. Bayer, 1996, for a theoretical account). That is, only *his, daughter* or the whole NP *his daughter* are appropriate foci in (13b).

(13)   a.   John only gave his daughter a new {$_F$ BICYCLE}.

       b.   *John gave only his daughter a new {$_F$ BICYCLE}.

Syntactic constraints on the association of focus and focus particle will play an important role in explaining the results of the aforementioned experiment, to which we now return. Consider first the paradigm shown in (14) and (15). For ease of judgment, the ambiguous pronoun *ihr* has been replaced by its respective unambiguous masculine counterparts *ihm* (dative) and *sein* (possessive).

(14)   a.   ... daß sogar {$_F$ IHM} Vertrauen entgegengebracht wurde
            ... that even him confidence shown was
            "that confidence was shown even in HIM"

       b.   ... daß sogar ihm {$_F$ VERTRAUEN} entgegengebracht wurde.
            ... that even him confidence shown was
            "that CONFIDENCE was shown even in him"

(15)   a.   ... daß sogar [$_{NP}$ {$_F$ SEIN} Vertrauen] mißbraucht wurde.
            ... that even his confidence abused was
            "that even HIS confidence abused was"

       b.   ... daß sogar [$_{NP}$ sein {$_F$ VERTRAUEN}] mißbraucht wurde.
            ... that even his confidence abused was
            "that even his CONFIDENCE was abused"

From the four combinations of accent position (either on the pronoun or the following noun) and syntactic structure (either dative or possessive), only three are well-formed. Excluded is the accentuation of the noun if it is preceded by a dative pronoun. This is due to the same adjacency constraint on the association of focus and focus particle that could be seen above in connection with example (13b). As shown in (16) and (17), the pattern in (14) and (15) replicates exactly in English.

(16)   a.   Mary gave even {$_F$ HIM} pictures.

        b.   *Mary gave even him {$_F$ PICTURES}.

(17)   a.   Mary liked even [$_{NP}$ {$_F$ HIS} pictures].

        b.   Mary liked even [$_{NP}$ his {$_F$ PICTURES}].

For the sentences without focus particles, the parallel paradigm is given in (18) and (19). In this case, all combinations of accent positions and syntactic structures are well-formed. The most important difference between the two accent patterns lies in the fact that accenting the pronoun allows only narrow focus on the pronoun itself, while an accent on the noun allows focus projection up to the whole clause.[6] This means that for these sentences, neutral intonation obtains if the noun is accented. As can be easily verified, the same holds for the English sentences in (16) and (17) after deleting the focus particle *even*.

(18)   a.   ... daß {$_F$ IHM} Vertrauen entgegengebracht wurde.

        b.   ... {$_F$ daß ihm VERTRAUEN entgegengebracht wurde}.

(19)   a.   ... daß [$_{NP}$ {$_F$ SEIN} Vertrauen] mißbraucht wurde.

        b.   ... {$_F$ daß [$_{NP}$ sein VERTRAUEN] mißbraucht wurde}.

The Prosodic Constraint on Reanalysis

The next step in accounting for the processing of sentences like (6) and (7) is to ask which stress pattern one assigns to these sentences on first-pass parsing, that is, before the sentences are disambiguated by the clause final verb. Intuitions suggest that one reads the string *ihr Vertrauen* with the accent pattern *ihr VERTRAUEN* rather than the pattern *IHR Vertrauen*. There are two reasons why this should be so. First, for the sentences without focus particles, this is the neutral intonation for the whole sentence, for both possessive and dative sentences. If subjects read sentences presented out of context - out-of-the-blue, so to speak - then it seems reasonable to assume that they read sentences with neutral intonation. After all, neutral intonation is the intonation appropri-

ate for out-of-the-blue utterances (cf. Rochemont, 1986), and there seems to
be no reason why readers should deviate from the only intonation that is
appropriate under the given circumstances. For the sentences with focus particles, the question of neutral intonation must be relativized to the phrase that is
the focus associated to the focus particle. Concentrating for the moment on the
possessive structure, which we assume is assigned on first-pass parsing, the
intonation *ihr VERTRAUEN* is the neutral intonation for this NP. A further
reason for assigning the stress pattern *ihr VERTRAUEN* lies in the fact that *ihr*
is a function word whereas *Vertrauen* is a content word. It is a well-known fact
that function words differ from content words phonologically, especially with
respect to prosodic properties. A basic difference between function and content words is that function words tend to be phonologically reduced in comparison to content words (cf. Selkirk, 1984). In particular, function words are
unstressed as long as there is no special reason to stress them. Content words,
on the other hand, always bear at least word stress. A special reason to stress a
function word is to focus this function word. For the sentences without focus
particles, and for the possessive sentences with focus particles, this reason
does not hold. In sum, the lexical status of *ihr* and *Vertrauen* favors the stress
pattern *ihr VERTRAUEN*.

If sentences like (6) and (7) are read with the noun accented and the pronoun unaccented, this has an important consequence for the parsing of these
sentences. Combining the grammaticality pattern shown in (14), (15), (18)
and (19) with the stress pattern ihr VERTRAUEN gives (20).

(20) a.   ... {$_F$ daß ihr VERTRAUEN entgegengebracht wurde}.
             (cf. (18b))

      b.   ... {$_F$ daß [$_{NP}$ ihr VERTRAUEN] mißbraucht wurde}.
             (cf. (19b))

      c.   *... daß sogar ihr {$_F$ VERTRAUEN} entgegengebracht
             wurde.(cf. (14b))

      d.   ... daß sogar {$_F$ [$_{NP}$ ihr VERTRAUEN]} mißbraucht wurde.
             (cf.(15b))

As can be seen, one of the four sentences in (20) is ungrammatical, namely
the sentence where *ihr* is a dative pronoun preceded by a focus particle. The
syntactic structure of (20c) is exactly the structure that leads to a garden-path
effect at the clause final verb. This seems to be no coincidence but instead
hints at the deeper reason why dative sentences containing a focus particle
lead to garden-path effects: one reads these sentences with the intonation

shown in (20c), which means that one assigns the false prosody - a prosody that makes the sentence ungrammatical at the point of disambiguation. For dative sentences without focus particles, on the other hand, the intonation initially assigned is correct, and no garden-path effect arises.

Let us consider this in more detail, beginning with the reanalysis that will become necessary in clauses without focus particles. Assuming that readers compute the possessive structure on first pass-parsing, reanalysis becomes necessary if the clause ends with a verb obligatorily requiring a dative object. The necessary revision is shown in (21). As indicated, only syntactic brackets have to be revised whereas the prosodic structure can be left intact.

(21)   ... daß man [ihr VERTRAUEN].
                  –> ... daß man [ihr] [VERTRAUEN] entgegengebracht hat.

For the sentences with focus particles, contradicting the initial structure has much more dramatic consequences. The reanalysis that becomes necessary in this case is shown in (22).

(22)   ... daß man sogar [ihr VERTRAUEN] entgegengebracht hat.
                  ->... daß man sogar [IHR] [Vertrauen] entgegengebracht hat.

(22) does not only show a rebracketing of the syntactic structure but also a revision of the initial prosodic structure. Due to the adjacency constraint on the association of focus particle and focus in the construction under consideration, when the NP [*ihr VERTRAUEN*] has to be split up into two separate NPs, the dative pronoun *ihr* has to be focused and accented accordingly. Thus, the syntactic revision from the possessive to the dative structure causes a shift of the focus-related accent from *Vertrauen* to *ihr*. Either the syntactic or the prosodic reanalysis process must be responsible for the fact that sentences of the kind shown in (22) are associated with a noticeable reanalysis effect. Since the syntactic reanalysis in (22) is essentially identical to the one necessary in (21), it cannot be the factor responsible for the garden-path effect. Otherwise, sentences of the type shown in (21) should exhibit the same kind of increased processing load, which they however do not. Therefore, the prosodic reanalysis must be the decisive factor. *The Prosodic Constraint on Reanalysis* (PCR), which is given in (23), captures this influence of prosodic reanalysis on syntactic reanalysis.

(23)   Prosodic Constraint on Reanalysis (PCR)
               Revising a syntactic structure is difficult if it necessitates a
               concomitant reanalysis of the associated prosodic structure.

It was just claimed that the syntactic reanalysis shown in (21) is essentially
identical to the one shown in (22). One might object to this claim by pointing
out that there is a phrase-structural difference between sentences with and
without focus particles. Could this difference be responsible for the results seen
in Figure 1? If we assume that a focus particle and its associated focus phrase
form a single syntactic constituent, then there clearly is a phrase-structural difference between the sentences with and without focus particles. This can be
seen in (24) and (25). With the structures in (24b) and (25b), we follow the proposal of Bayer (1996) that focus particles are syntactic heads without categor-
ical content which project a phrase of the same category as their complement.
As shown in (24) and (25), the introduction of a focus particle changes the
phrase-structural representation of the ambiguous string *ihr Vertrauen* by adding a further layer of bracketing.

(24)   a.   ... [$_{NP}$ ihr] [$_{NP}$ Vertrauen] ...

       b.   ... [$_{NP}$ sogar [$_{NP}$ ihr]] [$_{NP}$ Vertrauen]...

(25)   a.   ... [$_{NP}$ ihr Vertrauen] ...

       b.   ... [$_{NP}$ sogar [$_{NP}$ ihr Vertrauen]] ...

In principle, this additional layer of bracketing could be responsible for the
fact that reanalysis from the possessive to the dative structure is easy in sentences without focus particles but difficult in sentences with focus particles. If
this were so, then sentences that behave syntactically like sentences without focus particles but prosodically like sentences with focus particles, should be
easy to reanalyze, on a par with sentences without focus particles. This prediction can be tested by looking at sentences like (26), which contain a sentence
adverbial instead of a focus particle.

(26)   a.   ... daß tatsächlich ihr Vertrauen entgegengebracht wurde.
               ... that indeed her confidence shown was
               "... that confidence was indeed shown in her."

       b.   ... daß tatsächlich ihr Vertrauen mißbraucht wurde.
               ... that indeed her confidence abused was
               "... that her confidence was indeed abused."

A sentence adverbial and the phrase immediately following it do not form a constituent. This can be demonstrated by looking at root clauses. It is a general feature of German syntax that in a root clause only one constituent can be put in front of the finite verb. This constraint can be used as a test for constituenthood. Applying this test to the string *tatsächlich ihr Vertrauen* in (26b) results in (27). As indicated, (27) is ungrammatical. Therefore, *tatsächlich* and *ihr Vertrauen* cannot form a single phrase.

(27)   *Tatsächlich ihr Vertrauen hatte er mißbraucht.

                indeed her confidence had he abused

Since *tatsächlich* cannot form a constituent with following material, it follows that the phrase-structural representation of the ambiguous sequence *ihr Vertrauen* in (26) is identical to its representation in parallel sentences without a sentence adverbial. However, with respect to possible accent placements, sentences with a sentence adverbial are on a par with sentences containing focus particles. The possessive structure allows both accenting the pronoun and accenting the noun, whereas the dative structure is only compatible with an accent on the adjacent pronoun. This pattern is caused by a constraint on pronoun placement in German according to which unstressed pronouns must directly follow the complementizer or the subject (cf. Lenerz, 1992).

With respect to processing, two predictions are therefore possible. The PCR predicts that sentences with sentence adverbials should behave exactly as parallel sentences with focus particles. In contrast, if not the prosodic structure determines ease of reanalysis for this kind of ambiguity but the syntactic structure, sentences with sentence adverbials should pattern with sentences containing neither sentence adverbials nor focus particles. Intuitively, sentences containing sentence adverbials do not differ from corresponding sentences containing focus particles: there is a clear garden-path effect in clauses disambiguated by a verb requiring a dative object, whereas disambiguation by a verb not requiring a dative object is as easy as in comparable clauses without sentence adverbials. This intuition, which has been confirmed in a further selfpaced reading study (cf. Bader, to appear), strongly favors the PCR over any syntax-based account.

Consequences of the PCR

If the PCR as formulated above is basically correct, we should expect that it does not only apply to the examples already discussed but also to a much wider range of examples. In particular, we should find evidence for the PCR in all ambiguous constructions for which the alternative readings are associated with different prosodic structures. Furthermore, the severity of a given garden-path effect should vary with the amount of prosodic restructuring needed on reanalysis. Although one cannot say at the moment whether these predictions are fulfilled in general, a cursory glance at some further ambiguities of German confirms the role of the PCR for processes of reanalysis.

The example in (28), which is a real-life example, shows that prosodic misanalysis is not dependent on syntactic ambiguity. [7] The pun of this example can only be grasped if the determiner *einen (a/one)* within the NP e*inen reichen Onkel (a/one rich uncle)* is stressed and thereby focused. The result of stressing *einen* is that it is no longer understood as an indefinite determiner, but as a number word. In English, there would be no ambiguity, because focused *einen* corresponds to *one*, whereas unfocused *einen* corresponds to *a*.

(28)   "Gab es bei Ihnen auch so viele Schwierigkeiten bei der Namenswahl für ihren Jüngsten?" fragt Muckelmann seinen Nachbarn.
            "Did you have as many difficulties in finding a name for your newborn as we did?", Muckelmann asks his neighbor

            "Nein, wir haben nur einen reichen Onkel!"
            No we have only a/one rich uncle
            "No, we have only a/one rich uncle"

It was said above that function words are unstressed by default. Determiners are prime examples of function words. Accordingly, the preferred reading on initial encountering of *einen* has this word unstressed. Since the mini-discourse in (28) makes no sense with *einen* unstressed, one first gets the impression that something went wrong with this joke. Only after reanalysis, i.e. after stressing *einen*, does one grasp the intended meaning of (28). (28) has not yet been tested experimentally. However, several informants have been gardenpathed by this sentence, confirming the intuitive difficulty.

The next example shows an interaction of lexical-syntactic ambiguity and prosodic ambiguity. In (29a), the word *mehr* functions as a negative polarity item and the subordinate clause *als Maria anrief* is simply a temporal specification of the matrix clause. In (29b), on the other hand, mehr is a comparative operator and the subordinate clause *als Maria erlaubte* is a comparative clause.

(29)   a.   ... daß Fritz nicht mehr gegessen hat, als Maria anrief.
                  ... that Fritz not   more eaten has when/than Maria called
                  "... that Fritz was not eating any more when Mary called"

        b.   ... daß Fritz nicht MEHR gegessen hat, als Maria erlaubte.
                  ... that Fritz not more eaten has when/then Maria allowed
                  "... that Fritz did not eat more than Maria allowed"

The ambiguity of the word *mehr* is correlated with a prosodic difference in (29): In (29b), *mehr* must be stressed, whereas it must be unstressed in (29a), where it indeed may be phonologically reduced. The preferred reading for the *daß*-clause in (29) is with *mehr* unstressed, i.e. (29a). This leads to an intuitively perceivable difficulty in (29b) at the sentence final verb *erlaubte* because this verb makes no sense when completing the sentence under the intonation appropriate for (29a). These intuitions concerning sentences like (29a) and (29b) were confirmed in an experiment using the method of speeded grammaticality judgments (cf. Bader, 1996a, for details).

If the PCR applies to phrase-structure ambiguities in German, it should also apply to phrase-structure ambiguities in other languages. For English, it is easy to find examples that can be explained by recourse to the PCR. Consider again sentence pair (4), here repeated as (30), and the closely related ambiguity in (31). In contrast to (30), where both disambiguations are reported to be easy to process, sentence (31b) belongs to the class of garden-path sentences that cause conscious garden-path effects. This difference follows immediately from the PCR if the prosodic phrasing of the sentences in (30) and (31) is taken into account. How these sentences are divided up into intonational phrases (abbreviated as I) has already been indicated in (30) and (31) (cf. Nespor & Vogel 1986).

(30)   a.   [$_{IP}$ He gave her earrings on her birthday $_{IP}$]

        b.   [$_{IP}$ He gave her earrings to Sally $_{IP}$]

(31)   a.   [$_{IP}$ Without her contributions $_{IP}$] [$_{IP}$ the funds would be inadequate $_{IP}$]

        b.   [$_{IP}$ Without her $_{IP}$] [$_{IP}$ contributions would be inadequate $_{IP}$]

The sentences in (30) do not differ prosodically. For these sentences, the same holds as does for their German counterparts, as explained above. The sentences in (31) differ from each other with respect to prosodic phrasing. In both cases, the preposed PP forms an intonational phrase of its own. Since the preposed PP ends after *contributions* in (31a), but after *her* in (31b), a prosodic difference follows. The preferred syntactic structure for these sentences is the one with *contributions* as complement to the preposition *without*. If this structure has to be reanalyzed, the associated prosodic structure needs to be revised too. As predicted by the PCR, the reanalysis necessary in (31b) leads to a conscious garden-path effect.

Before leaving the topic of how prosody can influence the reading of syntactically ambiguous sentences, I will come back to a point already alluded to in the introduction, namely that some theories of syntactic ambiguity resolution see their main task in explaining which local syntactic ambiguities cause conscious garden-path effects and which do not. The formulation of the PCR in (23) only says that the need to revise a prosodic structure computed on first-pass parsing is difficult. Should this rather cautious statement be strengthened to the stronger claim (32)?

(32)   If a reanalysis involves a prosodic revision, then it will be
           perceived consciously.

The examples discussed in this section would all be compatible with (32), and there does seem to be a deeper reason why this should be so. What is the phonological code computed during reading, a part of which is the prosodic structure I have talked about in this section? This has been answered by Rayner and Pollatsek (1989, p. 214) in a concise form:

"In essence, we want to suggest that the phonological code that is established for words in silent reading results in your hearing a voice saying the words your eyes are falling upon. This kind of code is identical to the kind of code that occurs when you hear yourself think. This is not to say that all thinking is based upon speech processes; purely visual thinking clearly occurs. But we want to argue that the kind of phonological coding that occurs during thinking and reading are one and the same."

If this is indeed so, (32) follows immediately. If the result of phonological coding is what is consciously perceived during reading, then it must necessarily be the case that any reanalysis that involves the alteration of the initial prosodic structure leads to conscious difficulties. In this sense, an approach to reanalysis based on the interplay of syntax and prosody has a clear advantage over theories based on purely syntactic information. A purely syntactic theory of reanalysis must simply stipulate that certain revisions of the CPPM lead to conscious difficulties whereas others do not. Such a stipulation is superfluous in the theory proposed here.

SYNTACTIC FUNCTION AMBIGUITIES AND LEXICAL AMBIGUITIES

Syntactic function ambiguities (SFAs in the following) were already introduced at the beginning of this paper. They were defined as ambiguities that involve one or more NPs that are ambiguous with respect to their syntactic function. One of the challenges posed by SFAs lies in the fact that they lead to garden-path effects of very different degrees. While this is the same as with genuine phrase-structure ambiguities, the PCR, which was proposed above as a determinant for the ease of phrase-structure reanalysis, cannot be extended to reanalysis processes initiated by SFAs. The reason for this is that the different readings of most SFAs do not differ prosodically. Therefore the PCR simply does not apply. Nevertheless, SFAs support the general hypothesis that garden-path effects cannot be explained in purely syntactic terms. Besides syntactic factors, lexical-morphological factors play an important role in explaining the processing of SFAs: as will be shown below, certain cases of SFAs are hard to process only because decisions with respect to lexical properties of words have to be revised.

Subject-object ambiguities are the best known subtype of SFAs in German. Restricting our attention to embedded verb-final clauses, we can initially distinguish two kinds of subject-object ambiguities. One kind conforms to the scheme in (33). In (33), NP1 has been moved to the specifier of CP, either from in front of or behind of NP2, leaving a trace behind.

(33) $[_{CP}$ NP1j $[_{C'}$ ... (t_j) ... NP2 ... (t_j) ... Verb(s)]]

Since (33) involves an ambiguous A-bar-dependency, it is a subcase of a filler-gap ambiguity. NP1 in (33) can either be a relative pronoun (cf. (34a)) or a wh-phrase (cf. (34b)).[8]

(34)   a.   Das ist die Frau, die die Mädchen gesehen hat/haben.
            This is the woman who the girls seen has/have
            "This is the woman who has seen the girls/who the girls have seen"

       b.   Peter wollte wissen, welche Frau die Mädchen gesehen hat/haben.
            Peter wanted know which woman the girls seen has/have
            "Peter wanted to know which woman has seen the girls/which woman the girls have seen."

A second kind of subject-object ambiguity is found in embedded verb-end clauses that are introduced by a complementizer. The general scheme of this kind of subject-object ambiguity is illustrated in (35).

(35) $[_{CP} [_{C'}$ daß ...NP1 ... NP2 ... Verb(s)$)]]$

Clauses instantiating scheme (35) are often syntactically ambiguous between a subject-object and an object-subject reading, due to two properties of German syntax: many NPs are morphologically ambiguous with respect to their case, and German is a language with a relatively free constituent-order. Two examples illustrating (35) are given in (36) and (37).

(36)   a.   Jemand hat behauptet, daß Uli selten eine Postkarte geschickt hat.
            Someone has claimed that Uli seldom a postcard sent has
            "Someone claimed that Uli seldom sent a postcard"

       b.   Jemand   hat   behauptet, daß Uli selten eine Postkarte geschickt wurde.
            Someone has claimed that Uli seldom a postcard sent was
            "Someone claimed that a postcard was seldom sent to Uli"

(37)   a.   Anke$_i$ hat behauptet, daß sie$_i$ gestern die Eltern angerufen hat.
            Anke has claimed that she yesterday the parents called has
            "Anke claimed that she has called the parents yesterday"

       b.   Anke$_i$ hat behauptet, daß sie$_i$ gestern die Eltern angerufen haben.
            Anke has claimed that she yesterday the parents called have
            "Anke claimed that the parents have called her yesterday"

The following discussion will concentrate on ambiguities like the ones in (36) and (37), which have received far less attention so far than classical filler-gap ambiguities like those in (34). I will start in the next section with a short outline of the linguistic background which is essential for explaining the processing of SFAs (cf. Bader (1994a,b) and Meng & Bader (1997) for a comprehensive discussion of SFAs).

Linguistic Background

While there is widespread agreement that embedded wh-questions and relative clauses involve the movement of a constituent to the specifier of CP (but see Gorrell, this volume), no agreement has yet been reached with respect to the question of how the kind of word-order variability seen in (36) and (37) should be analyzed syntactically. For the purposes of this paper, I will follow some of the syntactic proposals made by Haider (1993), although much of what is said below will also hold under competing analyses. To begin with, consider sentence pair (38).

(38) a.   ... daß der Lehrer dem Schüler zugehört hat.   SUB < OBJ
             that the teacher the pupil listened has
             "that the teacher listened to the pupil"

      b.   ... daß dem Schüler der Lehrer zugehört hat.   OBJ < SUB
             that the pupil the teacher listened has
             "that the teacher listened to the pupil"

In (38a) the subject precedes the object; in (38b) the subject follows the object. (38a) and (38b) have the same truth-conditional meaning, but they differ with respect to the focus structures one can associate with them. (38a), where the subject precedes the object, allows for a variety of focus structures. With this sentence, one can answer questions like *What happened?, Who listened to the pupil?, Who did the teacher listen to?* or *What did the teacher do?* (38b) with the reversed word order is much more restricted in its possible focus structures. (38b) can only answer the question *Who listened to the pupil?*, i.e., only the phrase *der Lehrer* can be a focus in (38b).[9]

Of the possible orders between arguments, the one that is unrestricted with respect to its potential focus structures is the unmarked order, whereas all other orders are marked orders (cf. Höhle, 1982). Applying this terminology to the sentences in (38), we can say that (38a) is a sentence with an *unmarked* order whereas (38b) is a sentence with a *marked* order. One way to capture the distinction between unmarked and marked orders syntactically is by assuming that the unmarked order is base generated and that all marked orders are derived from the unmarked one by application of the rule Move α (This instance of Move α, which rearranges the arguments within a clause, is also known as scrambling, a term already introduced by Ross (1967)).

Whether a given order between arguments is unmarked depends on verb-specific information. For the majority of verbs, the subject precedes the object(s) in the base order. The verb *zuhören* belongs to this class of verbs. However, for a subset of verbs the order object before subject is the base order. In this class we find ergative verbs and certain psych-verbs (cf. Scheepers, this volume, for a different kind of psych-verbs). The verb *einfallen* is an example. For this verb, the order "subject before object" is marked (cf. (39a)) and the order "object before subject" unmarked (cf. (39b)). This means for example that sentence (39b) can answer the question *What happened?* but not sentence (39a), although this difference is not as clear-cut as for the sentences in (38).

(39) a. ... daß die Lösung dem Schüler eingefallen ist. SUB < OBJ
          ... that the solution the pupil occurred is
          "that the solution occurred to the pupil"

      b. ... daß dem Schüler die Lösung eingefallen ist. OBJ < SUB
          ... that the pupil the solution occurred is
          "that the solution occurred to the pupil"

The difference between the two verbs zuhören and einfallen with respect to their base orders must be somehow encoded in their lexical entries. Following Haider (1993), we can assume that the arguments in the lexical entry of a verb are ordered and that the base order directly reflects the order within the lexical entry. All serializations deviating from the order specified within the lexical entry are accordingly derived by an application of Move α (For the two verbs zuhören and einfallen, the lexical entries would contain the information shown in (40a) and (40b), respectively.

(40) a. *zuhören*: <Agent$_{Nominative}$, Theme$_{Dative}$>

      b. *einfallen* <Experiencer$_{Dative,}$ Theme$_{Nominative}$>

The hypothesis that sentence (39b) with its order "object before subject" is a base-order, derived without movement, has an important consequence. If the subject is located between an object and the verb, then the subject must be contained within VP, at least under the standard assumption that objects are dominated by VP. It had already been proposed in den Besten (1985) that the (surface-) subject of certain verbs can stay inside VP in German (and also Dutch), in contrast to English, where a surface subject is always located in the specifier position of IP. In terms of the VP-internal subject hypothesis (cf. Fukui, 1986; Kitagawa, 1986; Koopman & Sportiche, 1991), one way to capture this difference between German and English would be to say that the subject obligatorily moves to the specificier of IP in English whereas in German it may, but need not move.[10] However, there are reasons to take a further step and to assume a much more basic difference between English and German, namely that English has an IP projection whereas German does not (cf. Haider, 1993). Adopting this assumption, it follows that arguments are always contained within VP in German. The sentences in (38) will therefore receive the phrase-structure trees shown in (41)

(41) .

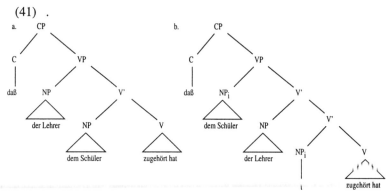

(41a) shows the representation of a sentence with unmarked word order. Both subject and object are in base-generated positions. In order to get the reverse order, with the object preceding the subject, the object must be moved to a position in front of the subject. The resulting phrase marker is (41b), where the object is in a derived position and a trace coindexed with the object is in the base-position of the object. For sentences like (39), which have the order "object before subject" as unmarked, the converse holds. Wording apart, the phrase-marker of sentence (39b), where the object precedes the subject, looks like (41a), and the phrase-marker of sentence (39a), where the object follows the subject, like (41b).

Taken together, the sentences in (38) and (39) show that there are two sources for the relatively free word-order found in German. Firstly, depending on the verb, the subject is either base-generated in front of or behind the object(s). Secondly, the order of subject and object can be rearranged via movement (scrambling). According to these two sources of word-order variability, we can classify syntactic function ambiguities as to whether they contain an ambiguous filler-gap dependency or not. The topic of the next section will be syntactic function ambiguities that involve only base-generated argument orders. Afterwards, sentences with filler-gap dependencies will be discussed.

Subject-Object Ambiguities Involving Base Orders

Consider again the sentences in (36), repeated here as (42). In a pilot sentence-completion study, where subjects had to supply the auxiliary in clause-final position, a strong preference for the order subject before object was found.

(42) a. Jemand hat behauptet, daß Uli selten eine Postkarte geschickt hat.
someone has claimed that Uli seldom a postcard sent has
"Someone claimed that Uli seldom sent a postcard"

  b. Jemand hat behauptet, daß Uli selten eine Postkarte geschickt wurde.
someone has claimed that Uli seldom a postcard sent was
"Someone claimed that a postcard was seldom sent to Uli"

If we assume again that results of sentence-completion studies reflect on-line parsing preferences, this means that one computes the order subject before object on first-pass parsing, and accordingly has to reanalyze when encountering a passive auxiliary as in (42b). Intuitively, this reanalysis is very easy to accomplish (experimental evidence confirming this intuitive judgment will be presented shortly). According to the syntactic assumptions introduced in the preceding section, this comes as no surprise. Above, it was argued that a certain subclass of verbs - in particular ergative verbs - exhibits the order object before subject as base-order. This holds generally in passive clauses derived from ditransitive verbs. A ditransitive verb like *schicken* has three thematic roles, namely agent, benefactive and theme, which are associated with the cases nominative, dative and accusative, respectively. (43) shows the base order of the thematic roles and cases.

(43)   *daß* Agent$_{Nominative}$ Benefactive$_{Dative}$ Theme$_{Accusative}$
     geschickt hat

(44)   *daß*   Benefactive$_{Dative}$ Theme$_{Nominative}$
     geschickt wurde

If a verb like schicken is passivized, both its theta-grid and the associated case features change: the agent role is suppressed and the accusative case deleted. The base order of the remaining arguments is shown in (44). As one can see, the theme still follows the benefactive. Case order, however, has changed to dative case in front of nominative case. This has two reasons: firstly, the former accusative object is now the subject while the dative object remains unchanged. In other words, the theme, which bears accusative case in active clauses, is marked as nominative in passive clauses whereas the benefactive is dative marked in both active and passive clauses. Secondly, in German the subject of a passive clause can remain in its base position. This is the same as with ergative verbs.

Together with the syntactic assumptions introduced in the last section, the two sentences in (42) will therefore receive identical phrase-markers, as shown in (45).

(45)   [$_{CP}$ daß [$_{VP}$ Uli [$_{V'}$ selten [$_{V'}$ eine Postkarte [$_V$ geschickt hat/wurde]]]]]

The assumption that the two embedded clauses in (42) do share the phrase-marker indicated in (45) predicts without further assumptions the fact that both (42a) and (42b) are easy to process. This is a welcome result, but it leaves us without an explanation for the preference for the subject-object order that was found in the sentence completion study mentioned above. Before proposing a solution to this problem, let me first present some more experimental results. In a speeded grammaticality judgment study, 30 sentences like (42) were compared to their unambiguous counterparts in (46). In contrast to proper names, pronouns show an overt distinction between nominative and dative case. The pronoun *sie* in (46a) is nominative marked whereas the pronoun *ihr* in (46b) is dative marked.[11,12]

(46)   a.   Uli hat behauptet, daß sie selten eine Postkarte geschickt
             hat.
             Uli has claimed that she seldom a postcard sent has
             "Uli claimed that she seldom sent a postcard"

       b.   Uli hat behauptet, daß ihr selten eine Postkarte geschickt
             wurde.
             Uli has claimed that her seldom a postcard sent was
             "Uli claimed that a postcard was seldom sent to her"

In this study, sentences were presented in the center of the screen, one word at a time. Each word appeared for 224 ms plus an additional 14ms for each character of the word. Immediately after the end of each sentence, three question marks appeared on the screen, signaling to subjects that they now had to indicate whether the sentence was grammatical or not. Subjects had to press the left shift-key on a standard computer keyboard for the answer "ungrammatical", and the right shift-key for the answer "grammatical". Both percentages of correct responses and reaction times were analyzed (cf. Bader, 1996c, for details). With respect to the percentages of correct responses, there was essentially no difference between the four sentences in (42) and (46). This confirms the intuitive impression one has when reading these sentences: all are easy to process. However, an interesting difference showed up in the reaction time data. There was no reaction time difference between ambiguous and unambiguous active clauses ((42a) versus (46a)), whereas ambiguous passive clauses needed about 230 ms longer to be judged as grammatical than their unambiguous counterparts ((42b) versus (46b)).

This reaction time difference between ambiguous and unambiguous passive clauses and the lack of such a difference for active clauses leads to two conclusions. First, the order "subject before object" is indeed preferred on first-pass parsing, as already indicated by the sentence completion study mentioned at the beginning of this section. Secondly, if the subject-object order computed on first-pass parsing is contradicted by a passive auxiliary, reanalysis becomes necessary. Since reanalysis needs some extra time, reaction times to ambiguous passive clauses become longer than reaction times to unambiguous passive clauses, which do not trigger any reanalysis processes.

If, as assumed above, sentence (42b) does not differ phrase-structurally from sentence (42a), how can it be explained that sentences of this kind exhibit a subject-before-object preference and that revising the initial subject-before-object reading is associated with increased processing costs? The key to answer these questions must lie in the fact that the ambiguity under consideration involves a case ambiguity. In particular, it involves an ambiguous NP that receives nominative case in the preferred structure but dative case in the reanalyzed structure. I propose that it is this case-ambiguity that is responsible for the slight garden-path effect elicited by (42b). That is, the case-ambiguous NP *Uli* is assigned nominative-case on first-pass parsing. If the case assignment has to be revised on second-pass parsing, a difficulty arises.

This proposal, which ties the garden-path effect of (42b) to a lexical-morphological case ambiguity, is suggested by an investigation of object-object ambiguities. Besides subject-object ambiguities, we also find ambiguities between accusative and dative objects in German. An example for such an ambiguity is given in (47). The verb *besuchen (to visit)* in (47a) assigns accusative case to its object whereas the verb *helfen (to help)* in (47b) assigns dative case. If the object NP contains a determiner, the distinction between accusative and dative case shows up at the determiner: *die Professoren* for accusative case but *den Professoren* for dative case. If the object NP is a bare NP like *Professoren*, there is no overt case distinction, and the fact that Professoren bears accusative case in (47a) and dative case in (47b) can only be determined by reference to the respective verbs.

(47)   a. $[_{CP}$ Peter$_i$ $[_{C'}$ will $[_{VP}$ t$_i$ $[_{VP}$ (die) Professoren besuchen]]]].
                Peter wants the professors visit
                "Peter wants to visit (the) professors"

        b. $[_{CP}$ Peter$_i$ $[_{C'}$ will $[_{VP}$ t$_i$ $[_{VP}$ (den) Professoren helfen]$
                Peter wants the professors help
                "Peter wants to help (the) professors"

Intuitively, both sentences in (47) are easy to process. This can be explained
- analogous to (42) - by assuming that clauses containing an accusative object
do not differ phrase-structurally from sentences containing a dative object. As
already indicated in (47), the object is a sister to the verb in both structures. Despite the lack of phrase-structural differences, under certain conditions ambiguities between direct and indirect objects lead to garden-path effects.
Consider the sentences in (48). In (48a), the NP beginning with the case ambiguous noun *Dirigenten (conductors)* is assigned accusative case by the verb
umjubeln (to cheer) while this same NP receives dative case in (48b) from the
verb *applaudieren (to applaud)*.

(48)   a.   Dirigenten, die ein neues Werk einstudiert haben, kann ein
                Kritiker ruhig umjubeln
                conductors who a new opus rehearsed have can a critic
                safely cheer
                "A critic can safely cheer conductors who have rehearsed a
                new opus"

        b.   Dirigenten, die ein neues Werk einstudiert haben, kann ein
                Kritiker ruhig applaudieren
                conductors who a new opus rehearsed have can a critic
                safely applaud
                "A critic can safely applaud conductors who have rehearsed
                a difficult opus"

In contrast to the two sentences in (47), which are intuitively both easy to
process, only (48a) is easy to process whereas (48b) leads to a garden-path
effect. At the point of disambiguation, i.e. at the clause final verb, one first
gets the impression that this sentence is ungrammatical because of a mismatch
between the case of the object NP and the case assigned by the verb. A certain
amount of reanalysis is needed in order to realize that (48b) is indeed grammatical, and that the initial NP is compatible with dative case.

By comparing (48b) to (49), one can see that the increased processing load
found at the disambiguating verb in (48b) is indeed an ambiguity effect, and not

just a general processing load associated with verbs assigning dative case. In (49), the case ambiguous noun *Dirigenten* has been replaced by the noun *Musikern* which is unambiguously marked for dative case (for accusative case, the correct form would be *Musiker*).

(49)   Musikern, die ein neues Werk einstudiert haben, kann ein
            Kritiker ruhig applaudieren
            musicians who a new opus rehearsed have can a critic
            safely applaud
            "A critic can safely applaud musicians who have rehearsed a
            new opus"

The difficulty associated with (48b) in contrast to (48a) and (49) has been experimentally confirmed in two studies (cf. Bader, Bayer, Hopf & Meng (1996)). The first experiment was a questionnaire study. 90 sentences were constructed, with three versions of each sentence: a dative ambiguous version (cf. (48b)), a dative unambiguous version (cf. (49)), and an accusative ambiguous version (cf. (48a)). Subjects had to judge the sentences, which were presented together with filler items in a sentence booklet, as "natural" or "awkward". Subjects were instructed to base their judgments not on semantic criteria, like real-world plausibility, but on grammatical criteria. Results from this questionnaire study showed a clear ambiguity effect: ambiguous sentences ending in a dative-verb were judged as "awkward" much more often than both unambiguous sentences ending in a dative verb and ambiguous sentences ending in an accusative verb.

In a second study, 60 sentences from the questionnaire study were selected and tested in an Event Related Brain Potentials (ERP) study. In this study, sentences were presented visually on a computer screen. After the presentation of each sentence, a word appeared on the screen and subjects had to indicate whether this word was part of the preceding sentence. ERP data for the disambiguating main verb in clause-final position showed an enhanced N400 for the ambiguous dative sentence compared to unambiguous dative sentences and the ambiguous accusative sentence. The latter two types of sentences did not differ from each other.

Taking the results of the questionnaire and the ERP study together, we may conclude that object-object ambiguities can lead the parser down the garden-path. Note that the sentences in (48) contain a further ambiguity besides the ambiguity between direct and indirect object. The noun *Dirigenten* is not only compatible with accusative and dative case but also with nominative case. Therefore, the NP beginning with *Dirigenten* is a potential subject. That it is not an actual subject in (48) can already be determined at the auxiliary, because it does not agree with the auxiliary in number. Intuitively, and according to the results of the ERP study, this extra ambiguity is not associated with an increased processing load (cf. Bader, Bayer, Hopf & Meng (1996) for further discussion).

Since sentences like (48a) and (48b) do not differ from each other phrase-structurally, they exhibit a pure case ambiguity, and the garden-path effect found for (48b) has to be explained in non phrase-structural terms. The occurrence of a garden-path effect in the absence of a phrase-structural difference between the alternative readings is reminiscent of what was found for subject-object ambiguities of the kind in (42), and the hypothesis I will propose will cover both object-object ambiguities like (48) and subject-object ambiguities like (42). Recapitulating the discussion so far, the following facts have to be explained:

- Before encountering the disambiguating clause-final verb, the NP beginning with *Dirigenten* is assigned accusative case in (48) (probably at the auxiliary, where subject-verb-agreement makes clear that the clause initial NP cannot be the subject).

- At the point of disambiguation, a garden-path effect can be observed for (48b).

- In contrast to sentence (48b), sentence (47b) is easy to process.

- Sentences like (42) show an initial subject-object preference.

- Sentence (42b), which is disambiguated in favor of the initially unpreferred object-subject order, elicits a slight garden-path effect.

The two garden-path sentences (42b) and (48b) have exactly one thing in common. In both sentences, a case-ambiguous NP receives dative case, a case that it does not receive in the corresponding non-garden-path sentence: the NP *Uli* bears dative case in (42b) whereas it bears nominative case in (42a); the NP starting with *Dirigenten* bears dative case in (48b), whereas it bears accusative case in (48a). This suggests that the two garden-path sentences are processed as follows. On first-pass parsing, the ambiguous NPs under consideration are marked for either nominative (42b) or accusative case (48b). After case has been assigned, the information that the morphological forms of the ambiguous nouns are also compatible with another case, namely dative case, gets lost. This information is thus not available at the point where the ambiguity is resolved. If the ambiguity is resolved in such a way that the verb assigns dative case to the ambiguous noun, a case mismatch arises. In order to remove this case mismatch, the lexicon has to be reaccessed in order to confirm whether the ambiguous noun is a legitimate dative form. Reaccessing the lexicon is an extra operation, and it is hypothesized that the garden-path status of (42b) and (48b) is a direct consequence of the need to reaccess the lexicon.

This hypothesis is in line with what is known about the processing of other kinds of lexical ambiguity. For example, for word forms that are ambiguous with respect to their meaning, usually all possible meanings are accessed; the selection of one of the possible meanings occurs only after lexical access has been completed (cf. Swinney, 1979; Rayner & Pollatsek, 1989; Simpson, 1994). If it later turns out that the wrong meaning has been selected, the lexicon must be reaccessed, resulting in an increased processing load. This has been shown for example in a study by Duffy, Morris & Rayner (1988). Sentence (50), which is from this study, contains the lexically ambiguous word *band*. After reading this word, the dominant meaning "music band" is selected. When the disambiguating subordinate clause forces readers to revise their initial selection, processing difficulties show up: reading times for the disambiguating region are longer for ambiguous sentences than for control sentences with *gold* replacing *band*.

> (50)   Of course the band was her favorite because it had such beautiful engraving.

The explanation that was just given for the two garden-path sentences (42b) and (48b) is the second instance of a reanalysis made hard by the need to revise decisions lying outside of the parser proper, namely at the interface of parsing system and lexical system. This explanation finds antecedents in the work of Ford, Bresnan and Kaplan (1982) and Ferreira and Henderson (1991). However, it is not yet complete. First of all, it seems to predict that all sentences containing a case ambiguous NP receiving dative case from a verb in clause-final position are hard to process. However, as shown by (47b), this is not the case. Furthermore, we have not yet explained why the garden-path effect elicited by (48b) is intuitively much more severe than that elicited by (42b). Finally, why does the dative structure lead to problems in (47), and why is the order "subject before object" preferred in the case of (42)? In order to answer these questions, we have to make some specific assumptions about the interplay of lexical and syntactic processing. At the moment, some of these assumptions are quite tentative, mainly due to the novelty of the effects reported here. However, all assumptions can be motivated by general features of the case system of German, and they are supported by what is known about the processing of case ambiguous NPs.

Consider a proper name like *Uli* that is ambiguous between nominative, dative and accusative case. If one hears or reads the word *Uli* in a sentence context, the lexical system must provide the parser with the information that this noun can bear any of the three cases mentioned. How might this information be coded? To answer this question, we have to look at some of the basic facts about case in German. First of all, we have to make a distinction between abstract and morphological case (cf. van Riemsdijk & Williams, 1986). Abstract case refers to the distribution of case features within syntactic representations, whereas morphological case concerns the way syntactic case distinctions are spelled out in the morphological component of a language. For German, one can show with respect both to abstract and to morphological case that nominative and accusative case belong together whereas dative case is distinct.

Beginning with abstract case, nominative and accusative case are what are called *structural cases* whereas dative is a *lexical* case. Structural cases are assigned in certain sentential contexts whereas lexical cases are assigned as a property of certain verbs. An argument that bears structural case A in context A may bear another structural case B in context B. An argument that bears a lexical case will bear this case independent of context. Consider passivization. If one passivizes a verb that assigns accusative case to its object, the subject is suppressed and the accusative object promoted to subject (cf. (51)). This contrasts sharply to what happens with dative case. Dative case is not affected by passivization. If an object bears dative case in a clause with active voice, then it will also bear dative case in the corresponding passive clause (cf. (52)).

(51)   a. Er_{nom} kann ihn_{acc} sehen.
            He can him see
            "He can see him"

       b. Er_{nom} / *Ihn_{acc} kann gesehen werden.
            He /Him can seen be
            "He can be seen"

(52)   a. Er_{nom} kann ihm_{dat} helfen.
            He can him help
            "He can help him"

       b.   *Er_{nom} / Ihm_{dat} kann geholfen werden.
            He/Him can helped be
            "He can be helped"

There are also contexts where an argument that normally bears nominative case is assigned accusative case. One context of this kind is provided by the ACI-construction, as illustrated in (53).

(53) a.   Maria sah, daß er$_{nom}$ kommt.
              Maria saw that he comes
              "Maria saw that he is coming"

      b.   Maria sah ihn$_{acc}$ kommen.
              Maria saw him come
              "Maria saw him coming"

The fact that dative case needs a specific licenser whereas structural case does not, is also supported by the behavior of cognate objects, i.e. objects to such semantically intransitive verbs like *schlafen (to sleep)* or *sterben (to die)*. As can be seen in (54), a cognate object bears accusative case, not dative case.

(54) a.   Fritz schläft [einen gesunden Schlaf]$_{Accusative}$.
              Fritz sleeps a healthy sleep

      b.   Fritz starb [einen grausamen Tod]$_{Accusative}$.
              Fritz died a cruel death

Nominative case and accusative case do not only pattern together in the syntactic component of German, but also in the morphological case system. For nouns, there is only a residual of case inflection. Many nouns are only differentiated between singular and plural. The burden of signaling the case of an NP is therefore left to the determiner. The case paradigm of the definite determiner is shown in Table 1. Note that plural determiners are not differentiated with respect to gender.

| | Singular | | | Plural |
	Masculine	Feminine	Neuter	
Nominative	der	die	das	die
Accusative	den	die	das	die
Dative	dem	der	dem	den
Genitive	des	der	des	der

Table 1: The inflection paradigm for definite articles

As one can see from Table 1, only masculine singular determiners distinguish between nominative and accusative case.[13] For feminine and neuter singular determiners, and for plural determiners in general, the accusative form and the nominative form are identical. Dative case sometimes is identical to genitive case (feminine singular), but it never coincides with either nominative or accusative case. What holds for definite determiners also holds for indefinite determiners (except that there are no plural indefinite determiners), determiner-like elements (e.g., quantifiers), pronouns and wh-words: whereas nominative and accusative case often coincide, dative case is always distinguished from these two cases. As a consequence of this, nominative and accusative NPs are often ambiguous whereas most dative NPs are unambiguously marked as such,[14] and one can state generalization (55) (to be revised below).

(55)   An NP that is not specifically marked for dative case is marked for structural case.
(Dative case needs an unambiguous morphological manifestation)

There are three types of systematic exceptions to (55), i.e. three types of NPs that can be ambiguous between nominative, accusative, and dative case: proper names, bare NPs and wh-phrases of the form *wessen Mutter (whose mother)*.[15] The former two have been shown above to elicit garden-path effects if disambiguated in favor of dative case. An example illustrating the third type is given in (56) which is analogous to (42). It has been shown by Meng (1997) that sentences like (56b), where *wessen Mutter* bears dative case, elicit garden-path effects.

(56) a.   Fritz wollte wissen, wessen Mutter ein Päckchen geschickt hat.
Fritz wanted know whose mother a parcel sent has.
"Fritz wanted to know whose mother had sent a parcel"

b.   Fritz wollte wissen, wessen Mutter ein Päckchen geschickt wurde.
Fritz wanted know whose mother a parcel sent was.
"Fritz wanted to know whose mother a parcel was sent to"

If, as seems to be the case, all three kinds of exceptions to the generalization (55) cause processing problems under certain circumstances, we can replace the structural generalization (55) with the processing generalization (57).

(57)   The assignment of abstract dative case to an NP that is not unambiguously marked for dative case by morphology is easy only within a short time span after that NP has been encountered.

Summarizing what has been said about the case system of German and about its morphological realization, we can now say that dative case must be lexically anchored, whereas structural case need not be. To represent this formally, I will introduce two kinds of case features, case features for abstract case and case features for morphological case. According to the Case Filter of the Principles- and Parameters Theory, every NP must bear an abstract case feature (with the exception of PRO, perhaps). With respect to morphological case features, I will assume the condition stated in (58).

(58)   Every lexical element realizing abstract dative case must bear a morphological case feature for dative case

(58) amounts to the claim that a nominal element is by default compatible with structural case (be it nominative or accusative) whereas it needs to be morphologically marked to realize dative case.[16] Some examples illustrating the assumptions about abstract and morphological case are given in (59), where abstract cases are in small letters and morphological cases in capital letters. Both the determiner and the noun in (59a) are compatible with structural case in general, and therefore these two words are not marked morphologically for any particular case. In (59b), the determiner is unambiguously associated with dative case, and therefore bears a morphological case feature *DATIVE*. The case ambiguous noun *Kind* can also bear dative case, and in (59b) it indeed must, due to the preceding determiner.

(59)

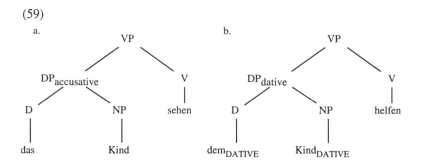

The processing of an ambiguous proper name like *Uli* will now proceed as follows. The lexical system will deliver the information to the parser that this noun is compatible with structural case, and that it can also bear the morphological dative feature. The parser's task is to integrate this information into the CPPM. How this is done depends on whether or not the CPPM uniquely determines a specific abstract case. If, for example, *Uli* is immediately preceded by the unambiguously dative marked determiner *dem*, the parser will compute a structure analogous to the one shown in (59b) for the NP *dem Kind*. If the CPPM does not contain disambiguating information, it must first be determined which abstract case to assign. In accordance with what is known about the processing of SFAs, Bader et al. (1996) have proposed the Case Preference Principles in (60) which determine which case is assigned in situations of ambiguity.

(60)   *Case Preference Principles*

     a.   Prefer structural Case to lexical Case

     b.   Prefer nominative Case to accusative Case.

The Case Preference Principles are what we should expect from a cautious parser that tries to make decisions that presuppose as little as possible. First of all, structural cases are preferred over lexical cases because a lexical case needs a specific verb through which it is licensed, whereas a structural case does not (cf. for example (54)). Secondly, nominative case is preferred over accusative case because the existence of an accusative object syntactically presupposes the existence of a subject but not vice versa.

Taking all assumptions together, the CPPM constructed for the sentences in (42) after processing the two NPs will look like (61a). Note that the representation in (61a) is essentially identical to the CPPM that would be computed for a sentence where the proper name is disambiguated by a determiner (cf. (61b)). This means that the CPPM contains no trace of the fact that the proper name *Uli* might also be a dative NP. From the perspective of the parser, after inserting *Uli* into the CPPM as bearing nominative case, it makes no difference whether this NP would also be morphologically compatible with dative case or not.

(61)

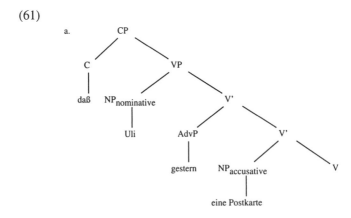

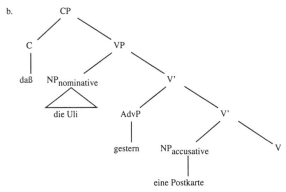

If either of the two structures in (61) is completed with a passivized verb like *geschickt* wurde, the same kind of case mismatch arises. This is as it should be, since from a phenomenological point of view, the garden-path effect elicited by sentence (42b) (or (48b), where it is easier to perceive, is identical to the perception of a truly ungrammatical sentence like (61b) completed by *geschickt wurde*. For (61b), the case mismatch cannot be removed, since completing (61b) with *geschickt wurde* results in a truly ungrammatical sentence. The structure in (61a) can be repaired, since the NP *Uli* is compatible with dative case. In order to do this, it must be checked whether the ambiguous noun can bear morphological dative case. This information was already made available at the point where *Uli* was first encountered. If we make the assumption that only information integrated into the CPPM is stored, the lexicon must be reaccessed to determine whether *Uli* can bear a morphological dative feature. As already pointed out above, there is independent evidence that reaccessing the lexicon is associated with extra processing costs (e.g. Duffy, Morris & Rayner, 1988).

However, it is not necessarily the case that the result of lexical retrieval decays immediately, even if not integrated in some larger structure. Let us therefore assume that the ease of reaccessing the lexicon is a function of the time that has elapsed since the word was first encountered. This last assumption is needed to explain (i) why sentence (47b) seems to be as easy to process as sentence (47a) and (ii) why the garden-path effect elicited by (48b) is stronger than the one elicited by (42b). The answer to the first question is that the ambiguity of (47b) is resolved immediately, at a point where the information that the noun *Professoren* may be the morphological spell-out of dative case might still be available. The greater difficulty of (48b) in comparison to (42b) can be explained by the greater distance between ambiguous noun and disambiguating verb in (48b) in comparison to (42b). Note that under our assumptions about the interplay of morphological and abstract case, it does not matter whether the ambiguous noun is assigned accusative case on initial encountering, or whether nominative case is assigned on first encountering and accusative case only later at the finite verb or the unambiguously nominative marked subject. In neither case will the morphological make-up of the initial noun have to be revised before encountering the clause final main verb.

The account just sketched might seem complicated, and one might wonder whether an easier account is available. An alternative which suggests itself would be an account in terms of thematic roles. Several theories of human syntactic processing rely heavily on thematic roles like agent, theme etc. (cf. Carlson & Tanenhaus, 1988; Trueswell & Tanenhaus, 1994; MacDonald, Pearlmutter & Seidenberg, 1994a,b). In the preceding discussion of the processing of SFAs, I made no appeal to thematic roles but to phrase-structure configurations and the distribution of case-bearing NPs within these configurations. Since thematic roles and cases correspond to a certain extent, one might suspect that it is not case information but thematic information that is decisive for the experimental results described in this section. It has been proposed by Carlson & Tanenhaus (1988) and MacDonald et al. (1994a) that in verb-final clauses thematic roles are tentatively assigned to arguments already before the verb is encountered. For a sentence fragment of the form *daß NP1 NP2* where NP1 is animate and NP2 inanimate, the parser may hypothesize that NP1 is an agent and NP2 a theme. That would be consistent with the fact that ambiguous sentences of this kind are preferentially understood as subject followed by object. The garden-path effect seen in ambiguous passive clauses like (42b) could then be explained by the need to replace the agent role of NP1 by the benefactive role that is assigned to NP1 in a passive clause.

There is direct empirical evidence against thematic roles having an influence on the ease of reanalysis. This evidence comes from a construction called *recipient passive*. This construction is shown in (62c). The sentences (62a) and (62b) are identical to the sentences (42a) and (42b), respectively. In sentence (62c), the perfect auxiliary *hat* of (62a) has been replaced by the quasi-auxiliary *bekam* (got). The meaning of (62c) is identical to the normal passive counterpart of (62a), i.e. (62b): The NP Uli bears the benefactive role and the NP *eine Postkarte* the theme role. With respect to syntactic functions, however, (62c) is identical to (62a). In both sentences, the NP Uli is the subject and the NP *eine Postkarte* the direct object.

(62) a.   Jemand hat behauptet, daß Uli selten eine Postkarte geschickt hat.

  b.   Jemand hat behauptet, daß Uli selten eine Postkarte geschickt wurde.

  c.   Jemand hat behauptet, daß Uli selten eine Postkarte geschickt bekam.
       someone has claimed that Uli seldom a postcard sent got
       "Someone claimed that Uli was seldom sent a postcard"

(63a) - (63c) show the distribution of cases and thematic roles in (62a) - (62c), respectively.

(63) a.   *daß* Agent$_{Nominative}$ Theme$_{Accusative}$ *geschickt hat*

  b.   *daß* Benefactive$_{Dative}$ Theme$_{Nominative}$ *geschickt wurde*

  c.   *daß* Benefactive$_{Nominative}$ Theme$_{Accusative}$ *geschickt bekam*

If case is the main determinant in the resolution of SFAs, then sentences like (62c) should pose no problem for the parser. The preferred analysis for sentences of this type is subject followed by object, and this analysis is confirmed by the quasi-auxiliary *bekam* in the same way as by the perfect participle *hat*. If, however, thematic roles are, completely or partially, responsible for the garden-path effect elicited by passive sentences like (62b), then sentences like (62c) should show at least some sign of a garden-path effect.[17] Intuitively, this is not the case. In a further speeded grammaticality judgment study (cf. Bader, 1996c), sentences like (62c) patterned with unambiguous passive clauses and not with ambiguous passive clauses. Therefore, either thematic roles are not assigned at all before the verb is encountered, or an initial thematic commitment can be withdrawn without any costs. In either case, a reanalysis account in terms of thematic roles would leave the fact unexplained that true passive clauses like (62b) lead to garden-path effects.

In terms of case, this fact is easily explained. I will therefore conclude that case is the decisive factor in explaining the data discussed in this section. To summarize, garden-path effects can be caused by the need to assign dative case to a case-ambiguous NP if the time-span between encountering the ambiguous NP and the point of disambiguation is long enough. The fact that dative case causes problems under certain circumstances can be motivated by the syntactic and morphological case system of German. Whereas nominative and accusative pattern together both syntactically and morphologically, dative case differs from these two cases, again both syntactically and morphologically.

Subject-Object Ambiguities Involving Non-Base Orders

So far, two non-syntactic sources have been identified that can make reanalysis hard: lexical case ambiguity and prosodic structure ambiguity. Does this mean that processes within the parser itself are irrelevant for the explanation of garden-path effects? This does not seem to be the case. Consider (37) again, here repeated as (64).

(64)   a.   Anke$_i$ hat behauptet, daß sie$_i$ gestern die Eltern angerufen hat.

                Anke has claimed that she yesterday the parents called has

                "Anke claimed that she has called the parents yesterday"

       b.   Anke$_i$ hat behauptet, daß sie$_i$ gestern die Eltern   angerufen haben.

                Anke has claimed that she yesterday the parents called have

                "Anke claimed that the parents have called her yesterday"

Whereas (64a) is as easy to process as comparable unambiguous sentences, (64b) induces a very strong garden-path effect at the point of disambiguation as will be shown below. The difficulty of (64b) is exclusively an ambiguity effect and has nothing to do with the order object before subject as such. The two sentences in (65) are the unambiguous counterparts to the ambiguous sentences in (64). In contrast to the feminine pronoun *sie*, the masculine pronouns *er* and *ihn* are unambiguous: *er* is a nominative pronoun and *ihn* an accusative one.

(65)   a.   Fritz$_i$ hat   behauptet, daß er$_i$ gestern die Eltern angerufen
               hat.

               Fritz has   claimed that he   yesterday the parents called
               has
               "Fritz claimed that he has called the parents yesterday"

       b.   Fritz$_i$ hat   behauptet, daß ihn$_i$ gestern die Eltern angerufen
               haben.

               Fritz has   claimed that him yesterday the parents called
               have
               "Fritz claimed that the parents have called him yesterday"

The verb *anrufen* specifies the order "subject before object" as base order.
Therefore, the order "object before subject" must be derived by moving the object in front of the subject. Together with the syntactic assumptions made in
section *Linguistic Background*, this means that the sentences in (64) will receive the syntactic representations shown in (66).

(66)   a.   [$_{CP}$ daß [$_{VP}$ sie$_i$ [$_{V'}$ gestern [$_{V'}$ die Eltern angerufen hat]]]]

       b.   [$_{CP}$ daß [$_{VP}$ sie$_i$ [$_{V'}$ gestern [$_{V'}$ die Eltern [$_{V'}$ t$_i$ angerufen
               haben]]]]]

Despite the superficial similarity between examples like (64) and sentences
like (38), there is an important difference: in (38b) moving the object in front
of the subject had the effect that only the subject could be a focus, but not the
whole sentence. The same is not true for (64b). (64b) allows for both narrow
focus on the subject and wide focus on the whole clause. The crucial difference between (38b) and (64b) is that in the former case a full lexical NP has
been moved, whereas in the latter case a pronoun has been moved. It is a general tendency of German pronouns to be located immediately after the complementizer, in the so-called Wackernagel Position. This holds for both object
and subject pronouns, and has no consequences for the focus structure. Therefore, sentences (64a) and (64b) do not differ with respect to their associated
focus structures. Furthermore, there is also no prosodic difference. In both
(64a) and (64b) neutral sentence stress falls on the NP *die Eltern*. All in all,
there is only one difference between (64a) and (64b), namely the syntactic difference shown in (66).

Given the syntactic structures in (66), the preference for the reading with the
subject preceding the object can be accounted for by assuming the Minimal
Chain Principle of De Vincenzi (1991).

(67)   Minimal Chain Principle (MCP)
                Avoid postulating unnecessary chain members at S-struc-
                ture, but do not delay required chain members.

Since the pronoun *sie* is not an obligatory filler, a parser abiding by the
MCP will hypothesize that *sie* is no filler at all, i.e. that *sie* resides in a base-
generated position. This leads to structure (66a). Therefore, if the sentence
ends in a plural auxiliary, reanalysis becomes necessary, resulting in a garden-
path effect. That this garden-path effect is a strong one is supported by experimental evidence both from self-paced reading studies and studies using the
method of speeded grammaticality judgments. In an experiment using the
speeded grammaticality judgment task described above, in connection with the
examples (36), sentences like (64) and (65) were tested (cf. Bader, 1996b, for
details). The results showed that unambiguous sentences did not differ from
each other. For ambiguous sentences, in contrast, a huge difference showed
up: if an ambiguous sentence was disambiguated in favor of the word order
"object before subject", the percentage of "grammatical" responses dropped
to approximately 30%, whereas the percentage of "grammatical" responses
for ambiguous sentences exhibiting the preferred subject-object order was as
high as for unambiguous grammatical. sentences. Similarly, in those cases
where subjects correctly judged ambiguous object-subject sentences as grammatical, it took them much more time than for all other sentence types. Taken
together, the results of the speeded grammaticality judgments study suggest
that subjects tend to perceive sentences like (64b) as ungrammatical on first-
pass parsing, and that they have great difficulty in revising their initial reading
of these sentences. However, is this conclusion justified, or is it an artifact of
the method used? If subjects have to quickly decide whether a sentence is
grammatical or not, perhaps they adopt a strategy of judging ambiguous sentences that do not confirm the preferred reading as ungrammatical even if they
would not have much difficulty in finding a correct analysis under more normal circumstances. Two reasons speak against such an interpretation. First,
the results of the speeded grammaticality study closely match the results of an
earlier self-paced reading study (Bader, 1994a). Secondly, it is not the case
that the unpreferred reading of a sentence always has a great impact on the
percentages of "grammatical" responses. This could be seen in the preceding
section in connection with the subject-object ambiguity exhibited by sentences like (42). Although these sentences display a clear subject-before-
object preference - as seen by sentence completion data and by the prolonged
time needed to decide that sentences with the unpreferred order are grammati-

cal -, sentences with the unpreferred order were judged as grammatical almost as often as sentences with the preferred order.

As is shown by data from the literature, what holds for filler-gap dependencies involving ambiguous pronouns also holds for other types of filler-gap dependencies, for example for ambiguous relative clauses (cf. (34a)) and ambiguous wh-questions (cf. (34b)) (cf. for example Bader (1990) and Schriefers, Friederici & Kühn (1995) for the former and Schlesewsky, Fanselow, Kliegl & Krems (this volume) and Bader & Meng (to appear) for the latter).

Garden-Path Strength and Syntactic Function Ambiguities

The preceding discussion has shown that both base-generated and filler-gap subject-object ambiguities are characterized by a preference for the subject-object-structure. In contrast to this shared preference, the garden-path effects that are observed when the initial subject-object-structure is contradicted by a clause final auxiliary vary widely in strength. The two relevant object-subject-sentences are repeated in (68), with (68a) exhibiting a base-generated word order and (68b) a derived one.

(68)   a.   Jemand hat behauptet, daß Uli selten eine Postkarte geschickt wurde.

someone has claimed that Uli seldom a postcard sent was
"Someone claimed that a postcard was seldom sent to Uli"

       b.   Anke$_i$ hat behauptet, daß sie$_i$ gestern die Eltern t$_i$ angerufen haben.

Anke has claimed that she yesterday the parents called have
"Anke claimed that the parents have called her yesterday"

Object-subject sentences like (68a) only lead to a weak garden-path effect which is mainly reflected in prolonged reaction times but not in a severe drop in the percentages of correct answers. Object-subject sentences like (68b), in contrast, cause a severe garden-path effect that results both in prolonged reaction times and in a sharp drop in the percentages of correct answers. This difference in garden-path strength is covered neither by the prosodic explanation proposed in *Phrase-Structure Ambiguities* ... nor by the lexical-morphological explanation proposed in section *Subject-Object Ambiguities involving Base Orders* Prosodically, passive sentences like (68a) do not differ from their active counterparts, and object-subject sentences like (68b) do not differ from their subject-object counterparts. Therefore, the PCR does not apply to either of these sentence types. Furthermore, the lexical explanation offered for passive sentences like (68a) is inapplicable to sentences like (68b) because these sentences do not involve dative case but only structural cases. The strong garden-path effect elicited by (68b) seems therefore to be due to the fact that its syntactic representation contains a filler-gap dependency that is overlooked on first-pass parsing. Whereas for sentences like (68a) only lexical revisions are necessary, a specific kind of syntactic revision becomes necessary for sentences like (68b): after processing the disambiguating auxiliary, a chain consisting of the pronoun *sie* and a trace has to be created. Might this additional syntactic reanalysis be responsible for the severity of the garden-path effect elicited by (68b)?

In terms of computational complexity, the creation of a chain does not seem to be very costly. And there is indeed some evidence that the need to create a chain by and of itself does not lead to garden-path effects. Consider the sentences in (69). Due to the determiners, the syntactic functions of the NPs *der Peter* and *der Maria* are not ambiguous. These sentences contain nevertheless a certain ambiguity. The verb *helfen (to help)* has the base order subject-before-object whereas the verb *auffallen (to strike)* has the base order object-before-subject. The NP *der Maria* is accordingly in a base-generated position in (69a) but in a derived position in (69b). According to the Minimal Chain Principle, the parser will hypothesize that both NPs are in base-generated positions and therefore the same kind of syntactic reanalysis will become necessary in (69b) as in (64b). Intuitively, (69b) does not elicit a garden-path effect, and surely not a severe one.

(69) a.   ... daß [der Peter]$_{nom}$ [der Maria]$_{dat}$ geholfen hat.
              ... that the Peter   the Maria   helped   has
              "that Peter helped Maria"

      b.   ... daß [der Peter]$_{nom/i}$ [der Maria]$_{dat}$ t$_i$ aufgefallen ist.
              ... that the Peter   the Maria   struck   is
              "that Maria struck Peter"

This means that the severity of the garden-path effect elicited by (68b) must be the result of the joint effect of morphological ambiguity and filler-gap ambiguity. How can this be the case if, as suggested above, nominative and accusative case are both structural cases and nouns are underspecified with respect to distinctions between structural cases? Consider the specific problem that is encountered with sentence (68b) on first-pass parsing. This problem is the lack of agreement between subject and object. Immediately before encountering the disambiguating auxiliary, the CPPM will look like (70). Into this structure, the singular auxiliary *hat* can be integrated without problems. Integrating the plural auxiliary *haben*, in contrast, leads to a temporary ungrammaticality due to the number mismatch between finite verb and subject.

(70)

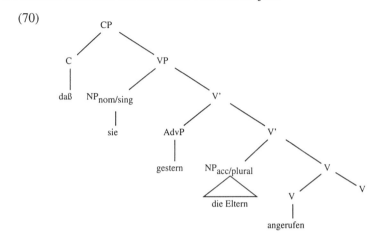

The important point to note with respect to structure (70) is the following. The problem that arises with the plural auxiliary *haben* is not the lack of a phrase-structural position but a problem that arises after having inserted haben into the position appropriate for auxiliaries. To see why this might be important, let us shortly digress to another ambiguity where the same problem arises in a more transparent way. Consider the English garden-path sentence in (71), which is claimed to exhibit a severe garden-path effect (e.g., Fodor & Inoue, 1994).

(71)   They told the boy that the girl met the story.

Under a modular architecture of the human sentence processing mechanism, syntactic parsing precedes semantic interpretation. In particular, the parser will integrate input into the CPPM without considering possible semantic consequences. These are computed shortly thereafter, in the module responsible for semantic interpretation. For the processing of (71), this means the following. At the point where the ambiguity arises, the parser analyzes *that* as beginning a complement clause. When encountering the NP *the story*, the parser attaches this NP into the CPPM as an object to the verb *met*. Syntactically, this is a completely legitimate option. Only later, during semantic interpretation, will it be determined that the story makes no sense as the object of met.

However, this seems to be too late to change anything at the CPPM responsible for the semantic incongruity of (71). Instead, the result of the semantic interpretation is immediately delivered to the central processor, or whatever processes are connected to our conscious perception of language, and one therefore perceives the sentence as nonsensical.[18]

The same reasoning that applies to (71) can be applied to (68b). Only one thing needs to be altered. Whereas for (71) a semantic mismatch arises, for (68b) a mismatch with respect to subject-verb-agreement occurs. Accordingly, the role played by the semantic module for the processing of (71) is played by the processes responsible for feature checking for sentence (68b). Since the checking of features - like case features or the number and person features involved in subject-verb agreement - is dependent on the prior availability of phrase markers, it automatically follows that checking processes lag slightly behind the construction of phrase-structural representations. That is, the auxiliary *haben* is inserted in the CPPM shown in (70). Immediately afterwards, the resulting phrase-marker is evaluated with respect to subject-verb agreement and a temporary ungrammaticality is found. In principle, there are two options at this point. These are shown in (72) (from Meng & Bader, 1996).

(72)

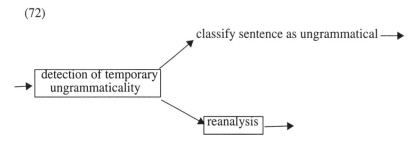

The first option is to reanalyze the CPPM in order to remove the ungrammaticality; this reanalysis might be easy or difficult. The second option is simply to classify the sentence as ungrammatical, without a prior attempt at reanalysis. For (68b), this latter option seems to be taken quite often. As with (71), the information that a mismatch has occurred is not used to initiate a revision process but to inform higher level processes that the current sentence contains a mismatch. In consequence, sentences like (68b) are judged as ungrammatical to a high degree, indicating quite a strong garden-path effect.

Is the account just given for the strong garden-path effect elicited by (68b) compatible with the prior account given for sentence (68a)? On first sight, the answer seems to be no. The CPPM computed for (68a) will also contain a temporary ungrammaticality - namely a mismatch between the case associated to the ambiguous NP *Uli* and the passivized verb *geschickt wurde*. Why does this temporary ungrammaticality only lead to prolonged reaction times in the speeded grammaticality judgment study but not to a reliable drop in the percentage of "grammatical" responses, like the ungrammaticality caused by sentence (68b). Or, put another way, why does the parser correct the temporary ungrammaticality instead of sending an error signal to the central processor for sentence (68a) but not for (68b)?

Meng &Bader (1997) have proposed that the answer to this question lies in the nature of the temporary ungrammaticality. If the temporary ungrammaticality that arises at the point of disambiguation is salient, the option of judging the sentence as ungrammatical will win over the alternative option of removing the ungrammaticality by some reanalysis process. If the temporary ungrammaticality is not salient, in contrast, the reanalysis option will win over the option of judging the sentence as ungrammatical. This particular relationship between garden-path strength and ungrammaticality detection has been termed the Mismatch Effect by Meng &Bader (1997) (cf. (73)).

(73)   *The Mismatch Effect*
            The more salient a temporary ungrammaticality is, the stronger the resulting garden-path effect will be.

The temporary ungrammaticality in sentence (68a) is due to the fact that the initial NP *Uli* is assigned nominative case on first-pass parsing, which is not compatible with the case requirements of the clause final passivized verb. The same kind of mismatch appears in (74a), albeit in a permanent way since the NP *die Frau* in (74a) can definitely not bear dative-case. The temporary ungrammaticality in (68b) is due to the fact the pronoun *sie* is assigned nominative case which leads to a failure of subject-verb agreement when the plural auxiliary *haben* is encountered. This temporary ungrammaticality corresponds to the permanent ungrammaticality in (74b), where the case ambiguous pronoun *sie* has been replaced by the unambiguously nominative-marked pronoun *er*.

(74)   a.   *... daß [die Frau]$_{nom/acc}$ selten   eine Postkarte geschickt wurde.
            that the woman seldom a postcard sent was

       b.   *... daß [er]$_{nom/sing}$ gestern die Eltern angerufen haben$_{plural}$.
            that he yesterday the parents called have

In experiments using the method of speeded grammaticality judgments, we have found that ungrammatical sentences like (74a) are judged as ungrammatical rather poorly, whereas sentences like (74b) are judged as ungrammatical with high reliability. This is shown in Figure 2, where percentages of correct answers for base-generated and filler-gap garden-path sentences together with their unambiguous control sentences are compared to percentages of correct responses for corresponding ungrammatical sentences like (74a) and (74b). It can be seen from Figure 2 that the slight garden-path effect in base-generated ambiguities corresponds to an ungrammaticality that is rather poorly judged whereas the strong garden-path effect in filler-gap sentences corresponds to an ungrammaticality that receives a very high percentage of correct responses.[19]

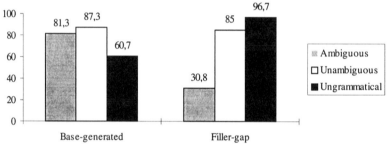

Figure 2: Performance on object-subject sentences for base-generated and filler-gap ambiguities

Assuming that performance in a speeded grammaticality judgment task reflects the salience of an ungrammaticality, we can conclude that violations of subject-verb agreement as in (74b) are much more salient than case mismatches as in (74a). Taking this finding together with the claim embodied in the Mismatch Effect gives a way to understand why the filler-gap ambiguity in (64b) causes a stronger garden-path effect than the base-generated ambiguity in (68a). When processing a sentence like (68b), a violation of subject-verb agreement arises after the disambiguating auxiliary has been inserted into the phrase-marker. The sentence can then either be judged as ungrammatical or the violation can be removed by altering the phrase-structure representation. In the case of (68b), the first option will win over the second one due to the salience of the temporary ungrammaticality. When processing a sentence like (68a), a case mismatch will arise, and the parser has again the option of judging the sentence as ungrammatical or removing the mismatch. The latter option will win this time since a case mismatch is not a salient type of ungrammaticality (cf. Meng & Bader, 1997, for details).

Since a sentence like (68a) differs syntactically from a sentence like (68b) (whatever the ultimate syntactic representation of this difference might be), the difference in garden-path strength between (68a) and (68b) does not strongly support the Mismatch Effect. However, the main evidence for the Mismatch Effect does not come from a comparison across different syntactic constructions but from comparisons within syntactic constructions. For example, consider the two sentences in (75). These sentences illustrate a further kind of filler-gap ambiguity. The case-ambiguous wh-phrase *welche Frau (which woman)* in the specifier-position of CP might be associated with a trace either in subject or in object position. In (75a) *welche Frau* must actually be related to the object position since the finite auxiliary is marked for plural and therefore the second NP *die Lehrer (the teachers)* must be the subject. In (75b) *welche Frau* is also the object but this time not because of subject-verb agreement but due to the fact that the second NP *der Lehrer (the teacher)* is unambiguously marked for nominative case.

(75) a. Ich will wissen, welche Frau$_{acc/nom}$ die Lehrer$_{acc/nom}$ t$_i$ getroffen haben$_{plural}$.

I want know which woman the teachers met have
"I want to know which woman the teachers have met?"

b. Ich will wissen, welche Frau$_{acc/nom}$ der Lehrer$_{nom}$ t$_i$ getroffen hat.

I want know which woman the teacher met has
"I want to know which woman the teacher has met?"

Sentences of this kind exhibit a subject-before-object preference, and the disambiguation in (75) accordingly leads to a garden-path effect. However, disambiguation by subject-verb agreement causes a much more severe garden-path effect than disambiguation by unambiguous case features on the second NP. This has been shown by Meng (1997) in several experiments. This difference in garden-path strength is accompanied by a difference in recognizing corresponding ungrammatical sentences. Sentence (76a) is the ungrammatical counterpart to (75a) and contains a violation of subject-verb agreement. (76b), which is the ungrammatical sentence corresponding to (75a), contains a violation of case-marking since there are two nominative-marked NPs.

(76) a. *Ich will wissen, welcher Mann$_{nom}$ die Lehrer$_{acc/nom}$ getroffen haben$_{plural}$.
I want know which man the teachers met have

b. *Ich will wissen, welcher Mann$_{nom}$ *der Lehrer$_{nom}$* getroffen
hat.
I want know which man the teacher known has

Sentences like (76a) are judged as ungrammatical much more reliably than
sentences like (76b) (cf. Meng, in prep.). This means that violations of subject-verb-agreement are more salient than case violations. Given the Mismatch Effect, this difference in the salience of the respective
ungrammaticalities entails that (75a) (disambiguation by subject-verb agreement) causes a more severe garden-path effect than (75b) (disambiguation by
case). The pattern seen in (75) and (76) has also been found within the class of
base-generated subject-object ambiguities. Under particular circumstances,
the subject-before-object preference in base-generated sentences (cf. (42))
reverses to an object-before-subject preference, eliciting a much more severe
garden-path effect than the one found in passive sentences like (68a). Again,
this correlates with a difference in correctly judging ungrammatical sentences
of the corresponding type (cf. Bader, 1996c, for details).

The repeated finding that - within one and the same syntactic construction
type - stronger garden-path effects correspond to more salient ungrammaticalities than weaker garden-path effects strongly supports the Mismatch Effect.
Furthermore, the fact that we can observe weak and strong garden-path effects
both within base-generated and within filler-gap ambiguities shows that there
is no overall difference between filler-gap ambiguities and base-generated
ambiguities. Therefore, the mere fact that one kind of ambiguity is a filler-gap
ambiguity whereas the other is not cannot explain the difference in garden-
path strength between the base-generated object-subject sentence (68a) and
the derived object-subject sentence in (68b). If the syntactic difference
between (68a) and (68b) has anything to do with the concomitant difference in
garden-path strength, then only indirectly, namely insofar as the respective
syntactic structures are a possible determinant of the salience of corresponding ungrammatical sentences. However, for the subject-object ambiguities discussed in this paper, syntactic properties do not seem to play a decisive role
for determining the salience of temporary ungrammaticalities. Instead, the
main factor seems to be how syntactic features like case or number and person
are related to sound and meaning (cf. Meng &Bader, 1997): salient ungrammaticalities seem to involve features that are usually unambiguously signaled
by morphological means and have semantic content (are interpretable in the

sense of Chomsky (1995)); less salient ungrammaticalities, in contrast, involve features that are neither unambiguously signalled in the morphology nor have semantic content.

Before leaving this topic, we have to make sure that the account of garden-path strength embodied in the Mismatch Effect is compatible with the Prosodic Constraint on Reanalysis. The main evidence for the PCR came from its ability to explain the contrast between (77a) and (77b) (repeated from above). Whereas sentence (77a) is easy to process, sentence (77b), which is identical to (77a) except that it contains a focus particle in front of the ambiguous pronoun *ihr*, elicits a garden-path effect.

(77) a. ... daß ihr Vertrauen entgegengebracht wurde.
          ... that her confidence shown was
          "... that confidence was shown in her"

      b. ... daß sogar ihr Vertrauen entgegengebracht wurde.
          ... that even her confidence shown was
          "... that confidence was shown even in her"

According to the PCR, the difference between (77a) and (77b) is due to the fact that reanalysis for (77b) involves a revision of the initial prosodic structure whereas reanalysis for (77a) does not. In terms of the model shown in (72), this means that the difference between (77a) and (77b) must reside in the reanalysis part of this model. This presupposes that these sentences do not differ with respect to their temporary ungrammaticality. Otherwise, the possibility would exist that it is not the prosodic revision but the prior temporary ungrammaticality that is responsible for the fact that (77b) does elicit a strong garden-path effect whereas (77a) does not.

Assuming that the possessive structure is preferred on first-pass parsing, the temporary ungrammaticalities ensuing in (77a) and (77b) correspond to the truly ungrammatical sentences in (78a) and (78b), respectively. In the sentences in (78), the ambiguous pronoun *ihr* has been replaced by the unambiguous possessive pronoun *sein*. These sentences are ungrammatical because the clause-final verb obligatorily requires a dative object but the sentence does not contain such an object. That is, the subcategorization requirements of the clause-final verb are violated.

(78)   a.   *... daß sein Vertrauen entgegengebracht wurde.
                that his confidence shown was
                "*... that his confidence was shown in"

       b.   *... daß sogar sein Vertrauen entgegengebracht wurde.
                that even his confidence shown was
                "*... that even his confidence was shown in"

Since the presence or absence of a focus particle has no bearing on the verb's subcategorization properties, sentence (78a) should not differ from (78b) with respect to ungrammaticality detection. This is indeed what has been found in an unpublished speeded grammaticality-judgment experiment. Whereas ambiguous sentences with focus particle (cf. (77b)) were judged poorer than ambiguous sentences without focus particle (cf. (77a)), ungrammatical sentences with focus particle (cf. (78b)) did not differ from ungrammatical sentences without focus particle (cf. (78a)). We can therefore conclude that the difference between (77a) and (77b) cannot be explained with reference to the Mismatch Effect. Instead, our explanation in terms of the Prosodic Constraint on Reanalysis still holds.[20]

CONCLUSION

This paper has discussed two types of syntactic ambiguities: phrase-structure ambiguities and syntactic-function ambiguities. With respect to phrase-structure ambiguities the Prosodic Constraint on Reanalysis has been proposed in order to account for certain garden-path effects that cannot be explained in syntactic terms. With respect to syntactic function ambiguities, two points have been made. First, certain garden-path effects found for subject-object and object-object ambiguities are caused by the need to reacess the lexicon. This holds for ambiguities where a case-ambiguous NP receives structural case on first-pass parsing but later, after disambiguation, is assigned dative case. Secondly, the Mismatch Effect has been introduced in order to explain why garden-path effects elicited by subject-object ambiguities vary widely in strength, both within and across particular types of subject-object ambiguities. According to the Mismatch Effect, ease or difficulty of reanalysis is not the only source of garden-path strength. A second source is the temporary ungrammaticality that ensues when an ambiguous sentence is disambiguated in favor of its unpreferred structure.

Although the role of syntax for reanalysis has been reduced in this paper, the role of syntax for sentence comprehension in general has been strengthened. For example, a prosodic effect on reanalysis as described in section

Phrase-Structure Ambiguities ... is only possible due to certain regularities of the syntax-phonology mapping. A prerequisite for applying this mapping is the prior computation of a syntactic structure. Without such a structure, there would be no such thing as a syntax-prosody mismatch that could lead to the kind of garden-path effect described in section *Phrase-Structure Ambiguities* .... A similar reasoning can be applied to the garden-path effects caused by the need to assign dative case on second-pass parsing. Such effects, which are located at the interface between lexical and syntactic processing, require syntactic representations for which case assignment can be defined.

Coming back to a point already made in the introduction, the approach to reanalysis sketched in this paper is compatible with a modular architecture of the grammar and the HSPM. Indeed, it is what is to be expected under such an architecture: since parsing does not proceed in isolation, the HSPM has to make many different commitments during the complete processing of a sentence, commitments not only with respect to the syntactic structure but also with respect to other kinds of grammatical information. Therefore, it is not too surprising that the need to revise commitments other than syntactic commitments can make a sentence hard to understand. The general idea that garden-path effects might caused be the need to revise non-syntactic decisions, is not a new one. For example, it has been proposed before that it is hard to revise certain semantic-thematic commitments (e.g., Inoue &Fodor, 1995). Interestingly, no evidence was found in this paper for an involvement of thematic information in processes of reanalysis. For the structures that seem a priori most suited to an explanation in terms of thematic information, empirical evidence speaks against such an influence (cf. the discussion of (62)). This does of course not exclude such an influence playing a role for other kinds of constructions, or that semantic commitments in general are irrelevant for processes of reanalysis. However, at the moment there is only strong evidence that reanalysis is influenced by non-syntactic information belonging to the PF-wing of grammar, i.e. pertaining to the articulatory-sensory interface in the sense of Chomsky (1995). Whether there is a deeper reason for this, or whether this is due to limited evidence, must be a topic for further research.

NOTES

[1] However, the use of the term garden-path is not necessarily related to the distinction between serial and non-serial parsing, as can be seen in Pritchett (1992)

[2] For further information on phonological coding, and for evidence that a phonological code is made available at least after lexical access is completed, cf.

e.g. Black, Coltheart & Byng (1987), Gathercole & Baddeley (1993), Patterson & Coltheart (1987). For prosodic structure as an aspect of phonological coding, cf. Wilkenfeld (1985).

[3] For reasons of space, the plausibility of this assumption cannot be discussed here. For the approach to reanalysis proposed in this paper, it actually does not matter whether there is a preference for the sentences under consideration or not. Cf. Bader (1994a) for an account that does not assume any preference at all.

[4] This difference for sentences without focus particles is reversed at the participle. For sentences with focus particles, in contrast, reading times at the participle show the same pattern as reading times at the auxiliary, although in a reduced and non significant manner.

[5] There are certain well-known exceptions to this claim, for example sentences like *The sun is shining*. For discussion, cf. for example Selkirk (1984) or Rochemont (1986).

[6] In these sentences, focusing the subject allows focus projection up to the whole clause because the subject of such passive clauses occupies the same phrase-structural position as the accusative object of the corresponding active clause (cf. the discussion of active and passive clauses in section *Linguistic Background*).

[7] I owe this example to Christine Haag-Merz, who found it in a bakery magazine called "Bäckerblume".

[8] There is a growing body of literature on the question of how ambiguous A-bar-dependencies are processed in German, including Hemforth, 1993; Farke, 1994; Meng, 1995; Schriefers, Friederici & Kühn, 1995 and the contributions of Gorrell, Scheepers and Schlesewsky et al. in this volume.

[9] This is to a certain extent comparable to the effect caused by the assignment of pitch accents. For example, *John* is obligatorily focused in *JOHN saw Mary*. In *John saw MARY*, on the other hand, either *Mary*, the VP *saw Mary*, or the whole sentence can be a focus.

[10] In a narrow range of cases, the subject of an English clause does not surface in SpecIP, cf. examples like *There arrived a man*. However, contrary to German, the subject position must nevertheless be filled, namely by the expletive *there*.

[11] The pronoun *sie* is indeed ambiguous between nominative and accusative. However, there is a strong tendency to read *sie* as a nominative marked pronoun (cf. the results presented in section *Subject-Object Ambiguities involving Non-based Orders*). Furthermore, the experiment also contained unambiguously nominative marked pronouns, namely the masculine pronoun *er*.

[12]The experiment also included unambiguous, ungrammatical sentences. These sentences, which were generally judged as ungrammatical with high reliability.

[13]In certain southern dialects of German, even masculine determiners show no difference between nominative and accusative case. However, for dative case the same holds as for standard German. Cf. e.g. Haag-Merz (1995) for Swabian

[14] With the exception that for feminine NPs, dative NPs are identical to genitive NPs. However, there is only a very small set of verbs in German subcategorizing for a genitive NP. Furthermore, like dative case, genitive case is a lexical case when assigned by a verb.

[15] Certain exceptions exist also in the pronominal system, for example for first and second person plural pronouns. However, pronouns also differ in other respects from full NPs, and will not be considered further here.

[16] I will leave open the question of how lexical elements are represented which are only compatible with either nominative or accusative case, e.g. *der Mann* (the man-nominative) versus *den Mann* (the man-accusative). Cf. Bader & Meng (in prep.) for discussion.

[17] Note that this effect does not depend on whether the NPs under consideration are ambiguous with respect to case or not. If a sequence of two NPs is assigned the thematic roles "agent" and "theme" per default, the only requirement is that they are compatible with nominative and accusative case, respectively (i.e., neither of the two NPs may be marked for dative case). This condition is fulfilled by the sentences in (62)) independent of the question of case ambiguity.

[18] In fact, there is a further reason why (71) should elicit a strong garden-path effect. The two readings of (71) do also differ prosodically. Therefore, the reanalysis becoming necessary on encountering *the story* will involve a prosodic revision, and, as proposed in section *Phrase-Structure Ambiguities ...* , prosodic revisions are difficulty.

[19] The results for the filler-gap sentences are all from the experiment described in section *Subject-Object Ambiguities involving Non-based Orders*. The results for ambiguous and unambiguous base-generated subject-object sentences are from the experiment described in section *Subject-Object Ambiguities involving Base Orders*; results for ungrammatical base-generated sentences come from a separate unpublished experiment. The original experiment described in section *Subject-Object Ambiguities involving Base Orders* also contained ungrammatical sentences but with pronouns instead of definite NPs which does not give an accurate estimation for ambiguous sentences containing proper names (cf. Meng & Bader, 1997).

[20] This does not necessarily mean that the Mismatch Effect is completely suspended in this type of ambiguity. At least with respect to the overall level of garden-path strength in sentences like (77b), the data suggest a correlation with performance on ungrammatical sentences like (78b).

REFERENCES

Abraham, W. (1995). *Deutsche Syntax im Sprachenvergleich. Grundlegung einer typologischen Syntax des Deutschen.* Tübingen: Narr Verlag.

Bader, M. (1990). *Syntaktische Prozesse beim Sprachverstehen.* Unpublished master's thesis, University of Freiburg.

Bader, M. (1994a). *Sprachverstehen: Syntax und Prosodie beim Lesen.* Unpublished doctoral dissertation, University of Stuttgart.

Bader, M. (1994b). Syntactic-function ambiguities. *Folia Linguistica, 28,* 5-66.

Bader, M. (1996a). *Prosodic effects and the distinction between primary and secondary phrases.* Poster presented at the 2nd Conference on Architectures and Mechanisms for Language Processing, University of Turin.

Bader, M. (1996b). *Reanalysis in a modular architecture of the human sentence processing mechanism.* Poster presented at the 7th CUNY Conference on Sentence Processing, CUNY, New York.

Bader, M. (1996c). *Syntactic and morphological contributions to processing subject-object ambiguities.* Unpublished manuscript, University of Jena.

Bader, M. (to appear). Prosodic influences on reading syntactically ambiguous sentences. In J. Fodor & F. Ferreira (Eds.), *Reanalysis in sentence processing.* Dordrecht: Kluwer.

Bader, M., Bayer, J., Hopf, J.-M., & Meng, M. (1996). Case-Assignment in processing German verb-final clauses. In *Proceeding of the NELS 26 Workshop on Sentence Processing* (MIT Occasional Papers in Linguistics, Vol. 9), 1-25.

Bader, M., & Meng, M. (to appear). *Subject-Object ambiguities in embedded clauses - An across the board comparison.*

Bader, M., & Meng, M. (in prep.). *Case attraction phenomena in German.*

Bayer, J. (1996). *Directionality and logical form.* Dordrecht: Kluwer.

Black, M., Coltheart, M., & Byng, S. (1987). Forms of coding in sentence comprehension during reading. In M. Coltheart (Ed.), *The psychology of reading* (Attention and performance XII) (pp. 655-672). Hove, London & Hillsdale: Lawrence Erlbaum.

Carlson, G. N., & Tanenhaus, M. K. (1988). Thematic roles and language comprehension. In W. Wilkins (Ed.), *Syntax and semantics. Vol. 21. Thematic relations* (pp. 263-288). San Diego: Academic Press.

Chomsky, N. (1995). *The minimalist program*. Cambridge, MA: MIT Press

Chomsky, N., & Lasnik, H. (1993). The theory of principles and parameters. In J. Jacobs, A. von Stechow, W. Sternefeld & T. Vennemann (Eds.), *Syntax: An international handbook of contemporary research* (pp. 506-569). Berlin: Walter de Gruyter.

den Besten, H. (1985). The ergative hypothesis and free word order in Dutch and German. In J. Toman (Ed.), *Studies in German grammar* (pp. ??). Dordrecht: Foris.

De Vincenzi, M. (1991). *Syntactic parsing strategies in Italian*. Dordrecht: Kluwer.

Duffy, S. A., Morris, R. K. & Rayner, K. (1988). Lexical ambiguity and fixation times in reading. *Journal of Memory and Language, 27*, 429-446.

Farke, H. (1994). *Grammatik und Sprachverarbeitung. Zur Verarbeitung syntaktischer Ambiguität*. Opladen: Westdeutscher Verlag.

Ferreira, F., & Henderson, J. M. (1991). Recovery from misanalysis of garden-path sentences. *Journal of Memory and Language, 30*, 725-745.

Fodor, J. D., & Inoue, A. (1994). The diagnosis and cure of garden paths. *Journal of Psycholinguistic Research, 23*, 407-434.

Ford, M., Bresnan, J., & Kaplan, R. M. (1982). A competence-based theory of syntactic closure. In J. Bresnan (Ed.) *The mental representation of grammatical relations* (pp. 727-766). Cambridge, MA: MIT Press.

Frazier, L., & Fodor, J. D. (1978). The sausage machine: A new two-stage parsing model. *Cognition, 6*, 291-325.

Frazier, L., & Rayner, K. (1990). Taking on semantic commitments: Processing multiple meanings vs. multiple senses. *Journal of Memory and Language, 29*, 181-200.

Frazier, L. (1979). *On comprehending sentences: Syntactic parsing strategies*. Unpublished doctoral dissertation, University of Conneticut, Storrs.

Fukui, N. (1986). *A theory of category projections and its applications*. Unpublished doctoral dissertation, MIT, Cambridge, MA.

Gathercole, S. E., & Baddeley, A. D. (1993). *Working memory and language*. Hillsdale, NJ: Lawrence Erlbaum Associates.

Gibson, E. (1991). *A computational theory of human linguistic processing*. Unpublished doctoral dissertation, Carnegie Mellon University, Pittsburgh, Pennsylvania.

Gorrell, P. (1995). *Syntax and parsing*. Cambridge: Cambridge University Press.

Haag-Merz, C. (1995). *Pronomen im Schwäbischen - Syntax und Erwerb.* Unpublished doctoral dissertation, University of Stuttgart.

Haider, H. (1993) *Deutsche Syntax - generativ. Vorstudien zu einer projektiven Theorie der Grammatik.* Tübingen: Narr.

Hemforth, B. (1993). *Kognitives Parsing: Repräsentation und Verarbeitung grammatischen Wissens.* Sankt Augustin: Infix Verlag.

Höhle, T. N. (1982). Explikation für "normale Betonung" und "normale Wortstellung". In W. Abraham (Ed.), *Satzglieder im Deutschen. Vorschläge zur syntaktischen, semantischen und pragmatischen Fundierung* (pp. 75-153). Tübingen: Narr.

Inoue, A., & Fodor, J. D. (1995). Information paced parsing of Japanese. In R. Mazuka & N. Nagai (Eds.), (pp. 9-63). . .

Jackendoff, R. (1972). *Semantic interpretation in generative grammar.* Cambridge, MA: MIT Press.

Jacobs, J. (1992). Neutral stress and the position of heads. In J. Jacobs (Ed.), *Informationsstruktur und Grammatik. Linguistische Berichte Sonderheft, Nr.4.,* 220-244.

Just, M. A., Carpenter, P. A., & Wolley, J. D. (1982). Paradigms and processes in reading comprehension. *Journal of Experimental Psychology: General, 111,* 228-238.

Kitagawa, Y. (1986). *Subject in Japanese and English.* Doctoral dissertation, University of Massachusetts at Amherst.

Koopman, H., & Sportiche, D. (1991). The position of subjects. *Lingua, 85,* 211-258.

Lenerz, J. (1977). *Zur Abfolge nominaler Satzglieder im Deutschen.* Tübingen: Narr.

Lenerz, J. (1992). Zur Syntax der Pronomina im Deutschen. Sprache und *Pragmatik, 29.*

MacDonald, M., Pearlmutter, N. J., & Seidenberg, M. S. (1994a). Lexical nature of syntactic ambiguity resolution. *Psychological Review, 101,* 676-703.

MacDonald, M., Pearlmutter, N. J., & Seidenberg, M. S. (1994b). Syntactic ambiguity resolution as lexical ambiguity resolution In C. Clifton Jr., L. Frazier & K. Rayner (Eds.), *Perspectives on sentence processing* (pp. 123-153). Hillsdale, NJ: Lawrence Erlbaum.

Meng, M. (1995). *Processing Wh-Questions in German and Dutch: Differential effects of disambiguation and their interpretation.* Poster presented at the 1995 "Architectures and Models for Language Processing" Conference (AMLaP), Edinburgh, December 1995.

Meng, M. (1997). *Die Verarbeitung von w-Fragen im Deutschen: Präferenzen und Reanalyseeffekte.* Doctoral dissertation, University of Jena.

Meng, M., & Bader, M. (1997). *Syntax and morphology in sentence parsing: A new look at German subject-object ambiguities.* Manuscript, University of Jena.

Nespor, M., & Vogel, I. (1986). *Prosodic phonology.* Dordrecht: Foris.

Patterson, K., & Coltheart, V. (1987) Phonological processes in reading. A tutorial review. In M. Coltheart (Ed.), *The psychology of reading* (Attention and performance XII) (pp.421-447). Hove, London & Hillsdale: Lawrence Erlbaum.

Pritchett, B. L. (1992). *Grammatical competence and parsing performance.* Chicago and London: The University of Chicago Press.

Rayner, K., & Pollatsek, A. (1989). *The psychology of reading.* Englewood Cliffs, NJ: Prentice Hall.

Riemsdijk, H. van, & Williams, E. (1986). *Introduction to the theory of grammar.* Cambridge, MA: MIT Press.

Rochemont, M. S. (1986). *Focus in generative grammar.* Amsterdam: John Benjamins.

Ross, J. (1967). *Constraints on variables in syntax.* Unpublished doctoral dissertation, MIT, Cambridge, MA.

Schriefers, H.,, Friederici, A. D., & Kühn, K. (1995). The processing of locally ambiguous relative clauses in German. *Journal of Memory and Language, 34,* 499-520.

Selkirk, E. (1984). *Phonology and Syntax: The relation between sound and structure.* Cambridge, MA: The MIT Press.

Selkirk, E. (1986). On derived domains in sentence phonology. *Phonology Yearbook, 3,* 371-405.

Simpson, G. B. (1994). Context and the processing of ambiguous words. In M. A. Gernsbacher (Ed.), *Handbook of Psycholinguistics* (pp. 359-374). San Diego: Academic Press.

Stechow, A. von (1991). Current issues in the theory of focus. In A. von Stechow & D. Wunderlich (Eds.), *Semantik: Ein internationales Handbuch der zeitgenössischen Forschung* (pp. 804-825). Berlin & New York: De Gruyter.

Swinney, D. A. (1979). Lexical access during sentence comprehension: (Re)consideration of context effects. *Journal of Verbal Learning and Verbal Behavior, 18,* 645-660.

Tanenhaus, M. K., Carlson, G., & Trueswell, J. C. (1989). The role of thematic structures in interpretation and parsing. *Language and Cognitive Processes, 3/4,* 211-234.

Trueswell, J. C., & Tanenhaus, M. K. (1994). Toward a lexicalist framework of constraint-based syntactic ambiguity resolution. In C. Clifton Jr., l. Frazier & K. Rayner (Eds.), *Perspectives on sentence processing* (pp. 155-179). Hillsdale, NJ: Lawrence Erlbaum.

Weinberg, A. (1993). Parameters in the theory of sentence processing: Minimal commitment theory goes east. *Journal of Psycholinguistic Research, 22*, 338-364.

Wilkenfeld, D. C. (1985). *Encoding prosody in silent reading.* Unpublished doctoral dissertation, University of Connecticut.

HEAD POSITION AND CLAUSE BOUNDARY EFFECTS IN REANALYSIS

Lars Konieczny, Barbara Hemforth and Christoph Scheepers
University of Freiburg

SUMMARY

Reanalysis cost has been demonstrated to be influenced by the distance of the semantic head of the ambiguous phrase to the disambiguating region (Ferreira and Henderson, 1991). F&H's original account, based on the assumption of decaying activation levels of multiple thematic frames, as well as its recently updated version (Ferreira & Henderson, in press), will be discussed in the light of empirical evidence from an eye-tracking study on German NP- vs. elliptic VP-coordination ambiguities. Head position was varied by using pre-nominal APs and post-nominal PPs or RCs.

The results suggest that the head position, i.e. its distance from the disambiguating material, does in fact influence the strength of the garden-path effect. However, Ferreira and Henderson's (1991) model of parallel thematic frame activation and decay fails to provide a straightforward explanation, since in the constructions investigated here, disambiguation does not (necessarily) coincide with the recovery of a recently abandoned thematic frame. Furthermore, the data also seem to be inconsistent with Ferreira and Henderson's (in press) latest proposal based on the introduction of additional thematic processing domains in the cases of PPs and RCs, but not in APs. In general, the results constrain the class of potential (de-)activation-based models such as Ferreira and Henderson's (1991) and Stevenson's (1993), and provide important insights in how these models have to be revised to be compatible with the empirical findings. We also offer an alternative explanation based on the amount of semantic unpacking required for re-interpretation.

INTRODUCTION

It has been shown in quite a few studies that the difficulty of reanalysis is influenced by the length of the ambiguous phrase that leads to a garden path

B. Hemforth and L. Konieczny (eds.), German Sentence Processing, 247-278.
© 2000 *Kluwer Academic Publishers. Printed in the Netherlands.*

(e.g. Frazier & Rayner, 1982; Warner and Glass, 1987). A classical proposal as to why this is so is that the number of syntactic commitments to be disentangled directly influences the cognitive load induced by reanalysis (Mitchell, 1989). In lengthening the ambiguous region, however, other factors, such as the syntactic complexity of the ambiguous region, might have been varied as well.

In their series of experiments, Ferreira and Henderson (F&H, 1991) tried to establish which factors determine the strength of the garden-path effect. Central to their approach is the *position of the semantic (thematic) head* of the ambiguous phrase, or better, its distance to the disambiguating region. F&H examine garden-path sentences with object-subject ambiguities like (1ab):

(1)   a.   Because Bill drinks *wine* beer is never kept in the house.

      b.   Because Bill drinks *wine* is never kept in the house.

The locally ambiguous NP "*wine*" can be attached as the object of the preceding verb "*drink*" (1a) or as the subject of the following matrix clause (1b). The preferred interpretation as the object of the preceding verb leads to the garden path, observable in sentences like (1b).[1]

Potential effects of syntactic complexity were tackled by lengthening the ambiguous region with either a relative clause (2b) or a PP (2c), assuming that relative clauses are syntactically more complex than PPs.

(2)   a.   short region
               When the men hunt *the birds* usually scatter.

      b.   long region, relative clause
               When the men hunt *the birds that cheetahs eat* usually scatter.

      c.   long region, PP
               When the men hunt *the birds with white plumage* usually scatter.

The position of the semantic head was varied by lengthening the ambiguous region by either a relative clause (3b) or a pre-nominal adjective phrase (3c).

(3) a. short region
         While the boy scratched *the dog* yawned loudly.

     b. long region, relative clause
         While the boy scratched *the dog that is hairy* yawned loudly.

     c. long region, pre-nominal adjectives
         While the boy scratched *the big and hairy dog* yawned loudly.

Judgements of grammatical wellformedness given by subjects after reading each sentence[2] showed no differential effects of syntactic complexity (PP vs. RC). On the other hand, a longer distance between the semantic head of the ambiguous NP (*dog*) and the disambiguating region appeared to increase reanalysis difficulty.

In F&H's (1991) account, the effects of head position are explained by a two stage parsing mechanism (based on Frazier & Rayner, 1982): in the first stage, syntactic structures are built considering only categorial and phrase structure information. The results of the syntactic processor are handed to the thematic processor, which yields the thematic structure of the sentence. In the *early closure* sentences, not only syntactic reanalysis has to be performed but also thematic reanalysis, since the NP *the dog* is initially attached as an argument of *scratched* and has to be reanalyzed as an argument of the verb *yawned*. According to Frazier and Rayner (1982), the longer a thematic attachment decision has been pursued, the more difficult reanalysis becomes. In F&H's (1991) approach, thematic attachment does not take place before the semantic head of a phrase has been encountered. Pre-nominal constituents of NPs like *the* or *the big and hairy* are not attached thematically. Furthermore, when a verb is encountered, all possible theta grids are activated, the strength of the activation depending on the relative frequency of the respective grid. Almost as soon as one alternative is chosen by thematically attaching an argument, the activation of the theta grids not used decays rapidly. If the disambiguating part of the sentence is close to the semantic head of the ambiguous phrase, the intransitive theta grid of the verb of the subclause *while the boy scratched* is still active and, thus, reanalysis is easier.

It is worthwhile mentioning that F&H's conclusion about the relevance of syntactic complexity in reanalysis is based on a statistical non-effect. However, since the experimental technique used by the authors (RSVP, grammaticality judgments) might not be sensitive enough for this kind of processes, the validity of this result has to be checked with more fine-grained on-line techniques. This is one of the aims of the eye-tracking experiment presented in this paper.

More importantly, there is some evidence that, contrary to F&H's proposal, thematic attachment is not delayed up until the semantic head of a phrase. In sentences with PPs that were semantically disambiguated towards the non-preferred NP modifying reading, such as (4), Strube et al. (1990) obtained a processing penalty even at the adjective within the PP, i.e. even before the head noun.

(4)   Peter watched the girl with the *blond* ...

Similar evidence comes from a series of self paced reading experiments by Hemforth (1993) on coordination ambiguities, such as (5).

(5)   Peter read the book and the hungry ... (dog watched him).

There is a strong structural preference to analyse the ambiguous NP *the hungry dog* as being coordinated with the preceding NP *the book*, such that the occurrence of the verb *watched* results in a garden path effect since it requires the ambiguous NP to be the subject in the coordinated sentence (see also Frazier & Flores d'Arcais, 1989, for similar results in Dutch). Crucially, increased reading times were obtained even on the pre-nominal adjective (e.g *hungry*), if it rendered the NP-coordination semantically implausible. Results like these strongly suggest that phrase fragments are interpreted at the thematic level before their thematic head is encountered.

This criticism, however, does not necessarily apply to the F&H's more recent approach (F&H, in press), in which they abandoned their original explanation of the data. The move was mainly motivated by the observation of a "head-position effect" in supposedly non-garden-pathing constructions, such as (1a). If no garden-pathing is to be expected, no head-position effect should be observable at all since the parser does not have to recover a structurally unpreferred thematic frame.

In their current account, the head-position hypothesis has thus been replaced by an explanation based on the number of interacting and embedded thematic processing domains (TPDs). A TPD roughly corresponds to the part of the input string that includes a thematic assigner, its arguments, and its modifiers (Frazier & Clifton, 1996). Sentences, for example, are TPDs as they include the verb and its arguments. A PP can also be a TPD if its preposition assigns a thematic role to the embedded NP. Following this definition, the relative clauses and PPs, i.e. the post-nominal modifiers used in F&H's studies, but not the APs, share the property of being TPDs. Therefore, the so-called head-position effect in their experiments might not be due to reanalysis at all, but to the processing load induced by encountering additional embedded TPDs in the form of a PP and an RC-modifier. This penalty can thus even be observed in non-garden-pathing constructions.

In garden-pathing examples, however, the reanalysis effort is mainly determined by the question of whether or not an initially assumed TPD (e. g. {NP_1 v NP_2} ...) *interacts* with a TPD required in the correct analysis (e. g. NP_1 v {NP_2 v ... }), i.e. whether an element of a TPD later turns out to be an element of a different, independent TPD (see also Pritchett, 1992; Frazier & Clifton, 1996).

The move towards a TPD-based explanation is substantial. Architectural assumptions become less relevant; e.g the idea of multiple thematic frames that have to be kept active until the integration of the semantic head of a potential argument allows the abandonment of non-matching frames. An account focussing on thematic processing domains is surely more transparent.

REANALYSIS IN COORDINATION AMBIGUITIES

In the remainder of the paper, we will present an eye-movement study set up to clarify the role of the head position and structural complexity in reanalysis. We used sentences containing a coordination ambiguity, as illustrated in (6).

(6) a.   NP-coordination
           Heinz schenkte der Nichte den Teddy und das Buch *zu Weihnachten.*
           Heinz gave the niece the teddy and the book *for Christmas.*

     b.   VP-coordination
           Heinz schenkte der Nichte den Teddy und das Buch *dem Neffen.*
           Heinz gave the niece the teddy and the book (to) *the nephew.*

Elliptic VP-coordinations can be expected to be more difficult to process for a variety of reasons, e.g. due to a violation of *Late Closure* (Frazier, 1987). In general, VP-coordinations go against a preference to attach the coordination phrase to the most recent phrase (Frazier and Fodor, 1978; Konieczny et al. 1994).[3] These predictions could be confirmed in several self-paced reading and eye-tracking experiments (e.g. Hemforth, 1993; Hemforth, Konieczny, & Scheepers, 1994). Figure 5 illustrates the syntactic reanalysis forced by the dative-NP *the nephew.*

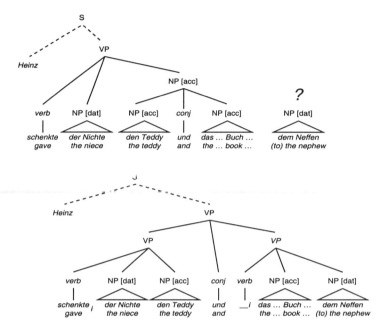

Figure 1: Reanalysis from NP-coordination to VP-coordination

There are two reasons for looking at this kind of construction: firstly, there is no thematic frame ambiguity involved here. In both cases the verb assigns three theta roles (*AGENS, RECIPIENT, THEME*) to its arguments. It would therefore be interesting if the "head-position" effect would still show up.

Secondly, reanalysis takes place within the same TPD (the entire sentence): since only the VPs are coordinated in the garden-pathing construction, there is no interaction of TPDs involved.[4] According to the TPD approach, reanalysis should be fairly easy, such that the processing load due to additionally introduced TPDs (e.g. PP or RC-modifiers) should shine through more clearly.

Materials and Design

Twenty-four sets of sentences like (aa–c, 8a–c) were constructed to investigate the effect of head position and syntactic complexity. The experimental sentences were manipulated according to a 2*3 within-subjects design with the factors *coordination type* (NP-coordination vs. VP-coordination) and NP-

modifier type (NP modified by an AP, a PP or a relative clause, RC). The order of the sentences was randomized. For each of the six conditions, four sentences were presented. The twenty-four sets were counterbalanced over subjects. Sentences were presented in two lines, the critical parts in the first line, the following subclause in the fourth line. Two empty lines were inserted so that we could unambiguously count fixations that were slightly below or above the relevant lines as fixations on the text. Additionally, subjects had to read 66 filler sentences of various types. Five of them were used as a training set.

NP-coordinations

(7) a. *pre-nominal adjective phrases*
Heinz schenkte der Nichte den Teddy / und das spannende und sehr lehrreiche Buch / *zu Weihnachten,* / *als er* / zu Besuch kam.

Heinz gave the niece the teddy and the exciting / and very informative book/ *for Christmas / when he* / came to visit.

b. *post-nominal prepositional phrases*
Heinz schenkte der Nichte den Teddy / und das Buch mit dem spannenden Titel / *zu Weihnachten,* / *als er* / zu Besuch kam.

Heinz gave the niece the teddy / and the book with the exciting title / *for Christmas/ when he/* came to visit.

c. *post-nominal relative clauses*
Heinz schenkte der Nichte den Teddy / und das Buch, das sehr spannend war, / *zu Weihnachten,* / *als er* / zu Besuch kam.

Heinz gave the niece the teddy / and the book that was very exciting / *for Christmas / when he* / came to visit.

VP-coordinations

(8) a. *pre-nominal adjective phrases*
Heinz schenkte der Nichte den Teddy / und das spannende

und sehr lehrreiche Buch / *dem Neffen*, / *als er* / zu Besuch kam.

Heinz gave the niece the teddy / and the exciting and very informative book /(to) *the nephew / when he* / came to visit.

b.   *post-nominal prepositional phrases*
Heinz schenkte der Nichte den Teddy / und das Buch mit dem spannenden Titel / *dem Neffen*, / *als er* / zu Besuch kam.

Heinz gave the niece the teddy / and the book with the exciting title / (to) *the nephew / when he* / came to visit.

c.   *post-nominal relative clauses*
Heinz schenkte der Nichte den Teddy / und das Buch, das sehr spannend war, / *dem Neffen*, / *als er* / zu Besuch kam.

Heinz gave the niece the teddy / and the book that was very exciting / (to) *the nephew / when he* / came to visit.

METHODS

Procedure

Prior to the experiment, the subject was fitted to a headrest to prevent head movements during reading. This was followed by a brief calibration procedure and a warming-up block consisting of five filler sentences. Then the experiment which was built up of 10 blocks began. Each block was initiated by a brief calibration procedure and contained 9 sentences, randomly taken from the full set of test and filler sentences, except for the first sentence presented, which was a filler in all blocks. As soon as subjects fixated a cross on the screen, which indicated the start-position of the sentence, the sentence was presented. When subjects had finished reading the sentence, they pressed a button, erasing the sentence from the screen. Each sentence was followed by a simple yes/no-question, which the subject had to answer by pressing one of two buttons (left-hand button: "yes", right-hand button: "no").[5] Subjects were told to read normally and that the purpose of the study was to determine where people look during reading.

Apparatus

The subjects' eye movements were monitored by a Generation 5.5 dual Purkinje image (DPI) eye-tracker, which has a resolution of less than 5 minutes of arc. Viewing was binocular, but eye movements were recorded only from the right eye. The eye-tracker was connected to an AT 386 computer which controlled the stimulus-presentation and stored the output from the eye-tracker for later data analysis.[6] The time sampling rate for data collection was 1 KHz (one measure per millisecond). The sentences were presented on a 20-inch color monitor, beginning at the 1st column of the character matrix. The subject was seated 80 centimeters from the face of the screen, so that 3 letters equaled 1 degree of visual angle. To prevent disturbing light reflections, the monitor was covered by a tube and the room was slightly darkened.

Subjects

Thirty-nine undergraduate students (native speakers of German) from the University of Freiburg were paid to participate in the study. All of them had normal, uncorrected vision and they were all unaware of the purpose of the study. During an experimental session of about 50 minutes at the Institute of Computer Science and Social Research in Freiburg, each of the subjects had to read 90 sentences while her eye movements were monitored.

Dependent Variables and Data Analyses[7]

First pass reading times, regression-path durations, load contributions (including *right-bounded reading times*) and *first pass regression probabilities* were calculated for three regions as indicated by the slashes in example (a) and (8): the ambiguous region (the conjunction *und* plus the following modified NP), the disambiguating region (a PP for NP-coordination, an NP for VP-coordination), and the two words following the disambiguating region, referred to as the *spill-over* region.

First pass reading times

The first pass reading time (FPRT) measure accumulates the durations of all fixations on a region beginning after the region is entered from the left until there is a saccade to another region. *First pass reading times* have been used for a considerable time now. Effects in FPRTs have often been interpreted as an indicator for garden-pathing, implying that longer FPRTs reflect processes of error detection and recovery. This assumption, however, implies that FPRTs collect the processing durations of both the first and the second (nth) analysis in the parser. Unfortunately, subjects do not always stay in a region after encountering an error until they find a consistent analysis. It happens quite often that subjects look back to earlier places in the sentence in order to read some portions of the sentence again. In these cases, FPRTs will not reflect all processes induced by a mismatch, namely pursuing a second analysis and, if it works, its semantic integration and evaluation. Thus, the FPRTs will probably be considerably short in these cases, because they only represent the time needed to detect the mismatch and to initiate a saccade to prior words in the sentence relevant in the reanalysis process. In the light of the fact that usually more regressive saccades can be observed after a local mismatch is detected, the average FPRTs are likely to be contaminated by the trials with regressions, so that, paradoxically, shorter average FPRTs might be observed in regions with material more difficult to process than in those with consistent material. For this reason, FPRTs might not be sensitive to garden pathing, if first pass reading is followed by a regressive saccade in too many cases (see Konieczny, 1996; Liversedge et al., in prep., for examples and discussions; see Altmann et al., 1992, for a potential solution).

Regression-path durations

Regression-path durations (RPDs; Konieczny, 1996; Konieczny et al. 1994) are suited to overcome the shortcomings of *first pass reading times*. RPDs accumulate the durations of all fixations in the *regression path*. The *regression path* is the stream of fixations starting as soon as a region is entered with a progressive saccade, and ending when the region is left or skipped with a progressive saccade.[8] Because RPDs include fixations in regions prior to the critical region following a regressive saccade from the critical region, they reflect the processing load induced in that region more realistically, because they include the first-pass reading time and the time needed to re-read previous portions when the region is left with a regressive saccade after first-pass reading.

Load contributions and right-bounded reading times

Along the *regression path*, some regions contribute more to the RPDs than others. Especially when reanalysis processes are to be investigated, it is of particular interest which regions are most intensively re-read after the initial analysis failed. For example, one might come up with the hypothesis that the ambiguous region is most important in reanalysis, or the potential attachment sites, or only thematic licensers, and so on. The *total reading times* of each region *within a regression path* reflect the amount of time spent on a certain region after a regressive saccade was initiated after first pass reading of a region further to the right. We will call this score *load contribution*. In contrast to the standard measures and the RPDs, *load contribution* is a two-place function $lc(reg_j, reg_k)$, namely the total reading time *in one region* (reg_j) *within the regression path of another region* (reg_k, called the *regression-path region*). The load contributions of all regions preceding and including the regression-path region sum up to the RPD of that region.

The *right-bounded reading time* measure (RBRTs, Liversedge, 1994) is a special case of the *load contribution* measure, namely the case in which both regions are identical, i.e. $lc(reg_i, reg_i)$. That is, RBRTs measure the local processing load including second pass (or *n*th pass) reading as long as the previous pass is followed by a regressive saccade. Otherwise, RPRTS are identical to the first-pass reading times.

RBRTs have been shown to be especially sensitive to certain garden-path phenomena (Liversedge, personal communication).

First pass regression probability

We also considered the probability of a regressive saccade after first pass reading as an indicator of garden pathing. The *first pass regression probability* is the number of regressive saccades following the first pass reading of a region, divided by the number of valid cases in the respective condition. Note that only those cases were considered, in which the first pass reading time was actually greater than zero (conditionalized analysis).

Regions

For data-analysis only, regions were built as indicated by the slashes ("/") in (a, 8), so that fixations could be assigned to particular regions. We concentrate on three regions: the *disambiguating region* (*the nephew* vs. *for christmas*), the region preceding it (i.e. the *ambiguous region*), and the region succeeding it (i.e. the *spill-over region*).

Hypotheses

If reanalysis difficulty is solely determined by the length of the ambiguous region, the magnitude of the garden-path effect should not differ between the modifier-types, because they are all equal in length. If, however, head position, i.e. the distance between the semantic head and the disambiguating region, or the embedding of an additional thematic processing domain is the critical property, sentences with ambiguous regions lengthened by a PP or an RC should be harder to reanalyse than those lengthened by an AP. If *head-position* is the critical factor for reanalysis load, according to F&H (1991) a reliable interaction of *coordination type* and *modifier type* is to be expected on the disambiguating region. However, if the embedding of an additional processing domain is the critical factor in general processing load (F&H, in press), no such interaction should be revealed but only additive effects. Instead, reading of the *ambiguous region* should take longer if it contains an additional TPD, such as a PP or an RC modifier.

Additionally, if reanalysis becomes more difficult in those cases in which the ambiguous region is syntactically more complex, sentences with ambiguous regions lengthened by a relative clause should be most difficult.

Data analysis

The data of four subjects had to be excluded from data analysis because of too many tracklosses and/or too many erroneous fixations (i.e. fixations on undefined regions of the screen). Consequently, the data of only 35 subjects will enter the analyses. Zero scores in FPRTs, right-bounded RTs, and RPDs were treated as missing values. The data, therefore, represent conditionalized scores (cf. Rayner et al., 1989).

The durations of fixations that were outside the stimulus area were added to the scores of the region fixated previously. Small y-deviations, i.e. fixations on either the (blank) line immediately above or below the stimulus line, were counted as fixations on the stimulus line. Note that in order to be able to unambiguously assign a y-deviating fixation to a character in the stimulus line, a blank line had to precede and follow each stimulus line, making two blank lines in between two stimulus lines.

In cases in which the (initial) first-pass reading time of a region was smaller than 100 ms, the respective fixations were treated as fail-fixations, and their durations were added to the relevant scores of the previously fixated region. Consequently, the region was considered not-yet fixated, so that all scores of that region were computed from subsequent fixations.

In order to eliminate the effect of word-length, the raw reading times were adjusted by subtracting 20ms for each character in the respective region beyond the fourth character[9] (see Konieczny, 1996, for a detailed discussion of various length adjustment procedures).

Extreme values were replaced by cutoff-values determined on the basis of the respective data distribution at a given region: for each (length adjusted) measure in each experimental condition, a range of values was determined (by subtracting the 25th percentile from the 75th percentile) which covered 50% of the observed data around the median score. An upper limit was then defined by adding this range times 1.5 to the 75th percentile, and a lower limit by subtracting the range 1.5 times from the 25th percentile. Data beyond these cutoffs were replaced by the upper limit or the lower limit, respectively.[10]

The adjusted data were then submitted to a full factorial 2*3 analysis of variance for repeated measures, including the factors *coordination type* (NP-coord vs. VP-coord) and *modifier type* (AP vs. PP vs. RC). Inferential statistics were computed for subjects (F1-analyses) and for items (F2-analyses), respectively.

Results

Ambiguous region

With respect to item analysis, there was a reliable main effect of *coordination type* in the *probability of first pass regressions* from the ambiguous region which was slightly higher in the NP-coordination condition (NP-coord: 0.10 vs. VP-coord: 0.07: $F1_{1,34} = 3.64$; $p < .07$; $F2_{1,23} = 5.80$; $p = .02$). This effect is hardly interpretable, since the materials do not differ across the coordination conditions up to that point.

No further influences of the experimental factors on first pass processing of the ambiguous region could be established (all Fs < 1.0) (cf. Table 1).

	NP-coord			VP-coord		
	AP	PP	RC	AP	PP	RC
FPRTs	638	599	638	692	641	682
RBRTs	761	732	745	761	718	804
RPDs	797	796	823	792	746	833
regr. prob.	.07	.11	.12	.06	.07	.07

Table 1: Mean length adjusted reading times (in milliseconds) for the ambiguous region: *first pass reading times* (FPRTs), *right-bounded reading times* (RBRTs) and *regression-path durations* (RPDs).The probabilities of regressions from the ambiguous region to a previous region are shown in the last row.

Disambiguating region

A reliable main effect of *coordination type* showed up in all relevant measures, indicating that subjects were strongly garden-pathed in the VP-coordination condition (cf. Table 2 and Figures 2 to Figure 5). The effect was found in *first pass reading times* (NP-coord: 385ms vs. VP-coord: 474ms; $F1_{1,34} = 12.69$; p = .001; $F2_{1,23} = 15.91$; p = .001), in *right-bounded reading times* (NP-coord: 493ms vs. VP-coord: 612ms; $F1_{1,34} = 23.31$; p < .001; $F2_{1,23} = 15.45$; p = .001), and in *regression-path durations* (NP-coord: 658ms vs. VP-coord: 953ms; $F1_{1,34} = 26.33$; p < .001; $F2_{1,23} = 36.58$; p < .001). Additionally, a significant increase in the *probability of regressions* from the disambiguating region to previous regions was observed in the VP-coordination condition (NP-coord: 0.28 vs. VP-coord: 0.41; $F1_{1,34} = 16.99$; p < .001; $F2_{1,23} = 12.37$; p = .002).[11]

The main effect of *modifier type* was reliable in right-bounded RTs ($F1_{2,68} = 13.09$; p < .001; $F2_{2,46} = 15.05$; p < .001), in *regression-path durations* ($F1_{2,68} = 25.64$; p < .001; $F2_{2,46} = 34.10$; p < .001), and in the *regression probabilities* on the disambiguating region ($F1_{2,68} = 15.14$; p < .001; $F2_{2,46} = 16.40$; p < .001), but not in *first pass reading times* (F1, F2 < 2.0; ns.). Planned comparisons regarding this main effect in the regression-sensitive measures showed that the disambiguating region is harder to process after PP-modifiers than after AP-modifiers (right-bounded RTs: AP: 561ms vs. PP: 629ms; $F1_{1,34} = 5.53$; $p < .03$; $F2_{1,23} = 7.38$; $p < .02$; *regression-path durations*: AP: 823ms vs. PP: 1008ms; $F1_{1,34} = 10.08$; $p = .003$; $F2_{1,23} = 20.74$; $p < .001$; *regression probabilities*: AP: 0.37 vs. PP: 0.45; $F1_{1,34} = 3.17$; $p < .09$; $F2_{1,23} = 3.82$; $p < .07$).

Quite surprisingly, with an RC-modifier, the regression sensitive reading times were significantly shorter and there were less regressions from the disambiguating region than in all other *modifier type* conditions (*right-bounded RTs*: AP: 561ms vs. RC: 467ms; $F1_{1,34} = 12.08$; $p = .001$; $F2_{1,23} = 10.46$; $p < .005$; PP: 629ms vs. RC: 467ms; $F1_{1,34} = 17.83$; $p < .001$; $F2_{1,23} = 23.93$; $p < .001$; *regression-path durations*: AP: 823ms vs. RC: 586ms; $F1_{1,34} = 26.81$; $p < .001$; $F2_{1,23} = 16.67$; $p < .001$; PP: 1008ms vs. RC: 586ms; $F1_{1,34} = 35.82$; $p < .001$; $F2_{1,23} = 59.78$; $p < .001$; *regression probabilities*: AP: 0.37 vs. RC: 0.23; $F1_{1,34} = 20.11$; $p < .001$; $F2_{1,23} = 10.21$; $p < .005$; PP: 0.45 vs. RC: 0.23; $F1_{1,34} = 25.14$; $p < .001$; $F2_{1,23} = 40.36$; $p < .001$).

	NP-coord			VP-coord		
	AP	PP	RC	AP	PP	RC
FPRTs	413	409	332	493	461	468
RBRTs	526	538	415	596	720	520
RPDs	692	753	530	954	1264	642
reg. prob.	.30	.34	.21	.43	.56	.24

Table 2: Mean length adjusted reading times (in milliseconds) for the disambiguating region: *first pass reading times* (FPRTs), *right-bounded reading times* (RBRTs) and *regression-path durations* (RPDs). The probabilities of regressions from the disambiguating region to a previous region are shown in the last row.

The interaction between *modifier type* and *coordination type* was significant in *regression-path durations* ($F1_{2,68} = 6.66$; $p = .002$; $F2_{2,46} = 6.14$; $p < .005$) and - restricted to subject analysis - in the probabilities of regressions from the disambiguating region ($F1_{2,68} = 4.16$; $p = .02$; $F2_{2,46} = 1.46$; ns.), but not in *first pass reading times* (F1, F2 < 1.5) or in the right-bounded RTs on the disambiguating region (F1, F2 < 2.0; $p > .15$) (cf. Table 2 and Figures 2 to 5).

A closer examination of this interaction in the *regression-path durations* on the disambiguating region showed significant processing difficulties for the VP-coordination condition in each *modifier type* condition (AP:NP-coord vs. AP:VP-coord: $F1_{1,34} = 9.06$; p = .005; $F2_{1,23} = 11.30$; p < .005; PP:NP-coord vs. PP:VP-coord: $F1_{1,34} = 25.00$; p < .001; $F2_{1,23} = 21.32$; p < .001; RC:NP-coord vs. RC:VP-coord: $F1_{1,34} = 3.04$; p = .09; $F2_{1,23} = 7.91$; p < .01).

Simple contrasts for the probabilities of regressions from the disambiguating region, however, revealed a significant simple effect of *coordination type* after APs and PPs, but not after relative clauses (AP:NP-coord vs. AP:VP-coord: $F1_{1,34} = 5.90$; p = .02; $F2_{1,23} = 4.32$; p < .05; PP:NP-coord vs. PP:VP-coord: $F1_{1,34} = 26.07$; p < .001; $F2_{1,23} = 7.19$; p < .02; RC:NP-coord vs. RC:VP-coord: F1, F2 < 1.5; ns.).

The simple effect of *modifier type* was significant both in the NP-coordination condition (RPDs: $F1_{2,68} = 6.95$; p = .002; $F2_{2,46} = 12.45$; p < .001; *regression probabilities*: $F1_{2,68} = 3.65$; p = .03; $F2_{2,46} = 3.80$; p = .03) as well as in the VP-coordination condition (RPDs: $F1_{2,68} = 20.77$; p < .001; $F2_{2,46} = 20.21$; p < .001; *regression probabilities*: $F1_{2,68} = 16.29$; p < .001; $F2_{2,46} = 8.07$; p = .001). Linear contrasts showed that, regardless of *coordination type*, the *regression-path durations* were reliably shorter and the *probability of regressions* from the disambiguating region was reliably decreased in the RC-modifier condition compared to all other modifier conditions (i.e. AP or PP, respectively). This holds true even for NP-coordination (*regression-path durations*: AP vs. RC: $F1_{1,34} = 7.74$; p < .01; $F2_{1,23} = 11.95$; p = .002; PP vs. RC: $F1_{1,34} = 12.02$; p = .001; $F2_{1,23} = 24.46$; p < .001; *first-pass regression probability*: AP vs. RC: $F1_{1,34} = 7.36$; p = .01; $F2_{1,23} = 3.97$; p < .06; PP vs. RC: $F1_{1,34} = 5.41$; p < .03; $F2_{1,23} = 6.68$; p < .02) as well as for the garden-pathing VP-coordination (*regression-path durations*: AP vs. RC: $F1_{1,34} = 17.47$; p < .001; $F2_{1,23} = 9.69$; p = .005; PP vs. RC: $F1_{1,34} = 32.56$; p < .001; $F2_{1,23} = 33.77$; p < .001; *first-pass regression probability*: AP vs. RC: $F1_{1,34} = 17.09$; p < .001; $F2_{1,23} = 6.16$; p < .03; PP vs. RC: $F1_{1,34} = 30.78$; p < .001; $F2_{1,23} = 19.83$; p < .001).

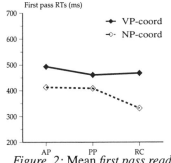

Figure 2: Mean *first pass reading times* on the disambiguating region. (length adjusted).

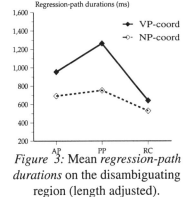

Figure 3: Mean *regression-path durations* on the disambiguating region (length adjusted).

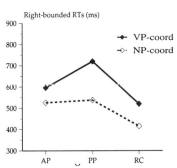

Figure 4: Mean *right-bounded reading times,* on the disambiguating region.(length adjusted)

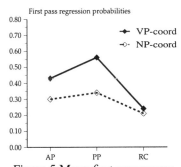

*Figure 5:*Mean *first pass regression probabilities* on the disambiguating region (length adjusted)

AP-vs. PP-modifiers

The data so far clearly demonstrate that subjects were garden-pathed in the VP-coordination condition, although this effect was less pronounced for RC-modifiers.

Importantly, the pattern of results suggests, that relative clauses are to be distinguished from the two other modifier types investigated. Contrary to what has been expected on the basis of the syntactic complexity hypothesis, processing times were generally *shorter* after relative clauses. Especially the measures which capture regressive saccades (i.e. the *regression probabilities,* the *regression-path durations* and - indirectly - the *right-bounded RTs*) indicate that subjects less frequently start regressions from the disambiguating region to earlier text passages after a relative clause. It seems that in this modifier condition re-reading of previous portions of the text is blocked, regardless of whether subjects are garden-pathed or not. This is reflected not only in the main effect of *modifier type*, but also in the significant contrasts between the relative clause condition and the other *modifier type* conditions within each of the *coordination type* conditions. Given this peculiar status of relative clauses, it seems reasonable to analyse the interaction between *modifier type* and *coordination type* in a reduced design which only includes AP- and PP-modifiers, in order to examine the influence of head position and/or the overlap of thematic processing domains.

Within this reduced design, we still found reliable two-way interactions between *modifier type* and *coordination type*, namely for right-bounded RTs ($F1_{1,34} = 3.90$; $p < .06$; $F2_{1,23} = 4.36$; $p < .05$) and for *regression-path durations* ($F1_{1,34} = 4.11$; $p = .05$; $F2_{1,23} = 5.30$; $p < .04$), but not for *first pass reading times* ($F1$, $F2 < 0.5$). After a PP-modifier, the disambiguating region took significantly longer to process than after an AP-modifier, but only in the garden-pathing VP-coordination condition (*right-bounded RTs*; VP-coord: AP vs. VP-coord: PP: $F1_{1,34} = 8.07$; $p < .01$; $F2_{1,23} = 8.16$; $p < .01$; *regression-path durations*: VP-coord: AP vs. VP-coord: PP: $F1_{1,34} = 9.18$; $p = .005$; $F2_{1,23} = 12.46$; $p = .002$). In the NP-coordination (control) condition, the corresponding simple effects of *modifier type* were far from being significant (*right-bounded RTs*; NP-coord: AP vs. NP-coord: PP: $F1$, $F2 < 0.5$; *regression-path durations*; NP-coord: AP vs. NP-coord: PP: $F1$, $F2 < 1.0$). Thus, the difference between APs and PPs (collapsed over coordination type) that we reported earlier can be reduced to the simple contrast in the garden-pathing condition (VP-coordination).

As already reported above, the simple effect of *coordination type* was significant in each of the modifier conditions for the RPDs. Similarly, there were prolonged *right-bounded RTs* for the VP-coordination condition in each of the modifier conditions (*right-bounded RTs*; AP:NP-coord vs. AP:VP-coord: $F1_{1,34} = 4.14$; $p = .05$; $F2_{1,23} = 2.54$; $p < .13$; PP:NP-coord vs. PP:VP-coord: $F1_{1,34} = 14.75$; $p = .001$; $F2_{1,23} = 10.25$; $p < .005$).

With respect to the probability of regressions from the disambiguating region, a similar pattern of results was observed as for the *right-bounded RTs* and for the *regression-path durations*, respectively. When subjects were garden-pathed (VP-coordination condition) there were more regressions from the disambiguating region in the PP-modifier condition than in the AP-modifier condition ($F1_{1,34} = 3.76$; $p = .06$; $F2_{1,23} = 5.00$; $p < .04$). In the NP-coordination condition, the simple effect of *modifier type* was not reliable (F1, F2 < 1.0). The two-way interaction of *coordination type* and *modifier type*, however, failed to reach significance in the *first-pass regression probabilities* (F1, F2 < 2.0; p > .15).

Spill-over region

There was a main effect of *modifier type* in the *first pass reading times* on the spill-over region which was reliable, however, only in the subject analysis ($F1_{2,68} = 3.96$; p < .03; $F2_{2,46} = 2.63$; p < .09) (cf. Table 3). Linear contrasts showed slightly prolonged FPRTs in the relative clause condition (AP: 188ms vs. PP: 199ms; F1, F2 < 1.0; AP: 188ms vs. RC: 235ms; $F1_{1,34} = 5.90$; p < .03; $F2_{1,23} = 3.39$; p < .08; PP: 199ms vs. RC: 235ms; $F1_{1,34} = 3.26$; p = .08; $F2_{1,23} = 3.40$; p < .08). A significant main effect of *modifier type* was also found for the *regression-path durations* ($F1_{2,68} = 9.35$; p < .001; $F2_{2,46} = 5.04$; p = .01). This effect was based on the same reading time pattern as was observed for the FPRTs, i.e. the spill-over region took longer to read in the RC-modifier condition than in the AP- or PP-modifier condition (RPDs: AP: 208ms vs. PP: 217ms; F1, F2 < 1.5; AP: 208ms vs. RC: 299ms; $F1_{1,34} = 15.78$; p < .001; $F2_{1,23} = 6.67$; p < .02; PP: 217ms vs. RC: 299ms; $F1_{1,34} = 7.99$, p < .01, $F2_{1,23} = 4.74$; p = .04).

In the *regression-path durations*, we also found an interaction between *modifier type* and *coordination type* ($F1_{2,68} = 7.27$; p = .001; $F2_{2,46} = 2.44$; p < .10) (cf. Table 3). Linear contrasts revealed that this interaction (which is significant only in the subject analysis) is mainly due to a simple effect of *coordination type* in the RC-modifier condition showing prolonged RPDs for VP-coordination ($F1_{1,34} = 6.98$; p < .02; $F2_{1,23} < 2.0$; ns.), whereas in the AP- or PP-modifier condition there is no significant effect of *coordination type* (all Fs < 2.0).

The simple effect of *modifier type* reached significance only in the VP-coordination condition ($F1_{2,68} = 11.03$; p < .001; $F2_{2,46} = 6.01$; p = .005) showing reliably prolonged RPDs for the RC-modifier condition (VP-coord: AP vs. VP-coord: PP: F1, F2 < 1.0; VP-coord: AP vs. VP-coord: RC: $F1_{1,34} = 14.21$; p = .001; $F2_{1,23} = 8.04$; p < .01; VP-coord: PP vs. VP-coord: RC: $F1_{1,34} = 10.09$; p < .005; $F2_{1,23} = 5.97$; p < .03). Since there was absolutely no reliable RPD-difference between the modifiers in the NP-coordination condition (all Fs < 1.5) the reported main effect of *modifier type* can be reduced to the simple effect in the garden-pathing (VP-coordination) condition.

At first glance, the RPD-pattern on the spill-over region (as compared to the corresponding FPRT-pattern) appears to contradict the hypothesis raised in the previous section, namely, that re-reading of earlier text passages during reanalysis is generally blocked by clause boundaries. Instead, the effect might just be delayed, such that regressions to an ambiguous relative clause are simply started later than regressions to an ambiguous AP or an ambiguous PP.

To clarify the matter we analyzed whether (and how long) people look back to material *beyond* the disambiguating region after they have read the spillover region. For that purpose, we treated the string including the disambiguating region and the spill-over region as one single region for all further measures sensitive to regressive saccades. That is, instead of the simple regression probabilities, which include regressive saccades to the disambiguating region, we only analyzed the probability of looking back to a pre-disambiguating region within the regression path of the spill-over region. Correspondingly, we computed the summed load contributions of all pre-disambiguating regions, which is the load contribution of the concatenation of all pre-disambiguating regions (R_p). Complementary, we replaced the simple *right-bounded reading times* for the spill-over-region with the sum of the load contributions of both relevant post-ambiguous regions, namely, the LC of the concatenation of the disambiguating region (R_d) and the spill-over region (R_s), R_{ds}.

	NP-coord			VP-coord		
	AP	PP	RC	AP	PP	RC
FPRTs	207	201	219	169	196	252
RPDs	223	221	236	194	213	362
LC(R_p,R_s)	13	26	36	67	69	32
[regr. prob]	[.01]	[.02]	[.04]	[.05]	[.05]	[.05]
LC(R_{ds},R_s)	175	190	178	145	166	269

Table 3: Mean length adjusted reading times (in milliseconds) on the spillover region: *first pass reading times* (FPRTs), *regression-path durations* (RPDs), and *load contributions* (LC) on the pre-disambiguating region (R_p), as well as on the string including the disambiguating region and the spill-over region (R_{ds}) within the *regression-path* of the spill-over region (R_s). The probabilities of regressions from the spill-over region (R_s) to the pre-critical region (R_p) are listed in brackets.

For the summed *load contributions* of the pre-disambiguating regions ($LC(R_p, R_s)$), we found absolutely no effects of the experimental factors (all Fs < 1.5) (cf. Table 3). In fact, as the corresponding *regression probabilities* in Table 3 indicate, there were only very few regressions from the spill-over region to the pre-disambiguating region. Hence, the increased RPDs for RC modifiers in the garden-pathing condition (VP-coordination) must be due to re-reading the disambiguating region and/or the spill-over region itself. This was confirmed by the data shown in the last row of Table 3.

The load contributions on the disambiguating region and the spill-over region ($LC(R_{ds}, R_s)$) exactly replicated the RPD-pattern on the spill-over region: there was a significant main effect of *modifier type* ($F1_{2,68} = 8.94$; p < .001; $F2_{2,46} = 4.30$; p < .02) which was due to reliably prolonged reading times in the RC-modifier condition (AP: 160ms vs. PP: 178ms; F1, F2 < 2.0; ns.; AP: 160ms vs. RC: 224ms; $F1_{1,34} = 16.65$; p < .001; $F2_{1,23} = 5.95$; p < .03; PP: 178ms vs. RC: 224ms; $F1_{1,34} = 6.55$; p < .02; $F2_{1,23} = 4.20$; p < .06).

Furthermore, the interaction between *modifier type* and *coordination type* was also reliable ($F1_{2,68} = 8.56$; p < .001; $F2_{2,46} = 6.62$; p < .005). Linear contrasts revealed significantly longer reading times for VP-coordination in the RC-modifier condition ($F1_{1,34} = 9.86$; p < .005; $F2_{1,23} = 7.90$; p = .01), but no effects of *coordination type* in the AP- or PP-modifier condition (all Fs < 2.0). The simple effect of *modifier type* was significant only in the garden-pathing VP-coordination condition ($F1_{2,68} = 13.55$; p < .001; $F2_{2,46} = 8.06$; p = .001) with reliably prolonged *load contributions* in the RC-modifier condition (VP-coord: AP vs. VP-coord: PP: F1, F2 < 1.5; VP-coord: AP vs. VP-coord: RC: $F1_{1,34} = 21.44$; p < .001; $F2_{1,23} = 10.70$; p < .001; VP-coord: PP vs. VP-coord: RC: $F1_{1,34} = 12.51$; p = .001; $F2_{1,23} = 7.81$; p = .01).

We conclude that there are regressive saccades even in the RC-modifier condition. These regressions, however, are qualitatively different from the regressions found in the other modifier conditions (AP and PP), in that they start later and, most importantly, in that they go back to pre-disambiguating regions to a much lesser extent; fixations merely stay in the region where the error was detected. This pattern therefore confirms that re-reading the ambiguous region is hindered by a right clause boundary that has already been passed.

DISCUSSION

The reliable interaction of *modifier type* and *coordination type* in regression-sensitive scores suggests that the additional processing cost induced by PPs is not independent of reanalysis processes, contrary to the predictions of Ferreira and Henderson (in press). The garden-path effect found after a PP-modified NP is much more severe than after an AP-modified NP, while no differential effect shows up in the control condition. In summing up, the "head position effect" was clearly established in the reduced design (only PP and AP modifiers). On the other hand, there was no sign of additional processing load due to additional embedded TPDs in any of the regions, contrary to Ferreira and Henderson's (in press) predictions.[12]

In general, the pattern of results obtained in this experiment suggest that the *head-position* is in fact the critical factor, whereas the embedding of another *thematic processing domain seems to be irrelevant*. Note, however, that in the constructions investigated here, the *head position* effect cannot easily be explained by parallel activation of thematic frames up to the point where the thematic integration of the head is possible, as suggested by Ferreira and Henderson (1991), because the structural ambiguity investigated here does not coincide with a lexical (i.e. thematic frame) ambiguity. Thus, the frame-activation model must be refined to cover situations with single frame activation. What is needed is a more detailed specification of the potential course of activation.

Thematic frame activation and decay

If we want to keep the thematic frame activation model proposed by Ferreira and Henderson (1991) consistent with the data, further specifications will be needed. Since there is no re-activation of a discarded thematic frame involved in reanalysis here, a thematic frame based explanation requires a more specific analysis of the course of activation of the single thematic frame that may (or may not) be kept active throughout the entire analysis.

Note that in the initially preferred NP-coordination, the ambiguous NP is coordinated with the final argument of the verb. Let us stipulate that

i.   *the thematic frame is kept activated until the head (noun) of the final argument of the verb is encountered.*

ii. *After that, activation decays quite rapidly.*

iii. *The thematic frame can be re-activated if needed, but the ease of re-activation depends upon the current activation level.*

In the constructions under investigation here, we would then expect a course of activation roughly as illustrated in Figure 6.

A post-nominal modifier prolongs the distance between the beginning of activation decay and the point of error detection, so that the activation level of

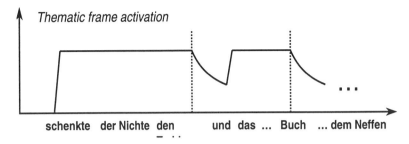

Figure 6: Course of activation of the thematic frame of the verb *schenkte* *("gave as a present").* Activation is kept high until the head of the final argument, and decays afterwards. At the conjunct *and,* the preferred NP-coordination opens up the final argument again, so that the thematic frame is reactivated. As soon as the head of the coordinated NP *(Buch, "book")* is encountered, activation decays again.

the thematic frame of the verb is supposedly much lower than without a post-nominal modifier, and the recovery of the thematic frame will therefore take longer. Since the frame is needed for the reanalysis of the correct coordination structure, an increased penalty is to be expected for post-nominal modifiers.

Although these assumptions are post-hoc stipulations, note that they make clear predictions: whenever the final argument is lengthened by a post-nominal modifier, recovery of the verb-frame should take longer. In *NP1-and-NP2* coordinations, the head-position effect is predicted for both NP2 and NP1 (*the teddy,* in the examples above), if *NP1* is also modified by an AP or PP: since the thematic frame of the verb has to be deactivated after the final argument and reactivated after the conjunct (otherwise the explanation would not work), an NP1-head-position effect is predicted at the conjunct or shortly afterwards (at NP2). Such a study is currently underway and further research will be necessary to evaluate this point.

NP-activation and decay

What happens after error detection? Throughout the reanalysis towards the elliptic VP-coordination, not only must a new VP be assembled, but also the thematic frame must be copied and instantiated with new arguments. The frame activation hypothesis discussed above suggests that the ease or difficulty of doing so depends upon the activation of the thematic frame to be copied. Alternatively, one could consider the activation of the *arguments* responsible for the head-position effect, rather than the activation of the *functor*. Such an approach looks more straightforward, since it is the position of the head of the final *argument* that yielded the effect in this study.

Suppose that binding NPs (or their referential manifestations, i.e. discourse entities, DEs) to argument-positions is a quasi-anaphoric process, and that binding takes longer the lower the activation of the filler gets. Let us further suppose that NPs (DEs) come with activations, which decay immediately after their head is encountered (perhaps unless activation is kept high through mechanisms such as *focussing*, etc., see Hemforth et al., this volume), as illustrated in Figure 7.

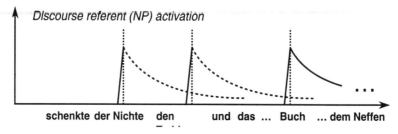

Figure 7: Course of activation of the argument NPs.

When it becomes clear (i.e. at the disambiguating NP *dem Neffen*) that a new thematic frame has to be allocated and instantiated with new arguments, the accessibility of the argument filler that has to be re-assigned to the new frame *(Buch, "book"*, in the example above) depends on its level of activation at that point in time. Its activation level, however, depends upon the time that has passed since the noun was encountered, i.e. upon the amount of material between its head and the point of binding to an argument position. This would clearly predict the head-position effect as well. No stipulations about the activation of thematic frames are required though.

We want to leave open whether such a process is anaphoric rather than syntactic in nature. Considering the latter possibility, the approach seems compatible in principle with Stevenson's (1993), and possibly with other activation based models.

Note that *no* NP1-head-position effect (in a *NP1 -and-NP2* coordination) is predicted here, since NP1 can be immediately bound to an argument variable in the thematic frame of the verb.

The semantic unpacking hypothesis

Alternatively, we propose that the reanalysis effect obtained might rather be due to incremental re-*interpretation* effort, without reference to activation levels of any sort.

Let us assume that the following propositions have been established after the ambiguous NP was read:

i.   gave1(j, k, l)

  ii. *Heinz(j)*

  iii. *niece(k)*

  iv. *teddy(l₁)*

  v. *book(l₂)*

When *the nephew* is read, the model must be modified to:

i.   gave1(j, k, l)

  ii. gave2(j, o, p)

  iii. *Heinz(j)*

  iv. *niece(k)*

  v. *teddy(l)*

  vi. *book(p)*

  vii. *nephew(o)*

The most substantial change here is that *book* must be unbound from an argument of *gave1* and re-bound to an argument variable of *gave2*.

Within this approach, the head-position effect might be due to the amount of semantic or conceptual elaborations (inferences) in the discourse model that have to be discarded as a consequence of re-interpretation. Conceptual refinements and elaborations are a consequence of the ongoing process of interpretation starting as soon as the *semantic head* of a phrase is integrated into a (thematic) proposition (or as soon as the semantic head can be predicted by conceptual means). Let us suppose that the semantic representation becomes enriched during the process of interpretation, so that more and more predicates are added to the model (or mental images of the scenery are constructed). This process will surely not be finished by the time the next word is read but will continue to proceed parallel to parsing. When it comes to reanalysis, these representations will have to be disentangled and partly destroyed.

The more information there is to revise, the harder the reinterpretation should be.

Rather than the decay of the activation of any sort, the proposed responsibility for the head-position effect here is the richness of the mental representations resulting from the interpretation and integration of semantic heads.[13]

Surface representation

What about the relative clauses? We propose that the fact that relative clauses are processed differently is related to working memory components in charge of a more concise internal representation of the input string. It is a well established fact that the surface representation of the preceding clause becomes much less readily accessible after the clause boundary is passed (cf. Caplan, 1972; Jarvella, 1979). The results obtained emphasize this phenomenon: after having passed a noun-modifier, readers are much less likely to re-read portions of it if they have to pass a right clause boundary simultaneously. Furthermore, garden-pathing is delayed until some words later, indicating that local processes interfere with other ongoing processes which supposedly spilled-over from the previous region. A plausible interpretation is that certain compacting and integration procedures (wrap-up) are triggered at subclause boundaries during which some surface-oriented representations of the sentence are discarded (while interpretation is deepened), supposedly to free the space for new materials to come in.

Interestingly, the lack of a functional surface representation then seems to block regressive saccades even though the input string is still visible. Such representations appear to be involved in the visual processing of the stimuli, so that saccade planning becomes hard to accomplish without them. This would explain the decreased probability of looking back to portions of the text read previously.

This effect can hardly be explained by properties of the grammar system alone. Even though most grammar theories focus on sentences as the relevant entities of theoretical investigation, there is no property of grammar theories that might predict that clause boundaries trigger such mechanisms. The explanation is thus genuinely architectural; i. e. it is tied to the properties of the performance system and its interaction with the representations assumed, in particular to its limited working memory capacity. Further research is necessary to clarify the role of the working memory in reading and eye-movement planning.

CONCLUDING REMARKS

Reanalysis difficulty was shown to depend on the internal structure of the ambiguous region, namely, on the position of the head of the ambiguous phrase as well as on the question of whether a right clause boundary had to be passed for re-reading.

With respect to the head-position effect, none of the current approaches discussed in the literature offer a straightforward explanation for the kind of construction investigated here: F&H's (in press) recent account, based on the assumption that the so-called "head position effect" is in fact due to the existence or non-existence of embedded thematic processing domains, is clearly disconfirmed by the data.

F&H's (1991) original account, based on the activation pattern of discarded thematic frames, is hardly applicable to the structures investigated, since no thematic frame ambiguity is involved here. Nevertheless, only minor modifications to the model were shown to suffice in providing a post-hoc explanation of the data.

We offered two more potential accounts, nevertheless. The first was based on the activation pattern of discourse entities, which becomes crucial during the supposedly anaphoric process of thematic frame instantiation. The second approach emphasizes the role of conceptual re-interpretation. We are aware of the fact that this approach shifts the problem of reanalysis to the field of semantic / conceptual processing - and it will be necessary to set up further experiments that will enable us to dissociate the processes involved and to distinguish the alternative proposals.

Acknowledgements

This research was supported by grants from the German National Research Foundation (Deutsche Forschungsgemeinschaft, DFG, grant no. Str 4-1/3, He 2310/2) and by the Cognitive Science Graduate Program located at the University of the Saarland, Saarbrücken. We want to thank Gerhard Strube for numerous fruitful discussions, and our students Thomas Mulack, Thilo Weigel, Christoph Hoelscher, and Nick Ketley, for running the experiments and for their helpful comments on earlier versions of this manuscript. We also like to thank Don Mitchell, Marica de Vincenzi, Fernanda Ferreira, Janet Fodor, and two anonymous reviewers for their valuable comments on an earlier version of this paper.

NOTES

[1] This preference is predicted by a number of parsing principles, the best known of which is late closure (Frazier & Rayner, 1982; Frazier, 1987). But principles from various accounts, for example theta attachment (Abney, 1987: Pritchett, 1988, 1992) or the principle of head attachment (Konieczny, Hemforth, & Strube, 1991; Konieczny, Scheepers, Hemforth, & Strube, 1994; Konieczny, Hemforth, Scheepers, & Strube, 1997), predict the same preferences for this kind of structures.

[2] Sentences were presented following the RSVP-technique, with roughly 4 words per minute.

[3] In addition to this, the second part of the VP-coordination in (6b) is not parallel to the first part in its constituent order: whereas the indirect object precedes the direct object in the first part of the conjunction, which is the unmarked order, the direct object comes first in the second part. For present purposes it is irrelevant which of these factors mainly causes problems.

[4] Note, however, that the second VP in the VP-coordination is elliptic and requires the verb to be copied.

[5] Subjects answered with a high degree of accuracy (85% correct responses).

[6] We want to thank Chuck Clifton, whose software for stimulus presentation and data recording was the basis for the version used in this study.

[7] Data analysis was carried out in four stages: First, raw data were compacted to single fixations, if they were continuously located in one of the rectangles in the 80 x 25 VGA character matrix of the screen for at least 10 ms. These fixations were then related to the positions of the words of the respective stimulus item on the screen. This second step was computed with the program Analyse1, written in C by Thilo Weigel. The output, consisting of sequences of fixations on words, and the lengths of the particular words, thirdly, was fed into the program Eye2Mind (Konieczny, in prep.), written in ObjectiveC (and based on Openstep, running on Nextstep 3.3 or higher). Eye2Mind computes all higher-level scores that entered the statistical analysis as dependent variables.

[8] RPDs and related measures have been used under different names recently, such as *cumulative region reading times* (Brysbaert, 1994). A similar measure was developed by Kennedy et al. (1989), called *total pass per word*. We will adhere to the term *regression-path duration*, because it will allow us to focus

on different aspects of the *regression path* needed for the definition of other measures.

[9] Just and Carpenter (1987) found a linear increase of about 30 ms per character. In our own regression analysis, however, we found a slope of about 20 ms per character.

[10] The definition of extreme values is implemented in the SPSS-procedure *EXAMINE*.

[11] Also the accuracy in responding to the questions significantly decreased in the VP-coordination condition, as was obtained by loglinear analyses (NP-coord: 93% correct answers vs. VP-coord: 77% correct answers; *likelihood ratio chi square change* = 51.00; df = 1; p < .001).

[12] Note that this result raises the question of how the "head-position" effect found in the non-garden-pathing conditions in the experiments of F&H (1991, in press) are to be explained. It might be too strong a claim that readers are *never* garden-pathed in the control sentences (especially considering the context of a psycholinguistic experiment containing a substantial number of early closure constructions). Readers might just be *less often* garden-pathed in the control condition. Also note that such a stance is not a commitment to probabilistic models. The data might just reflect various noise inducing artifacts, such as whether or not the immediately preceding sentences at a given point in the experiment consisted mostly of non-preferred constructions (priming), or such as intra-sentential aspects like the lexical aspects of the words used, pragmatic factors, etc. Therefore, one would expect for a minority, say 20%, of the cases that readers are garden pathed even if the construction read supposedly supports the preferred first analysis (and, of course, that readers are *not* garden-pathed in supposedly unpreferred constructions in a comparable number of cases). Under such a premise one would expect factors that amplify a garden-path effect in the garden-path condition to be effective in the non-garden-pathing condition as well, although to a lesser extent.

[13] In one of their experiments, F&H (in press) varied the subject-object ordering within the RC-modifier. The additional processing load induced by object-RCs should be independent of the reanalysis load and thus show up as a penalty in both early and late closure sentences. Interestingly, they established a processing penalty for object-RCs only in early closure constructions, not in the late-closure controls.

REFERENCES

Abney, S. (1987). Licensing and parsing. *Proceedings of the 17th Conference of the NELS, Cambridge, MA*. ??.

Abney, S. (1989). A computational model of human parsing. *Journal of Psycholinguistic Research, 20* (3), 233-250.

Altmann, G. T., Garnham, A., & Dennis, Y. (1992). Avoiding the garden path: eye movements in context. *Journal of Memory and Language, 31*, 685-712.

Baddeley, A. D. (1986). *Working memory.* Oxford: Oxford University Press.

Berwick, R. C., & Weinberg, A. S. (1984). *The grammatical basis of linguistic performance.* Cambridge, MA. MIT Press.

Branigan, H. (1995). *Language processing and the mental representation of syntactic structure.* Unpublished doctoral thesis, University of Edinburgh.

Brysbaert, M. (1994). *Sentence reading: do we make use of non-audible cues.* Paper presented at the 4th Workshop on Language Comprehension, Giens, 13-14 May.

Caplan, D. (1972). Clause boundaries and recognition latencies for words in sentences. *Perception & Psychophysics, 12,* 73-76.

Ferreira, F., & Henderson, J. (1991). Recovery from misanalyses of garden-path sentences. *Journal of Memory and Language, 30,* 725-745.

Frazier, L. (1987). Sentence processing: A tutorial review. In M. Coltheart (Ed.), *The psychology of reading* (pp. 559-586). Hove/London/Hillsdale: Lawrence Erlbaum.

Frazier, L., & Clifton, C. (1996). *Construal.* Cambridge, MA: MIT Press.

Frazier, L,. & Flores d'Arcais, G. (1989). Filler driven parsing: a study of gap filling in Dutch. *Journal of Memory and Language, 28,* 331-344.

Frazier, L., & Fodor, J. D. (1978). The sausage machine: a two stage parsing model. *Cognition, 6,* 291-325.

Frazier, L., & Rayner, K. (1982). Making and correcting errors during sentence comprehension: eye movements in the analysis of structurally ambiguous sentences. *Cognitive Psychology, 14,* 178-210.

Gibson, E. (in press). Memory limitations and linguistic processing breakdown. Cambridge, MA: MIT Press.

Hemforth, B. (1993). *Kognitives Parsing: Repräsentation und Verarbeitung sprachlichen Wissens.* Sankt Augustin: Infix.

Hemforth, B., Konieczny, L,. & Scheepers, C. (1994). On Reanalysis: Head position and syntactic complexity. In B. Hemforth, L. Konieczny, C. Scheepers & G. Strube (Eds.), *First analysis, reanalysis and repair.* (IIG-Berichte 8/94) (pp. 23-50). Freiburg: University of Freiburg, Institute for Computer Science and Social Research.

Hemforth, B., Konieczny, L., & Strube, G. (1993). Incremental syntax processing and parsing strategies. *Proceedings of the 15th Annual Conference of the Cognitive Science Society.* Hillsdale, NJ: Erlbaum, 539-545.

Hörmann, H. (1976). *Meinen und Verstehen. Grundzüge einer psychologischen Semantik.* Frankfurt am Main: Suhrkamp.

Jarvella, R. J. (1979). Immediate memory and discourse processing. In G. H. Bower (Ed.), *The psychology of learning and motivation (Vol. 13).* New York: Academic Press.

Kennedy, A., Murray, W. S., Jennings, F., & Reid, C. (1989). Parsing complements: Comments on the generality of the principle of minimal attachment. *Language and Cognitive Processes, 4,* 51-76.

Konieczny, L. (1996). *Human sentence processing: a semantics-oriented parsing approach (IIG-Berichte 3/96).* Freiburg: University of Freiburg, Institute for Computer Science and Social Research.

Konieczny, L. (in prep.). *Eye-movement data analysis with Eye2Mind* (IIG-Bericht). Freiburg: University of Freiburg, Institute for Computer Science and Social Research.

Konieczny, L., Hemforth, B., & Scheepers, C. (1994). Reanalysis vs. internal repairs: Nonmonotonic processes in sentence perception. In B. Hemforth, L. Konieczny, C. Scheepers & G. Strube (Eds.), *First Analysis, reanalysis, and repair (IIG-Berichte 8/94)* (pp. 1-23). Freiburg: University of Freiburg, Institute for Computer Science and Social Research.

Konieczny, L., Scheepers, C., Hemforth, B. & Strube, G. (1994). Semantikorientierte Syntaxverarbeitung. In S. Felix, C. Habel & G. Rickheit (Eds.), *Kognitive Linguistik: Repräsentationen und Prozesse.* Opladen: Westdeutscher Verlag.

Konieczny, L., Hemforth, B., Scheepers, C., & Strube, G. (1997). The role of lexical heads in parsing: Evidence from German. *Language and cognitive processes,* 2-3.

Lewis, R. (1993). *An architecturally-based theory of human sentence comprehension.* Unpublished doctoral thesis, Carnegie Mellon University, Pittsburgh, PA.

Liversedge, S. (1994). *Referential contexts, relative clauses, and syntactic parsing.* Unpublished doctoral thesis, University of Dundee.

Mitchell, D. C. (1989). Verb-guidance and other lexical effects in parsing. *Language and Cognitive Processes, 4,* 123-155.

Pritchett, B. L. (1988). Garden path phenomena and the grammatical basis of language processing. *Language, 64,* 539-576.

Pritchett, B. (1992). *Grammatical competence and parsing performance.* Chicago: University of Chicago Press.

Rayner, K., Sereno S. C., Morris, R. K., Schmauder, A. R., & Clifton, C. (1989). Eye movements and on-line language comprehension processes. *Language and Cognitive Processes, 4,* 21-50.

Scheepers, C. (1996). *Menschliche Satzverarbeitung: Syntaktische und thematische Aspekte der Wortstellung im Deutschen.* Freiburg: Unpublished doctoral dissertation, University of Freiburg, Freiburg, Germany.

Stevenson, S. (1993). *A constrained active attachment model for resolving syntactic ambiguities in natural language parsing.* Unpublished doctoral dissertation,University of Maryland.

Strube, G., Hemforth, B., & Wrobel, H. (1990). Resolution of structural ambiguities in sentence comprehension: On-line analysis of syntactic lexical and semantic effects. *Proceedings of the 12th Annual Conference of the Cognitive Science Society* (pp. 558-565). Hillsdale, NJ: Erlbaum.

Warner, J., & Glass, A. L. (1987). Context and distance-to-disambiguation effects in ambiguity resolution: Evidence from grammaticallity judgments of garden path sentences. *Journal of Memory and Language, 26,* 714-738.

SUBJECT-VERB AGREEMENT IN GERMAN: EVIDENCE FROM PRODUCTION AND COMPREHENSION EXPERIMENTS

Christoph Hölscher and Barbara Hemforth
University of Freiburg

INTRODUCTION

In many languages the subject and verb of a sentence agree in number. The grammatical rule of subject-verb number agreement is rather basic and straightforward, so that most children at the age of 4 years master it quite well (Keeney & Wolfe, 1972).

Nonetheless, agreement violations are found quite frequently in both spoken and written language:

(1)   The readiness of our conventional forces are at an all-time low.
        (quoted from Bock & Miller, 1991)

(2)   Obwohl die Versuchsperson weiß, was in diesen Situationen wichtig sind...
        (W. Kintsch, quoted from Schriefers & van Kampen, 1993)

The examples (1) and (2) have a singular subject. Therefore a singular verb would have been appropriate. Looking at the examples one can see that in between the subject and the verb there are one or more nouns which do not agree with the number of the subject. The verb falsely agrees with these local or proximal nouns which seem to have disrupted the agreement process. This phenomenon has been called attraction error or proximity concord (Quirk, Greenbaum, Leech & Svartvik, 1972).

In recent years, agreement errors in spoken production have received increased attention in the literature, while agreement phenomena in written production and in language comprehension have only occasionally been investigated. In fact, with respect to processing German sentences these questions have not been addressed at all.

279

B. Hemforth and L. Konieczny (eds.), German Sentence Processing, 279-310.

In this paper, we will present two experiments on agreement phenomena in German: Experiment 1 addresses the domain of written production, while Experiment 2 - an eye-tracking study - looks into the comprehension of constructions that are known to elicit high rates of agreement errors in sentence production. The design and materials were held constant across both experiments to allow for a comparison between these two domains.

AGREEMENT IN PRODUCTION

To investigate the production of agreement errors in a laboratory setting, Bock and colleagues (Bock & Miller, 1991, Bock & Cutting, 1992, Bock & Miller, 1993; cf. Bock, 1995 for an overview) introduced a sentence completion task which is capable of eliciting such errors: a sentence initial fragment (preamble) such as: *"The key to the cabinets"* is presented aurally. Subjects then repeat the preambles and complete them to full sentences as rapidly as possibly. Usually the subjects immediately continue the fragment with a verb so that the noun of the second NP can be seen as a local noun. The number marking of both the local and the head noun are varied systematically.

Significantly higher error rates were found across a number of experiments when the head noun mismatched the local noun in number, compared to control conditions with matching nouns. This effect corresponds to the proximity concord or attraction errors introduced above. Furthermore, there is an asymmetry between the two mismatch-conditions *singular-plural* and *plural-singular*. Most errors are found for sentences with a singular head noun and a plural local noun. Eberhard (1993) has argued that the singular is to be seen as a default and that only plural forms are marked for number. Applied to the asymmetry between the mismatch conditions this means that most errors occur when the head noun does not carry any agreement marker while the local noun is overtly number-marked, rendering it a salient distractor.

Bock and others (Bock & Miller, 1991, Bock & Cutting, 1992, Bock & Miller, 1993) investigated a number of semantic, lexical and phonological factors that might contribute to agreement violations: the length of intervening material between subject and verb showed only a weak effect on agreement errors. Phonological aspects seem to be negligible since singular local nouns which are homophones of plural forms do not elicit increased error rates. No semantic influences could be demonstrated in these experiments either: neither animacy nor notional number (comparing regular nouns such as "ship" with collective nouns such as "fleet"), nor the comparison of single-token preambles ("the key to the cabinets") to multiple-token preambles ("the picture on the postcards") showed any effects. From this pattern of results,

Bock and her colleagues concluded that agreement processes are syntactic in nature and that they are computed on an abstract-syntactic level without influences from semantic-conceptual sources.

This view has been further explicated by Nicol and colleagues (Vigliocco & Nicol, 1995; Nicol, 1996). They adopted Eberhard's (1993) view that singular is the default number marking and that only plural-marked nouns can interfere with the agreement process. In the case of subjects marked for plural, Vigliocco & Nicol (1995) see the normal agreement process as a percolation of the plural-marker from the head noun to the verb. If no plural-marker is percolated to the verb, a singular verb is produced. But there can also be an erroneous or "slippery" feature percolation (Nicol, 1996) from a plural local noun to the verb, which then leads to falsely producing a plural verb. Nicol's model thus accounts for the fact that most agreement errors occur with a singular head noun and a plural local noun because this is the only case where an erroneous percolation of a plural feature from the local noun to the verb yields the incorrect verb form. Further support for this model comes from experiments by Vigliocco and Nicol (1995) using complex NPs with three nouns such as (3) and (4):

(3)   The helicopter for the flights over the canyon ...

(4)   The helicopter for the flight over the canyons ...

Higher error rates were detected for constructions such as (3) in which the mismatching noun phrase was closer to the head of the NP compared to constructions with a more deeply embedded noun phrase such as (4), although the mismatch in (4) occurs closer to the verb in the surface structure of the sentence. These results are in line with the hypothesis that mismatch effects can be characterized by "slippery" feature percolation.

In the domain of written production, Branigan and her colleagues (Branigan, 1995; Branigan et al., 1995) used a written sentence-completion task and obtained somewhat different results from Bock et al.'s data. For singular head nouns the basic attraction effect was replicated with British subjects showing the general applicability of the written task for the investigation of agreement errors. The notable difference to the spoken production data was the fact that higher error rates were found after plural heads compared with after singular heads. Most errors occurred in the plural-plural match condition, a result that cannot be accounted for by a mismatch effect.[1] Branigan (1995) suspects that an explanation can be found on the level of conceptual integration into a mental model. Following Fodor (1982), she assumes that the many-to-many mappings necessary for building a mental model of plural-plural preambles are the most difficult and, therefore, interfere most with the agreement process. Unfortunately, most experiments on agreement use only singular heads, so that the specific effects of head noun plurality are not yet fully understood.

Vigliocco and others (Vigliocco et al., 1995; Vigliocco et al., 1996) also found significant semantic-conceptual effects on agreement processes in Italian, Dutch and French. Multiple-token head nouns consistently yielded more errors than single-token heads (see examples (3) and (4) above) in these 3 languages. Since North-American speakers were insensitive to the semantic variable "distributivity" (cf. Bock and Miller, 1991), one has to look for inter-lingual differences between (North-American) English and Italian, Dutch and French. The morphology of number-marking on the verb was identified as the crucial interlingual difference to English (Vigliocco et al., 1996). While the verb is often not unambiguously marked for number in English, it always is in the other three languages. The authors argue that verbal number inflection in English no longer carries any semantic information (no information about the number of participants in a scenario) due to the reduced morphology. As a consequence, the notion that number agreement is produced on an abstract-syntactic level in English cannot be generalized to other languages.

In German, spoken production of number agreement was investigated by Schriefers and van Kampen (1993). They contrasted phonological and syntactic factors making use of the fact that the accusative but not the dative form of a plural noun and its determiner is phonologically identical to the nominative case. Making a local noun phonologically compatible with the sentence's subject should increase the likelihood of attraction errors but only if the phonological level influences the agreement process.

Two types of constructions were used in this experiment: complex noun phrases with quantificatory heads such as (5) and (6) were compared to NP-PP preambles with non-quantificatory heads such as (7) and (8).

(5)   Eine Anzahl Filme über diese Themen... (local noun: acc, plural)
            (A number of movies about these subjects ...)

(6)   Eine Menge Vögel in den Wäldern... (local noun: dat., pl.)
            (A number of birds in the forests...)

(7)   Der Hinweis auf die Akten... (local noun: acc., plural)
            (The reference to the files...)

(8)   Der Hinweis in den Akten... (local noun: dat., plural)
            (The reference in the files...)

There appears to be no clear grammatical rule for quantificatory heads in German: native speakers judge both singular and plural verb forms as equally acceptable. It may be suspected that the processes underlying agreement in these special cases differ from the processes of agreement in general. Therefore, we will only concentrate on non-quantificatory heads.

For non-quantificatory heads - which are equivalent to the constructions usually employed in Bock's experiments - agreement effects could only be established with some constraints: the head noun has to be feminine and - contrary to the phonological hypothesis - the local noun has to appear in the dative case. For such materials the determiner of the head noun is ambiguous with respect to number marking, while the determiner of the distracting local noun is unambiguously number-marked (see Vigliocco et al., 1995, for similar morphological influences in Italian). These constraints were adopted for the construction of the materials for the present experiments to increase the probability of attraction errors.

PLAUSIBILITY AS A CONFOUNDING SEMANTIC FACTOR?

The experiments by Branigan et al. (1995) and Vigliocco and colleagues (Vigliocco et al., 1995; Vigliocco et al., 1996) challenge the idea that agreement effects must be described on a purely syntactic level, at least when generalizing to different languages.

Systematically varying the number of the head noun and local noun in the design of a study may at the same time change the plausibility of an item:

(9)   The key to the cabinet...

(10)   The key to the cabinets...

Sentence fragment (9) and (10) differ in the plausibility of the situations that they describe: the syntactically simple singular-singular match version (9) is at the same time conceptually simple, while the critical mismatch version (10) represents the special case of some kind of master key.

Consider also example (11) and (12):

(11)   The statue which stood in the courtyards at the mansion...

(12)   The statue which stood in the courtyard at the mansions...

A single statue standing in more than one courtyard is either hard to imagine or requires a generic reading in (11), while example (12) poses no such problem on a conceptual level.

Plausibility differences become even more obvious when animate, human participants are involved. A sentence fragment like "the king of the subjects" describes the standard situation, while "the kings of the subject" needs some additional inferences like the subject being rather long-lived.

Such differences in plausibility, if they are in fact systematically confounded with syntactic variation, could be an alternative explanation for agreement errors. It appears that the critical mismatch conditions are frequently the conceptually more complex or unusual ones and hence the less plausible ones. Increased error rates in these conditions might not only be due to syntactic but also to semantic-conceptual difficulties. Vigliocco et al. (1996) have shown a possible confound of plausibility and agreement errors in Dutch.

For the following two experiments the plausibility of the items was systematically controlled, contrasting especially the two mismatch conditions singular-plural and plural-singular. Plausibility ratings were obtained for full sentences with initial complex NPs. The sentences' initial fragments were used as stimuli in Experiment 1, while in Experiment 2 full sentences were presented.

Three different sets of materials were constructed:

(13)   S-P mismatch (a.) more plausible

    a.   Die Göre mit den Büchern wartet an der Telefonzelle. (S-P)
         The girl with the books waits at the phone booth.

    b.   Die Gören mit dem Buch warten an der Telefonzelle. (P-S)
         The girls with the book wait at the phone booth.

(14)   P-S mismatch (b.) more plausible

    a.   Die Pflanze vor den Fenstern vertrocknet in der Hitze.
         The plant at the windows withers in the heat.

    b.   Die Pflanzen vor dem Fenster vertrocknen in der Hitze.
         The plants at the window wither in the heat.

(15)   both mismatch conditions equally plausible

    a.   Die Tanne neben den Eichen verliert ihre Nadeln im Winter nicht.
         The fir tree next to the oaks loses its needles in Winter not.

b.   Die Tannen neben der Eiche verlieren ihre Nadeln im Win-
       ter nicht.
       The fir trees next to the oak lose their needles in Winter not.

In a. the critical mismatch condition S-P, which usually yields the highest
error rates, is constructed as highly plausible compared to the opposing
mismatch condition P-S, while in a. this relation is reversed. As a control
condition items such as a. are constructed where all four syntactic variations
are equally plausible.

EXPERIMENT 1

In this experiment, a written sentence completion task was used to investigate
agreement errors in written production. The number of both head noun and
local noun were varied independently to capture the agreement processes for
singular and plural head nouns. Together with a three-level factor of plausibility, this manipulation resulted in a 2*2*3 design. Correct and incorrect
number inflections of the verb were scored as dependent variables.

Methods

Participants

Twenty-four undergraduate students (German native speakers) from the University of Freiburg and the Ruhr-Universitaet Bochum participated in the
study. They received either payment or course credits for participation.

Materials

In pretests an item-pool of 48 sentences was constructed with 16 items for
each of the following plausibility conditions: A. mismatch condition S-P more
plausible than mismatch condition P-S, B. mismatch condition P-S more plausible than S-P, C. all syntactic variations equally plausible (control condition).
In all three plausibility conditions the match conditions S-S and P-P had to be
of about the same above-medium plausibility. These materials were selected
and confirmed with a paper-and-pencil questionnaire and a computer-assisted

questionnaire with 20 participants each. Average ratings on a 6-point scale (0= highly implausible, 5= highly plausible) are shown in table 1.

Number condition	Plausibility condition A (S-P more plausible)	Plausibility condition B (P-S more plausible)	Plausibility condition C (control)
S-S	3,38	3,63	3,92
S-P	3,65	1,78	3,93
P-S	1,87	3,90	3,58
P-P	3,65	3,74	3,47

Table 1: Mean plausibility ratings from pre-tests.

Four versions of each item were used, resulting from independently varying the number of the head and local noun. Only the initial complex noun-phrases of the target sentences were used in Experiment 1. Four lists were constructed, so that each item was included in each list once and an equal number of items of each syntactic version was included in each list.

In addition, 48 filler items were used to distract from the experimental variation. None of these filler items had a PP in its initial noun phrase. Since all the experimental items were constructed with a feminine head noun, masculine or neuter head nouns were employed in the filler items. The number of the head noun was balanced across all materials (target and filler items).

The lists were randomized and four different versions of completion booklets were printed. After each sentence fragment an empty line was provided for its completion.

Procedure

The experiment was run individually for each subject. One of the four versions of the completion booklets was given to each of the subjects. They were instructed to read the fragments and complete them to full sentences as rapidly as possible. It was stressed that a spontaneous and hence fast completion was important for this study.

Data Analysis

Sentence completions were scored in one of three categories: correct responses were scored when the fragment was immediately followed by a correctly inflected verb and the rest of the sentence was also grammatical. "Agreement errors" were scored when a verb immediately followed the preamble but was incorrectly inflected for number. "Miscellaneous" responses were scored for completions that did not form a complete sentence, had other material before the verb, or did not interpret the preamble as the sentence subject. Two sentences from plausibility condition B had to be eliminated due to a typographical error in the booklets.

Each subject completed 4 fragments per condition, i.e., 48 target fragments, as required by the 2*2*3 design with the factors *match* (match vs. mismatch of the two nouns), *local* (local noun singular vs. plural) and *plausibility* (S-P more plausible vs. S-P less plausible vs. control).

An analysis of variance (ANOVA) was performed with these three independent factors. Additionally, separate ANOVAs were computed for each level of plausibility, as well as an ANOVA with data collapsed across all plausibility conditions. These analyses of variance were carried out with participants (F1) and with items (F2) as random factors. All effects that achieved significance were reliable at or below the .05 level. The percentages of agreement errors, correct responses and miscellaneous completions were used as dependent measures.

Hypotheses

Across all plausibility conditions: according to Bock and colleagues an increased error rate should occur only in the S-P mismatch condition compared to its control condition S-S. The other mismatch condition P-S should yield no significant differences to its control P-P. Therefore an interaction of the factors *match* and *local* is to be expected. In addition to the attraction error, increased error rates may be found following plural head nouns compared to singular head nouns, following Branigan (1995).

If a plausibility difference does underlie the phenomenon, no differences in error rates between S-S vs. S-P can be expected in plausibility condition A, because the critical mismatch S-P is very plausible in this condition. At the same time, the implausible P-S version should show more errors than its control version P-P. For the plausibility condition B (S-P less plausible than P-S), the contrast of the S-P mismatch to its control S-S should be pronounced, while for the difference between the (highly plausible) P-S mismatch and the P-P control condition no effects are to be expected.

No significant effects are expected in plausibility condition C if plausibility is the main source of errors. If plausibility rather has a modulating influence on agreement errors, similar effects to the general analysis could emerge, but in a less pronounced fashion.

Results

A total of 989 correct responses (89.5%), 73 agreement errors (6.6%) and 42 miscellaneous completions (3.9%) were scored.

Results for the dependent measure "agreement errors" are presented here. The overall 3-way interaction of *match, local* and *plausibility* was significant in the F1-Analysis ($F1_{2,43}=4,28$, $p<.020$), but not in the F2-Analysis ($F2_{2,46}=2,69$, $p<.080$). This 3-way interaction is caused by the differing interactions of the factors local and match on the individual levels of plausibility.

But let us first consider the influence of *local* and *match* across all levels of plausibility: the percentage of errors for the four syntactic variations is shown for data collapsed across all levels of plausibility in Fig. 1.

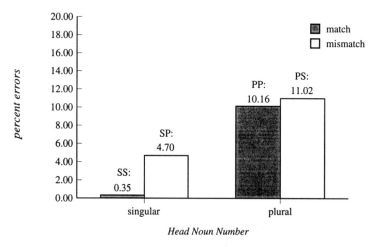

Figure 1: Percentage of agreement errors across all levels of plausibility

Analysis of variance revealed no significant main effects of the factors *local* and *match*. The interaction of these factors however was significant across subjects ($F1_{1,23}=11.16$, $p<.01$) and items ($F2_{1,45}=15.36$, $p<.01$). To investigate the nature of this interaction, planned comparisons of the mismatch conditions to their respective match conditions were computed. The contrast S-S vs. S-P reached significance in both the F1- and F2- analysis ($F1_{1,23}$=13.99, p<.01; $F2_{1,45}$=9.47, p<.01), while the contrast P-P vs. P-S failed to do so. This means that a significant effect of a matching vs. mismatching local noun can only be found following singular head nouns. Nonetheless, most agreement errors were found following plural heads, irrespective of local noun number ($F1_{1,23}$=11.16, p<.01; $F2_{1,45}$=15.36, p<.001). Percentages of agreement errors for the individual levels of the plausibility variation are shown in Fig. 2.

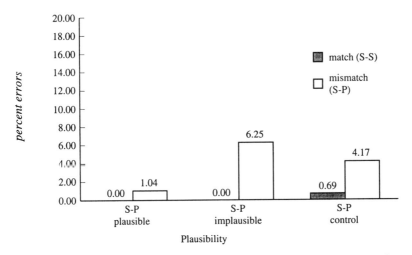

Figure 2: Percentage of agreement errors within individual levels of plausibility.

Plausibility condition A: S-P more plausible than P-S

Analysis of variance revealed no significant main effects of the factors *local* and *match* in this subgroup of items. The interaction of these factors however was significant across subjects ($F1_{1,23}$=13.31, p<.01) and items ($F2_{1,15}$=15.00, p<.01). Again the contrasts of the mismatch conditions to their respective match conditions were computed. None of these contrasts reached significance, although numerically more errors were found for the highly implausible P-S than for its P-P control.

Plausibility condition B: S-P less plausible than P-S

The main effect of the factor *match* reached significance ($F1_{1,23}$=5.90, p< .03; $F2_{1,13}$=6.78, p<.03), while neither the factor *local* nor the two-way interaction showed reliable effects. A significant contrast was established between the S-P mismatch condition and its S-S control across items ($F2_{1,13}$=4.79, p<.05), but not across subjects. Numerically, the contrast is more pronounced in this subgroup of items than in the global analysis with more agreement errors occurring in the mismatch condition than in the match condition. Failing to reach the level of significance can be explained by the lower number of data points in this analysis (only one third of global analysis).

For plural head nouns, no significant contrast between the mismatch condition P-S and the respective control condition P-P was found.

Plausibility condition C: control

While no significant main effects for the factors *match* and *local* could be established for this subgroup of items, the interaction of the two factors was significant in both F1- and F2-analyses ($F1_{1,23}$=5.79, p< .03; $F2_{1,15}$=7.30, p<.02). This interaction is based on the contrast between the mismatch condition S-P and match condition S-S, which reached significance across items ($F2_{1,15}$=5.00, p<.05), but not across subjects. The contrast S-S vs. S-P implies that even with plausibility fully controlled, a mismatch of head noun and local noun yields more agreement errors, as long as the head noun is singular.

No significant contrast between matching and mismatching local nouns could be found for plural head nouns. The error rates are substantially higher following plural heads compared to singular heads ($F1_{1,23}$=5.79, p<.05; $F2_{1,15}$=7.30, p<.05), irrespective of local noun number.

Comparison between plausibility conditions A and B:

Since significant differences between match and mismatch conditions were found only following singular heads, the comparison between plausibility conditions was restricted to singular head nouns.

An analysis of variance was conducted with the factors *match* (match vs. mismatch of head and local noun) and *plausibility*. This analysis suffered from a lack of variance in so far as no errors were found in the match condition S-S so that the relevant planned comparisons could not be computed. Therefore, an additional hierarchical loglinear analysis was performed with the factors *match* and *plausibility* (and *error* as a dummy factor for loglinear analysis).

Significant 2-way interactions of *plausibility* and *error* (L.R. Chisq Change = 6,149, p<.0132) and *match* and *error* (L.R. Chisq Change = 11,400, p<.001) were found. These correspond to main effects of *plausibility* and *match* in an analysis of variance. Furthermore the contrast between plausibility levels A and B within the critical mismatch condition S-P was significant (L.R. Chisq Change = 6,149, p<.02).

Discussion

The comparisons across all plausibility conditions reveal the fundamental effects of number variation. The classic congruence effect was found for singular head nouns: a mismatching local noun yielded increased error rates compared to a matching one. This represents the attraction errors which have been shown a number of times by Bock and her co-workers. The present result establishes this basic phenomenon for the domain of written production in German. It can be concluded that the written task is a viable means for investigating agreement phenomena.

While these results are in line with Bock and colleagues' findings, the data for plural head nouns presents a different picture. In accordance with Bock, no significant influence of the number of a local noun was found here. At the same time, however, the number of errors following plural heads is reliably increased - in fact more than doubled - compared to singular heads. This increase is in line with Branigan's data from written production of British English.

The plausibility variation was shown as having a significant impact on the production of agreement errors in this experiment. In plausibility condition A the critical S-P mismatch is constructed as highly plausible. As a consequence, the congruence effect, which is so reliably found across numerous experiments, drops below significance. Making the critical mismatch highly implausible (condition B) increases the congruence effect numerically. The difference between these plausibility conditions was found to be significant in the loglinear analysis.

No reliable statistical effects were found for fragments with plural head nouns with respect to the plausibility variation. Numerically, in particular the P-P condition varied rather unsystematically. Due to large variance, none of the numerical differences in the distribution of errors reached significance.

But plausibility by itself did not prove to be the only basis of agreement errors. In the control condition C, in which all syntactic variations of the items are equally plausible, the basic syntactic effects remained. Plausibility has a rather modulating influence on the agreement process. Hence the above statements about syntactic effects and processes hold, irrespective of plausibility differences. This result nonetheless shows that semantic-conceptual differences indeed have an effect on agreement in German, casting further doubt on the claim that agreement processes are purely syntactic when generalizing to languages other than English.

COMPREHENSION OF NUMBER AGREEMENT

Research on agreement phenomena has generally focused on the production of agreement and less on potentially analogous processes of comprehension. Such an analogous process does not necessarily have to exist. Production and comprehension have different goals in human communication and some models of human language processing assume different mechanisms and processes for production and comprehension. In the production mode the speaker must actively avoid grammatical errors in order to convey the message appropriately, while the listener or reader is primarily concerned with interpreting the content of the message, a task that does not necessarily require grammatically correct input.

Studies using event-related potentials (ERP) have shown that listeners are sensitive to agreement violations (Osterhout & Mobley, 1995). A P 600 shift, which is assumed to be an electro-physiological indicator of syntactic processing difficulties, was found after presentation of materials violating the required agreement of subject and verb. But these studies only show that subjects are sensitive to the ungrammaticality in agreement violations. The sentence fragments used by Bock and co-workers were grammatical per se, yet produced high error rates in mismatch conditions. The interesting question is whether such constructions produce processing difficulties in fully grammatical sentences.

In a pioneering experiment, Nicol et al. (1996) presented their subjects with full sentences beginning with complex noun phrases. The number of both the head noun and the local noun was systematically varied.

(16)   The statue in the courtyard was beautiful beyond belief.
            (S-S)

(17)   The statue in the courtyards was beautiful beyond belief.
            (S-P)

(18)   The statues in the courtyard were beautiful beyond belief.
            (P-S)

(19)   The statues in the courtyards were beautiful beyond belief.
                (P-P)

A so-called "Maze task" was used involving a type of serial presentation where each word is presented together with an irrelevant word. It required pressing the corresponding button for the word in the pair which best continues the sentence. This button-pressing again initiates presentation of a following pair of words. The main finding of this experiment was that reaction time on the verb was increased for materials with a singular head noun and a plural local noun, directly corresponding to the agreement effects shown for production. A mismatching plural local noun interfered with the agreement process in comprehension as well as in production. The authors suggest that a plural feature percolates from the local noun to the head noun in comprehension just as it does in production. The agreement check initiated from the verb then encounters a mismatching feature leading to increased processing time on the verb.

To rule out the possibility that the Maze task required covert production in addition to comprehension, and that this covert production was the source of the effects, the experiment was replicated with a whole-sentence grammaticallity judgement task. Measuring the total reading times for the sentences, the same pattern of results was found, replicating the agreement effect.

Nicol et al. (1996) also addressed potential biases in plausibility by repeating the experiment with the same materials, but altering the verb forms so that they no longer had to carry agreement markers (e.g. *The authors of the speech will be rewarded*). Mismatch effects in these constructions should be due to plausibility differences, since no agreement computation is necessary. No mismatch effects could be established, leading to the conclusion that there were no such plausibility differences in the materials. Yet one might still suspect that plausibility differences between matching and mismatching versions of items could interact with the agreement process and become effective only when agreement is computed rather than being a completely independent source of processing load. In the present study a different approach to plausibility differences was taken, namely, establishing plausibility differences in pre-tests and systematically varying this semantic variable in the main experiments.

To summarize, Nicol et al. (1996) were able to show that processing difficulties can be found for the same structures that elicit agreement errors in production. Still some methodological concerns have to be mentioned. While their Maze task did not eliminate the possibility of unwanted covert production, the whole-sentence grammaticallity judgement does not allow for identifying at which point in the sentence processing difficulties actually occur. Furthermore, the necessary use of ungrammatical sentences as fillers may have caused strategic effects. Readers performing this type of task may be much more attentive to grammatical relations than those who are asked to read for comprehension and not grammatical correctness. Therefore a generalization of this finding to "normal" reading processes is not fully justified.

Similar objections can be raised with respect to experiments reported in Pearlmutter et al. (1995). In two experiments, one using self-paced reading, the other using eye-tracking, the authors looked at singular head nouns, varying the number of a local noun and the verb, so that half the materials violated the subject-verb agreement rule.

(20)   The key to the cabinet was rusty from many years of disuse. (S-S)

(21)   The key to the cabinets was rusty from many years of disuse. (S-P)

(22)   The key to the cabinet were rusty from many years of disuse. (S-S, ungrammatical)

(23)   The key to the cabinets were rusty from many years of disuse. (S-P, ungrammatical)

In self-paced reading a mismatch effect could be established for the grammatical sentences by showing longer reading times for the region of the verb and the next word. Eye-tracking revealed no effects for First Pass Reading Time, but significantly more regressions from the verb region were found for mismatching local nouns, again showing the agreement effect.

But methodological concerns have to be raised again. The basic question is whether or not a mismatch of the head noun and the local noun interferes with agreement processes in normal reading, i. e., reading for comprehension. In these two experiments ungrammatical materials were used which may well have led to undesirable strategic effects. This concern is much stronger here than for the Nicol et al. (1996) study, because the ungrammaticality is always located at the verb in these experiments, leading to strong demand characteristics in the verb region.

In a third experiment, however, Pearlmutter et al. (1996) compared singular and plural head nouns, this time presenting only grammatical materials. Self-paced reading times on the verb region replicated the mismatch effect for singular head nouns, while no such effect was found for plural head nouns.

These effects, however, are not as stable as one would want them to be, as a series of experiments by Branigan et al. (1995) demonstrates. While Nicol et al. (1996) and Pearlmutter et al. (1995) identified mismatch-effects in time measures for the verb-region, Branigan et al. (1995) found no effects of number mismatch in the verb region, either for First Pass Reading Times or for Total Reading Times. However, they did find a significant mismatch effect for the Total Reading Time of the region of the local noun. Finding an effect in this rather early region is surprising, because no computation of number agreement is necessary while reading the local noun. But one must keep in mind that the Total Reading Time is a quite broad measure which may also contain regressions from a later region, e.g. the verb. Unfortunately, no regression measures were reported for this experiment which would permit a comparison to the experiments by Pearlmutter et al. (1995). Another remarkable finding is that the mismatch effect was found for both singular and plural head nouns in this experiment, contrasting sharply with findings from production experiments and with the data on comprehension presented by Nicol et al. (1995) and Pearlmutter et al. (1996).

In a replication of this eye-tracking experiment the agreement effects virtually disappeared. Even the numerical tendencies towards agreement effects were only weak. A result like this challenges the claim that mismatching local nouns lead to processing difficulties for the agreement process, especially since the experiments reported by Branigan et al. do not face the problems of possible strategic effects caused by ungrammatical materials.

Experiment 2

In this second experiment an eye-tracking technique was used to investigate the comprehension of structures which are known to elicit agreement errors in production. Materials consisted of complete, grammatical sentences with initial complex noun phrases, embedded in neutral contexts. Eye-movements were recorded during reading for comprehension. The number of head nouns and local nouns were varied systematically to capture the agreement processes for singular and plural head nouns. Together with a three-level factor of plausibility this manipulation resulted in a 2*2*3 design. First pass reading times and regression measures were scored as dependent variables.

Method

Participants. Twenty-four undergraduate students (German native speakers) from the University of Freiburg were paid to participate in the study. All of them had normal, uncorrected vision and were unfamiliar with the purpose of the study.

Materials. The full sentence versions of the materials for Experiment 1 were used in this experiment. The 48 target sentences consisted of 16 items for each of three plausibility conditions as established in pre-tests (see Experiment 1 for details):

A. mismatch condition S-P more plausible than P-S
B. mismatch condition P-S more plausible than S-P
C. all syntactic variations equally plausible.

Four versions of each item were used, resulting from independently varying the number of the head and local noun. The experimental target sentences were embedded in neutral contexts. Contexts were constructed such that four raters agreed that none of the context sentences made one of the syntactic variations of a target more or less plausible than the other. Small texts were created, consisting of one syntactic version of a target sentence (such as (25) through (28)), two context sentences (such as (24) and (29) and a content question (such as (30)).

(24)   Wind und Regen peitschten über den Landstrich an der Atlantikküste.
            (Wind and Rain whipped across the countryside at the Atlantic coastline.)

(25)   Die Leitung zu dem Haus übersteht den Sturm unbeschadet. (S-S)
            (The power line to the house withstands the storm undamaged.)

(26)   Die Leitung zu den Häusern übersteht den Sturm unbeschadet. (S-P)
            (The power line to the houses withstands the storm undamaged.)

(27)   Die Leitungen zu dem Haus überstehen den Sturm unbeschadet. (P-S)
            (The power lines to the house withstand the storm undamaged.)

(28)   Die Leitungen zu den Häusern überstehen den Sturm unbeschadet. (P-P)
            (The power lines to the houses withstand the storm undamaged.)

(29)   So haben die Bewohner wenigstens Strom und Telefon.
            (At least the residents have electricity and the telephone
            working.)

(30)   Stürmte es an der Küste?
            Was there a storm at the coast?

The target item was the second sentence in half of the texts and the third
sentence in the other half of the texts. The content question always related to
one of the context sentences. These measures were taken in order to distract
from the experimental items. The context sentences also served as fillers in
this experiment and were therefore syntactically diverse, avoiding sentence
initial complex noun phrases with PPs.

Four lists were constructed from these texts, including each text in each list
once and an equal number of items of each syntactic version as well. Across
the four lists each four number versions of each target sentence were included
once. The lists were automatically randomized individually for each subject
by the experimental control software to minimize sequence effects.

Procedure. The experiment was run individually for each subject with a
session length of about 60 minutes. Subjects were instructed to read the texts
for comprehension and answer content questions at the end of each sentence.
Eye-movements during reading were monitored with a Dual Purkinje Image
Eyetracker. A chin rest was used to prevent head movements during reading.
A brief calibration procedure was performed at the start and following regular
pauses. Two filler texts were presented after calibration. Before a sentence
was presented, the subject had to fixate a cross marking on the screen indicating the starting position of the sentence-string. When the subject had
finished reading a sentence, he or she pressed a button to initiate presentation
of the next sentence. The questions at the end of the texts had to be answered
by pressing one of two buttons (left-hand button: "yes", right-hand button:
"no").

Materials were presented on a 20-inch color display at a distance of 83 cm,
so that 3 letters equaled 1 degree of visual angle. Eye-movements of the right
eye were recorded at a sampling rate of 1KHz for the second and third
sentence of each text and stored for later analysis.

Three to five days after the eye-tracking experiment, subjects completed a
questionnaire containing the 48 target sentences (no contexts) in the respective
versions, which the subject had been presented with in the main experiment.
Plausibility ratings were obtained with this questionnaire to test whether the
subject of this experiment rated the plausibility in the way expected from the
pre-tests.

Data Analysis

For data analysis the sentences were divided into regions, shown as slashes in
(31).

(31)   Die Göre / mit dem Buch / wartet / an der / Telefonzelle.
              (The girl/ with the book/ waits / at the / phone booth.)

Dividing into regions appeared necessary because the critical parts of the
items contained a considerable number of function words like determiners and
prepositions. Such function words are often skipped so that wordwise analysis
is not indicated.

The data were summarized for each region resulting in the dependent variables *first pass reading time, first regression path duration* (FRPD) and *total
regression path duration*(TRPD). *First pass reading time* is defined as the
duration of all fixations on a specified region from first encountering that
region from the left until the eyes move away (either to the left, or to the right)
from that region. Regression path durations accumulate the durations of all
fixations in the regression path and add them to the first pass reading time. The
regression path is defined as the set of all fixations following a regressive
saccade from a region until the region is fixated again or skipped, i.e., until the
right boundary of the critical region is crossed (cf. Konieczny, 1996 for a
detailed description of these reading time measures).

Sentences with more than 300 msec of tracking errors (resulting from
blinking and head movements) were excluded (ca. 5% of the data). When
incorrect answers were given to the content question of a text, the data from
that text was also excluded after establishing an independence of the experimental factors from correct vs. incorrect answers in an analysis of variance.
Reading times lower than 100 msec were excluded from further analyses, so
that the data reported represent *conditionalized fixation durations* (see Rayner
et al., 1989).

In order to reduce statistical noise, extreme values were eliminated from
the data. Taking word length into account, all data points diverting more than
2.5 standard deviations from the mean were excluded for each measure. To
account for word-length effects the Trueswell et al. (1994) method was used,
so that subsequent statistical tests were performed on residual reading time
measures.[2]

Hypotheses

Across all plausibility conditions: if the comprehension of agreement resembles production, the S-P mismatch condition should be more difficult to process than its corresponding match condition. Furthermore, items with plural head nouns should be more difficult to process than those with singular head nouns, irrespective of the local noun, paralleling the error distribution in Experiment 1.

If plausibility also influences agreement processes in comprehension, no contrast between the S-P mismatch condition and its control should be found for the plausibility condition A, because S-P is highly plausible here. At the same time, mismatch condition P-S should show processing difficulties, because it is constructed as very implausible for plausibility condition A.

For the plausibility condition B (S-P less plausible than P-S) the contrast of the S-P mismatch to its control condition should be pronounced, while for the difference between the (highly plausible) P-S mismatch and its control no differential effects are to be expected.

In plausibility condition C, no significant effects are expected if plausibility is the main source of processing difficulty. If plausibility rather has a modulating influence on agreement processes in comprehension, similar effects to the general analysis might emerge, but in a less pronounced fashion.

Results

Each subject read 4 target items in each condition as required by the 2*2*3 design with the factors *match* (match vs. mismatch of the two nouns), local (local noun singular vs. plural) and *plausibility* (S-P more plausible vs. S-P less plausible vs. control).

Separate analyses of variance (ANOVA) were performed with these three independent factors for each level of plausibility. Additionally ANOVAs were computed with data collapsed across all plausibility conditions. Theses analyses of variance were carried out on all reading time measures with participants (F1) or items (F2) as random factors, respectively. All effects achieving significance did so at or below the .05 level.

The relevant statistical effects could only be established for *first pass reading times*. The regression measures FRPD and TRPD did show similar patterns numerically, but no interpretable effects showed up. Therefore only the *first pass reading times* are presented in detail here for the region of the local noun (N2-region) and the region of the verb.

The separate analyses for each level of plausibility revealed only weak effects, even for the *first pass reading time* measure. Two possible reasons may be responsible for this lack of effects. Only one third of the data points were entered into each of the separate analyses, so that the empirical basis may have been too weak to detect any effects. The other, more likely possibility is that the experimental plausibility variation was not successful in this second experiment. Analyses of the post-experimental plausibility ratings revealed that plausibility judgements were not as clear-cut in this experiment as in the pre-tests. Plausibility scores were much higher in this post-test (i.e., sentences were generally judged as more plausible) and the variance of the ratings was much lower. For more than half of the items all syntactic variations of the item were roughly equally acceptable for the subjects. The post-experimental ratings are correlated with the pre-test scores with a coefficient of only r=.43, giving some further indication that the plausibility variation failed to be fully effective in Experiment 2. Hence, we will concentrate on analyses of data collapsed across plausibility conditions in the following presentation.

N2 region

Residual reading times of the N2-region for the analysis collapsed across all plausibility conditions are shown in Fig. 3.

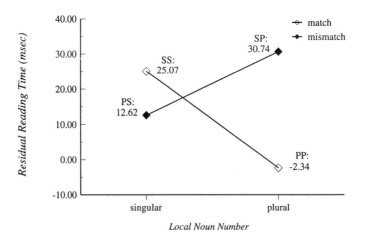

Figure 3: Residual Reading Times: N2 Region

Analysis of variance revealed no significant main effect for the factors *local* ($F1_{1,23}<1$, $F2_{1,47}=1.06$) and *match.*($F1_{1,23}=1.01$, $p<.32$, $F2_{1,47}<1$), but a significant two-way interaction across subjects ($F1_{1,23}=7.09$, $p<.02$) and across items ($F2_{1,47}=4.34$, $p<.05$).

To investigate the nature of this interaction, the contrasts of the mismatch conditions to their respective match condition were computed. Note that different contrasts were computed for the N2 region and the verb region. Contrasts were computed between those conditions that contain the same material (and hence have the same length) in the respective region. Therefore, mismatch condition S-P was compared to match condition P-P in the N2 region (plural marked local nouns), while mismatch condition P-S had match condition S-S as its control (singular marked local nouns). This is reversed in the verb region, because here S-P corresponds in length to S-S (singular marked verbs) and P-S corresponds to P-P (plural marked verbs). The figures are designed according to the same logic, grouping the data by the local noun for the N2 region and by the head noun for the verb region.

The contrast S-P vs. P-P was significant in the F1-analysis ($F1_{1,23}=5.46$, $p<.03$), but only marginally so in the F2-analysis ($F2_{1,47}=3.75$, $p<.06$). Numerically, this corresponds to the fact that when following a singular head noun a mismatching local noun increases reading times for the N2 region by ca. 30 msec. The contrast S-S vs. P-S failed to reach significance across both subjects and items ($F1_{1,23}<1$, $F2_{1,47}<1$).

Comparisons of the two match conditions S-S and P-P reveal an oddity. The S-S match condition, which should be easiest to process according to all theoretical assumptions encountered so far, seems to bear a much higher processing difficulty than the other mismatch condition P-P, for which processing difficulties were actually expected. Fig. 4 shows the raw scores for the same region, allowing a comparison.

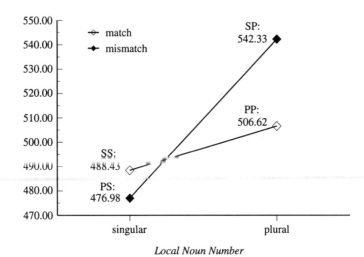

Local Noun Number

Figure 4: N2 Region (First Pass Reading Time, raw scores)

The raw scores make it obvious that the highly increased residual reading times for the S-S match condition are most probably a consequence of the length correction, which seems to have been an over-correction in this case. The contrasts that were computed in the above analysis were not affected by this problem of the length correction procedure, because conditions of equal region length are compared in these statistical contrasts.

Verb region

Residual reading times of the verb region for the analysis collapsed across all plausibility conditions are shown in Fig. 5.

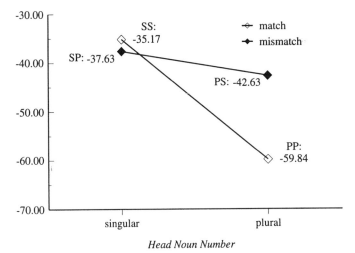

Head Noun Number

Figure 5: Residual Reading Times: Verb Region

The main effect of the factor *match* did not reach significance ($F1_{1,23}=1.27$, $p<.27$, $F2_{1,47}=1.02$, $p<.31$), while the factor *local* was significant across items ($F2_{1,47}=4.04$, $p<.05$), but not across subjects ($F1_{1,23}=,3.32$ $p<.09$). The two-way interaction however reached significance in both analyses ($F1_{1,23}=7.38$, $p<.02$, $F2_{1,47}=5.46$, $p<.03$). Again contrasts between corresponding match and mismatch conditions were computed to reveal the nature of the interaction (S-S vs. S-P and P-S vs. P-P, respectively).

The contrast S-S vs. S-P, i.e., the mismatch effect following a singular head noun, remained far from significant ($F1_{1,23}<1$, $F2_{1,47}<1$). Actually numerically slightly lower residual reading times are found for the mismatch condition S-P compared to the S-S match. A mismatch effect of about 25 msec could be established for materials with a plural head noun. The contrast P-S vs. P-P failed to reach significance in the F1-analysis ($F1_{1,23}=3.95$, $p<.06$), but was significant across items ($F2_{1,47}=4.15$, $p<.05$).

Similar to the data for the N2 region, the S-S match condition shows highly increased residual reading time scores compared to the P-P match condition. Since this result contradicts all hypothetical expectations, raw scores for the verb region are shown in Fig. 6.

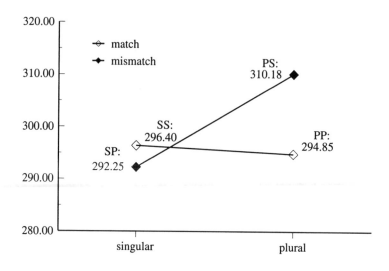

Head Noun Number

Figure 6: Verb Region First Pass Reading Time (raw scores)

Once more the raw scores reveal that the difference between S-S and P-P is likely to be an artifact of the length correction technique proposed by Trueswell et al. (1994).

Discussion

First of all, it is remarkable that significant effects were found only for first pass reading times. Both Pearlmutter et al. (1995) and Branigan et al. (1995) failed to find effects for this measure. Instead they established effects for regression measures or total reading times, again potentially containing fixations which result from regressions.

Although the regression measures from the present experiment revealed a similar pattern, no significant effects were found. To interpret this finding one should keep in mind that the regression measures used here contained the sum of both first pass reading times and regression times. Fixations in the regression path may have mainly added unsystematic variation, thus reducing the strength of this measure. Another less methodological interpretation is also available: all materials were grammatically correct and there was no need to resolve ambiguities like those found in garden-path sentences, for example. At the same time, the number of words between the beginning of the sentence and the critical region was rather small. With these constructions, the language processing system might not be forced to look back over prior material in order to resolve agreement conflicts caused by erroneous feature percolation. Instead, local conflict resolution on the critical region may be more appropriate, revealing effects only in first pass reading times. When using ungrammatical sentences or when explicit grammaticallity judgments are required, different strategies might become effective which would then increase the number of regressions.

On the more methodological side, this experiment revealed some dangers that lie in the choice of length-correction techniques. In German, the plural forms of nouns and verbs are usually longer than the singular forms, so that a confound of region-length and experimental conditions cannot be avoided. Therefore, length correction is mandatory. The confounding of experimental variation and word length, however, seems to have led to an overestimation of word-length effects. In this experiment, the regression of word length on reading times, which is the basis of Trueswell et al.'s (1994) formula, was computed over all regions in the target sentences, including the critical regions. Using filler sentences as the basis of the required regression may be a better solution for the future.

The relevant planned comparisons presented in this paper are unaffected by differences in word length and therefore seem to be the most reliable statistical source of information for this experiment.

In the N2 region a mismatch effect was identified following a singular head noun. This finding is generally compatible with the feature percolation hypothesis of Nicol et al. (1996). Surprisingly though, the effect was found in quite an early region, before the verb was read and before agreement processing should have been initiated by the verb. This early effect contrasts findings by Nicol et al. (1996) and Pearlmutter et al (1995) who found effects on the verb or even later.

In the verb region no mismatch effect was found for singular head nouns, again conflicting with the data from Nicol et al. (1996) and Pearlmutter et al. (1995). Instead, a mismatch effect was found following plural head nouns. Plural head nouns have usually been unaffected by mismatch effects in both production and comprehension experiments. In fact, the asymmetry between singular-plural and plural-singular mismatch conditions is reversed in the present study.

This unexpected result might be attributed to an artifact of the eye-tracking method since the pattern of results for the verb region is a mirror image of the results for the N2 region. Materials that took longer to read in the N2 region subsequently required shorter reading times in the immediately following verb region. Longer reading times in a preceding region also included more opportunities for a parafoveal preview of later material. Parafoveal preview can be eliminated with "gaze contingent" presentation techniques, where only the currently fixated word is displayed in clear text, while words in the parafoveal area are replaced with meaningless letter strings. A replication of the study using such a technique might clarify this issue.

Since no other data on the comprehension of complex noun phrases with respect to verb agreement processes is available to date, interlingual differences could be an alternative interpretation for the results obtained in the verb region. This alternative will be addressed below.

No clear effects of the plausibility variation could be established in this comprehension experiment, although the same materials with the same plausibility variation did show reliable effects in Experiment 1. The tentative explanation for these differences in the influence of plausibility is that the items in Experiment 2 were presented in contexts. The contexts were constructed to be neutral, i.e., without biasing the plausibility of any number variation. They may have had the unwanted side-effect of diminishing all plausibility differences in the materials, because the contexts made even those versions plausible that were implausible when presented in isolation. The reduced plausibility differences found in the post-experimental rating support this interpretation.

GENERAL DISCUSSION AND CONCLUSIONS

Experiment 1 investigated the consequences of mismatching local nouns for subject verb agreement in the written production of the German language. The basic agreement effects which had been established for spoken production of English by Bock and co-workers (Bock & Miller, 1991, Bock & Cutting, 1992, Bock & Eberhard, 1993) and for spoken production of German by Schriefers and van Kampen (1993), were replicated. A mismatch between a singular head noun and a plural local noun increased error rates, while after plural heads, a mismatch has no consequence on error rates. In addition, largely increased error rates were found after plural head nouns compared to singular head nouns, a pattern that is not readily explained by a feature percolation hypothesis.

At least two processes must be assumed to account for these results. First, mismatching local nouns can interfere with the agreement process if the head noun is singular. Nicol (1996) describes this as slippery percolation of a plural feature from the local noun, a hypothesis which is compatible with the results from Experiment 1. This idea also accounts for the non-effect of the local noun after plural heads, since singular is the not explicitly marked default and would not percolate. An erroneous percolation of the plural marking in P-P constructions, on the other hand, would not lead to an agreement error.

But the overall increase of errors after plural heads, irrespective of the local noun, remains to be explained. An additional process has to be assumed. When subjects lose track of the correct verb number they might be more likely to produce a singular verb inflection by default regardless of the potential local distractor noun. This tendency of using a singular when inattentive or uncertain, has no effect as measured by error rates if the head noun is also singular, but increases the error rates following plural head nouns.

Why the difference between singular and plural head nouns is so pronounced in written production is still puzzling. Plural head nouns have been omitted in many of the experiments in the literature, thus obscuring potentially similar tendencies for spoken production. No data on the spoken production following plural head nouns has been published for German to date, leaving a number of questions unanswered.

What about plausibility effects? Bock et al. have shown in a number of experiments that semantic-conceptual variables hardly ever influence the agreement process in speech production in English. However, the present study has established a significant modulating influence of the semantic variable plausibility for German. These results clearly indicate that the view on agreement processes being purely syntactic in nature cannot be generalized to German. Since Vigliocco et al. (1996) also showed semantic-conceptual influences for Italian, French and Dutch, it would seem that English might be the exception, one where semantic aspects are not effective on agreement processes.

Experiment 2 looked into the comprehension of similar structures with respect to agreement phenomena. A number of results were found that differed from those reported for English. First, effects were limited to first pass reading times rather than regression measures. This may have been the consequence of not using ungrammatical materials in the present study. Those studies that did report effects for regressions had employed such materials. Introducing ungrammaticality in an experiment probably changes the strategies of the participants and these different strategies might effect reading time measures differently.

A mismatch effect for singular head nouns, well known from production studies, was found in the N2 region prior to the verb. Such an early effect is not immediately compatible with Nicol's feature-percolation hypothesis because the verb has not yet been read and could not yet have initiated an agreement check. One speculation might be that it is not the verb agreement processing that is responsible for the early effect. The integration of a mismatching local noun into the complex noun phrase could be more difficult, because it could increase the processing load in computing the number of the complex noun phrase itself, assuming that a plural feature in fact percolated from the local noun to the head noun. This difficulty might be independent of an agreement check initiated by the verb.

In the verb region, the results were reversed. Singular head nouns no longer showed a mismatch effect. Instead, the mismatch effect was found after plural head nouns, contradicting all expectations based on earlier research. These findings could be an artifact of the eye-tracking method, namely a consequence of parafoveal preview. But interlingual differences could also provide a source for this surprising outcome. The literature reviewed earlier focused on comprehension in English only. A major difference between German and English is reflected in verb morphology. In English most verb forms are ambiguously marked for number, but such ambiguities do not arise in German.

MacWhinney, Bates & Kliegl (1984) compared German, English and Italian with respect to the influence of a number of variables on comprehension of short sentences. They found that Germans rely much more on agreement cues than English readers do. These results have to be interpreted with caution, since these experiments contained ungrammaticalities for both German and English materials. There is no assurance that these differences in the use of agreement cues can be generalized to normal comprehension of fully grammatical sentences. Nonetheless, this cross-lingual study points at possible differences between German and English that may play a role in agreement processes of comprehension.

It is not clear which specific interlingual differences would be responsible for the reversal of effects between German and English in comprehension, but the difference between a rich and a reduced verbal morphology seems to be a likely candidate worthy of further investigation. Comparisons with languages other than German and English might also help to further clarify this issue.

NOTES

[1] Bock (1996, personal communication) points out that a meta-analysis of her own data reveals some similarity to this finding: the plural-plural match conditions show higher error rates than the singular-singular match conditions, indicating that plural heads are more difficult to process irrespective of attraction

by a local noun. This difference however is much smaller than the one obtained by Branigan et al. (1995).

[2] For each subject the regression of word length on first pass reading times was computed based on all regions in the target sentences. Residual reading times result from subtracting the intercept and the product of region length and slope from first pass reading times.

REFERENCES

Bock, J.K. (1995). Producing agreement. *Current Directions in Psychological Science, Vol. 4, 2,* 56-61

Bock, J.K., & Cutting, J. C. (1992). Regulating mental energy: Performance units in language production. *Journal of Memory and Language, 31,* 99-127.

Bock, J.K., & Eberhard, K.M. (1993). Meaning, sound, and syntax in English number agreement. *Language and Cognitive Processes, 8,* 57-99.

Bock, J.K,. & Miller, C.A. (1991). Broken agreement. *Cognitive Psychology, 23,* 45-93.

Branigan, H.P. (1995). *Language processing and the mental representation of syntactic structure.* Unpublished doctoral dissertaion, University of Edinburgh.

Branigan, H. P., Liversedge, S. P., & Pickering, M. J. (1995). *Verb agreement in written comprehension and production.* Paper presented at the 8th Annual CUNY Sentence Processing Conference, Tuscon, AZ.

Eberhard, K.M. (1993). *The specification of grammatical number in English.* Unpublished doctoral dissertation, Michigan State University, East Lansing.

Fodor, J. (1982). The mental representation of quantifiers. In S. Peters & E. Saarinen (Eds.), *Processes, beliefs and questions* (pp. 129-164). Dordrecht: Reidel.

Keeney, T.J., & Wolfe, J. (1972). The acquisition of agreement in English. *Journal of Verbal Learning and Verbal Behavior, 11,* 698-705.

Konieczny, L. (1996). *Human sentence processing: A semantics-oriented parsing approach.* Unpublished doctoral dissertation, Albert-Ludwigs-Universität, Freiburg.

MacWhinney, B., Bates, E., & Kliegl, R. (1984). Cue validity and sentence interpretation in English, German, and Italian. *Journal of Verbal Learning and Verbal Behavior, 23,*127-150.

Nicol, J.L. (1996). Effects of clausal structure on subject-verb agreement errors. *Journal of Psycholinguistic Research, 24*, 6, 507 - 516.

Nicol, J.L., Forster, K.I., & Veres, C. (1996). *Subject verb agreement processes in comprehension*. Manuscript in preparation.

Osterhout, L., & Mobley, L.A. (1995). Event-related brain potentials elicited by failure to agree. *Journal of Memory and Language, 34*, 6, 739-773.

Pearlmutter, N. J., Garnsey, S. M., Bock, K. (1995). *Subject-verb agreement processes in sentence comprehension*. Paper presented at the 8th Annual CUNY Sentence Processing Conference, Tuscon, AZ.

Pollard, C., & Sag, I.A. (1988). An information-based theory of agreement. In D. Brentari, G. Larson, & L. MacLeod (Eds.), *Papers from the 24th Annual Regional Meeting of the Chicago Linguistic Society. Part Two: Parasession on agreement in grammatical theory* (pp. 236-257). Chicago, Ill.: Chicago Linguistic Society.

Quirk, R., Greenbaum, S., Leech, G., Svartvik, J. (1972). *A grammar of contemporary English*. New York: Seminar Press.

Rayner, K., Sereno, S. C., Morris, R. K., Schmauder, A. R., & Clifton, C. (1989). Eye movements and on-line language comprehension processes. *Language and Cognitive Processes, 4,* SI 21-50.

Schriefers, H., & van Kampen, A. (1993). Syntaktische Prozesse bei der Sprachproduktion: Zur Numerus-Kongruenz zwischen Subjekt und Verb. *Sprache & Kognition, 12*(4), 205-216.

Trueswell, J.C., Tanenhaus, M.K., & Garnsey, S.M. (1994). Semantic influences on parsing: use of thematic role information in syntactic ambiguity resolution. *Journal of Memory and Language, 33*, 285-318.

Vigliocco, G., Butterworth, B., & Semenza, C. (1995). Constructing subject-verb agreement in speech: The role of semantic and morphological factors. *Journal of Memory and Language, 34*, 186-215.

Vigliocco, G., Hartsuiker, R.J., Jarema, G., & Kolk, H.J. (1996). One or more labels on the bottles? Notional concord in Dutch and French. *Language and Cognitive Processes, 11*, 4, 407-442.

Vigliocco, G., & Nicol, J. (1995). *The role of syntactic tree structure in the construction of subject-verb agreement*. (submitted)

AUTHOR INDEX

SUBJECT INDEX

STUDIES IN THEORETICAL PSYCHOLINGUISTICS

STUDIES IN THEORETICAL PSYCHOLINGUISTICS

KLUWER ACADEMIC PUBLISHERS – DORDRECHT / BOSTON / LONDON